THE SCIENCE GAME

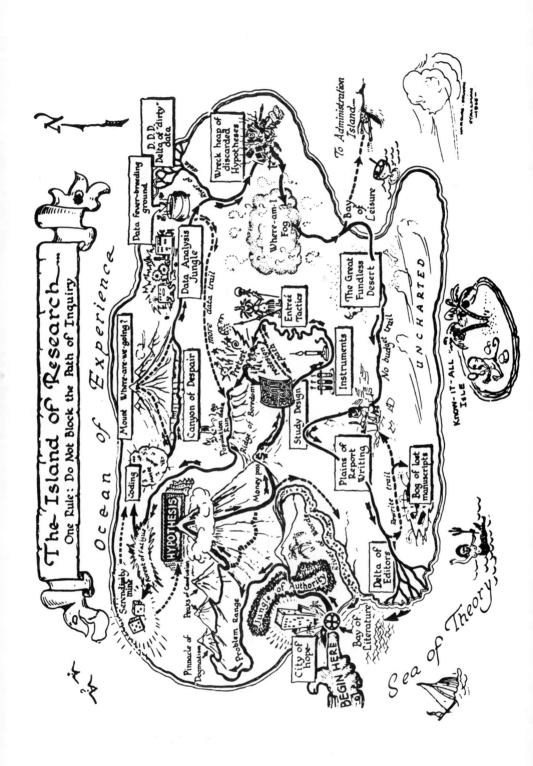

fourth edition _____

THE SCIENCE GAME
GAME
An Introduction to Research in the Social Sciences

Neil McK. Agnew
Sandra W. Pyke
York University

Prentice-Hall, Inc., Englewood Cliffs, New Jersey 07632

Library of Congress Cataloging-in-Publication Data

Agnew, Neil McK. (date)
  The science game.

  Bibliography: p.
  Includes index.
  1. Psychology—Research. I. Pyke, Sandra W.,
(date)   . II. Title.
BF76'.5.A36   1987   301'.072   86-11260
ISBN 0-13-795295-3

Editorial/production supervision and
  interior design: Barbara DeVries
Cover design: Wanda Lubelska Design
Manufacturing buyer: Barbara Kelly Kittle

The third edition of this book was published under the title *The Science Game:
An Introduction to Research in the Behavioral Sciences.*

Printed in the United States of America

10 9 8 7 6 5 4 3 2 1

ISBN 0-13-795295-3 01

Prentice-Hall International (UK) Limited, *London*
Prentice-Hall of Australia Pty. Limited, *Sydney*
Prentice-Hall Canada Inc., *Toronto*
Prentice-Hall Hispanoamericana, S.A., *Mexico*
Prentice-Hall of India Private Limited, *New Delhi*
Prentice-Hall of Japan, Inc., *Tokyo*
Prentice-Hall of Southeast Asia Pte. Ltd., *Singapore*
Editora Prentice-Hall do Brasil, Ltda., *Rio de Janeiro*

iv

Contents

PART II   SIEVES OF SCIENCE

PART III   FROM DESCRIPTION TO EXPERIMENTATION

To Aryn, Kyra, Tim, Wendy

Preface

A number of changes have been incorporated into the fourth edition of *The Science Game* including:

a. Chapter 1: Major revisions.
b. Chapter 4: A Case for the Counselor
c. Chapter 14: The Animal Controversy and the Implementation of Ethical Principles.
d. Chapter 16: A new chapter on the effects of sex bias on research.

The organization of both the text and other material has been edited to varying degrees to reflect the advice of professors, reviewers, students, and editors.

Even a small book, with a 20-year history, accumulates a huge debt. To the many people who routed us through past editions once again, our thanks: To John Isley, who initiated the fourth edition and never rained on any parade, our sincere affection: To our secretary, Nancy Yake, for maintaining her cool in the face of apparent author capriciousness, our gratitude: To our families, a promissory note for more attentive ministrations in the future: To Susan Willig, Dee Josephson, and Barbara DeVries of Prentice-Hall, our appreciation for shepherding us through the publication process: To Ernest Harburg, our grateful acknowledgment of his permission to use the Island of Research map: To our mentors, especially the Donalds—Campbell and Hebb—whose creative conceptions of science excite and challenge, our great esteem. Professor Campbell continues to send us profoundly nourishing "intellectual care packages"—such a mind!

Last, but obviously not least, we thank the university and college teachers who adopted the previous edition, and whose comments, along with those of their students, stimulated and shaped this fourth edition. As well as those in psychology, sociology, and education, we thank those in law, economics, business, medicine, nursing, social work, community planning, etc. Finally, we thank our own students who have the uncanny knack of almost immediately identifying confusions exactly where we unwittingly put them.

Neil McK. Agnew
Sandra W. Pyke

chapter 1

This Thing Called Science

— Science vs "Common-Sense"

Most attempts to divide our observations into two piles—like the good guys and the bad guys, the bald and the hairy, the anxious and the calm, the feminine and the masculine—end up with two relatively small heaps at each extreme end of the scales and a great big leftover pile of uncategorized people in the center.

The less we know, the easier it is to divide things into two heaps. Such simple division usually requires that we wear blinders of bias or unfamiliarity that allow us to ignore an important similarity here and to magnify a difference there. Although dividing things into two piles is too simple and ignores differences, assigning each individual or event to its own unique category is too complex, ignores similarities, and leaves us with an unmanageable number of piles or categories.

In this book we will not end up with two piles, one for science and another for nonscience. Rather, we will propose that scientific problem solving differs from common-sense problem solving in terms of the emphasis it places on a combination of dimensions. To the degree you combine driving curiosity, systematic observation, systematic experimentation, probabilistic thinking, and a theoretical framework; to that degree you practice the scientific method; to that degree you move beyond the simple methods and oversimplified, temporary, or unreliable solutions of many common-sense approaches.

In this section we shall view science as a news service, enabling you to bring to bear on scientific news the critical wisdom you periodically use to evaluate or interpret daily news that captures your attention. Thus, as your curiosity is aroused, you take second and third looks, and have second or third thoughts, about an item of news—an observation or explanation—and in so doing you enter into the spirit of science. You can think of carefully applied common-sense methods as overlapping with some of the simpler scientific methods, which we will discuss in Part Two of the book, then move on to more powerful methods in Part Three.

Also, since we are all victims as well as beneficiaries of scientific news, it is important to distinguish observational science from speculative science, and to distinguish both from pseudoscience. In Chapter 2 we remind you that scientists, like the rest of us, speak with different tongues—one describing what the outer eye "sees" and another describing what the inner eye "sees." Without a good ear, and little familiarity with the language, you can mix them up. Sometimes even scientists mix them up. Sometimes it's hard to tell whether they believe *because they see* or, conversely, that they see *because they believe*.

> Whoever undertakes to set himself up as a judge in the field of Truth and Knowledge is shipwrecked by the laughter of the Gods.
>
> Einstein, 1972, p. 920.

A SAMPLE OF NEWS

- The average person has 8 sexual fantasies a day, and 16 laughs.
- Pepsi must sell 875,000,000 cans of pop to recoup the cost of its Michael Jackson commercial.
- 10 percent of the Japanese have I.Q.'s above 130.
- 2 percent of Americans have I.Q.'s above 130.
- There was a 400 percent increase in government seizures of LSD "tabs" in 1982–83.
- The average length of sexual intercourse for humans is 2 minutes; for chimpanzees, 7 seconds.
- There is a 300 percent increase in teenage suicides since 1953.
- 60,000,000 Americans read below the ninth-grade level.
- 95 percent of Americans break their New Year's resolutions within a week of making them.
- Approximately 15,000 scientific and technical articles are published each day.

Where do these numbers come from? Are they true? What do they mean?*

If you read these observations and numbers in a Sunday newspaper you would probably have less confidence in them than if you saw them in a scientific journal. Why?

*Items 1, 3, and 4 are from *Harpers Magazine,* May, 1984, p. 9. Item 6 is from *Harpers Magazine,* February, 1985, p. 13.

Scientific journal vs newspaper ⎱ What's the difference ... they both tell a "story"?

Both publications provide a news service. What are the similarities and differences between the popular press on the one hand and scientific coverage on the other? Both rely on observers—reporters in the first instance and researchers in the other. And both also rely on commentators or explainers—the newspaper editors and columnists in the one case, and scientific journal editors and theorists in the other.

CONSUMER'S GUIDE TO SCIENCE

You don't believe everything you read in the papers—on the news pages, the sports pages, the entertainment pages, or in the editorials—because you know that some reporters are lazy or rushed, and some editors blatantly biased. On reflection, you also know that there are several "layers" to most stories—surface news and deep news, casual as opposed to probing observation.

You recognize a big difference between the reporter who simply takes his or her story as a handout from the political press secretary, compared to the investigative reporter who digs into the story from different angles. From Watergate, and life, we learn that there is always more to any story than meets the eye, that news comes in endless layers. Furthermore, you understand that any news— surface, middle, or deep—has several explanations and that usually something can be said for each of them.

Similarly, scientific news has endless layers, many more than meet even the scientific eye, or the scientific imagination. If you take your accumulated wisdom about news services in general and apply it to scientific news and commentary, you will take one more step toward becoming a more critical and appreciative consumer of scientific information and speculation.

Now take your accumulated wisdom and a critical perspective and reconsider the "news" reported at the beginning of this chapter. Notice first that these are all news stories rather that editorials or commentary—they are the products of reporters or researchers.

Read through them quickly and pick out which observations and numbers you consider to be "hard" news and which ones you judge to be only surface, soft, or fuzzy news.

First-year students usually list all the observations as hard news with the exception of the following:

8 sexual fantasies
Only 2 percent of the Americans have I.Q.'s above 130
The average length of sexual intercourse for humans is 2 minutes.

These three items the students categorized as "fuzzy" or questionable items.

How do their choices compare with your selection of hard and soft news items from the list? What might a second look, a little digging, a little investigative reporting, or research, uncover?

THE QUALITY OF NEWS

Most news, scientific or otherwise, we simply ignore, or skim uncritically as you probably did on first reading the items on page 2. This is just as well, otherwise reflective and critical reading of a newspaper would take days.

A Second Look: Personal Experience

But when our attention becomes focused on an item through personal interest we take a second, and maybe even a third and fourth look. In bringing to bear your curiosity and your critical faculties on an observation, you are being a personal scientist (Kelly, 1955). You are deciding whether it "makes sense" on the basis of your experience, on the basis of your observations, beliefs, and expectations. If from a second look the observation makes sense to you, your curiosity drops it, becoming available for other things. If not, it takes more looks until satisfied, exhausted, or bored.

For example, take a second look at the observation that: "The average person has 8 sexual fantasies a day." How on earth would you go about getting that number?

If you were a reporter, or a researcher, how could you obtain reliable information about sexual fantasies? Interview people? Send them a questionnaire? How well do you remember your sexual fantasies? Do you keep a tally? When does a romantic daydream become a sexual fantasy? The boundaries are frequently vague or fuzzy. How would you respond in an interview, or fill out a questionnaire? Would you report "high" (to create a macho image) or report low (because of guilt)? Or would you have trouble even figuring out what "high" means, so then maybe discuss it with a trusted friend and together invent a "reasonable" number? So what does it mean when a researcher reports that: "The average person has 8 sexual fantasies a day"? Among other things it means there is a large margin of error, perhaps as large as when you try to count ghosts, where you learn more about the person making the observation than about the ghost population.

So by taking a second or third look at a news item, or a "scientific" observation, you discover that what first appears to be "facts" turns out to be fuzzy. We can use our personal experience, just as scientists use their research experience, to examine critically the validity and the plausibility of other people's observations and numbers.

So in science, as well as in daily news, we must learn to question observations that "count fuzzies"—that tie numbers to events that, on second thought, we know from personal experience don't come packaged in hard, easily counted containers—experiences like fantasies, passing thoughts, suicides, or the I.Q.'s of 250 million people.

A Second Look: Beliefs and Expectations

On closer examination, why might you question the news item that only 2 percent of Americans have I.Q.'s above 130?

When asked, the main reason first-year students gave was that they didn't like that observation; they just didn't like having the Japanese scoring higher. So if consumers don't like some particular "news" they typically become more careful critics. First-year students asked various critical questions, such as:

"Where did they get the Americans (in the civil service) and where did they get the Japanese (in the universities)?"
"I read that group I.Q. tests aren't all that accurate, so how can they be sure?"
"How many Americans did they measure?"
"Who scored the Japanese tests—the Japanese I'll bet."

So we become more critical and perhaps more sophisticated consumers not only when personal experience and a second look tell us the information is hard to get (for example, fantasies), but also when we encounter observations or numbers we don't like or believe (such as numbers that put us or our beliefs in a bad light).

Personal and professional scientists alike concentrate their curiosity and critical faculties around *unexpected* observations. Why might you question the unexpected news that the average length of sexual intercourse for humans is 2 minutes? One first-year student summed up the response of many when he said: "Maybe two minutes in the laboratory, but not in the bedroom." Another asked: "When did they start timing?" A third student said: "If that's true a lot of my friends are liars." So this "observation" was questioned both on the basis of personal experience and on the basis of reports and beliefs concerning the experience of others.

A fourth student commented: "Where do they get all the 'average people' for these stories?" Where do average people, and average time, come from? Do they ask 10 people, then add the scores and divide by 10 and generalize to the whole population? Who do they choose? Where do they get them? As Bill Cosby wonders, How come those people in the ads never choose Coke? Who buys all the stuff?

So when you take second, third, or more looks at a given observation, you as a personal scientist are behaving in the *spirit* of the scientific tradition, which recognizes that all observations contain regions of uncertainty that are exposed by asking such questions as:

1. Where did they get those numbers, or observations?
2. Who was the reporter or researcher (casual; rushed; probing; Republican; Democrat; pro-life; pro-choice; creationist; evolutionist; male; female; and so forth)?
3. At what level (surface; middle; deep) were those observations made? Even if you had excellent reporters and researchers would this news, these numbers, be tough or almost impossible to get? If so, the news is probably a fragment of surface news supported by counting or measuring fuzzies (the observers reported seeing an average of 3.73 ghosts, having an average of 8.52 sexual fantasies per day, while drinking an average of 4965.1329 beers a year!).
4. What "paper" does he/she work for? What "side" of the news are they looking for? Reporters' and researchers' observations are screened by the news editor, who decides whether they go on the front page, the back page, or in the garbage. Did you know that the majority of articles submitted by researchers are rejected by scientific-journal editors?

But even if you don't know anything about the competence of the researcher, or the editorial policy of the source of the news story, you can be certain that most observations, scientific or otherwise, include enough uncertainty surrounding them, and embedded in them, to warrant further critical examination. Furthermore, you can be certain that such critical examination will expose many more questions than the original observation or explanation can handle. In this sense, then, all scientific observations and explanations are *temporary* and *tentative.*

Think of any observation as being surrounded by a region of doubt, or uncertainty, and of containing an area of uncertainty. We recognize these fuzzy regions in everyday language when we say: "We had a few beers, *more or less.*" We recognize these regions of uncertainty in scientific language when we say: "Life originated 2 billion years ago, plus or minus 500 million years"; or "The average person has 8 sexual fantasies a day, plus or minus 7"; or that "Teenage suicide is up 300 percent, more or less."

FIGURE 1–1

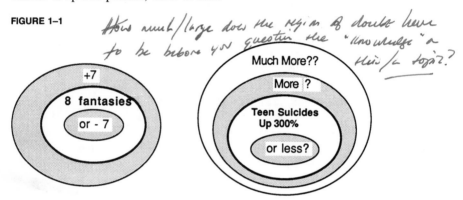

Teenage suicides up 300 percent? Give that a second look and a bit of reflection. Would you guess that number was high or low? Is there bias operating against accurate reporting of suicides: a family bias (hiding suicide notes), a medical bias (protecting the family), a religious bias (it's a sin), an economic bias (loss of insurance), and so forth? All these factors acting in concert would affect the statistics. So a more accurate statement might be that: "*Reported* teenage suicides are up 300 percent." Perhaps an even more accurate statement would be that "Reported teenage suicides are up by at least 300 percent, but actual suicides are probably up by much more!"

On the other hand, with computer linkages we are probably getting more of the *reported* suicides into the national data bases, so better bookkeeping rather than more suicides might account for most of the increase. As we said, "Teenage suicide is up 300 percent . . . more or less!" There's more to most observations than meets the eye, more uncertainty than can be solved with only a second, or third, look.

Stop and think of how much of our experience consists of observations that contain a "more or less' rider attached to them, implicitly if not explicitly. Some contain large regions of uncertainty, such as the origins of life, fantasies, the potential duration of a marriage, or the number of suicides. Others possess relatively smaller regions of uncertainty, such as your weight, skunk odors, precise time of death, and the labels on Coke, Pepsi, and Tylenol. For the last three, the region of uncertainty is not on the surface; it's on the inside. Is there any real difference between Coke and Pepsi? Advertisers would have us believe so. Is there only Tylenol inside the bottle?

So-called *objective observations* involve small regions of uncertainty, in the sense that different observers agree (for example, assign the same numbers) even without peeking at each other's notes. For instance, both Republican and Democratic reporters can agree that the President spoke for 17 minutes, plus or minus a few seconds, but strongly disagree about what he "really" said or what it meant (large regions of uncertainty or subjectivity).

Similarly, different observers can agree that one can is *labeled* Pepsi and the other Coke (small region of uncertainty), but disagree over which tastes best (large region of uncertainty or subjectivity). Notice what happens when you cover the labels and ask people to identify, by taste alone, their favorite—you will probably find that over a series of trials most "observers" can't tell the difference when they can't see the labels.

Thus, we have several ways of making decisions or choices when operating in high uncertainty regions. We can rely on external surfaces or labels; we prejudge the hidden layers on the basis of the surface appearance or labels, whether judging soft drinks or people. Although "you can't judge a book by its cover," most of the time we do; we can't spare the time to perform blindfolded taste trials and "get to know" everyone.

So the confidence we have in surface observations or labels serves as a very powerful decision aid in the myriad of choices we must make every day.

When we lack subjective confidence, or time, or energy, we rely on others to guide us—"trusted" others, or "experts" like family, friends, priests, professionals, technicians, and of course scientists. Society provides science with the time and technology to explore beneath the surface, to conduct our blindfold trials for us, gradually to shrink given regions of uncertainty, and pass its "more or less" findings down the imperfect communication channels to the professionals (for example, doctors) and technicians (for instance, electronic experts) who, in turn, pass them on down to us.

But we have only discussed one side of a news service—the observational side (reporting and research). There was no editorial or explanatory material attached to these stories; they only covered observations—fuzzy, surface, limited, or otherwise.

Commentary or theory focuses on explaining the news, on speculating about what key factors led up to or produced the news, and what the key consequences might be. Commentary and theory draw linkages between a given piece of news and other events—earlier events, current events, future events. Commentary and theory place news in a larger frame of reference—a larger conceptual frame, a larger experience frame, a larger time frame.

Consider the following news item, which lists the top seven discipline problems in public schools in 1940 and the top 17 in 1982:

1940	1982
1. Talking	1. Rape
2. Chewing gum	2. Robbery
3. Making noise	3. Assault
4. Running in the halls	4. Burglary
5. Getting out of turn in line	5. Arson
6. Wearing improper clothing	6. Bombings
7. Not putting paper in wastebaskets	7. Murder
	8. Suicide
	9. Absenteeism
	10. Vandalism
	11. Extortion
	12. Drug abuse
	13. Alcohol abuse
	14. Gang warfare
	15. Pregnancy
	16. Abortion
	17. Venereal disease

Where do they get these "observations"? Who counted the rapes? the suicides? the extortions? the pregnancies? the abortions? the venereal disease?

Notice, no editorial comment is included, but with the two lists placed side by side, and given the dates, most readers spontaneously generate commentary and explanations. What comments come readily to your mind?

Make a guess as to where this "news" item was published.

(a)   A Harvard University research institute journal?
(b)   A school board newsletter?
(c)   An evangelical church publication during the presidential election?
(d)   A police circular?

If you guessed item (c) you are correct.*

To appreciate the powerful role different points of view or vested interests can play in interpreting an event, refer to the news clipping at the end of this chapter. It describes the radically different frames of reference used by the prosecuting and defense attorneys in a trial involving the bombing of three abortion clinics.

EXPLANATION, SPECULATION, THEORY

Observations—facts or fuzzies—piled on a table or merely listed page after page cry out for organization. Whether scientist or citizen we seek linkages.

---

*From *Harpers Magazine,* March, 1985, p. 25.

Which current events are tied together?
What events in the past caused them?
What events will they cause or lead to in the future?

Once again, scan the news items at the beginning of this chapter. Which ones seem linked together in some way?

The mind's eyes of first year students reported the following possible linkages:

1. The linkage (contrast) between the American and Japanese I.Q. figures.
2. The possible causal linkage between increased LSD use and teenage suicide.
3. The possible causal linkage between 60,000,000 Americans reading below the grade-nine level and American I.Q. levels below the Japanese.

Cause and Effect

Our flow of observations—facts, fantasies, or fuzzies—demand organization. The mind's eye provides linkages that the real eye can't or doesn't see. The mind's eye spontaneously looks for "cause-effect" linkages, for explanations. The outer eye tries to focus on "what" questions, and the mind's eye on "why" questions.

Some linkages are so obvious and so close in time and space that the real eye can detect them without much help from the mind's eye:

Question: What caused the broken window?
Answer: This baseball that just came through it.

Some linkages are pretty obvious, with the real eye providing most of the answer and the mind's eye (speculation and memory) adding some supporting arguments.

Question: What led to the touchdown?
Answer 1: The intercepted pass.
Answer 2: Yes, but that was caused by poor blocking.
Answer 3: Yes, and don't forget about the intended receiver being out of position.
Answer 4: Yes, and don't forget that the coach threw that new quarterback in without having prepared him for such an emergency by giving him some previous big-game experience.

So . . . what really "caused" the touchdown?

In this puzzle we have the real eye and the inner or mind's eye working together on direct and indirect, or additional, causes or linkages. We see an expanding list, even a flood, of proposed causes or explanations.

Some linkages are hard to see or trace, and the mind's eye must do most of the work, with selected supporting arguments provided by the real eye.

Question: What caused his death?

Answer 1: A gunshot wound to the head.

Answer 2: He was in with a fast crowd.

Answer 3: I heard he was on drugs.

Answer 4: No, it was an accident; he was cleaning a gun.

Answer 5: I heard he had cancer or maybe it was just the flu.

Answer 6: He was down in the dumps about his girlfriend.

Answer 7: Depression runs in his family. . . .

So . . . what "caused" the death or suicide?

FIGURE 1–2

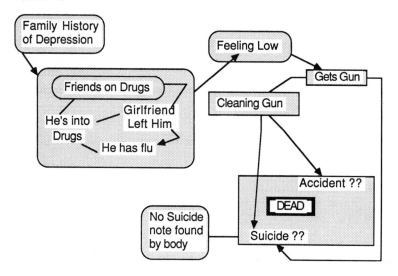

Notice that the only "hard" observations are probably the gunshot wound and presumably the death. All the rest are the work of the mind's eye puzzling away inside different heads.

What caused the death? The simplest answer is: A gunshot wound to the head (more or less, until an autopsy is performed). But what caused the gunshot wound? Obviously a gun, probably the one found beside his body, (more or less, until ballistic tests reduce that region of uncertainty). But surely it was an accident. Maybe, but he knew how to handle guns, more or less. Probably suicide then, but he left no suicide note, more or less (at least the person who found him reported no note was found). Still, he was feeling low, more or less; and he and his friends were on drugs, more or less; and his girlfriend had walked out on him, more or less; and he had the flu, more or less; and depression ran in the family, more or less.

Of all these "causes," which were relevant? How much did each one contribute? Was his mother right: "He must have sneezed because of his flu and the gun went off accidentally"?

We see, from this example, that talking about "what caused what" can become very complicated with hidden, imaginary, or invisible linkages going off in all directions further and further back in time. So although the term *cause* is still widely used in daily conversation, and in common-sense explanations, most scientists avoid the word. They avoid it because it only designates the last explanation you have—the one you are holding when you stop asking questions, or when due to confusion, fatigue, or boredom, the mind turns its eye away from that particular puzzle.

Antecedents and Consequences

Instead of talking about cause and effect, scientists talk about *antecedents and consequences*. Notice, they don't talk about *the* antecedent, but about antecedents (plural), which is a way of acknowledging that there are usually many antecedents—usually more than the mind's eye can perceive, more than the real eye can see even when the mind's eye gives it hints about where to look. Moreover, each antecedent has an endless network of ancestors stretching back in time.

The best that investigators can hope for in their search for explanations is to attempt to trace a few of many possible antecedents part of the way back in time, whether they are attempting to explain the origins of life; of subatomic particles; of depression; of touchdowns; or of an accidental death or suicide.

> **Most interesting questions facing citizens, or scientists, come surrounded with more antecedents than the outer eye can see, or the inner eye can manage or imagine.**

Therefore, the reach of science, like the reach of common sense, is limited. Nevertheless, with the use of certain methods, and certain ways of thinking, science extends her reach by using what we popularly think of as *the scientific method*.

THE SCIENTIFIC METHOD: THREE KEY INGREDIENTS

Since antecedents and consequences frequently contain large regions of uncertainty, and since interesting questions come surrounded with more antecedents than we can see or imagine, we require more than casual curiosity and casual observation to solve them.

Common-sense problem solving, on the one hand, typically involves having the external eye take a second or third look at one or two antecedents, and having the mind's eye take a second or third look at how they might be linked to each other (the flu to a sneeze to an accidental gun shot), and how these in turn might be linked to the consequence in question (the death . . . the accidental death?). Scientific problem solving, on the other hand, typically involves having *many* external eyes—plus their technical extensions and magnifiers—take repeated looks at various antecedents in an effort to reduce their regions of uncertainty, and having *many* mind's eyes take repeated looks and run repeated tests on possible linkages. This process, known as the *scientific method*, draws its power from a variety of sources that will be discussed throughout the book. But let us begin with three key ingredients.

The first and most important ingredient is *driving curiosity,* otherwise we have no questions or observations or solutions or explanations other than those generated by casual or temporary cur‸ ›sity—those generated by the short reach of common-sense problem solving.

A second ingredient is *systematic observation*—involving repeated, magnified examinations—aimed at reducing the regions of uncertainty surrounding selected antecedents and their linkages, and aimed at reducing the size of the "more or less" or "plus or minus" regions in which all our observations lie nested.

A third ingredient is *systematic experimentation,* which involves testing different antecedents to see which one, or combination, produces a given consequence.

So one way of comparing the scientific method with common-sense methods of problem solving is in terms of the relative emphasis each one places on these three key ingredients, which are illustrated in Figure 1–3.

As indicated on the left-hand side of Figure 1–3, *common-sense* solutions mainly arise from a combination of casual or temporary curiosity, observation, and experimentation. This combination of casual or temporary problem-solving activity typically yields a grab bag of conflicting solutions: The death was accidental . . . . No, it was suicide . . . . It was due to drugs . . . It was due to bad genes . . . .

On the other hand, *scientific problem solving* relies on a combination of factors: driving/persistent curiosity; systematic observation; systematic experimentation—a combination likely to generate more reliable solutions.

As noted on the right-hand side of Figure 1–3, by combining persistent curiosity with systematic observations we generate the *observational sciences* in which researchers become increasingly accurate in describing, predicting, and explaining a host of phenomena ranging from the heavenly movements of stellar bodies to the earthly movements of political opinion and voting patterns.

When the third ingredient—systematic experimentation—is combined with driving curiosity and systematic observation, we generate the *experimental sciences.* This combination represents our most powerful puzzle-solving strategy, leading not only to accurate predictions and sophisticated explanations and models but also to potent control and shaping powers.

In the experimental sciences, researchers not only track public opinion but also manipulate it; they not only observe and predict human behavior, but they shape it—with information, drugs, advertising, indoctrination, rewards, training, and so forth.

But remember, scientific predictions, manipulations, controls, and explanations operate within different margins of error—some small, some large, some unknown. This is true not only because all researchers are "casual" common-sense problem-solvers some of the time (and a few are casual most of the time) but also because certain dimensions of the physical world and of human nature continue to surprise and confound science and its most dedicated researchers using

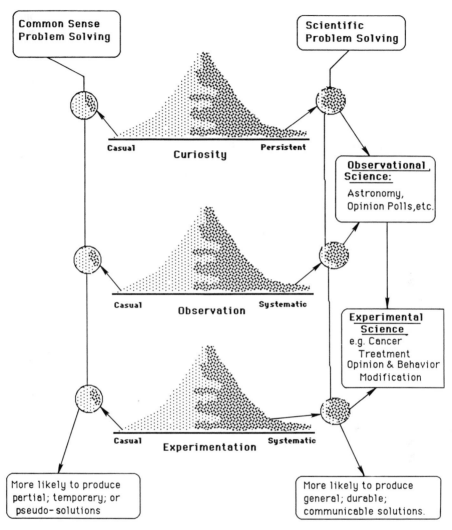

FIGURE 1-3

its most powerful probes and magnifiers. Thus, even science cannot penetrate some regions of uncertainty.

Next we will examine these three vital components of the scientific method: compelling curiosity, systematic observation, and systematic experimentation.

Compelling Curiosity

A colleague named Grayson is "hooked" and has been for the past five years on exploring "human" thinking, feeling, and acting in relation to making *resolutions* about all kinds of behavior: smoking, eating, drinking, worrying, daydreaming, sleeping, speaking out, test anxiety, procrastinating, cramming, and so forth.

Whereas you or I temporarily focus our attention on a particular puzzle (a resolution to stop cramming, or to cease smoking), Grayson focuses his on a general puzzle (many people's resolutions about *many* types of behavior) and his attention remains locked on it; his career revolves around it.

He looks forward to New Year's just as a child looks forward to Christmas; he avidly collects resolutions and tracks their limited spans; he publishes papers in learned journals that describe the few success stories he discovers and which present alternative explanations why these few smokers, or boozers, or crammers succeeded in changing their behavior whereas thousands of others failed.

At cocktail or dinner parties he corners unsuspecting guests, interrogating them about their resolutions, collecting treasured specimens for his growing collection. His wife pleads with him to stop badgering friends and acquaintances, to limit his lectures to the classroom and his research to his laboratory at the university. She even got him to make a New Year's resolution that he would, but she doubts he'll keep it . . . "Doctor, heal thyself!"

Compelling curiosity is the engine of science. Whether the goal is prediction, control, or understanding, it requires a combination of persistence and fascination to map and untangle the complex and shifting network of antecedents and consequences.

But while such driving curiosity is a necessary tool of the researcher and the theorist, it alone does not distinguish scientists from the rest of us. Each of us gets hooked on something: our careers, our children, our lover, music, football, the stock market, fashion, foods. Furthermore, each of us knows that "getting hooked" rarely follows a tidy, predictable path; trial and error seems to play a larger role than planning in establishing our "addictions" or our fascinations.

Similarly, a scientist's compelling curiosity usually hooks on to a problem or a puzzle by trial-and-error gambits rather than by rationally picking a "good one" off the scientific shelf. Like some people, not all scientists get hooked, so they end up going through the motions.

As with some people, some scientists get hooked on "bad" or insoluble puzzles. While walking one spring day with a colleague and his three-year-old daughter, Leslie, we commenced to climb the river bank. After a few unsuccessful attempts Leslie sat down and lisped: "That hill is too big for my shoes!" Her father, a cancer researcher, looked down, smiled, and replied gently: "Leslie, that hill is like daddy's work. Sometimes it's too big for his mind, maybe too big for all our minds . . . time will tell."

However, like many people, some scientists hook on to compelling engagements, and their driving curiosity sustains them through the unpredictable ups and downs that arise in any complex relationship—whether engaging a person; a career; or one of "human nature's" knotty puzzles.

But while compelling curiosity is a necessary ingredient of science, it is not enough; it is not sufficient. It must be combined with at least one other ingredient: systematic observation.

Systematic Observation

Solid research requires driving curiosity generating and focusing the power to build a foundation of reliable observations.

Our colleague Grayson's foundation of observations includes the fate of thousands of New Year's resolutions. Each December, through student questionnaires, interviews with faculty, television appearances, and newspaper ads, he collects hundreds of resolutions. Then starting in January he and his research assistants, using questionnaires or interviews, follow the fate of each fragile resolve.

Grayson's observations indicate that over 90 percent of the resolutions have dissolved or self-destructed by the end of January. Approximately another 5 percent have actually been broken but reported as still in force through "white lies," wishful thinking, or poor memory. Grayson and his sleuths conduct investigations on a sample of "successful" resolutions by such methods as checking ashtrays, interviews with family and friends, weight checks . . . . They even go as far as to smell the fingers of "ex-smokers."

Like tenacious investigative reporters, these researchers don't necessarily believe everything they're told. They learned early that data come in all shapes and sizes, and some data on close scrutiny turn out to be garbage. GIGO (garbage in/garbage out) is a favorite acronym of computer scientists to highlight the point that if you start with bad data no amount of fancy analysis will transform it into "the truth." All researchers live with the vague awareness that today's data may be tomorrow's garbage. Well, all jobs involve some risk—even scientific jobs; all solutions are "more" or "less" solutions.

Society provides scientists and researchers with time and money so they can aim driving curiosity and systematic observation at important puzzles so they will come up with more accurate predictions than we can using our more casual common-sense methods.

In his research on resolution making and breaking, not only does Grayson make general predictions covering large numbers of observations, but notice he also couches his predictions in terms of probabilities—the odds are 9 to 1 against keeping a New Year's resolution. Like race track touts and professional gamblers, researchers understand that unknown antecedents always play a role, that chance sits in on every game and plays its cards. If we're lucky, chance plays from a weak hand; if not, it confounds our arrogant predictions and exposes our fragile understanding.

By assigning different probabilities, or odds, to their observations, scientists attempt to estimate the size of the regions of uncertainty surrounding and embedded in their observations and to acknowledge the potentially powerful influence hidden or unknown antecedents can exert.

Furthermore, experienced researchers know they can't believe everything they see or hear. Some of their sources talk a good game but can't play one, or even if you actually "see" them play one it may be a flash in the pan—maybe it was luck playing its cards in their favor. Therefore, experienced researchers invariably seek several lines of evidence. That is why Grayson and his sleuths probe below the surface of the few "success" stories they encounter and indeed find over half of those claiming success were talking a better game than they played. That is why Grayson tenaciously follows up those who start out playing a better game, to determine whether the change is fragile and temporary.

Therefore, when driven by persistent curiosity, scientists via systematic observation, and repeated examinations of a puzzle, aim to reduce the regions of uncertainty in which all antecedents and their linkages reside. Otherwise we settle for temporary or unreliable solutions that arise from casual first and second looks and the simple cause-effect logic of common-sense explanations—fuzzy antecedents fuzzily linked to each other and to fuzzy consequences.

For example, observe the common-sense problem solving of a student who crams for exams—if you happen to know one: procrastination, plus or minus; leads to cramming, plus or minus; leads to anxiety, low grades, self-disgust, plus or minus; leads to resolutions to start studying earlier, plus or minus; leads to drawing up a study schedule and/or a few days studying, plus or minus; leads back to procrastination and repeating the cramming cycle.

This familiar recycling of ineffective common-sense solutions suggests that casual or temporary curiosity combined with casual observation frequently fails to identify clearly important antecedents and critical linkages or leverage points and so produces pseudo-solutions.

Without systematic observations we end up linking one vague observation to another, like glibly tying "teenage suicide" to "a history of depression in the ancestors." And yet simply reducing the size of the more-or-less regions of uncertainty surrounding the incidence of one antecedent (family history) and one consequence (teen suicide) remains a formidable challenge to systematic observation before we can even address the question of whether they are tied together in some way—weak, moderate, or strong.

In brief, without compelling curiosity we don't have the engine to drive systematic observations, and without systematic observations we end up with fuzzy explanations of fuzzy networks of antecedents and consequences. We end up with New Year's resolutions, and with "right wing" and "left wing" explanations of any fuzzy puzzle you can name.

All science, whether observational or experimental, whether aimed only at description and prediction, or also aimed at control, is at the mercy of the regions of uncertainty surrounding and embedded in its observations. The goal of systematic observation is to reduce continuously that uncertainty—to shrink the size of the more-or-less rider attached to all our measurements, our counts, our "solutions."

Systematic Experiments

By necessity or preference, some scientists, like astronomers and pollsters and New Year's resolution trackers, limit themselves to making increasingly accurate descriptions or predictions of accessible portions of a given network of antecedents and consequences. They can't or don't try to manipulate or control the network under observation—the astonomers can't manipulate the orbits or position of the planets, and pollsters presumably don't try to influence the vote.

In contrast, the popular view of science highlights gaining control over physical and social networks through experimentation.

Experimentation is not the exclusive domain of scientists. All of us experiment. But our "experiments" are typically casual, trial-and-error affairs that involve manipulating one fuzzy antecedent (a New Year's resolution) and casually observing what happens to a fuzzy consequence (studying). If that doesn't seem to work, we usually throw a bunch of fuzzy antecedents into a bag (drawing up a study schedule; asking your boyfriend not to ask you out weeknights; putting a "do not disturb" sign on your door; turning off the T.V., and so forth) and see what happens.

What happens? Not much more or less, but it's hard to say because you didn't make systematic observations, and looking back your memory is a bit vague, but as you recall your boyfriend had hurt his knee playing football so needed extra time and attention, and somebody stole your "do not disturb" sign, and there were some important educational programs on T.V. you "had" to watch.

But what about your studying? Well . . . I think it improved . . . more or less! How did you keep track? Did you keep a record of minutes studied per day? Or pages read and underlined? Or pages summarized? Well, no, none of those, but my general impression is that it improved, more or less, and I've drawn up a new schedule so . . . .

Yes, we all experiment, but it's complicated for many reasons: (1) You have to decide which antecedents are important; (2) then try to put them in place; (3) then try to keep them in place; (4) while keeping accurate records of all that, plus what's happening to your studying.

Experimental science faces the same problems, for it must:

1. Decide which antecedents and consequences in the network to focus on.
2. Reduce the regions of uncertainty enough so that we can keep track of them.
3. Decide which antecedent we're going to manipulate and which ones we're going to control (eliminate or hold steady).
4. Figure how to do that, then do it.
5. Systematically observe what's happening:
   –Is the antecedent we're manipulating behaving itself?
   –Are the antecedents we're controlling staying controlled?
   –Are the consequences changing in the direction and by the amount our hunch or theory predicted they would?
6. Wonder why it didn't work.
7. Repeat the above using a more precise measure of consequences.
8. Wonder why it still didn't work.
9. Try bigger dose of favorite antecedent.
10. Wonder why it still didn't work.
11. Try more precise control of other antecedents.

12. Aha, finally getting some changes in one of the consequences.
13. Better repeat the experiment again. It might have been due to chance, or some hidden antecedent we can't even see.

Yes, there's a difference between the common-sense and casual "experimentation" versus the systematic experiments that researchers employ. And not only do they have to be systematic but they have to be lucky enough to pick relevant antecedents—to pick one, or a combination, that is "really" linked to an important consequence. Otherwise that careful one-by-one testing, while keeping all the other antecedents quiet (controlled), can take a lifetime or more, and frequently does. Think how complicated it is to try to untangle the relative influence on human behavior of such complex antecedents as heredity on the one hand and environment on the other. What is their relative contribution to depression, for example?

To help us untangle these two powerful yet complex types of antecedents we can sometimes capitalize on *natural experiments*; for example, studying identical twins who have been separated at birth and raised in different environments. If one twin subsequently suffers from depression, what is the probability of the other showing similar symptoms?

If the probability turns out to be high for a number of such pairs, then because their hereditary antecedents are identical and their environmental antecedents are different, it suggests that their hereditary antecedents are playing a significant role—more or less. Since we can't "experiment" with people's heredity, identical twins raised apart offer social scientists a rare opportunity to *more or less* untangle the relative contribution of hereditary and environmental antecedents as they relate to everything from intelligence to abnormal behavior. As you will find in subsequent chapters, our current explanations contain large regions of uncertainty and generate heated debates.

Although we can't systematically experiment with human heredity as it relates, for example, to depression, we can do so with various treatments for depression. When you or I feel low we unsystematically experiment with a bagful of "treatments" and usually give credit to the last one we tried before we got better, completely forgetting that feeling low usually lasts a week, more or less, no matter what we do about it. That's common-sense problem solving, and no harm done.

Systematic experimentation, on the other hand, would involve a group of depressed patients divided into two "matched" groups, with one getting the traditional treatment, or a placebo (sugar pill), and the other group getting the new treatment, then systematically observing any changes in symptoms, with other antecedents being controlled, or held more or less equal; for instance, time on treatment, ward environment, food, ward staff, number of visitors, and so forth.

Future chapters will examine the increasingly powerful methods of observation and experimentation scientists use continuously to reduce the regions of uncertainty surrounding their observations and their solutions. We shall also discuss how they attempt to extend the reach of science in exploring the shifting network of human experience. But before concluding this chapter we must make an important point.

Although compelling curiosity, systematic observation, and experimentation form the foundations of science, several other vital ingredients must be acknowledged.

PROBABILISTIC THINKING ABOUT ANTECEDENTS
AND CONSEQUENCES

We have already discussed a *fourth dimension* that characterizes scientific problem solving and helps distinguish it from common-sense approaches—namely the way scientists think about a problem in terms of antecedents and consequences, rather than in terms of simple cause and effect. Not only that but in order to acknowledge the regions of uncertainty that always surround their observations and explanations, scientists attempt to assign odds to the reliability of those observations, or estimate the probability that a particular antecedent, or combination of antecedents, is "really" tied to a given consequence.

When lacking experience or strong beliefs, nonscientists can also think in terms of odds—what are the *chances* the letter will arrive; the horse will place; the other person agree, or the dice are loaded? You carry around crude maps of chance in your head and start getting nervous when a seven comes up "too often" or the coin lands heads "too often." But whereas you may rely on intuition to compute crude odds, many scientists rely on highly sophisticated mathematical and statistical models to help them estimate the degree of certainty they can afford to have in their observations, predictions, and conclusions. We discuss some of these statistical models—or maps of chance—in later chapters.

If only chance is operating, a coin has a 50–50 probability of coming up heads, otherwise more than chance is influencing the toss. But there's another antecedent in addition to chance—a bias of some kind. Similarly, if only chance is operating, certain patients have a 50–50 chance of getting better. If, however, following treatment on a new drug more than 50 percent improve, maybe there's a bias operating, a positive treatment influence over and above chance. But you know you can get a run of heads even from a true (unbiased) coin by chance. So how far do your results have to deviate from 50–50 before you decide that something more than lady luck is playing in your game?

Scientists go to great lengths to estimate how much their findings are merely due to lady luck on a roll and how much to the antecedents they're manipulating, or the treatment they are administering. Most scientists acknowledge the significant role chance or unknown antecedents play in their findings. So a fourth dimension characterizing science is a probabilistic way of thinking about reality as composed of complex networks of antecedents, consequences, and chance, in contrast to a simple cause-effect way of thinking typically employed in common-sense problem solving.

We must also acknowledge a frequently neglected fifth dimension of science—the vitally important role played by hunch, intuition, and theory in guiding scientific discovery.

INTUITION AND THEORY

Although there are thousands of systematic researchers conducting careful, one-by-one screenings of thousands of potential antecedents, the famous scientists are the few who by good luck or brilliant hunch guide the rest of us to selected regions in the infinite network where we can find surprisingly powerful antecedents.

How complicated and time-consuming it is to test even three or four antecedents one by one; then in different quantities or durations; then in different combinations; in different quantities; for different durations; then on different consequences. Two different drugs, in three different quantities, for three different durations, on patients at three levels of severity of illness, of different ages, married and unmarried, receiving two different levels of nursing care—we're already up to hundreds of experiments on this one relatively simple network puzzle.

Such brute force science is not enough. It needs help. To help narrow its focus on to relevant regions of the network, and then on to powerful though hidden antecedents, science needs guidance and help from brilliant hunches and from inspired theory. And while, during their university training, we can identify *potential* scientists—those with compelling curiosity, which drives systematic observation and careful experimentation—we can't reliably separate those with "crazy" hunches from those with brilliant ones; or determine without years of work which theorist will lead hundreds of researchers either on a wild goose chase or to surprisingly powerful antecedents, such as the potential forces locked inside the atom; the chromosomes; the hormones; the unconscious; conditioned responses; partial reinforcement; mother-child bonding; peer pressure; cultural mores; and so forth.

You can perhaps gain a crude feel for the vital role intuition and theory play in science by using the analogy of the scientist as safecracker.

Scientist As Safecracker

As any safecracker knows, you don't gain access to major vaults by one or many casual twirls of the dial; the safe's combination contains several numbers where both the sequence and timing count, and only one combination out of potentially thousands will work. Similarly, any good scientist knows you don't gain access to nature's major vaults by casually manipulating several antecedents.

Even when you decode the combination you may find

A.   The door opens to disclose only a little secret, or

B. To disclose another vault requiring another combination. Good puzzles keep expanding, keep a jump ahead of the mind and technology of the researcher. Remember, "That hill is too big for my shoes," or

C. The combination may change. Just when you seem to have captured a stable truth the trusted combination doesn't work anymore. Remember, *chance* reserves a seat in every game. She decides when she'll play the aces up her sleeve or even change the rules of the game.

D. Sometimes the big secret you seek doesn't even reside in the vault you're working on; often it lies, in another bank entirely . . . but which one?

Recall the drunk down on his hands and knees under a streetlight looking for his car key. When asked when he last remembered seeing it he replied: "I just dropped it a few minutes ago when I was trying to get into my car on the other side of the street."

When asked why he wasn't looking for it where he dropped it, he said, "Don't be silly. How could I find it over there. There's no light."

Sometimes researchers also look in the wrong place—for instance, in laboratories because there's more light and their familiar search tools are anchored there. In other words, when looking for solutions to puzzles some researchers work on vaults that fit in the lab, which may or may not contain significant secrets or solutions.

E. So researchers may be in the right bank but working on the wrong safety deposit box, or they may be in the wrong bank altogether. Sometimes the solution's not even locked away in vaults but rather it's lying right out in the open but can only be perceived from a hilltop when walking with a child . . . or sitting under an apple tree and an apple falls . . . .

F. And of course, sometimes researchers wouldn't recognize an answer if it landed in their hands.

Recall researchers trying to figure out what caused swamp fever and malaria while busy swatting those pesky mosquitoes. Or doctors blaming "humors in the air" for killing so many young mothers with childbed fever, when all along it was due to live, invisible dirt on the doctor's hands.

So the answer to the puzzle of malaria and the puzzle of childbed fever literally lay in the palm of their hands, but because they were expecting a different kind of solution they were "blind." The idea of germs hadn't been planted in the scientific mind—*the mind was blind.* Later, after the idea of germs was planted, we had to wait for the invention of the microscope so the actual eye could see what the mind's eye imagined.

So, if the mind's eye is looking in the wrong direction, the real eye may see everything . . . except the solution.

If you keep in the back of your mind the analogy of the scientist as a safe-cracker seeking the right combination to the right vault, you have a crude but useful model of science. The analogy highlights not only the need for systematic experimentation to solve the combination but also highlights the overriding importance of selecting, by luck, hunch, or theory, the right vault—the "right" region of the network.

We know much more about working on combinations, about systematic experimentation, than we know about choosing the right vault—about pointing the mind's eye in the direction where powerful antecedents and solutions are likely to lie.

Consider then the cast of players involved at various levels in the scientific enterprise.

Great scientists   combine a wizard's mind with a safecracker's touch.

Great theorists   possess a wizard's mind; they point to richly stocked vaults, to regions where powerful antecedents can likely be found by skilled researchers.

Great researchers   possess "great hands" that make them master safecrackers, that enable them to expose the validity or error of the theorist's predictions.

As you can well imagine, a popular theorist can keep an army of researchers and technicians occupied for years, as did Einstein, Darwin, Freud, and Skinner, for example.

Technicians   help design and build equipment to aid researchers in their magnification of the very far, the very fuzzy, and the very small, and they also take the discoveries of theorists and researchers and turn them to practical use, and/or keep them "tuned" (for example, engineers of all kinds, electricians, computer specialists).

Professionals   borrow some of this technology and combine it with professional custom and common sense, and apply the mixture to our daily problems (doctors, dentists, clinical psychologists, social workers, and others are examples of these professionals).

UNDERSTANDING HUMAN BEHAVIOR

Where do we look for the origins of human behavior—for the really powerful antecedents? There are just too many potential antecedents to be tested; even those within our reach are beyond counting, let alone testing via systematic observation or experimentation. Where in the network should we search and test? Which of the millions of vaults should we work on?

As we noted earlier, we rely on favorite theorists to guide us, and we select search spaces—our vaults—according to our theoretical preference. Some theorists and researchers look inside the individual for the major antecedents—in their genes, their hormones, their brains, or their minds—while others look outside— at their parents, their institutional ties, their cultures.

So we see theorists and researchers specializing at different levels of speculation, observation, and experimentation as portrayed in Figure 1–4.

When you ask questions about depression, the answer you get—the powerful antecedents proposed—will depend on which levels, or vaults, the theorist or researcher is working. If at the level of the gene, you will get the results of genetic observations (remember the identical twins raised apart) and experiments tied together by genetic theories or editorials. If at the level of the culture, you will get the results of cultural observations tied together by sociological or anthropological theories (depression is concentrated among poor, single mothers, and other lower socioeconomic classes).

Levels of Observation and Speculation

"To produce an individual put genes and culture
in a bag and shake just right"

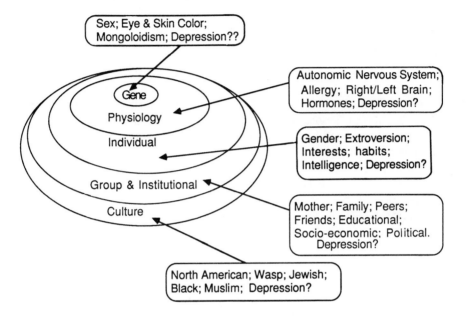

Sex; Eye & Skin Color;
Mongoloidism; Depression??

Gene
Physiology
Individual
Group & Institutional
Culture

Autonomic Nervous System;
Allergy; Right/Left Brain;
Hormones; Depression?

Gender; Extroversion;
Interests; habits;
Intelligence; Depression?

Mother; Family; Peers;
Friends; Educational;
Socio-economic; Political.
Depression?

North American; Wasp; Jewish;
Black; Muslim; Depression?

Specialization

Different social sciences tend to focus their observations, speculations,
and theories at certain levels; for example:

Gene/Physiological Level: Physiological/Experimental Psychologies.

Individual Level: Developmental/Clinical/Personality Psychologists.

Group/Institutional Level: Social Psychologists; Sociologists; Economists, etc.

Cultural Level: Anthropologists; Sociologists.

Note: Increasingly scientists are crossing traditional boundaries and creating
new interesting and controversial fields like sociobiology.

FIGURE 1-4

Also, within each layer will be subspecialists—theorists and researchers
working perhaps on the twenty-first chromosome vault. Within these subgroups
will be cautious theorists and researchers not straying too far from what is known,
exploring a limited, close-to-home region of the more-or-less uncertainty space.
But there will also be the risk-takers, speculating and probing in highly uncertain,

improbable regions—working on "way out" vaults but within the same bank, or same level.

And then there will be theorists who, to the dismay of some of their colleagues, will pogo-stick around within and across layers, picking up an antecedent here and there and tying them together into a provocative theory that attracts young or bored or disenchanted researchers who then excitedly hammer away at vaults all over the place, to the delight of the press and to the disgust of "real" specialists.

Just like everyone else, theorists and researchers come in temperaments ranging from the cautious and conservative to the grand speculators and gamblers. So at what levels they choose to work is not merely a matter of theoretical preference, but also of personal style. But regardless of level and style, luck, hunch, and theory play powerful roles in determining what vaults they work on and what they find inside.

What's found is always a composite picture compiled by both the outer and inner eye. As two researchers peer into a newly opened vault, one "sees" only a mosquito; the other "sees" the answer to malaria; one "sees" a fuzzy pattern on a microscopic slide; the other "sees" the antecedent of mongolism; one "hears" a funny story; the other "detects" the structure of prejudice.

SUMMARY

We don't believe everything we read in the newspaper, nor should we believe everything that scientists tell us. For in each case news comes in layers—surface, middle, deep—and also in each instance it comes nested in a region of uncertainty.

Nevertheless, we understand that scientific problem solving is more powerful than common-sense problem solving. We rely on science to explore regions of uncertainty we can't reach, even though the reach of science itself is limited, and even though each scientific probe reveals new and often larger puzzles.

Common-sense and scientific problem solving can be distinguished by the relative emphasis they place on five ingredients: (1) casual versus persistent curiosity; (2) casual versus systematic observation; (3) casual versus systematic experimentation; (4) simple cause-effect versus probabilistic antecedents-consequences thinking; (5) atheoretical versus theoretical thinking.

Beginning in Chapter 3 we will commence discussing the increasingly powerful methods scientists and researchers use to reduce the regions of uncertainty located in certain regions of "reality"—in certain networks where antecedents generate consequences, of course, with help from the fickle hand of chance, more or less.

But in order to get into the mind-set of scientists and researchers it may be helpful to become a bit more familiar with their way of thinking and talking—they speak with three tongues. You use these languages on occasion too, so you won't find them foreign.

Reality In The Mind's Eye of The Beholder

ABORTION BOMBERS LIKE 'KNIGHTS' NOT TERRORISTS, LAWYERS TELL TRIAL

By Tim Harper, Toronto Star
Pensacola, Fla.

Four young people who embrace religion, old-fashioned family ethics and have ''an abiding sense of American values'' went on trial yesterday charged with bombing three Florida abortion clinics last Christmas Day.

The four were described by a defense lawyer as ''knights in shining armor,'' not terror-ists.

''The government has brought charges against innocents, as [in] the trial of Jesus and the trial of Socrates,'' lawyer T. Patrick Monaghan said in his opening statement as he outlined plans for an insanity defense.

The trial of the four anti-abortion youngsters has put the spotlight on what can happen when the ongoing, increasingly violent abortion debate in the United States gets out of hand.

Lawyers defending the four youngsters are attempting to turn the trial into a referendum on the abortion issue.

The prosecution wants to keep the focus on the charges of bombing the three clinics and conspiracy to build weapons.

STRANGE BLEND
In opening statements at a U.S. courthouse in the middle of the Gulf Coast, dubbed the Redneck Riviera, the defense introduced a strange blend of ol' time religion, Bible quota-tions and American apple pie in its address to the jury of six men and six women.

The abortion debate careened out of control when three blasts within 20 minutes rocked this town near the Alabama border in the foggy predawn of last Christmas Day.

Charged are Matthew Goldsby, 21; his fiancee, 18-year-old Kaye Wiggins; James Sim-mons, 21; and his 18-year-old wife of eight months, Kathren.

''Matthew Goldsby is not a terrorist,'' said Monaghan, a Kentucky lawyer who is chief spokesman for the defense.

''James Simmons is not a terrorist and Kathren Simmons and Kaye Wiggins are not terrorists . . . just two young girls very much in love with their knights in shining armor.''

Monaghan said abortion is not an issue in this case.

''But we'll see how the controversy hits on young people individually and particularly these young people,'' he continued.

''We'll see how abortion is okay—it's in the Yellow Pages—and how it conflicts with the story of Luke these kids were taught.''

Abortion has been legal in the United States since a 1973 Supreme Court ruling.

But Monaghan also alluded to recent anti-abortion remarks made by U.S. President Ronald Reagan as fuelling the defendants' confusion.

Monaghan said the defendants were getting conflicting signals from authority figures. Their religious training and even Reagan, who he called a national ''father figure,'' led them to believe abortion is evil while the Supreme Court says it is legal.

''They saw unborn children being killed at three abortion clinics and what they saw were people being taken there to be killed,'' Monaghan said.

He called the defendants ''four outstanding young people.''

''They don't smoke. They don't drink. They don't engage in drugs. And they believe sex is properly a part of marriage.''

"They have a deep and abiding sense of God, America and American values. They identify with the American way of helping the underdog."

Monaghan said it was their virtues, not their vices, which brought them to the court-room.

"These are four of our own kids. Try to understand what in American youth—their beauty, their idealism, their zaniness or their craziness—compelled them to do this."

Pensacola lawyer Paul Shimek, who earlier had backed down on his attempt to represent all four, went further in his remarks in defense of Wiggins.

"They are horses in a race," he said, "and God is their jockey. They are winners.

"They obey God's law, not man's law. Take it or leave it. There are absolutes."

Prosecutor Susan Novotny said there was nothing symbolic about the Christmas bombings. She said Goldsby told agents he chose that morning because there would be fewer police officers on duty.

ESCAPE DETECTION

The four went to great lengths to prepare the bombs, plan the bombings and escape detection, she said.

She also said she would introduce evidence to show the four bought powder in one- to two-kilogram installments until they had enough for their bombs.

The four are all devoutly religious. None had ever had a criminal conviction before and they are the epitome of clean-cut, good-looking, pure-living southern young achievers, Shimek said.

Goldsby was arrested after attending church.

There have been 29 bombings of abortion clinics in the United States since 1982. Last year, federal authorities reported 24 acts of vandalism, including bombings, on U.S. abortion clinics.

Reprinted with Permission of the *Toronto Star*, Wednesday, April 17, 1985, A25.

chapter 2

The Language
of Science

SCIENCE SPEAKS WITH THREE TONGUES

If you think of reality as multilayered—some layers visible to the outer eye, and others only perceived, or imagined, by the mind's eye—you gain a clearer understanding of science. Scientific language acknowledges these distinctions between observation, speculation, and theory.

Similarly, our everyday language acknowledges a multilayered reality and identifies surface as well as hidden layers:

Laughing on the outside, crying on the inside.

Which layer is true—the visible laughing layer or the invisible crying layer? Both are true—in their way.

The visible laughing layer is *publicly* true. The words "laughing on the outside" are tied to *objective* behavior. It is a public fact that you are laughing. This statement, with supporting evidence (direct observation or a photograph) would stand up in a court of law, or in a court of science.

Fine. But how can we determine the "facts" about the invisible layers? How do we determine the truth about the part of the statement that describes "crying on the inside"?

We have at least three obvious options in deciding the accuracy of statements describing the invisible layers of nature and experience.

First, we can conclude that such a statement as "crying on the inside" cannot either be proved *or* disproved because it isn't tied to anything objective—to anything available for public inspection. Furthermore, we can continue to adopt such an "open-minded" stance until someone figures out how to make "inside crying" objective—until someone figures out how to "part the curtains" that cover that hidden event so we can measure it, see it, photograph it, or weigh it.

Our second alternative in deciding the accuracy of statements is to agree that the statement is *subjectively* true, even though its public truth remains indeterminant. In this second option the truth or falsity of the statement becomes a matter of personal opinions or convictions anchored to internal images and feelings—a matter of *phenomenology*.

Or third, we can agree that both kinds of information—objective and subjective—help us explore and map nature's many layers. This third position anchors confidence in objective evidence but recognizes that we must make many critical decisions in the absence of adequate objective evidence (choosing a mate, prescribing a new treatment for depression, evaluating the risk of nuclear waste). Therefore we must learn to get by with a few concrete observations, bolstered by a network of subjective, invisible, or indirect evidence—we must rely on "guesstimates," on what we feel, or sense, or hypothesize lies below the surface or behind the curtains of the future.

This third alternative reflects the view of science as a news service that not only relies on objective observations (facts) but also relies heavily on speculative frameworks concerning: (1) what lies beneath the surface facts; (2) what lies beyond current facts; and (3) hypotheses about hidden relationships, or mechanisms, that tie available facts together.

By means of objective and speculative descriptions, or maps, science reduces our sense of uncertainty in selected regions of that infinite antecedents-consequences-chance network we call reality.

Science = Observations + Speculations

Sophisticated consumers of science appreciate that "facts" represent the tip of the scientific iceberg—appreciate that the underlying superstructure of science consists of logical and speculative frameworks that support and link the surface facts together.

The simple local bit of news that "She's laughing on the outside but crying on the inside" contains the basic ingredients of complex scientific puzzles. It includes *observations* and *speculations*.

Observation 1:
"She's laughing."—*All* observers agree!
Observation 2:
"The laughing seems forced.'—*Some* observers agree.

Speculation 1:
"She's happy. She's really happy! Simple as that."—*Some* observers make this speculation.

Speculation 2:
"She's happy, but a bit nervous in a new situation."—*Some* observers make this speculation.

Speculation 3:
"She's really sad, but putting up a good front."—*Some* observers make this speculation.

Like scientific news, the analysis of this statement includes some observations about which all reporters agree, some observations about which only some reporters agree, and alternative conflicting explanations or speculations about possible but "invisible" connections or relationships between the surface layers and the hidden layers, or regions of uncertainty.

Many times each day you spontaneously make such differentiations; distinctions between "hard" news (he spoke for 45 minutes) and "soft" news and speculation (he's a closet Democrat, not a real Republican); or his *reported* I.Q. score is 103 (hard news), but he's much brighter than that; his academic potential is very high (soft news or speculation).

Furthermore, we recognize that what is perceived to be hard news by some (he definitely has high academic ability) may only be confident speculation masquerading as fact. On the other hand, such "observers" may be the early detectors of "emerging hard news" that will eventually become publicly available—everybody laughed at poor Ignaz Semmelweis and his crazy belief that invisible bugs cause disease until emerging germ *theory,* the invention of the microscope *(technology),* and a host of systematic observations and experiments *(research)* brought the ghostly bugs into public view and scientific respectability.

Just as you now distinguish between hard and soft, or fuzzy observations, and between casual and disciplined speculations in attempting to make sense of local news, you will learn to make sense of scientific news with the aid of the same distinctions. And you would be wise to do so because each day "you bet your life" on scientific observations and speculations and their subsequent technical spin-offs, and professional and "expert" interpretations, with each layer in the communication chain inheriting and contributing regions of uncertainty—more or less—to the air you breathe; the water you drink; the brake pedal you push; the aircraft you recline in; the nuclear power station down the road; the health advice and treatment you take; the counseling and "expert" advice you receive on everything from diets to dying.

Science and its technological and professional satellites constitute "strong stuff"—for good or ill—and so are worthy of some appreciative and critical attention. If you learn to listen, most scientists and many technicians and professionals will freely disclose the degrees of confidence they have in different observations, predictions, and speculations or theories. In our search for peace of mind and certainty we often filter out the qualifiers scientists build into their language.

Each individual scientist, and each scientific specialty, must work not only with the "facts," but also with the logic, and the hunches of their era. Our purpose in this book is to discuss how scientists evaluate alternative guesses about reality and how you, as a consumer of science, can evaluate scientific guesses by fine-tuning skills you already possess. As you improve these skills you will better learn to distinguish robust scientific observations from flimsy ones and to distinguish casual and sloppy scientific speculations from disciplined ones.

This view of science as an evolving speculative map with observational checkpoints not only helps protect you from pseudoscience but also can yield an enriched understanding of your world. Such a perspective might even lead you into a scientific career, where you join others exploring and mapping the fascinating and shifting surfaces of human experience.

Consumers of science, like its practitioners, will understand and appreciate its products as well as its arguments to the degree they understand the three types of language that scientists use to describe nature's many layers.

Each of the three languages focuses on different levels of description. The first, *observational language,* focuses on the exposed, currently accessible, or "factual" layers of nature. The second, *speculative language,* focuses on the hidden, speculative, or subjective layers of nature. The third, *formal language,* focuses on the logical, mathematical structures or models that scientists use to build frameworks formally linking together their observations and their speculations. A famous example of such a formal framework is Einstein's proposal that $E = MC^2$.

OBSERVATIONAL LANGUAGE (SEMANTICS)   Observational or "objective language deals with the high certainty surfaces, or regions, discussed in Chapter 1, deals with clear observations, and with clear linkages between antecedents and consequences—so clear that even traditional opponents like Republicans and Democrats, feminists and male chauvinists, experimental psychologists and anthropologists, can agree; so clear that it's unnecessary to peek at each other's notes, call a committee meeting, or take a vote because different observers "see" no uncertainty, or only a tiny plus or minus region of uncertainty, surrounding the observation—198 pounds plus or minus 1.

All language consists of symbols (spoken or written) and rules for their use. Observational language (semantics) employs

1. symbols or labels, and
2. rules for linking them to concrete objects or events.

The key rule in using objective language states: "Different observers, familiar with the symbols and the events in question, can *independently* and *consistently* tie a particular label to a particular object or event."

The following examples will help clarify the rule as well as indicate how it is both practiced and broken regularly in everyday language.

1. *"That man weighs 198 pounds."* In this example you are familiar with the symbols (the language); you can identify the key object as it (the man) has

been *pointed* out to you; and you are familiar with the rules for tying them together—that is, with the procedures for weighing the man. You know how to assign weight numbers to him—you can do it independently (alone) and consistently (repeatedly) and within a reasonable time period assign more or less the same numbers.

Here we have a clear instance of objective language: We know the symbol system; the key objects (the man and the scales) are publicly available; the procedures for combining them (weighing) is common knowledge; the procedure for labeling the result (assigning a weight number to the man) is agreed upon. So we end up with a solid observation that can be made independently and consistently by most adult members of the culture.

2. *"Tuo mies painaa yhdeksankymmenta kiloa."* Since you probably don't understand this particular symbol system, you cannot judge the objectivity of the statement—not until you learn the language or have someone translate it for you. If you did, it would translate from Finnish as "That man weighs 90 kilograms"— which is about 198 pounds.

But for all you know, it might have said, "198 angels can dance on the head of a pin." So to judge whether a statement meets the rules of objective language you must know the language, or system of labels; the object or events in question; and the rules for labeling them. Just because numbers are used doesn't mean that the statement is objective.

3. *"That woman is highly intelligent."* Here you are familiar with the symbols (the language), and you can identify the woman objectively (she's being pointed at). But how do you decide *objectively* whether the label "highly intelligent" can be tied to her? Although the woman is publicly visible, her intelligence is not.

Unlike her weight, you don't know how to measure her intelligence. After watching her and asking her questions, the same observers who could agree about her weight cannot agree about her intelligence—some label her as being of average intelligence, some label her as highly intelligent, and a few label her as stupid.

One way to handle such problems is to delegate them to an expert, in this case to a psychologist to "test" the woman and "label" her. The psychologist reports back that the woman's I.Q. (intelligence quotient) is 132, and since, by custom, all people with I.Q.s over 125 are labeled "highly intelligent," she is so labeled.

As a consumer of science, are you satisfied? You may know nothing about I.Q. testing; however, you need to know little to decide whether you're dealing with objective language. First, you know that numbers may mean nothing. Next, you know that to be classed as objective language, labels must be assigned independently *and* consistently by different observers or, if delegated, by different experts. Since only one expert has tested the lady and tested her only once, the argument can't be settled, not until at least two independent experts each test her twice. Let's say this is done and the first expert reports scores of 132 and 129, while a second reports scores of 125 and 128.

So, the different consumers of science may now agree that the woman has a high I.Q.—125 or higher. But they will probably continue arguing about whether or not she is "highly intelligent"—some observers saying, "If she's so smart how come she can only get high marks in math and not history, and how come she's so stupid socially, and so dumb with her money?"

In brief, wise consumers of science learn to distinguish objective language—independent and consistent labeling—from speculative language—from subjective language, and special interest group labeling. They learn as well to recognize that similar labels can differ greatly in their degree of objectivity—as do the labels "intelligence quotient" and "intelligence." Finally, informed consumers of science learn to see science as an evolving landscape, as an expanding system of guesses, spotted with objective outcroppings around which scientists cluster and explore different lines of speculation that disappear behind the horizons and surface layers of multilayered reality.

When using observational language—which identifies these objective outcroppings, or hard news surface layers—we will enclose the object or event under discussion in a heavy bordered circle

or in a heavy bordered circle nested in a narrow, dotted, surrounding circle to indicate a small region of uncertainty:

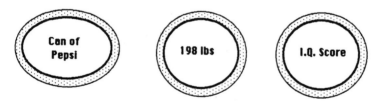

When a scientist or any expert makes a statement, a consumer has every right to inquire (1) what parts of the proposition describe an observed outcropping, (2) what parts represent speculation—disciplined or casual, or (3) whether the statement is a stewpot of observational and speculative language. We now turn our attention to speculation and to stewpot labels—to speculative language.

SPECULATIVE LANGUAGE (PRAGMATICS)   We can cast our mind's eye into regions of "pure speculation"—such as imagining what "heaven" or "hell" or "life from outer space" or "the edge of the universe" might look like.

Such speculations are "pure" in the sense that they are devoid of objective outcroppings; observational language is inappropriate except when used in an obvious metaphorical or analogical sense: "I imagine heaven to be like Miami Beach on a big expense account with me controlling who comes and goes." Or "I imagine life from outer space would look like . . . ." Through history, professional "healers" have speculated about and prescribed treatments on the basis of demons, humors in the air, invisible bugs, nerves, and so forth.

Similarly, theorists explore high uncertainty regions with their mind's eye *inventing possible*, hidden networks of linkages concerning cures for the common cold or cancer; or concerning the structure and dynamics of intelligence, personality, learning, forgetting, and so forth.

When using speculative language, which identifies high uncertainty regions, we will enclose the contents in dotted or hatched circles

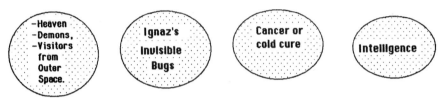

or show spreading—concentric—regions of uncertainty, and nested in them small, heavy bordered circles to indicate that they contain some isolated or linked objective outcroppings—crude empirical reference points:

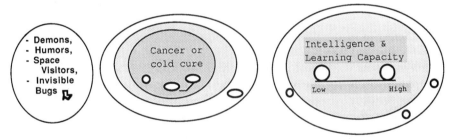

Objective outcroppings or discoveries, represented by observational language, are the bench marks of science. It is from such "observational checkpoints" that scientific explorations usually commence; it is from such checkpoints that scientists take their bearings to avoid becoming lost in speculative space; it is new objective landfalls they seek to discover or uncover in their explorations and experiments. Although these objective checkpoints represent the navigational aids of science, the bulk of scientists spend their time drawing and exploring speculative maps between or beyond observational checkpoints—some staying close to observational outcroppings, some ranging "far out" in speculative space into high uncertainty regions of the network, where antecedents, consequences, and chance play unfamiliar—sometimes weird—games.

As you can appreciate, every observational checkpoint (like an intelligence quotient) can spawn a host of speculations (about its genetic or environmental origins, about its importance in shaping your personal and professional future).

Therefore the large speculative maps of science are relatively sparsely spotted with observations and will remain so, for each new observational checkpoint generates a cornucopia of speculative maps—some focusing their guesses closely around the observational outcropping, some linking the observation to other close or distant outcroppings, some linking it to safe, and some to radical guesses.

This view of science, as perhaps one part observation and many parts speculation, is what led Einstein to refer to science as "a system of guesses" (Einstein & Infeld, 1966, p. 30).

This multilayered view of reality is also reflected in the following quotation by Einstein:

> Physical concepts are free creations of the human mind, and are not, however it may seem, uniquely determined by the external world. In our endeavour to understand reality we are somewhat like a man trying to understand the mechanisms of a closed watch. He sees the face and the moving hands, even hears it ticking, but he has no way of opening the case. If he is ingenious he may form some picture of a mechanism which *could* be responsible for all the things he observes, he may never be quite sure his picture is the only one which could explain his observations. He will never be able to compare his picture with the real mechanism and he cannot even imagine the possibility or the meaning of such a comparison. But he certainly *believes* that, as his knowledge increases, his picture of reality will become simpler and simpler and will explain a wider and wider range of his sensuous impressions. He may also believe in the existence of the ideal limit of knowledge and that it is approached by the human mind. He may call this ideal limit the objective truth (Einstein & Infeld, 1966, p. 31).

If science is to be viewed as a system of guesses or speculations, sparsely dotted with observational checkpoints, then the consumer of science must become skilled in sorting disciplined from casual or sloppy speculation and must develop a sense of the way our guesses or maps of reality evolve.

For example, consider how a series of observational checkpoints and speculations helped us zigzag our way to a more powerful system of guesses and treatments of illness, including "fever deaths."

LANGUAGE TYPE	OBJECTS AND EVENTS COVERED
1. Objective checkpoint (observational language)	Some people get recurring fever and die.
2. Popular speculation (speculative language—invisible layer or cause)	Fevers caused by "demons" occupying person's soul or body.
3. Observational checkpoint	Poor Harold Winch who died of fever was cursed by old Nell Blackstock at tavern last Michaelmas.
4. Enlightened speculation (invisible humors)	Illness not caused by demons, but by humors in air—by bad air. Keep windows closed.
5. Observational checkpoint	People who live in swampy areas get the fever.
6. Speculation	Fever caused by swamp "gas"—fits bad-air speculation theory.

7.	Observational checkpoint	People who live on high ground or move from swamp areas don't get fever (further support for bad-air speculation).
8.	Observational checkpoint	Some people who live in swampy areas don't get fever, and some people who live on high ground do.
9.	Speculation	Supporters of demon speculation see this as support for their theory—demons travel everywhere.
10.	Alternative speculation	Supporters of bad-air theory generate patch-up speculations—some bad air drifted to high ground, some swamp dwellers live on second floor so don't get so much bad air.
11.	Emerging speculation	Maybe illness not caused by demons *or* bad air, but by invisible bugs (beginning of germ theory).
12.	Observational checkpoint	Many mosquitos in low swampy areas.
13.	New speculation	Maybe mosquitos carry fever—maybe they inject invisible bugs into you when they bite you.

With the aid of further speculation and the discovery of the microscope, the "malaria" carried by mosquitos was identified.

Notice the leapfrogging from observations to speculation to observations—with observations providing a focal point around which speculations gravitate and fan out. Some speculations stimulate the search for and discovery of additional observational checkpoints, some of which fit the given speculation, some of which don't, thus generating patchwork speculations. Here we get a sense of the rhythm of science as it wends its zigzag way through nature's veils, very much a joint venture of the outer and inner eyes, very much a complex mix of observational and speculative language, which to the untrained ear sounds "observational."

The malaria example provides a view of multilayered reality; an *objective surface layer* including fever, death, and concentration of fever in certain areas. We see too the selective linking of *observations*: death by fever is linked to encounters with old women or death by fever is linked to living in swamp areas. We see as well *speculations* about invisible or vague layers or causes: demons, humors in the air, invisible bugs.

Notice the mosquitos were "invisible" in a sense, as were hundreds of other "swampy" objects or events until a chance observation or speculation made them suspect. Certainly germs were invisible and remained so until a mutually reinforcing combination of speculation (Ignaz Semmelweis' emerging invisible bug theory) and improved technology (the microscope) moved germs from the level of crude guesses to a sophisticated framework of speculation linking hundreds of internationally tested observational checkpoints.

Of course, speculation continues. Speculation, and science, gravitated around differences, around exceptions. For example, not all people who get fever

have been publicly cursed by an old woman (a witch). So "believers" speculate
that witches could curse you secretly from a distance—a patchwork, but effective,
speculation for those who believe in witchcraft.

Not all people who get germs get the disease. Why? Well, maybe they have
"something" inside—a stronger disease-fighting system. Here we go again! Some
scientists focus their speculation and research on outside sources of disease—
cigarettes, liquor, bad air (pollution), new invisible bugs (viruses)—while others
focus their speculation and research on inside sources of explanations like the
body's "immunological system"—much of which is still vague and invisible.

So then how do we decide which speculations "to back"—to publish, to
give research funds to, to teach, to try out? We can't rely only on the objective
rules because they illuminate only a tiny fraction of our vital questions. While
scientists can usually agree that the patient died or got better—an observational
checkpoint—there are always several schools of thought (schools of speculation)
as to why the patient died or got better. Some speculators bet that it's due to a
new virus; others that it has something to do with the immunological system, or
God's will, or the patient's will to live.

Since we don't get *independent* and *consistent* agreement among the observers about the answers to many important questions, we have to resort to other
decision rules for deciding which speculations to accept. The decision rules or
methods we use to judge speculative language are the rules of majority vote,
expert *judgment,* group pressure, force, and argument. The guesses, or maps, of
science are judged by rules similar to those used in the courts of justice.

The court of speculation.   Proponents of a given theory or speculation each
present their stewpot of objective evidence and speculative linkages, and then
the jury of scientific "peers" or a group of scientific "judges" chooses the
"stronger" case, which prevails until a theory with a stronger case evolves.

The courts of justice represent our most sophisticated public means of labeling stewpots of objective and speculative evidence. They give up all pretense of
aiming for independent labeling—relying instead on coaching and group pressure
to achieve agreement. In the courts, observers are coached first by lawyers of the
prosecution and then by defense lawyers concerning which parts of the stewpot of
evidence to "see" as hard objective evidence and which parts as soft; they are
coached and cajoled concerning what should be seen as a reasonable speculation
and what as weak conjecture. Even then each jury member is not permitted to
retire to a private place to *independently* reach his/her decision. No, they are
locked together in order to let group pressure, argument, and fatigue generate
agreement on what labels to apply to the regions of uncertainty—to the fuzzy
antecedents-consequences-chance network.

Although foregoing the rule of observer independence, courts still provide
opportunities to test the consistency of labeling through the appeal process. While
costly, retrials and review boards provide tests for the consistency of judicial labeling—tests of the consistency with which the important labels "innocent" or
"guilty" are applied.

In some "courts" we use a judge rather than a jury. Here we still provide
for argument and coaching but delegate the labeling not to a jury of peers but to

one "expert," who does not pretend to be completely objective but rather aims to choose and label the "stronger" case. Once again (recognizing that even for experts guilt or innocence lies partly, perhaps significantly, in the eye of the beholder) opportunities for appeal and retrial are provided.

In the case of the Supreme Court, we have several judges (a panel of experts) hear the arguments and then vote—relying ultimately on a majority rule to assign the label of guilt or innocence.[1]

In science as well as the courts, majority vote by peers and by senior judges (journal editors, research grant committees) plays a powerful role in deciding which mix of observational evidence and speculation receives grant funds, is published, or is awarded Nobel prizes. In science as well as the courts, such judgments are influenced by which judges preside—whether, as is usual, a preponderance are "establishment" scientists or whether, by accident or sloth, a majority of "radical" speculators or a block of "reactionaries" have gained control, of a journal, a research funding agency, or an award-giving institution.

Nevertheless, "cases" are continuously under review in science, through its journals and conferences. Granted, certain cases receive more press and more sympathetic judgments than others, but the popularity of given observational checkpoints and related speculations shift with time.

Thus to what extent the scientific "bench" is loaded by "demonologists," "pollutionists," "germ sleuths," or "immunologists" strongly influences the flow of scientific funds, information, and awards.

As a consumer of science you need not, and cannot, be informed about the intricacies of the judging process, but you would be wise to keep informed about which "school" of scientists presides on the major courts of science—in the main they will probably be "establishment" scientists bracketed by small numbers of scientific reactionaries and radicals. Gradually, as was the case with fever, the reactionaries (the demonologists) will be displaced by the current establishment members (the germ hunters) who in turn will be displaced by one of the new radical schools (immunology), who then become the establishment school, *for a while*. Then of course new "radicals," or scouts, will vie for positions on the leading edge of the discipline.

And so science evolves, with each passing theory or speculation giving way to a more powerful successor but having played a significant role in its time in providing science with observational and speculative bench marks and stepping stones on its zigzagging exploration of multilayered reality.

FORMAL LANGUAGE (SYNTACTICS)   Not only do scientists rely on objective language to provide observational checkpoints and on speculative language to help map the endless uncharted regions between and beyond observational checkpoints, but science relies too on formal language to provide powerful simplifications and models of nature's Chinese puzzle boxes.

---

[1]For one fascinating "picture" of how the U.S. Supreme Court labels its stewpots of evidence, see Woodward and Armstrong (1981).

SYMBOL RELATIONSHIPS. Whereas observational language deals with rules of procedure for tying symbols to concrete objects and events and speculative language deals with rules and procedures for tying symbols to subjective or hypothesized objects and events, formal language deals with rules for tying symbols to other symbols. Thus formal language deals with abstractions, with relations between symbols:

$$1d + 2d = 3d$$

These abstract relations are powerful shapers of our thought patterns. They carry with them (or suggest) observational chunks and speculative packages that restrict or channel our thinking into habitual modes, along habitual tracks. Deviation from these modes is jarring.

$$1d + 2d = 1d$$

"That's not right! What are you talking about?"
1 drop + 2 drops = 1 big drop
"Oh, well, I thought you were talking about solid things—you didn't say that *plus* meant *pouring* and that *d* meant wishy-washy things like drops."

That's right; we didn't. But in playing such a trick, we make the point that when you describe relations in abstract, or observational, or speculative language keep an eye on the underlying and surrounding assumptions. When you're not sure what the symbols mean, enclose them in a dashed circle: e.g., $\left(+\right)$ $\left(d\right)$.

Some important abstract relations that provide habitual tracks for scientific minds to run along include the following:

a. *Equivalence relations*
$A = B$
Which can mean:
1.   There are one or more ways in which $A = B$ even though there are lots of ways in which they differ. For example, they're both male, or both psychologists, or both depressed, or both possess triangles.

2.   *A* and *B* are identical on *all* dimensions. All dimensions? Well, that certainly doesn't apply to people, even identical twins, so that particular kind of equivalence relationship will have limited application in the behavioral sciences.

b. *Order relations*
A is greater than *B*, and *B* is greater than *C*, therefore is *A* greater than *C*.

$A > B$, and $B > C$, therefore $A > C$

which can mean that if *A* precedes or is taller than *B*, and *B* is taller than *C*, then *A* is taller than or precedes *C*.

This kind of abstract relation can provide a valuable track for the mind to carry *physical* information like height and weight and interestingly enough helps the mind make predictions about some physical observations that it has not yet made. But notice that this track is not so useful for carrying more complex information or making complex predictions. For example, just because the Dallas Cowboys can beat the Pittsburgh Steelers and the Steelers can beat the Houston Oilers doesn't mean that the Cowboys can beat the Oilers:

$$A > B, \text{ and } B > C, \text{ but } A \text{ may not be } > C$$

So, abstract statements which fascinate logicians and mathematicians and furthermore that can help describe and predict certain observations (stable physical observations) may be quite inappropriate for describing and predicting other kinds of complex and unstable observations.

In dealing with less stable phenomena which combine in dynamic ways, we rely on other abstract relations or complex mental pathways. For example, when we want to say that a given phenomenon A is tied in vague ways to many other phenomena we may say:

$$A = f, B, -C, D \ldots T \ldots e$$

which may mean that the consequence A is a function of (is somehow tied to) the antecedents $B, -C, D, T,$ and e.

Now here is the kind of abstract relation, or mental track, that may be useful to help describe relationships (observations and speculations) of interest to behavioral scientists and their consumers—the kind of mental track that can do justice to multilayered, shifting reality.

Notice when we ask how someone will behave, the answer, whether from a scientist or a friend, will include a statement equivalent to "It all depends." This is like saying A's behavior depends on (is a function of) a lot of antecedents: $B, -C, D \ldots T \ldots e$.

For example, it might depend on B (on what his best friend does) *and* depend on $-C$ (which means the opposite of what his parents advise) *and* depend on D (on what his girlfriend wants), *and* it might depend on T (on the time of day or the time of the week), *and* it will depend to a certain extent on e (on irreducible errors of prediction, on *chance* factors, on the fact that even scientists and best friends get surprised). Here we see that in certain areas the minds of scientists and knowledgeable laypeople run along similar paths of complex relations. Usually, however, when we're busy, or ignorant, or new to a field, or in a crisis, we rely on simple tracks like:

$$A = f(B + e)$$

which means A can be explained almost wholly by B, with a little unpredictability left over in e.

Such simple mental tracks reduce intellectual effort, allowing one so-called expert to conclude that personality *(A)* depends on genetics *(B)* or, just as simple-mindedly, on environment *(B1)*.

Similarly, as a result of being a novice or a bigot, other simple tracks let our brains compact complex information into oversimplified mind-sized packages:

$$(\widehat{A}) \quad = \quad (\widehat{f}) \qquad\qquad (\widehat{B}) \qquad (\widehat{e})$$

Behavior	depends on	Sex	
		or skin color	?
		or intelligence	?
		or political affiliation	?
		or area of experience	?
		or genetics	?
		or etc.	?

So although over a lifetime our brains perform magnificent feats of storing and processing information, nevertheless our short-term memory is very limited, and we can normally handle only one short train of thought at a time.[2] Therefore most of our mental traffic involves messages about simple relationships. However, when we focus on something repeatedly, our minds develop more sophisticated paths to do justice to the multilayered and shifting relationships—like those we explore in science and in friendship.

The scientific answer to a question generally takes the following form:

> **In any network a given consequence *depends upon* a variety of antecedents, acting independently and in various combinations—and don't forget the tricks those two rogues time and chance can play.**

This is the kind of answer that a multilayered, changing universe deserves.

Special symbols.   Although formal language focuses on "relations" (such as additions, subtractions, multiplications) between number symbols and letter symbols, such statements can also be used to describe parts of the objective world.

1 doctor + 2 doctors = 3 doctors

When we use formal language as a shorthand way to describe concrete objects and events, we will use special symbols in order to indicate that we are talking about established observational checkpoints—ones that can pass the test of independent and consistent labeling—and we will enclose the symbol in a **solid** circle:

$$\left(1d\right) \;+\; \left(2d\right) \;=\; \left(3d\right)$$

[2]Did you ever try to remember a new phone number as you walked through a noisy room?

Such solidly enclosed symbols are reserved for objects which have pretty clear boundaries—that is, things that strongly excite our senses: our sight, like the sun does; and our smell, like a skunk does; and our hearing, like a child's shriek of pain does; and our touch, like a needle does.

However, in science we don't rely only on our unaided senses; we multiply our senses and their power in order to detect additional boundaries by extending our nervous system with technical probes and instruments.

Such extended sensory probes enable us to map multiple boundaries of nature—tiny boundaries like those of the virus; fragile boundaries like those of a single cell; distant boundaries like those of Venus and Mars, and not only their spatial boundaries but their temperature and weight boundaries as well.

In the behavioral and social sciences we extend our casual observations by designing more sensitive probes and recording devices, ranging from carefully structured interviews to intelligence tests and questionnaires, and including careful case histories and the systematic study of historical documents and records; one-way observation rooms; Skinner boxes; automatic, computer-assisted systems which deliver a preset program of antecedents and record a variety of responses or consequences, all precisely timed and with careful attempts to keep stray or chance suspects out of the "network."

The "reality" you locate depends on the probes and detectors you use; the surfaces or boundaries you identify, or invent, depend on what you bring with you to the network; for example, your world is much emptier of smells and sounds than the rich variety a dog detects in the same "location"—the same space/time network. Similarly, while you can't locate snowflakes in a darkened room by throwing a baseball—baseballs don't bounce back from striking snowflakes— you can, however, readily locate them by throwing photons at them (by using a flashlight) because light waves or particles bounce back off snowflakes. And sometimes when we're strongly "set" to see or hear or catch a given signal, our mind's eye or ear can manufacture it out of the noise that emanates from every network.

Some of our social science probes are so "heavy" they demolish the event we seek—probes like clumsy interviews and questionnaires—while others are so "light" they don't penetrate below the surface of white lies, or contrived responses, and so we record and count lies and fuzzies— 8 sexual fantasies.

Does this kind of thinking make you stop and wonder how many boundaries or layers of reality remain to be explored and how many "teeming" regions of a network appear empty only because the "inhabitants" are demolished by our social science baseballs, or if they do respond we fail to see, hear, feel, smell, or catch the "bounce back"?

As a notational aid, in the remainder of the book we use solid circles (ⓓ , ○) to indicate those parts of experience where our senses or probes do locate clear or firm boundaries.

However, much of science and daily experience deals with vague and shifting boundaries and speculations about their relations—speculations about vague subatomic particles, viruses, genes, ailments, talents, futures, heavens, or hells.

For such fuzzy objects and events we need special symbols to indicate when we are talking about uncertain or imaginary boundaries.

1 demon + 2 demons = 3 demons

$$\{\overline{1d}\} \quad + \{\overline{2d}\} \quad = \{\overline{3d}\}$$

$$1 \{\overset{\cdot}{\cdot}\} \quad + 2 \{\overset{\cdot}{\cdot}\} \quad = 3 \{\overset{\cdot}{\cdot}\}$$

For most observers the term "demon" is empirically fuzzy or empty. Therefore, it can be symbolized by a fuzzy, hatched circle. We put a point in the middle. This point occupies no space, but it reserves a place just in case a speculative concept later captures some empirical content.

In addition to highly speculative terms like demons, undiscovered viruses, and distant futures that are currently empirically empty, there is a myriad of important terms that possess some empirical or observational content surrounded by an area of doubt or speculation—terms that have captured some observational content about which independent observers can agree but surrounding which there remain significant regions of disagreement or vagueness, like genes.

We are not here referring to concepts like your weight of 162 pounds, plus or minus a small region of speculation due to measurement errors, variations in the scales used, or angle of vision of the person reading the scales. Such concepts represent observational checkpoints and can be symbolized as a solid circle (O) or for accuracy's sake a solid circle surrounded by a very narrow band of uncertainty or speculation ($\{\overset{\cdot}{O}\}$).

Between such empirically full concepts as weight and height on the one hand and such empirically empty concepts as demons or imaginary subatomic particles on the other lie a host of concepts with varying degrees of observational content. Here we refer to important empirically anchored concepts like intelligence, cancer, health, love, habits, genetics, learning, or marijuana. While surrounded by a fluctuating region of speculation, all these terms contain some reliable observational checkpoints about which independent observers can usually agree. We symbolize such empirically anchored, but not empirically full, concepts by enclosing one or more solid circles inside a dotted or fuzzy circle:

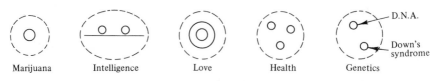

| Marijuana | Intelligence | Love | Health | Genetics |

For example, concerning genetics, while experts speculate and argue about the genetic contribution to most behavioral characteristics, they can agree specifically that Down's syndrome (mongolism) is strongly anchored to an observable abnormality on the twenty-first chromosome. Furthermore, different specialists can agree that a variety of observations indicate that I.Q. and certain forms of mental illness have genetic components. While they argue about how strong the genetic contribution is, they all assign it some empirical space.

Concerning intelligence, for example, specialists from very different schools would probably endorse the following general formula:

Intelligence = f(Genetics + Environment + e)

Some specialists argue for a large genetic contribution and a small environmental one; they "see" a large genetic contribution:

while other specialists argue just as strongly for the reverse weighting of environmental influences, "seeing" a large environmental component:

Not only should the key terms in these statements be surrounded by circles of uncertainty but also the linking symbols (= ,f, +). In social science we probably assign these relating or linking symbols more precision than they deserve because of our experience with them in mathematics.

For example, anyone with a little high school math can determine the value of X given the value of Y, Z, and e in the following formula:

$$X = f(Y^2 + Z + e)$$

So if $Y = 2$ and $Z = 3$ and $e = 1$, then it can be readily determined that $X = 8$. Anyone who knows the language of algebra can make such calculations independently and consistently.

Furthermore, we all understand what it means to "add" together things with solid boundaries:

1 doctor + 2 doctors = 3 doctors

Here the plus sign means placing the objects physically together in one place, or in one bag, or in one room:

However, what does "adding" or a plus sign mean when you're trying to combine things that don't have clear boundaries?

1 demon + 2 demons = 3 demons

$$(d) + (d)(d) = (d)(d)(d)$$

Most of our students accept this equation, but a few question it. One says, "No! Demons combine not like blocks, but like drops of water." Therefore:

1 demon + 2 demons = 1 big demon

$$(d) + (d)(d) = (D)$$

Another student says, "Nonsense. When demons come together they instantly multiply, faster than rabbits, as fast as the speed of light." So:

1 demon + 2 demons = millions of demons

$$(d) + (d)(d) = \begin{matrix}(d)\\(d)\end{matrix} \text{ etc., etc.}$$

Without belaboring the point further, remember that our mathematical and logical ways of thinking are usually based on the big assumption that we are combining or subtracting relatively stable things with clear boundaries.

Now keeping this point in mind, what does it mean to say:

$$X = f(Y^2 + Z + e)$$

where X = Intelligence (o)

Y^2 = Genetics (o^2)

Z = Environment (o)

e = error and chance factors (o)

In this formula all the key terms have vague boundaries, and furthermore we don't know whether the plus signs mean:

1. to add together like balls of wool or sticky marshmallows; or
2. to pour like water on Alka-Seltzer or like hot chocolate on ice cream; or to insert like seeds in soil, or a host of other alternatives.

Although very vague, the formula is not empty.

First, the formula is not speculatively or theoretically empty. It advises us *where* in multilayered reality to look for linkages—it instructs us to look for linkages in genetic layers and in environmental layers, and furthermore it instructs us not to expect to find all the answers in either or both of these layers combined.

This is so because errors of measurement and chance factors play tricks with intelligence.

Second, the formula is not empirically empty; it includes some observational checkpoints. For example, while we may argue about who is the smartest student in a high school history class, nevertheless we have no difficulty in differentiating their intellectual abilities, individually or as a group, from the intellectual abilities of students with Down's syndrome. In other words, we can independently and consistently label such obvious and extreme differences in intellectual ability.

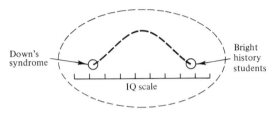

Furthermore, chromosome studies and studies of identical twins provide crude observational checkpoints for estimating genetic influences on all kinds of physical and psychological characteristics—some of which may or may not be linked to intelligence. Therefore, although our methods of studying genetic effects are still crude, we do possess some methods, such as microscopic studies of chromosomes and twin studies, that are starting to provide some observational checkpoints in the field.

In addition, reliable observational checkpoints have been mapped within the broad concept of *environmental* influences. Various specialists have mapped *extreme* differences in nutritional and social environments—for example, differences in nutritional deprivation and disease (e.g., measles) in pregnant females—and have reliably mapped as well some of the extreme differences in amount of parental "cuddling" given different infants. Therefore independent observers can consistently detect extreme differences on these dimensions, thus providing some observational checkpoints that may or may not be tied to intelligence.

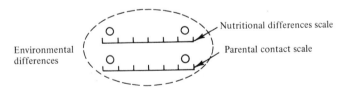

Once having mapped some of these extreme differences in intellectual abilities, in genetics, and in environment, we can then start to determine whether extreme differences in one appear to be linked to extreme differences in the other. Indeed, we discover that some linkages exist—strong linkages, for example, between some chromosome abnormalities and intellectual deficit. We also find evidence, some of it controversial, showing that identical twins (genetically identical) score very much alike on I.Q. tests, even when raised apart.

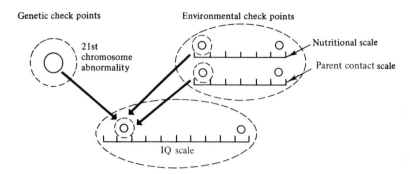

Thus we get some observational evidence supporting the speculation linking intelligence to genetics but only crude evidence, limited usually to extreme cases. Similarly we have evidence linking extreme nutritional and social deprivation to low intelligence.

Now having some evidence supporting our overall speculation linking intelligence both to genetic and environmental factors, how do we put the genetic *and* environmental influences together—how do we combine them? What does the first plus sign in the following formula mean?

$$\underset{IQ}{\bigcirc - \bigcirc} = f\left(\underset{Genetic}{\bigcirc} + \bigcirc + \underset{Environment}{\bigcirc - \bigcirc} + \underset{Chance}{\bigcirc} \right)$$

Does it mean that they're to be added together in the traditional sense: 2 units of genetics + 2 units of environment = 4 units of intelligence? Not likely!

Some people think of "add" in the sense of putting a seed in the soil—a genetic contribution represents the seed, and the environmental contribution represents the soil. As you can see, such a metaphor for "addition" suggests many questions about the relative contribution of the seed and the soil on a host of human characteristics.

Another popular way of defining how genetic and environmental influences combine, or add, involves using a rubber band analogy—with genetics representing the band and environmental factors the stretching forces. Notice that this analogy provides for very large environmental influences and so reflects a particular theoretical bias. Similarly, using the seed and soil analogy to represent the addition sign represents a theoretical bias as well—a genetic bias. These widely differing analogies indicate that we are a long way from any precise knowledge of how genetics and environment combine. Therefore we should write our formula without plus signs or multiplication signs, merely saying that intelligence is "some" function of genetic factors, environmental factors, chance factors, combined in complex, yet-to-be-determined manners:

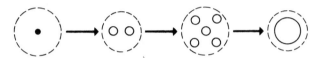

The preceding formula involves large speculations dotted with observational checkpoints and linked together in complex and mysterious ways.

The life expectancy of a scientific concept. When first appearing on the scene, new concepts and linkages possess little empirical content—possess few observational checkpoints. No one knows how durable or expandable are these observational checkpoints. For example, do the new diseases (AIDS) and new treatments (Interferon) represent recently discovered stable layers of reality, unreliable speculations, or passing tricks of chance? Will they grow into durable observational checkpoints:

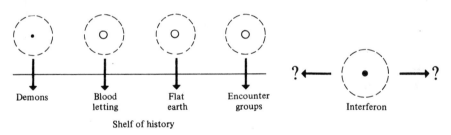

or will they melt away under the heat of close scrutiny? Or will they perhaps for a time reach a high respectability—like bloodletting—and then retreat to occupy a small or large space on the shelf of the history of failed speculations and chance observations?

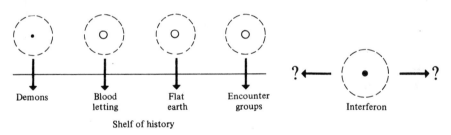

We have no Scientific Insurance Company to insure the life of a young scientific concept or speculation. For some people a concept may die in infancy; for others it may live on even after an official scientific burial. Demonology still lives in some cultures for you can still kill a person with words or cast a spell and call it hypnosis. For many, mysterious humors in the air prevail, and we call it "pollution."

Perhaps we should use a verb rather than a noun to describe our explanations—call them "sciencing," rather than science. In this way we build an image of endless explorations through nature's infinite veils, of perpetual attempts to unveil and map the invisibles in the air, in the ground, in the organism, in the past, in the future, and map as well how they are all linked together.

Using formal language to decode scientific news. When examining a piece of scientific news, or an argument favoring a particular speculation or theory, you can better distinguish the observational from the speculative language by translating the story into formal language. Consider two examples, one dealing with drugs and the other, a bit more controversial, dealing with doctors.

Example 1: Consider the news story that Valium may be linked to cancer. Translated into formal language we have:

Consider the *quantity and quality* of the observational checkpoints in the key terms "Valium," "cancer," "linked to." The reporter, however, is sloppy, focusing on the millions of people who may be "eating cancer pills," rather than providing details concerning how many cases were involved in this study and how much Valium they were taking for how long. Nor does the reporter even mention alternative speculations. In science there are always *legitimate* alternative speculations. So we are left to do our own speculations concerning what the news release might mean. Certainly the statement remains essentially meaningless until the key term "linked to" is given some observational anchors. The following are examples of what the term "linked to" might mean in observational terms:

1. "I noticed my last four cancer patients were heavy and prolonged Valium users." (What a tiny observational checkpoint that is!) or,
2. "We found 60 percent of 4000 cancer patients used Valium regularly for three or more years." (Now here we have a larger observational checkpoint, but where is the evidence for using the words "linked to"? What about the other 40 percent, and what about the hundreds of thousands of people who have used Valium for three or more years with no evidence of cancer?)
3. "We find that many cancer patients are Valium users *but* that most started receiving Valium only after they learned they had cancer."(So . . . Valium may be more a symptom of cancer than a cause.)
4. "Valium users are frequently heavy smokers and drinkers so it may be alcohol and nicotine that link Valium users to cancer—if indeed there is a linkage." (So again Valium may be found near cancer cases but as an innocent bystander or merely as a friend of the real villains, nicotine and alcohol.)

In brief, translating the statements of experts into formal language can frequently expose the claims to be loose, rather than disciplined, speculations and can help protect the consumer of science from "scientific noise." Appended to this chapter is an example of not only good press coverage of the Valium-cancer controversy but also the risks a scientist runs by challenging the establishment.

As indicated in the preceding examples concerning Valium and cancer, consumers must learn to distinguish between the sloppy and the disciplined use of linking terms like "caused by," "tied to," and "linked to" and to spot qualifiers like *"may* cause," *"reportedly* linked to," *"suspected* tie between." Sure, creatures in outer space "may cause" your headaches, but on the basis of current observational checkpoints, it isn't ruddy likely. Now consider another unlikely example; or is it?

Example 2: "Doctors cause illness." We have a tendency to assume because two things or events appear frequently together that they are somehow *intimately* tied together or that one "causes" the other. Often that's a useful assumption, but it can also be misleading or result in gross oversimplification. For example, because they appear together frequently or "hang around" together, someone might actually assume that:

Doctors cause illness

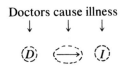

However, you "know" that's silly, and so you rewrite the statement as follows:

Illness leads to doctors leads to getting better,

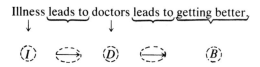

But wait. According to my doctor it's not quite that simple. He says, "Never go near a doctor unless you're really sick," because:

Doctors can lead to illness

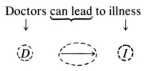

He writes the following formula covering doctors and illnesses:

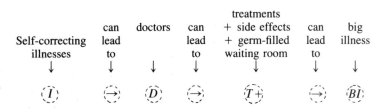

So my doctor argues that because most illnesses are self-correcting, you should stay away from doctors. Furthermore, he observes that because all treatments carry some risk (side effects, addictions) and because germs gravitate to, and hang around, doctors, you could really get sick going for treatment. Now you see what a powerful tool formal coding can be. Or is this an example of irresponsible speculation?

SUMMARY

As both beneficiaries and victims of science, consumers require a clearer understanding of this most awesome human enterprise.

To understand science better, consumers must become more familiar with its three tongues. *Objective* language provides observational checkpoints on the surfaces of multilayered reality. *Speculative* language describes guesses about the unmapped regions lying between or beyond observational checkpoints. *Formal* language helps scientists describe in a shorthand, abstract manner, alternative ways in which observations, and ideas, may be linked together.

In the remainder of the book we examine various methods scientists use to establish observational checkpoints and to test speculations—in brief to explore multilayered, moving reality.

EXAMPLE

Consumers Worry While Experts Disagree

Scientist fired in pill controversy[3]

The Valium controversy springs from a David-and-Goliath conflict involving an outspoken Montreal researcher, cautious international scientists, and a wealthy multinational drug company.

Dr. David Horrobin, 41, who sounded the alarm that there could be a link between Valium-like tranquilizers and cancer, lost his $40,000-a-year job at a Quebec research centre for his efforts.

Hoffmann La Roche, the Swiss-owned company with $3 billion in total world revenue last year, responded to Horrobin's claims by citing sparse details of an unpublished private study and by relying on a hired consultant who refuted Horrobin and said no further studies were needed.

Now a significant number of leading scientists agree that tests to date are inadequate to assure that Valium is safe for public use, though it's been on the market for nearly two decades.

WON'T SPEAK OUT

The scientists say they've been reluctant to speak out on Horrobin's behalf because of traditional avoidance of publicity outside the academic community, and because of increasing financial restraints on new research.

Dr. Emmanuel Farber, of the University of Toronto, said emphatically, "In the case of a drug that millions of people are taking, somebody should be doing studies. There are many different ways available for studying tumor promotion. It's not mysterious."

Horrobin, widely considered to be a brilliant if unorthodox scientist, is a medical doctor and neurophysiologist trained at Oxford University. He discovered, in 1977, that when he fed diazepam [Valium] to rats with implanted breast tumors, the tumors grew to three times the size of those in rats without the drug.

[3]By Ellie Tesher, reprinted with permission of the *Toronto Star,* Monday, April 16, 1981, A2.

Horrobin found the diazepam effect worked only with low doses that were disturbingly close to the usual daily dose of tranquillizers for humans.

Yet the scientist was refused funds for further research by the two main Canadian funding agencies—the National Cancer Institute of Canada and the Medical Research Council.

In March, 1979, Horrobin read published studies of Dr. Basil Stoll of St. Thomas' Hospital in London. Stoll found that women who had taken tranquillizers, and were later found to have breast cancer, had more rapidly spreading tumors at the time of diagnosis. Stoll suggested anxiety might produce the effect.

But Horrobin said the tranquillizer drug might have promoted tumor growth. The coincidental facts that a drug widely used by women—an estimated 25 percent—could enhance breast cancer, now affecting one in every 11 women in North America, caused him to raise a warning flag on diazepam.

Horrobin spoke out in a letter to the British medical journal *Lancet*. Newspaper interviews followed. A week later, he was asked to resign as director of a research laboratory at the Clinical Research Institute in Montreal, which is largely funded by the Quebec government and medical research grants.

Dr. Jacques Genest, 61-year-old founder and director of the centre, wrote Horrobin: "Either your head has become too big for your feet or your feet have become too big for the institute. . . . It is preferable for you to seek another place where you will find total freedom for such behaviour."

Horrobin resigned as requested, and left in July, 1979. During that summer Dr. Rashida Karmali, who had worked on diazepam with Horrobin in Montreal, quietly published a report of a second similar test she undertook as a researcher at the University of East Carolina University. Karmali's study also found diazepam caused transplanted tumors in rats to increase in size.

A year later, Dr. James Trosko, a scientist at Michigan State University, applied Horrobin's theory to his own study of substances that promote tumors on bacteria in test tubes. Tosko found diazepam has properties similar to known tumor promoters such as saccharine.

PLAN OF ACTION

Alerted that Horrobin planned to renew his call for broad scrutiny of diazepam at an international science symposium in Toronto last January, Hoffmann La Roche executives went into action.

Roche, whose sales of Valium in Canada alone total at least $4 million (a company estimate), hired British consultant scientist, Dr. Francis Roe, to review Horrobin's claims.

Two weeks later, Roe, who had been consultant on a previous Roche-commissioned study of Valium that has yet to be published, said Horrobin's work was "inconclusive and trivial," and that transplantable tumors were unreliable for measuring tumor growth.

Roche quickly released Roe's statement that Horrobin's findings "provide no grounds for concern or alarm. They also provide no basis for requiring any further laboratory studies."

But in an interview with *The Star*, Roe said he'd like to see further testing of diazepam, unrelated to Horrobin's work. He said he'd like to see the drug tested on mice in view of earlier studies that show diazepam's metabolite drug, oxazepam, causes cancer when given to mice in large doses.

A two-year study Roche commissioned from Huntingdon Research Laboratories in England, on which Roe consulted, was on rats.

Roche says the Huntingdon results were recently released to Canadian and U.S. health officials. The company says they are standard tests that show conclusively that Valium does not cause cancer.

Roche executives also claim that the Huntingdon study can be interpreted to prove that Valium doesn't enhance tumor growth, and that specific tests for tumor promotion aren't possible.

But Dr. Ian Henderson, of Ottawa's health protection branch, says he has yet to see the full data of the British study. So far he's only received a summary.

Henderson said it was "odd" that the study only used rats when conventional tests for cancer call for experiments with three animal species.

Dr. Donald Zarowny, 41-year-old medical director for Roche's Canadian operations, speaks with conviction.

"We feel that there is excellent data that totally absolves diazepam and Valium from causing or increasing the growth of tumors."

chapter 3

The Field Study

Few human tools surpass in importance those used to sift fact from fancy. We next consider the nonexperimental techniques evolved to date to unmask fact and fancy, those two delightful knaves who love to masquerade in each other's costumes. These two masters of disguise are embraced with vigor by scientist and nonscientist alike. At unmasking time, scientists, much to their embarrassment, may discover themselves clutching an armful of charming fancy instead of a beautiful fact.

You will learn of the imperfect methods that scientists employ to sift fact from fancy. Such methods cannot eliminate error. Rather, they help increase the durability of the data packages scientists produce. Some methods help us produce more durable packages than others. The different research methods scientists use may be thought of as sieves. Some sieves help us collect relatively durable chunks of information, while other sieves collect an indistinguishable mixture of perishable and durable data. Usually, the more durable you want the chunk to be, the greater the cost involved in designing and using the appropriate sieves. The sieves discussed in this section include: naturalistic observation in field settings; the after-the-fact, or case, method; archival and survey research.

If you want to know the rituals practiced by the pygmies in their worship of the forest god Ituri, or what people do when they win at the roulette table, or if bees exhibit social behavior, or how apes communicate, or whether teachers encourage creative thinking in their pupils, the most obvious recourse is to "go and see." In some scientific circles the technique of crude observation of events without technical apparatus is known as the *eyeball technique,* and this is the core of the field-study method.

The essence of this science sieve is the observation, description, and interpretation of events as they occur in nature or naturally (a stew of observational and speculative language). This method requires no manipulation, no controlled experimentation, but rather the careful observation of episodes as they take place in their usual surroundings. It is perhaps the earliest (and, in some ways, crudest) of science's methods. The "primitive" strategies of careful, methodical observation and classification predate the use of complex experimental designs and elaborate apparatus. However, even with the more advanced methods, observational skills are essential, and increasing awareness of the limitations of laboratory technologies has prompted a revival of interest in the field study and its principal technique—naturalistic observation.

Darwin's (1936) picture of evolution provides an excellent example of this method. By his own admission Darwin devoted five years to the careful, detailed "field" observation of thousands of plants and animals, both domestic and wild. These observations were meticulously (even compulsively) recorded in prose and picture form and subsequently grouped into categories which in turn led to a grand speculation—*the theory of evolution.* If we were to represent this process schematically, we would start with a series of O's (observations) and then impose some grouping scheme on our O's so that they are combined according to certain rules.[1]

$$O_1, \quad O_2, \quad O_3, \quad O_4, \quad O_5, \quad O_6, \quad O_7, \quad O_8, \quad O_9 \cdots O_n$$

then combining the observational and formal language systems:

$$O_1 = O_2 \text{ in some respects}$$

$$O_1 \neq O_2 \text{ in other respects}$$

$$O_3 < O_4 \text{ in some respects}$$

$$O_3 > O_4 \text{ in other respects}$$

Finally, the groups are integrated into a higher classification at the speculative level of language—*survival of the fittest!*

There are four key components to the field-study strategy (1) the setting, (2) the observational task, (3) the role of the observer, and (4) the classification of observations. In the discussion to follow, we examine each of these in turn. In

---

[1]Each O stands for a different observation. If there were 19 observations, then n would be 19, and O_n would represent the nineteenth observation.

actual practice, however, these facets of the method do not necessarily operate sequentially or independently.

THE SETTING

Field studies obviously belong in field settings—that is, in nonlaboratory environments—but research in the field implies a lack of control, implies unpredictability. Although investigators have hunches about how their observations are causally linked, cause-and-effect relationships cannot be established via this method of research; it is descriptive rather than inferential. If other science sieves promise more precision, why use a field approach? As we gain precision and control, we lose *validity*. Would people in a laboratory who passively obey an experimenter's instruction to shock an innocent victim display this same blind obedience in a real-life setting? Perhaps not. There is good reason to assume that people behave differently in natural settings than they do in the lab where they may be on their "best" behavior. Also some areas of interest (for example, the reaction to natural catastrophes) cannot be duplicated *realistically* in a laboratory environment.[2] For these important reasons the field study is one essential arrow in the scientific quiver.

Once investigators decide what they want to know, the next decision involves selecting the setting(s). Choosing the setting depends on various factors: the question to be answered; the feasibility and cost of the appropriate setting—this depends on how broadly or narrowly the researchers wish to apply their findings. Suppose our budding scientists are interested in the characteristics of people who burglarize and vandalize abandoned vehicles. They live in New York so they observe an abandoned car in the Bronx. Within the first ten minutes they see a white family of three (father, mother, and young son) remove the battery and the contents of the trunk and glove compartment. By the end of the day, adult vandals have extracted every removable part from the automobile. In succeeding days acts of random destruction occur (breaking windows, denting the hood) mostly perpetrated by well-dressed adult whites. Aha, conclude (speculate) our researchers, vandalism is primarily an adult activity which will occur in any urban center. But is it legitimate to draw this conclusion?

Zimbardo (1970) who actually conducted this study, reports not only that a car similarly abandoned in Palo Alto, Calif., was not vandalized, but also that one man thoughtfully lowered the hood of the car when it was raining so the engine wouldn't get wet. Zimbardo's speculation is that high population density creates conditions of anonymity and loss of identity. Such conditions, he argues, foster a reduction in one's sense of responsibility and social consciousness. Hence the individual performs acts which appear reprehensible. Certainly Zimbardo's analysis is supported by much of the available data, but it is worth noting that the

---

[2]One respected book on decision making excludes data from "contrived" situations because of the questionable validity of such studies (Janis & Man, 1977).

two settings employed (New York and Palo Alto) differ in many respects, not just population density (Milgram, 1970), but some of these other factors may be just as relevant.

A number of questions must be addressed by researchers choosing an appropriate setting. (1) Is this a setting in which the event(s) of interest are likely to occur? (2) Is this a representative setting in terms of most settings in which the event(s) of interest are likely to occur? or is it unique in all the world? If the latter, then as consumers of science we have less confidence that this particular research project provides us with "the big picture."

THE OBSERVATIONAL TASK

Harry's old Chevy died, much to his disgust, five blocks from the "Greasy Spoon" where he works as a short-order cook. He decides to walk and call the tow truck from the cafe. As he trudges crankily past the school playground, he glances idly at the children playing. Two future National Hockey League stars are high-sticking each other on the ice, another boy is inscribing a particularly nasty piece of graffiti on the school wall, a big girl is washing a small boy's face with snow, and one little imp noticing Harry's interest hurls a snowball with deadly accuracy hitting him on the temple. Harry angrily shakes his fist and speculates, "Bloody juvenile delinquents—damn kids could sure use a kick in the ass."

Harry has observed a number of events in their natural surroundings, has integrated or grouped them, and has generated some speculations. However, Harry's observational procedure is casual, and so we should question both the validity of his observations and his conclusion. For example, Harry didn't notice that the feisty hockey players were really just trying to disentangle their sticks which were caught in skate blades. Ineptitude, rather than aggression, accounted for their behavior: ⦂O⦂ . Harry also failed to observe the dancing pair of figure skaters at the other end of the rink. Harry was gone when the big girl picked up the little boy, hugged him, dusted off the snow on him, and carefully retied the laces of his boot. And how could Harry know that the miniature Nolan Ryan had actually been aiming for the fence post: ⦂O⦂ ?

Defining what to look for in any observational task becomes the most crucial aspect of the field-study method. As consumers of science we must focus on the quality of the data base or observational checkpoints that researchers use in generating their speculations.

Distortion

Personal experience in observing an event is obviously not a guarantee of truth. Since human senses are fallible, what we think we see isn't always what has occurred. Our observations are not pure—that is, we do not perceive only forms, contours, and certain wavelengths of light or sound, but we also impose an organization on them. One might say with some justification that we do not in fact see light waves of 75 microns; we see red. Similarly, we do not hear a sound of 80 decibels; rather we hear a pneumatic drill. Thus any event that is observed is not experienced "in the raw" but is altered by our past learning or, as in Harry's case, our mood. Sometimes our interpretations (organization) of what we see can be quite misleading. For example, psychologists have constructed rooms built on a slant in which an individual standing at one side of the room looks like a midget. Viewers, instead of perceiving the room as distorted, distort the size of the individual in the room (Weiner, 1956). If we press this argument further, it will be seen that our opinions, beliefs, and attitudes can also alter our observations since they form part of our past learning. When we are observing the movement of planets, the pelvic bone structure of the apes, the strength of a magnetic field, or the electrical conducting properties of copper, you might argue that political affiliation, religious denomination, skin color, or nationality would not affect our observations. Is this in fact the case? Religious beliefs supporting the theory that the earth was flat prevented many people from making the simple observation that the mast of a ship appeared on the horizon before the rest of the ship. If the area under study involves human behavior, how much more will we distort our observations to fit our beliefs, hopes, or fears? (See Chapter 16—Sex and Science.)

Scientists using the field-study method and the techniques of naturalistic observation strive to be as objective as possible; they consciously try to observe without evaluating. They try not to make value judgments like good or bad, wrong or right, beautiful or ugly. In other words they attempt to prevent their own biases, opinions, values, and beliefs from coloring their observations. They try to keep observations as pure as possible. Although scientists have set an impossible task for themselves, at least knowing how beliefs can distort observations makes them more careful, more cautious about accepting observations, their own or others', at face value. Also scientific training and the use of certain instruments, like hidden cameras, can help get a more objective picture: this (O) rather than this (o) .

Selection

We know that biases play a role in the selection of information. In other words, we see or notice those things we want to see and screen out information that doesn't fit in with our particular point of view. For example, the biased observer who is convinced that civilization corrupts people and who believes that people living in primitive societies are happier may fail to notice all the negative aspects of primitive life. The poverty, the suffering that is due to lack of medical attention, the grueling hard work with improvised tools—these things escape attention. The scientist being aware of this pitfall attempts to make *detailed, value-free observations*.

Selection operates not only on our observations but also on our recording and report writing. We don't see everything that happens nor do we record everything we see. We can't record all our observations (even if we wanted to) because we forget things, and we forget selectively. We tend to forget those things that don't fit well with our established biases and preferences and to remember those things that do. We have no trouble remembering an appointment to go out for dinner and to the theater, but dental appointments easily slip the mind. In addition, time can distort the memory of observation. Since our memories are both leaky and creative, it is essential to make accurate notes when making observations, a practice most good researchers have developed. Alternately, in order to avoid relying on our imperfect and creative memories, we may use tape recordings, films, sketches, graphs, or counters. There is still the danger that valuable data may be lost, but such recorded observations are not as subject to distortion, decay, or growth as are the ones we deposit in memory. A further advantage accrues because the data may be perused in all its rich detail at some later date and may be examined again and again, by us or by others.

Even if our memories did not erase some observations from our minds, we still can't record everything that we observe. Secretaries know that exact reproduction of even a short conversation leads to a copious report. Minutes of meetings represent highly condensed and abbreviated versions of what actually occurred; much of the discussion must be omitted. Similarly, researchers must select from what they remember of the events observed. They must decide what to record and what to omit and ignore material that is not relevant to the thesis being developed. Notice that while not trying to discard observations that contradict their views, they still must discard those observations that add nothing to the point of the research. Such observations are tangential to the topic under study. If one wishes to describe in detail the puberty rites of the Hopi Indians, it is perhaps irrelevant to record that homes of the Indians are constructed of thatched straw and adobe.

The researchers' bias or point of view helps them select what is worth recording. Such biases may prevent them from considering alternatives but are vital in terms of providing guidelines for selection from the flood of data surrounding them.

An Example

If Harry is really serious about studying the aggressive behavior of little girls and boys on the playground, he must first decide (1) what constitutes aggression, (2) which children he will watch (he can't observe all of them), (3) at what time of the day, (4) for how long, (5) who will do the observing and recording, (6) how many observers he will need, (7) how will the observations be recorded and checked for accuracy.

To illustrate the complexity of the observational task, consider the following excerpt from a study conducted by Bem (1975). Bem investigated the extent to which a person's playfulness (with a kitten) was related to the individual's sex and sex-role orientation. Although not a field study, the observational strategies employed are similar to those that might be adopted in a field setting. Notice particularly how the experimenter establishes reliable observational checkpoints.

> During the period of forced and spontaneous play, the subject's interaction with the kitten was time sampled every 10 seconds by one of four female coders, all of whom

were blind with respect to the subject's sex role and all of whom observed an approximately equal number of masculine, androgynous, and feminine subjects of each sex. For each subject, the coder made 30 2-second observations during forced play and 60 2-second observations during spontaneous play. Ten behaviors were coded as present or absent: Was the subject looking at the kitten? Speaking to the kitten? Petting the kitten? Nuzzling the kitten? Was the subject playing with the kitten? If so, was he holding it in his hand, on his lap, on his chest, or face-to-face?

In order to establish the reliabilty of these various measures, two of the four coders simultaneously observed 12 subjects. These double coding sessions were scheduled so that all possible pairs of coders were together twice and so that 2 subjects from every sex role received double coding. The reliability of a given behavior was determined by combining forced and spontaneous play for a total of 90 observations per subject and then by calculating the percentage of observations on which the two coders agreed perfectly. The results indicated very high reliability (over 95% perfect agreement) for all 10 behaviors (Bem, 1975, p. 640).

Do you have any questions about the independence of observers? Do we know from this description whether they peeked at each other's notes during the session? How might independence have been assured?

THE ROLE OF THE OBSERVER

We have already seen how past learning and current mood can affect what the observer sees. As consumers of science we are justifiably interested in the strategies employed by the investigator to counteract these sources of error.

Multiple Observers – Multiple Observations

Making several observations and having several observers make repeated observations of the same event (the strategies Bem employed) increase the probability of producing durable packages of information. This principle is utilized by those practicing the technique of naturalistic observation. In an attempt to partially overcome or reduce observer bias, scientific investigations often make use of two or more independent observers who later come together and discard any observations on which they do not agree. Or, more commonly, a third observer is called in to resolve the disagreement. Also, the same observer may try to observe the same event many times in order to ensure that s/he has noticed all the relevant details and to rule out the possibility that the initial observation was a once-in-a-lifetime event. Thus anthropologists may visit the same primitive tribe many times and observe the tribe's activities over long periods. For the same reason another investigator may repeat a colleague's experiment, and the extent of similarity in their findings adds to the durability of their observations.

Nonparticipant Observation

The work of anthropologists such as Margaret Mead and Dorothy Eggan who studied so-called primitive societies is based on the field-study method. In research of this kind one aspect of the method is of prime importance: nonparticipant observation. Nonparticipant observation means that the observer is a passive entity who merely observes and does not actively participate in any way in the event he or she is studying—however, just being there watching can influence some events, can't it?

This concept applies to all methods of science, including the one under discussion. The researcher can be seen as an influence to be studied in his or her own right. For example, in well-designed and controlled laboratory experiments involving human subjects, the sex of the experimenter can affect the results obtained. In studies dealing with inanimate matter, observers have less effect on the material. It is difficult, for example, to conceive of a situation in which the sex of the geologist affects the rocks one is sampling. Still, in some experiments in physics or chemistry, the electric potential in the human body or perspiration on the hands can affect the phenomenon under study.

Like the well-trained spy, experimenters or observers try to remain as unobtrusive as possible. They do not join in the activities of the children's play group being studied; they try not to mix their own bacteria with the bacillus being cultivated; they do not help the rat find its way out of the maze. They are *passive* observers. They play as minute a role as possible in the events they are studying. They really try to refrain from influencing the phenomena they observe. For this reason naturalists studying the behavior of birds or animals may hide themselves in blinds or use long-range cameras, and psychologists and sociologists may use the one-way mirror (as did Bem).

Nevertheless, those of us studying humans (and some other primates, too) are well aware of the sensitive and *reactive* nature of our subjects. When people know they are being observed, their behavior changes—they put on their company manners, and spontaneity vanishes. Field researchers studying humans may be passive and unobtrusive, but it is difficult to disguise the research entirely. The research participants are often aware that they are on display—that they are being observed, judged, evaluated. In fact, strict adherence to ethical principles (see Chapter 14) requires that subjects be aware of the nature of their participation (principle of informed consent).

One procedure commonly used by researchers to counteract this "on-stage" effect involves observing the group (be present in the group) for some time before actually beginning the study. This gives the group members a chance to acclimatize themselves to the outsider. Eventually the researcher seems to fade into the woodwork. Another procedure employs two or more researchers observing the same ceremony or event at different times. If their observations are discrepant, one explanation for the discrepancy might be that the two observers had different effects on the group.

Participant Observation

Another creative strategy for overcoming the reactivity problem is to employ undercover confederates who infiltrate and become participant members of the group (Whyte, 1943). However, care must be exerted to ensure that the confederate does not shape or mold the group to perform in a manner dictated by the investigator's hypotheses or predictions. This tactic also raises some thorny ethical issues.

An alternative approach was adopted by Barker and Schoggen (1973) in their comparison study of life in two small towns—one in the U.S. Midwest and the other in England. The researchers and their families established residences in the towns and fully explained the purpose of the study to the local inhabitants. They attempted to participate normally in community affairs, following their own interests but avoided initiating new activities.

CLASSIFICATION/INTERPRETATION

The final component of the field-study method involves classification of observations—their linkages, order, or pattern. This discovery or invention of pattern is the basis of science.

The development of the periodic table in chemistry represents a most fruitful use of one aspect of the field-study method—that of classification. In the nineteenth century, elements were being discovered rapidly, but as each element had different properties, no obvious sense of order or relationship could be perceived among elements. However, science doesn't just create heaps of facts; it puts facts in a framework. Attempts to classify, group, or arrange elements into some kind of order were made by several investigators, including chemists and a geologist. Mendeleev's periodic table was the most successful attempt at classification. Mendeleev believed that the properties of elements were more important than their atomic number; when arrangement by number would not work neatly, Mendeleev left holes in the table for elements still to be discovered. He even predicted the properties of some of the missing elements on the basis of his table. With knowledge of the hypothesized properties of these missing elements, their eventual discovery was stimulated. Thus classification proved valuable in the progress of a science.

The development of the system for the classification of plants and animals by Carolus Linnaeus (1707–1778), the Swedish botanist, is another famous example of the fruitfulness of taxonomy to science. Classification of organisms, both past and present, into kingdoms, phyla, classes, orders, families, genera, and species is an obvious example of an attempt to replace disorder and confusion with order. To develop such a taxonomic system, close observation of the properties of organisms had to be undertaken. Again, the technique of naturalistic observation proved invaluable.

Barker and Schoggen (1973), whose field study was briefly described earlier, attempted to produce a complete inventory and classification of the behavior settings (public places or occasions) in each community. The Midwest town was found to have considerably more public behavior settings, which in turn was reflected in the different activities of the inhabitants, ranging from public attention toward children to religious pursuits.

The construction of classification systems is very much a function of bias or point of view. In fact, classification can be seen as a primitive form of theorizing that allows for the expression of opinion or inference. With any set of data there are usually a variety of ways in which these data may be ordered or grouped, and the researchers' hunches or biases determine which particular grouping they will develop—will the researchers group people on the basis of intelligence, or skin color, or sex, or political persuasion, or aggression, or genetics, or what?

$$(A) \quad = \quad f((B) \quad (?))$$

$$\begin{array}{ccc} & & \text{Sex} \\ \text{I.Q.} & & \text{Skin color} \\ & & \text{Social class} \end{array}$$

CONCLUSION

Just because naturalistic observation is employed to study somewhat gross behavior units and requires little in the way of elaborate equipment, don't conclude that it is no longer in vogue, has outlived its usefulness, or is a simple method that requires little training. All these inferences are wrong. There are many areas of study in which it is impossible—for ethical, moral, political, or practical reasons—for the researcher to manipulate events or to experiment. In addition, certain kinds of information can only be obtained in field or naturalistic studies. For example, if we want to investigate the phenomena of hibernation, famine, or juvenile gangs, we must use naturalistic observation for at least some portion of our study. The work of Piaget, the famous child psychologist, was based on the technique of naturalistic observation and is the foundation for much of the current research in some areas of psychology today. Although a crude sieve, the field study remains a valuable source of important and durable data in the hands of a skilled researcher.

One obvious advantage of this method is its superiority to casual observation and hit-or-miss recording or tabulating of events. A second advantage accrues because it does not require manipulating or controlling events; therefore many subjects normally taboo to experimental science become open to this form of study. Furthermore, the four principles of the field study (the setting, the observational task, the role of the observer, and the grouping or classification) apply, to some degree, to all the other sieves of science. Often the data gathered by the field-study method provide guidelines for later inquiry with more sophisticated sieves, as has been the case with Piaget's work. Finally, this method can be practiced by the young student scientist who has limited resources. By being analytical, passive, and accurate, novice researchers can establish important observational checkpoints and can offer fascinating speculations.

SUMMARY

As distinguished from sloppy or casual observation, the field-study method contributes the following data-collecting, storing, and sorting tools: (1) detailed and concentrated observation, (2) accurate recording and record keeping, (3) sophisticated observational strategies, and (4) identification of patterns and classes among carefully recorded, detailed observations. All scientific methods rely on these four basic tools in mapping multilayered nature.

EXAMPLE

The following is an excerpt from Charles Darwin's *Origin of Species*.[3] It illustrates the utilization of the field-study method by a master.

Slave-making Instinct
This remarkable instinct was first discovered in the *Formica (Polyerges) rufescens* by Pierre Huber, a better observer even than his celebrated father. This ant is absolutely dependent on its slaves; without their aid, the species would certainly become extinct in a single year. The males and fertile females do not work. The workers or sterile females, though most energetic and courageous in capturing slaves, do no other work. They are incapable of making their own nests, or of feeding their own larvae. When the old nest is found inconvenient, and they have to migrate, it is the slaves which determine the migration, and actually carry their masters in their jaws. So utterly helpless are the masters that when Huber shut up thirty of them without a slave, but with plenty of food which they like best, and with their own larvae and pupae to stimulate them to work, they did nothing; they could not even feed themselves, and many perished of hunger. Huber then introduced a single slave *(F. fusca)*, and she instantly set to work, fed and saved the survivors; made some cells, and tended the larva; and put all to rights. What can be more extraordinary than these well-ascertained facts? If we had not known of any other slave-making ant, it would have been hopeless to speculate how so wonderful an instinct could have been perfected.
    Formica sanguinea was likewise first discovered by P. Huber to be a slavemaking ant. This species is found in the southern parts of England, and its habits have been attended to by Mr. F. Smith of the British Museum, to whom I am much indebted for information on this and other subjects. Although fully trusting to the statements of Huber and Mr. Smith, I tried to approach the subject in a skeptical frame of mind, as any one may well be excused for doubting the existence of so extraordinary and odious an instinct as that of making slaves. Hence I will give the observations which I have myself made, in some little detail. I opened fourteen nests of *F. sanguinea,* and found a few slaves in all. Males and fertile females of the slave-species *(F. fusca)* are found only in their own proper communities, and have never been observed in the nests of *F. sanguinea.* The slaves are black and not above half the size of their red master, so that the contrast in their appearance is great. When the nest is slightly disturbed, the slaves occasionally come out, and like their masters are much agitated and defend the nest; when the nest is much disturbed, and the

[3]Charles Darwin, *Origin of the species.* New York: Random House, 1936, pp. 193–196.

larvae and pupae are exposed, the slaves work energetically together with their masters in carrying them away to a place of safety. Hence, it is clear, that the slaves feel quite at home. During the months of June and July, on three successive years, I have watched for many hours several nests in Surrey and Sussex, and never saw a slave either leave or enter a nest. As, during these months, the slaves are very few in number, I thought that they might behave differently when more numerous, but Mr. Smith informs me that he has watched the nests at various hours during May, June and August, both in Surrey and Hampshire, and has never seen the slaves, though present in large numbers in August, either leave or enter the nest. Hence he considers them as strictly household slaves. The master, on the other hand, may be constantly seen bringing in materials for the nest, and food of all kinds. During the present year, however, in the month of July, I came across a community with an unusually large stock of slaves, and I observed a few slaves mingled with their masters leaving the nest, and marching along the same road to a tall Scotch-fir-tree, twenty-five yards distant, which they ascended together, probably in search of aphides or cocci. According to Huber, who had ample opportunities for observation in Switzerland, the slaves habitually work with their masters in making the nest, and they alone open and close the doors in the morning and evening; and, as Huber expressly states, their principal office is to search for aphides. This difference in the usual habits of the masters and slaves in the two countries probably depends merely on the slaves being captured in greater numbers in Switzerland than in England.

One day I fortunately chanced to witness a migration of *F. sanguinea* from one nest to another, and it was a most interesting spectacle to behold the masters carefully carrying their slaves in their jaws instead of being carried by them, as in the case of *F. rufescens*. Another day my attention was struck by about a score of the slave-makers haunting the same spot, and evidently not in search of food, they approached and were vigorously repulsed by an independent community of the slave species *F. fusca;* sometimes as many as three of these ants clinging to the legs of the slave-making *F. sanguinea*. The latter ruthlessly killed their small opponents, and carried their dead bodies as food to their nest, twenty-five yards distant; but they were prevented from getting any pupae to rear as slaves. I then dug up a small parcel of the pupae of *F. fusca* from another nest, and put them down on a bare spot near the place of combat; they were eagerly seized and carried off by the tyrants, who perhaps fancied that, after all, they had been victorious in their late combat.

At the same time I laid on the same place a small parcel of the pupae of another species, *F. flava,* with a few of these little yellow ants still clinging to the fragments of their nest. This species is sometimes, though rarely, made into slaves, as has been described by Mr. Smith. Although so small a species, it is very courageous, and I have seen it ferociously attack other ants. In one instance I found to my surprise an independent community of *F. flava* under a stone beneath a nest of the slave-making *F. sanguinea;* and when I accidentally disturbed both nests, the little ants attacked their big neighbors with surprising courage. Now I was curious to ascertain whether *F. sanguinea* could distinguish the pupae of *F. fusca,* which they habitually make into slaves, from those of the little and furious *F. flava,* which they rarely capture, and it was evident they did at once distinguish them; for we have seen that they eagerly and instantly seized the pupae of *F. fusca,* whereas they were much terrified when they came across the pupae, or even the earth from the nest of *F. flava,* and quickly ran away; but in about a quarter of an hour, shortly after all the little yellow ants had crawled away, they took heart and carried off the pupae.

One evening I visited another community of *F. sanguinea,* and found a number of these ants returning home and entering their nests, carrying the dead bodies of *F. fusca* (showing that it was not a migration) and numerous pupae. I traced a long file of ants burthened with booty, for about forty yards back to a very thick clump of heath, whence I saw that last individual of *F. sanguinea* emerge, carrying a pupa, but I was not able to find the desolated nest in the thick heath. The nest, however, must have been close at hand, for two or three individuals of *F. fusca* were rushing about in the greatest agitation, and one was perched motionless with its own pupa in its mouth on the top of a spray of heath, an image of despair over its ravaged home.

Such are the facts, though they did not need confirmation by me, in regard to the wonderful instinct of making slaves. Let it be observed what a contrast the instinctive habits of *F. sanguinea* present with those of the *F. rufescens*. The latter does not build its own nest, does not determine its own migrations, does not collect food for itself or its young, and cannot even feed itself; it is absolutely dependent on its numerous slaves. *Formica sanguinea*, on the other hand, possesses much fewer slaves, and in the early part of the summer extremely few: the masters determine when and where a new nest shall be formed, and when they migrate, the masters carry the slaves. Both in Switzerland and England the slaves seem to have the exclusive care of the larvae, and the masters alone go on slave-making expeditions. In Switzerland the slaves and masters work together, making and bringing materials for the nest; both, but chiefly the slaves, tend, and milk, as it may be called, their aphides; and thus both collect food for the community. In England the masters alone usually leave the nest to collect building materials and food for themselves, their slaves, and larvae. So that the masters in this country receive much less service from their slaves than they do in Switzerland.

By what steps the instinct of *F. sanguinea* originated I will not pretend to conjecture. But as ants which are not slave-makers will, as I have seen, carry off pupae of other species, if scattered by their nests, it is possible that pupae originally stored as food might become developed; and the ants thus unintentionally reared would then follow their proper instincts, and do what work they could. If their presence proved useful to the species which had seized them—if it were more advantageous to this species to capture workers than to procreate them—the habit of collecting pupae, originally for food, might by natural selection be strengthened and rendered permanent for the very different purpose of raising slaves. When the instinct was once acquired, if carried out to a much less extent even than in our British *F. sanguinea*, which, as we have seen, is less aided by its slaves than the same species in Switzerland, natural selection might increase and modify the instinct—always supposing each modification to be of use to the species—until an ant was formed as abjectly dependent on its slaves as is the *Formica rufescens*.

chapter 4

After-the-Fact Method

When something unexpected happens and we want to know how or why it happened, we go back in time and attempt to reconstruct the past—or at least those aspects of the past that *appear* to be connected with the unexpected event. (This method differs from naturalistic observation, which focuses upon presently occurring events.) We face a variety of after-the-fact questions: Who or what led to the stomachache, the car breakdown, the fall of Rome, or the murder? Some of the suspects will be innocent, and some will be guilty. How do we sort guilty from innocent or fact from fancy—after the fact?

A CASE FOR THE COURT

Our courts attempt to sift fact from fancy, to sift durable evidence from perishable evidence. An event occurs, and we trace back in time to find a likely suspect. For example, a crime is committed—a murder—and the investigators look out over the city, faced with an apparent impossible task—"Who did it?" Of all the thousands or perhaps millions of people out there, which person or mob played the key part in the crime? The prosecution must go back in time and attempt to tie the crime to a few selected people.

First, they must sort suspects from nonsuspects and then gradually separate the most likely suspects from the least likely. They continue screening until a group of neutral people, the jury, can decide beyond a reasonable doubt whether the crime can be tied to a given suspect. The jury must decide how closely the crime and the suspect are tied together. Is the suspect, for example, a lone plotter and executioner and therefore strongly tied to the crime? Or is he an unwitting accomplice and therefore only tied to the crime by a thin line?

The problem facing the court is a stewpot of observations and speculations collected after the event has occurred—or, as we call it, *after the fact*. After-the-fact situations face us daily, whether in the courtroom, the history class, the doctor's office, at an afternoon tea, a pub, or a garage. The problem is to select from a variety of suspects the one most strongly tied to, or leading to, the event of interest—whether it be a murder, a war, a pain in the stomach, an elopement, a lost football game, a car that won't start, or the causes of lung cancer.

The most common approach used in sifting suspects in these after-the-fact situations is sometimes known as the *case method*. It is a sieve with relatively big holes, one that permits a large amount of fancy to slip through with the facts. Nevertheless, this kind of sieve can be a powerful aid in narrowing down the number of suspects or alternatives, particularly when the person using it is aware of its limitations. We must be aware of the limitations of the particular method used in selecting the suspect; otherwise it is impossible to decide how much confidence the selection of a particular suspect warrants.

Consider the following methods of selecting suspects in a murder case:

Method 1: fortune teller using crystal ball ("A tall dark stranger is the guilty one.")
Method 2: opinion of murdered man's wife ("The business partner is the guilty one.")
Method 3: pretrial judgment of the district attorney ("A hired gun from the West Coast is the guilty one.")
Method 4: decision of jury ("The jealous mistress is the guilty one.")
Method 5: retrial decision of jury ("Yes, the jealous mistress is the guilty one.")

It is apparent that these five different methods of deciding between suspects deserve different degrees of confidence.

In science, too, different methods of selecting suspects warrant different degrees of confidence. While the case method, for example, warrants more confidence than does casual opinion, it usually warrants less confidence than does the controlled experiment. Since the case method, however, is used in many fields in which other methods are difficult or impossible to employ, we must examine its strengths and weaknesses carefully.

The After-the-Fact or Case Method

This model is simple. An observation (O) is made. A murdered man is found, or a patient is diagnosed as depressed, or Elizabeth slaps Richard. Next we attempt to decide what previous event (X) led up to O or what previous events were necessary in order for O to happen. In the language of common sense we are asking what caused O. In the language of science we are asking what key antecedent(s) (X's) were linked to the selected consequence (O). There are usually several possible X's; that is, several antecedents (independent variables) that could lead to a given consequence (dependent variable) and the problem is to select the most probable one or ones: X_1? X_2? X_3? . . . , X_n? When our murder victim is first discovered, there are a large number of X's or suspects.

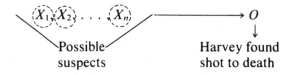

How do we narrow down the number? What aids do we use to sort the most likely suspects from the least likely ones? Our decision aid is *time*. When the time of death is determined to within two hours, all suspects who have reasonable alibis for the shooting time (1:00 A.M. to 3:00 A.M.) are separated from those who do not. Notice we say "reasonable alibi" because we can't be dead certain in each case; hence an area of uncertainty remains.

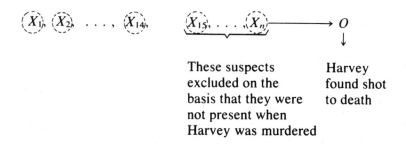

Thus perhaps all but 14 of the original suspects go free.

Let us narrow the list of suspects still further, this time using the decision aid of *motive;* twelve others are now eliminated because they have no obvious motive. Notice we say no "obvious" motive; again, circles of uncertainty always remain. That is one reason hired guns are used—they have no obvious connection with the victim.

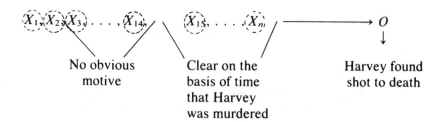

Of the suspects who still remain after the "time" and "motive" screening, Suspect 1 is focused on when it is found that the murder weapon is his. This, plus the fact that he had a motive and has no alibi, links him to the death with three lines of evidence. Nevertheless, Suspect 1 is quickly replaced by Suspect 2 when the latter's fingerprints are found on the murder weapon. As well as being the suspect most closely tied to the murder weapon, he has a motive and no alibi.

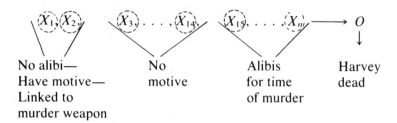

No alibi—   No   Alibis   Harvey
Have motive—   motive   for time   dead
Linked to   of murder
murder weapon

So gradually, with the aid of the time and motive sieves, we have eliminated some X's and tied others to the crime in question—some with only one fine thread of evidence (motive) and others with several lines of evidence (motive, no alibi, murder weapon).

The case method consists of eliminating certain suspects and then attempting to determine which of the remaining ones are most heavily tied to the observation or event being studied. Its main strength probably lies in helping rule out certain suspects rather than in guaranteeing the selection of the best suspect from among those who remain. It is not a foolproof procedure, as wrongly condemned men will hasten to tell you (at least those who still have use of their vocal cords).[1] Nevertheless, it has great advantages over the crystal ball or the casual opinion or the widow's bias or the D.A.'s hunch.

A CASE FOR THE HISTORIAN

This same after-the-fact method is used by historians to explain what led to what in the past. Whereas the problem for the courts is to determine what preceding events and people are tied to a given crime, the problem for the historian is to determine what preceding events and people are tied to a given historical observation. What key events (X's) led to or were tied to the circumstances that provoked the beginning of World War II (O)? Were the key events economic, growing out of Germany's need for raw materials and markets? Were they psychological, growing out of the personality structure of the German people, coupled with the resentment over their defeat in World War I? Was the single key

---

[1]We noted that although none of the methods is perfect all are designed to reduce the risk of error—the risk of certain types of error. Our courts are presumably set up to reduce the risk of condemning an innocent person on the principle that it is better to let a hundred guilty persons go free than to condemn one innocent individual.

event the mistake of allowing a clever madman to gain control during troubled times? Or did the war result from a combination of all these, and if so, what relative importance should we assign to each?

$$X_1, X_2, \ldots, X_n \quad 1X_1, 1X_2, \ldots, 1X_n \quad 2X_1, 2X_2, \ldots, 2X_n \longrightarrow O$$

Economic   Psychological   Political   Beginning
                                                             of World
                                                             War II

    This is the task of the historian, to make a case for his or her particular selection of suspects—a challenging task because there are so many. This fact leads many to conclude that history is an art rather than a science. Thus any one interpretation of history must leave many suspects unnoticed or unaccounted for; the risk of error is so high that the historian may be seen as an artist rather than as a scientist. According to this view historians faced with a formidable number of suspects develop a point of view to help them in their task; otherwise they would literally be driven to distraction.

    Many historians look for economic suspects as explanations for historical events, and as a result they miss or ignore other types of explanation. Nowadays many historians look for sociological or psychological suspects as well as economic ones. But if the kinds of suspects on the historical hit parade change, how are we to tell a good historian from a bad one? The good historian is one who can sell other historians on using his or her theory or point of view in selecting suspects. In addition, good historians carefully document the suspects they have the time, inclination, and techniques to consider.[2]

    Notice that when faced with an overwhelming number of suspects, many of them fuzzy, historians require a theory, a bias, or a point of view in order to focus their limited resources on one or two main suspects—economic, psychological, or religious. In brief, anyone using the after-the-fact method requires a theoretical viewpoint, or bias, to reduce the problem to mind size.

A CASE FOR THE PHYSICIAN

Consider another situation in which the after-the-fact or case method is employed. You have a stomachache, and you present your case to the physician. The doctor is faced with the same problem as the court and the historian—that of narrowing down the list of suspects and then attempting to deal with the many that remain. Just as historians are governed in their approach by current theories or points of view about history, so doctors are influenced by current medical theory, which leads them to bet on one suspect or group of suspects over others. Thus a mixture

---

[2]In an impressive effort to make their work more objective and quantitative, an increasing number of historians are adopting some of the methods of the social and behavioral sciences.

of experience, current medical theory, and personal biases determines what types of sorting devices your doctor uses and therefore what kinds of suspects he or she will select from the many available.

For example, what happens when you present your physician with a stomachache that comes and goes?

$$X_1, X_2, X_3, X_4, X_5, X_6, \ldots, X_n \longrightarrow O$$
$$\downarrow$$
Stomachache

Various alternative suspects come to mind. Some are remembered from classes at medical school, some have been encountered often in practice, and others are remembered from reading recent articles—if your doctor has had time to read and digest them. What are some of the suspects that might be considered: appendicitis, ulcer, mild food poisoning? Your physician does not concern him/herself with *all* of the alternatives but initially focuses on one at a time. The doctor examines the stomach and attempts to localize the site of discomfort. He or she tries to determine the time of onset and the kind and degree of pain. These bits of information are applied to each of the possible common suspects. Perhaps none of the common suspects gets much support, and so all are discarded. Also, to limit the number of suspects, your doctor has focused on recent events and now looks further back in your history—the doctor extends his or her time frame, asks about similar illnesses in parents and grandparents. If nothing is found there, the physician will likely consider rarer causes, seeking information from lab tests, X-rays, or specialists. Thus facing this stewpot of evidence, the doctor with the aid of theory, observations, and *hunches* gradually reduces the large number of possible suspects, eventually choosing one that emerges within the scope of his or her medical vision.

A CASE FOR THE COUNSELOR

This fourth example of the after-the-fact method in action derives from the experiences of a client in counseling who reported concerns related to the initiation, development, and maintenance of interpersonal relations with women. In seeking to understand the nature of the client's impediments to the formation of rewarding relationships with females, the counselor explores the personal history of the client and endeavors to enhance the client's insight through the use of a cognitive templating technique (Pyke, 1979). Essentially, this technique is a mechanism to identify key suspects and their interrelations. Readers wishing to try their hand at after-the-fact researching should read through the history below and attempt to isolate suspects, subsequently comparing those selected with those identified by the counselor.

The Client's Chronicle

Michael, at 38, is in the second year of a Ph.D program in political science. He is the eldest and favorite son of upper-class conservative parents. His father, a devout and moralistic Christian, was an extremely successful businessman whose work frequently required that the family live for extended periods in foreign locales. About his father, Michael says, "He was always serious, up-tight, sometimes petulant, a chronic worrier, but always just and fair and I was proud of his success and status. He's extremely sensitive to criticism and nonemotional, self-possessed."

Although well-educated, Michael's mother had never supported herself but assumed the demanding role of charming and capable social hostess for her spouse's many business associates in addition to her child-care responsibilities. Recurring bouts of serious depression resulted in repeated suicide attempts, but her children had no knowledge of these acts until long after they had left home. Michael noted that he valued some of his mother's qualities—her sensitivity and interpersonal skills.

Family interactions were not characterized either by overt displays of affection or acrimonious, angry scenes. Maintaining a calm, civilized, and cultured demeanor was stressed. Rational and intelligent behavior, reflecting good self-control, was expected. Academic achievement was especially rewarded. Michael observed, "Having someone say, 'You're stupid' was the worst thing that could happen."

At the age of 14, Michael was enrolled in a private boys' school, which he described as a brutal authoritarian environment. "I was traumatized on so many fronts when I was at Parkdale. I was totally ignorant about sexual matters, and being knowledgeable in this area was an important issue at the school. I tried to avoid situations where my ignorance would be apparent, with the result that there was relatively little diminution in the depth of my naivete. Physical violence was commonplace, and there was a constant undercurrent of tension that frequently erupted into vicious combat. There was absolutely no emphasis on academic achievement although I continued to get excellent grades. Other kids taunted me, called me 'Brainy' and tried to pick fights. For my own protection I developed a relationship with one of the enforcers; I helped him with his assignments and he, in turn, kept the other kids off my back. I felt like a coward and still do. I reacted in a cowardly way, responding by withdrawal rather than confronting. I always want to win without risk. That's a pattern in my life."

At 16, Michael entered a university, majoring in philosophy. "I saw myself as a failure in male-female relationships—felt emasculated and upset. I was also preoccupied about having my inexperience exposed." Divergence from the family values crystallized during this period. "I became an atheist, adopted a Marxist political orientation, and was extremely active in a campus radical group. We were superintellectual, strongly idealistic, and totally alienated from the university academic structure, which to us appeared antithetical to learning and challenge. Although I rarely attended classes, I worked hard on assignments and maintained good grades. I was incredibly arrogant and so openly disrepectful to some of my professors that I was thrown out of several classes. I didn't date during the four years I was there—much too busy with the political and philosophical issues. Again, it's the same pattern, more withdrawal. So, I was still a virgin at 20.''

After a year working with the peace movement, during which, on a "one night stand," Michael experienced the mysteries of intercourse, he enrolled in a graduate school in California. Once again, Michael joined a group of activists and was soon recognized as part of the upper echelon of organizers in the group. An 18-year-old fellow activist, Laura, initiated contact with Michael and they began cohabiting in a commune setting. "I had more status so I probably looked attractive to her. I mentioned that because I'm a bit paranoid about attraction and success. It was a good relationship, both emotionally and physically, but we were intellectually competitive. Laura strived to be equal and to be perceived as equal although, being older, I had the edge.''

Michael's disenchantment with academic environments continued unabated and he was debarred after participation in a series of rather dramatic protest activities, the last of which culminated in his arrest for civil disobedience. Michael referred to the university's action as an attempt to "purge the department of dissident elements." Coinciding with the escalation of Michael's difficulties with the university and the police was a deterioration of the relationship with Laura. "It was a bad period politically. I didn't know what I wanted and that showed. I felt held back by any kind of monogamous relationship and was openly engaging in extracurricular sex with other women. Nevertheless, I was hopeful about future relationships because I had had very positive experiences with Laura over the couple of years we were together.''

Now denied access to the university, Michael and some comrades founded a New Left Marxist group off campus and established a radical newspaper. Headquarters for the group was a large, old private home in which 15 to 30 core organizers lived and worked communally for about four years. Soon after the establishment of this new movement, which included nonstudent radicals, Michael developed a friendship with Sharon, "a very gutsy, beautiful, sexy, and sexually active woman." Michael reports, "She initiated sexual contact and I was delighted. It was a status symbol to relate to her in sexual terms—it was a real conquest. And, as for her part, I was becoming an increasingly important figure in the movement and was receiving a fair amount of public recognition. The relationship was doomed from the beginning.''

In a short time Michael became the designated leader of the group and his responsibilities included the organization of protest marches, public rallies, speaking engagements, writing for the newspaper, and maintenance of security (from police infiltration). Sharon wanted a child and although Michael was initially opposed, believing the revolution to be more important, Sharon persuaded him, arguing that, "If the Vietnamese can do it, so can we.''

Concurrently, the tension on the political scene was mounting. "Violence was in the air—from the right, from the police, and even from within our own ranks. I was extremely ill-at-ease under conditions of violence. I felt responsible for my people and worried about sending them out into the streets. Our activities received a lot of media coverage and since I was the spokesperson it was my face on the T.V. and my words in the paper. I received a certain number of threats and hate literature and was picked up by the police several times, even shot at. Once she became pregnant, Sharon seemed to be becoming more and more dependent on me and that was an added strain.

"Then there was a challenge to my leadership. Both Sharon and I were accused of being undercover cops and I was removed from the leadership pending an investigation by the Security Committee. When this happened, Sharon decided to get an abortion. I was very upset. I helped set it up and paid for it but with tears in my eyes. I felt threatened by what I saw as her withdrawal of solid love and affection, and I became defensive, not only because of the abortion but also because she decided to work in a night club as an erotic dancer. She asked me if I would come with her if she left the movement and I said no, and maybe that was the end, but we continued on and then she publicly humiliated me by going out and sleeping with an old boyfriend who'd come to town. The relationship finally terminated a month or so later when she took up with a fellow on the Security Committee—one of my detractors. When I had high status it was okay to relate to me, but when I was under siege, I was abandoned. Sharon's abortion was a watershed. I haven't had a satisfactory relationship with a woman since then. When I'm rejected I withdraw, retreat, and deploy resources. I shift gears and go someplace else."

Michael was exonerated from the "police informer" allegation but he was devastated by these experiences in his personal and political life and he looked for something different. He moved to the East Coast and joined a Marxist-Leninist group oriented more toward working-class politics. The group seemed promising and the leader inspired confidence. He also obtained a teaching position and essentially held two full-time jobs working 80 to 85 hours a week. Michael spent seven years with this organization. Increasing recognition of the inadequacy of the theoretical philosophical model underlying the movement led ultimately to its demise.

"The feminist critique of the Marxist model of social change was particularly telling. At a mass self-analysis meeting of all members and hangers-on, it became apparent that the criticisms of the feminists couldn't be handled within the model and since the organization had no better alternatives to propose, the group decided to disband," Michael explained.

"Part of what was wrong with the movement was the denial, the absence of common-sense selfishness. After the collapse of the New Left movement, I had to rethink some basic assumptions. Concern with myself and my own happiness is legitimate, not selfish. Twenty years of my life have been devoted to being a professional activist. I sacrificed my career for the sake of the movement, but I can't say that I regret the activity nor do I see it as over. My experiences in these groups were overwhelmingly positive and opened up all sorts of choices. I still have libertarian views but no longer want to give voice to them within a framework of Puritan self-denial. I am no longer prepared to give up everything for the movement. And, I needed to establish myself; to increase my capacity to earn my bread and butter. I chose the high road—more education—because the academic lifestyle is more appealing to me than the technical route.''

Concerning his problem, Michael commented, ''I've never seen it as legitimate to ask someone out: it's a shame thing or a Christian thing. I don't like to admit an interest in someone in front of anyone else. If I get rejected and other people know I was interested, I'll look bad. Maybe sexuality is associated in my unconscious mind with something evil or dirty or it could be the competitive thing—fear about revealing any weakness at all. Perhaps I've narrowed myself down to activities I know I'll succeed in. I'm relatively cautious, prudent, or conservative, I guess.''

About his general sense of himself, Michael observed, ''I have a positive self-concept when my self is object but not when it's subject. I seem to be preoccupied with my presentation of self—how I'm coming across to others. My sense of ideal self is so strong that I'm driven by my sense of what should ideally be the case. What I want is so much greater than what is. Do I have hidden desires to exploit others: Is this why I feel guilty? I have difficulty stating baldly that these are my needs, maybe because of my Christian training. When I say I want *X*, it comes out cynically—my moralistic attitude poisons it.

''I don't feel inferior to others; my basic self-concept is positive yet I have a strong sense of not being worthy. My failure to establish intimate relations with women threatens my sense of myself. My self-concept is fragile, though. I seem to have a need to hit back if someone doesn't recognize and respect me. I'm too easily insulted.''

On another occasion Michael confessed, ''I seem to be worried that people will see through me but I'm not sure what I'm hiding. When I'm with others I seem to be play-acting. I'm truthful in that I show both the positive and negative aspects of myself, but somehow I maintain control in how it comes across. Because I anticipate criticism I use a variety of strategies to allay it—humor, taking on the role of the clown, invective, even self-criticism. My principal concern when I'm involved with a woman is how other men will see me with that woman. The woman herself is incidental. I'm playing for the audience. It's not nice to say it, but I see a woman as a commodity, as a potential contributor to status. The woman is not even part of the audience; she's a prop. The audience isn't necessarily real. I'm still playing to that bunch of guys in Parkdale or the jocks in the club. I want to look good to others; to put on a good face. I have to battle with myself to bring up negative things and I spend a lot of time justifying myself.

''I'm judgmental (but am afraid of being judged) and have a strong sense of what's right. I've always had to be better than everyone else—more revolutionary, more feminist—then I'm invulnerable to reproach. But no matter how well I do, I feel it's not good enough. It may be good enough for some people but not for me. I can't handle praise because although I want it and appreciate it, I always feel the achievement wasn't good enough. Also, I tend to analyze the motives of the person giving me praise. What's their status? Are they manipulating me? I have high expectations for others and always see their strengths before their weakness. I find it hard to believe they will be base. To avoid being taken in or gulled I superanalyze everything so I won't make a false move. It's a strategy to help handle my naivete and innocence.''

With respect to his future, Michael reflected, ''I'm playing make-up now, racing against time. I'm impatient because I'm in the second half of my life and in some sense I'm just starting. But I don't really like the idea of achieving adult status. I really enjoy being young and don't want to surrender my youth. I worry about being caught in the straight life. I feel there's not much time left. I need to get on the offensive again—to stop reeling from the punches. Many of the ways I had for dealing with the world were wrong or if they were right, the object of the change was wrong.''

Summing up his difficulties in the area of developing intimate relationships with women, Michael said, ''I have a great capacity for forming superficial relationships. It was a habit not to get too deeply committed as a kid because I knew we would likely move soon. But I've always been well-liked even by my political adversaries. I like social situations and thrive in them. It's unusual for me to be this withdrawn from people. I'm preoccupied with not blowing my academic work. My problem is one of timidity or shyness in situations where there is a possibility of loss, especially in the area of initiating relationships with women. I'm just not bonding well with women. That's the crux of my feelings of inferiority. It threatens my sense of my own masculinity. I don't feel normal vis-à-vis other males. What blocks me from taking emotional risks?''

Cognitive Template

Faced with the myriad of potential suspects embedded in Michael's narrative, how does the counselor sort key suspects from less influential factors? Helpful clues available to the counselor include: (1) the number of different times Michael mentions a feeling or incident; (2) the total amount of time Michael spends describing an issue; (3) the intensity of the affect or emotion associated with the experience; (4) Michael's own assessment of the importance of a particular event or feeling; (5) any obvious reluctance on Michael's part to explore a particular issue; (6) the counselor's theoretical orientation, which will lead to a focus on suspects related to behavioral habits, or feelings experienced in the ''here and now,'' or illogical thought processes, or sex and gender-role socialization, or on the resolution of the oedipal complex.

Figure 4–1 represents the counselor's attempt to depict the personal history variables (key suspects) relevant to the presenting problem. From the client's chronicle, the key suspects are identified and tied to the client's cognitions (his descriptions) of his life experiences and of himself. Figure 4–2 presents abstracted themes representing clusters of key events that seem interrelated and, additionally, the connections among themes.

The feminist orientation of the counselor is clearly apparent in the analysis below. Counselors of other theoretical persuasions (and readers) would no doubt have selected a different complex of key suspects. The ultimate test of who's right

Michael's Cognitive Template

Key Suspects

| *Family* | *Other* |

Family	Other
1. Mother—failure/weak 2. Father—success 3. Achievement (task-oriented) emphasis 4. Intellectual emphasis 5. Emotionality discouraged (cool, objective, calm, rational) 6. Parental relationship (lack of intimacy) 7. Christian/Puritan/conservative tradition 8. High status & class 9. Masking/disguise	10. Travel (instability, isolation, special) 11. Private school—no females, new 12. Private school milieu—negative emotionality 13. Cultural influences—sex stereotypes 14. Experiences with female friends & lovers 15. Political ideology—priorities & communal intimacy 16. Political experiences

FIGURE 4–1

lies in the utility of the approach, and the ultimate judge of that is the client—the consumer.

Interpretation

Michael's sense of his own *specialness* derived in no small measure from his father's success in achieving a prestigious position of extraordinarily high status and respect. The benefits of travel (familiarity with other cultures, facility in several languages) contributed to this specialness. As horrendous as the private school was for Michael, attending the school added to his differentness. Adoption of an unpopular political position combined with atypical experiences (getting arrested) further enhanced Michael's sense of his own uniqueness.

Related to the specialness was Michael's development of high *standards* and expectations for both self and others. Again, several family variables were instrumental in this development as well as the idealism and self-sacrifice expectation inherent in the political ideology embraced by Michael. One by-product of the high standards was *low self-esteem;* Michael could never measure up to his own expectations and hence had developed a number of strategies for dealing with constant failure (withdrawal; intellectualization and rationalizations to *justify* his own performance). Another by-product was that Michael was frequently disappointed in the behavior of others because they too failed to meet his standards.

Themes

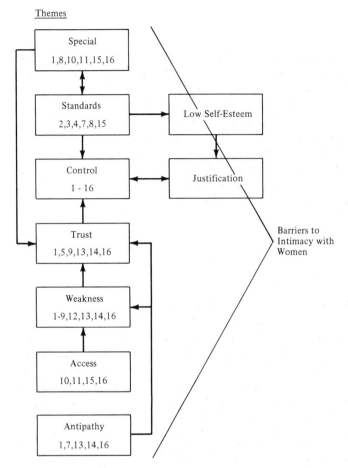

FIGURE 4–2

Attempting to live up to high standards required that Michael maintain iron *control* and self-discipline. This theme of control seemed central to Michael's cognitive style and was certainly reinforced in the family environment where emotional expression was regarded as inappropriate or immature or sloppy while a dispassionate, objective, and cool style commanded respect. Coping with fears of looking foolish, inept, or ignorant, coupled with the need to put on a good face, necessitated the maintenance of a high degree of control.

Michael grew up in a family where surface serenity was highly valued—not surprising given that the family was on frequent public display. Family conflicts or personal problems were kept under wraps. Even the enormity of the mother's suicide attempts could not penetrate the wall of respectability, the facade of the well-adjusted family. Such an environment, with its emphasis on masking and disguise, is not conducive to the development of *trust* or to learning how to establish trust in an interpersonal relationship. More specifically, with respect to relationships with women, Michael's mother's erratic behavior indicated she couldn't be relied upon (trusted), and exposure to the general cultural stereotypes would suggest that women in general can't be trusted. With few exceptions, subsequent personal experiences with women only reinforced this bias. Michael's involvement in a revolutionary political movement also reinforced a pre-existing bias. The constant concern about police infiltration, informers, police entrapment, and the like inspired constant suspicion. And Michael's specialness also contributed to the general lack of trust. "People like me not for who I am but rather what I am."

This lack of trust encourages the tendency to maintain control, as does Michael's abhorrence of *weakness*. It would never do to let anyone perceive a vulnerability, a chink in the armor. A self-declared weakness exists in the area of relations with women, which derived in part from the limited *access* or opportunity to forge and maintain relationships with females. Perceiving women as weak and not to be trusted is part of a general *antipathy* toward women. This antipathy stems from several factors: the unsatisfactory female model provided by Michael's mother; his exposure to the Christian view of women; his social conditioning into the traditional masculine role; his personal unfulfilling relationships with women. The death knell might well have been the role women played in the destruction of a political movement near and dear to his heart.

REDUCING THE RISK OF ERROR

In the foregoing discussion we considered examples from the fields of law, history, medicine, and counseling in which a large-hole sieve—the after-the-fact method—is employed. The same method is employed in economics, political science, anthropology, sociology, and business administration. We use the after-the-fact method when it is impossible, or too difficult, or too late to experiment.

You will have noticed that any time we can reduce the number of suspects we increase our chances of picking the correct one. The same principle holds in drawing for a car. Which would you prefer: to have your ticket in a drum with 1000 other tickets, with 100 other tickets, or with 10 other tickets? Any method that helps reduce the number of suspects appeals to the scientist as much as any method of reducing the number of tickets in the drum appeals to the ticket holder. Notice then the two main ways we use to reduce the number of suspects in the after-the-fact method: the time frame and the theory frame.

Whenever you draw a *time frame* around the event or observation under study, you include some suspects and exclude others. Recall how the knowledge of the time of death of poor Harvey helped rule out a large number of suspects and so helped shrink the scope of the investigation. A time frame helps us exclude certain suspects, whether the problem faces the court, the historian, or the physician, thus enabling them to focus their limited investigative resources on a few suspects—hopefully the right ones.

Another method of cutting a problem down to investigative size is to place it inside not only a time frame but inside a *theory frame* as well. A theory frame reduces your decision burden or search space by focusing your attention on certain kinds of cues: motive cues, economic cues, psychological cues. Notice in the instance of Harvey's death that we first drew a time frame around those suspects that had no alibi and then reduced that group still further by applying a theory frame, by focusing only on those with a motive.

The application of time frames and theory frames doesn't guarantee that you'll find the right suspect—the after-the-fact method, no matter how skillfully applied, offers no guarantees—but by shrinking the investigative space, time frames and theory frames protect juries, historians, physicians, and citizens from drowning in an ocean of speculative-observational evidence.

Consider the case of Elvis, a tall, blond, good-looking young man of 20 who is referred to a psychiatrist. Elvis has difficulty sleeping, is tense and anxious, and seems to spend a lot of time worrying about his courses at the university, his looks, and his dates. We start then with Anxious Elvis as our observation (O), as our dependent variable.

The psychiatrist has the job of attempting to see what led to O. How many suspects are there? The number of suspected reasons or events contributing to Elvis's unhappy state is infinite. Everything that has happened from the moment of his conception is a potential suspect, is a potential independent variable.

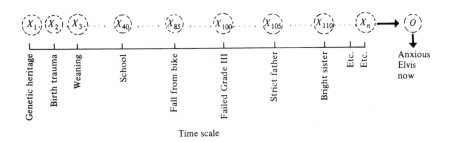

Time scale

Elvis's problem, then, may be due to a lot of things: a genetic factor (bad genes—"his grandfather was the same way"); a mother who did not want him, handled him roughly, and weaned him too early; a witch of a first-grade teacher who terrorized the boy; a bang on the head received from a fall off a bike at the age of eight; a stern father who was always smiling but never satisfied, no matter how hard Elvis tried to please; or any one of a thousand things or combination of things. Like historians, psychiatrists must have some biases or theories about what events lead to anxious people; otherwise the avalanche of possible suspects could drive them . . . well, to see a psychiatrist. Thus some psychiatrists look to your genes and your biochemistry (using genetic or biological sieves), others to your weaning and toilet training (usually early experience sieves), others to your attitude toward authority. If Elvis has been anxious for years, the doctor needs a theory frame to help reduce his or her medical search space down to a size where the doctor can sift through a certain class of suspects—biochemical, genetic, or psychological.

Notice how using a time sieve can reduce the overwhelming search space facing the psychiatrist. If Elvis has only been anxious for a month think how this time frame drastically reduces the number of suspects.

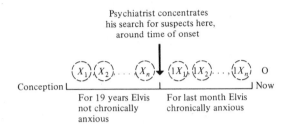

Time scale

Now the psychiatrist has a better chance to home in on some contributing suspects by examining events just preceding the onset of anxiety. This is not to say that events during the first 19 years are irrelevant, but at least they were not sufficient alone to lead to an anxiety state. The psychiatrist can use a time frame (the last month), a theory frame (a biochemical frame—allergies), or a psychological stress frame (fight with his girlfriend). The doctor now has at least a chance of reaching a reasoned conclusion—right or wrong.

SUMMARY

Before we proceed to an extension of the case method, a summary is in order. Using the case method we attempt to go back in time after an event has occurred to find the most probable cause or suspect. However, two major problems plague us: (1) there are usually a great number of possible causes or suspects; (2) it is often extremely difficult to get reliable information about past events or symptoms (possible causes or suspects). For example, the courts must rely heavily on the memory of the witnesses, and such memories prove time and again to be unreliable. Also much of the evidence becomes unavailable as eyewitnesses melt in the crowd or fail to volunteer evidence for fear of getting involved in lengthy or unpleasant court proceedings. Your doctor, too, relies heavily on the fragmentary bits of information you provide—bits you select from the large file of fact and fancy you call your memory, that wonderful data swamp. The historian also deals in fragments of the past, documents written perhaps from the fallible recollections of someone who knew someone who knew someone who saw "it" happen. We rarely know how time has taken an event and shaped and reshaped it to fit the minds and tongues through which it passes. Remember playing the party game "Rumor," in which a message is passed from person to person in the same room, and recall how quickly the message became unwittingly distorted and reshaped by each person in the chain.

Thus the case method with its large numbers of suspects—some lost to view, some distorted by time—presents a great challenge to those who would sort fact from fancy. With an awareness of the difficulties, however, and in the knowledge that no more practical method is readily available, dedicated men and women in law, medicine, and history have demonstrated that useful and durable packages of information can be produced. Others in the same fields, less dedicated or less aware of the limitations of the method, have posed and have been accepted as authorities, only to be unmasked later as pushers of perishable goods. Some people are a double threat: a threat to themselves, in that they assume they know and so are less open to other evidence, and a threat to those who rely on their advice. Perhaps the best safeguard exists when both the experts and the public are aware of the strengths and weaknesses of the various methods used to sift fact from fancy.

In spite of its limitations, do not reject this after-the-fact method simply because it cannot guarantee to produce the correct suspect. In many situations it remains the best method we have. It is useful in narrowing down the field of suspects so that we can at least make a decision—probably a more durable one than those produced by the rules of evidence of the armchair, the pub, or the afternoon tea party.

In the next chapter we consider a special form of the after-the-fact method. It can be called the archival method and is also applied in situations that involve going back into the past for suspects.

In this archival method, we employ time frames and theory or bias frames to reduce the number of suspects to manageable size and to enable us to critically examine the framed or enclosed observations and speculations.

EXAMPLES

Before proceeding to the next chapter, we include here two brief case studies. The first was part of a project designed to help students narrow down the field of suspects before proceeding to more sophisticated methods. The second is a case described by David Premack (1970) a creative researcher and theorist, that demonstrates how case studies can be useful in helping to clarify theoretical issues. Both cases concern people who have given up smoking without professional help.

Case I

This is the case of a 35-year-old female who had been smoking between a package and a package and a half of cigarettes per day for 15 or 16 years. She is a married professional woman with three degrees and two children.

She reported that she inhaled and enjoyed every cigarette she ever smoked. She stated she had attempted to stop smoking only once before on a rash $100 bet made at a cocktail party. She lost the bet the following morning with no regrets. At the time of our interview, several years later, she had not smoked for eight months. While she didn't miss it all the time, a day never went by that she didn't strongly want a cigarette on several occasions.

As a consequence of giving up smoking she reported that she had gained 15 pounds and can't seem to control her overeating. If the weight gain continued, she felt she would have to return to smoking, and she appeared to enjoy that possibility. When asked what eventually led her to give up smoking, she said she wasn't sure, but she thought it was the result of several factors. She listed the following suspects: (1) a period of poor health; (2) pressure from her children, the oldest of whom consistently repeated all the antismoker advertisements she heard, while the younger child repeatedly pretended to smoke in imitation of his mother; (3) pressures from nonsmoking colleagues at meetings and from friends at parties. The pressure was not directed particularly at her but against smokers in general and was often subtle—like no ashtrays at a dinner party. When asked to name the main reason responsible for her giving up cigarettes, she found it difficult, responding that she felt that none of the factors alone would probably have been sufficient.

DISCUSSION
This after-the-fact example illustrates the difficulty of clearly determining what suspect or combination of suspects leads to a given event or observation. It also illustrates how easy it would be for theorists with different biases to each cite this case as supporting their own particular theory.

Some theorists could focus on the "poor health" suspect as support for a "threat-to-life" hypothesis. Others would point to the effectiveness of the antismoking advertising campaign as delivered through the oldest child. Still others would focus on the "modeling" of the youngest child "getting to" the mother; while other theorists would point to "group pressures" at meetings and parties as the key influence.

However, as the woman said, it was probably a complex combination or interaction of all these suspects acting in concert and would take a more sophisticated research design to untangle their influences.

Case II
A 40-year-old male smoked two packages a day for 20 years before quitting abruptly and completely; he has not smoked in 7 years. Despite the lengthy period of abstinence, he is not able to discuss the topic dispassionately. "It is humiliating to be duped by those goddam cigarette companies. They know their product causes cancer, but they do absolutely nothing to prevent it. Instead they spend millions on advertising to keep all the old suckers smoking and to start as many new suckers as possible. Can you see those bastards down there sitting around a pool—Virginia, Kentucky—counting the loot, patting one another's back, laughing it up and not one of them smoking? You're right, absolutely, the blacks are the ones you see smoking down there." The tirade could be enriched along numerous lines, but the speaker's attitude has already been adequately conveyed. If this person were to contemplate the possibility, he might be able to hear, not so much the clinical warning, "You may get cancer," as a sniggering invitation in a southern accent calling to him across the splashing of a pool, "Smoke, suckah, and make me rich!"[3]

Notice in this case the person quit smoking abruptly; therefore the time frame focuses on events immediately preceding his breaking the habit. He focuses on one critical event— that in which he is made to see himself as a sucker. Theorists who favor personal critical events as explanations of changes in behavior would probably concur. However other theorists who believe in the power of advertising and social pressure would probably suggest that such factors paved the way for his so-called sudden insight—that without such "priming" events the insight would never have occurred.

[3]Premack, D. (1970) Mechanisms of self-control. In W. Hunt (Ed.), *Learning and mechanisms of control in smoking*. Hawthorne, N.Y.: Aldine, 107–123. (Reprinted by permission of the American Cancer Society, Inc.)

Chapter 5 ———————

Archival Research or Spoor Analysis

In many instances you don't have to observe behavior directly to know what has occurred; you only have to observe the marks, tracks, spoor, or deposits it leaves. One of the byproducts of the revolution in communications technology is the development of information pools of oceanic proportions—data pools, rich and ready for the nets of eager scientific sailors. Newspapers, magazines, books, films, plays, songs, census statistics, radio broadcasts, suicide notes, letters, diaries, gravestones, and paintings all provide valuable information for researchers. The analysis of these existing materials, of these people-tracks or traces, is known as *archival research*. Employing this method allows the scientist to capitalize on and exploit already collected or deposited data chunks. Moving one or several steps away from direct observation, the investigator relies on the accumulated behavioral spoor and creatively analyzes, groups, combines, and juxtapositions these indirect data.

A study by Sir Francis Galton (cited in Webb, Campbell, Schwartz & Sechrest, 1966) provides an example of the creative use of archival research. Since the long life of a monarch was prayed for more frequently than was the case for less august persons, greater longevity should be observed for royal personages, if praying is effective. The data revealed that in fact royalty had shorter life spans than did the gentry. As sophisticated consumers of science you are quick to note that people of royal birth differ from gentry on a host of other variables, and

Galton's study doesn't seem to have taken these other differences into account—some of them, like inbreeding, perhaps much more relevant in affecting life span than prayer. So Galton's research on this question has only anecdotal value.

CONTENT ANALYSIS

Just as the principal technique of the field study is naturalistic observation, so one of the frequently employed tools of the archival researcher is *content analysis*. Naturalistic observation, it will be recalled, involves detailed, objective, and systematic observation of events in their typical surroundings. Similarly, content analysis requires detailed, objective, and systematic observation of verbal or symbolic communications.

Consider the following research question derived from a study by Pyke (1976). "To what extent do children's books depict traditional sex roles?" Assume that two researchers collect a representative sample of books. They then undertake an analysis of the prose and picture (verbal and symbolic) content of these books. Two coding categories are established: (1) a female figure is performing a traditional female sex-role function (mother squirrel is dusting the nest with her tail); (2) a male figure is performing a traditional male sex-role activity (a fireman is holding the net for the lady in the burning building). For comparison purposes the researchers include two more categories which are the converse of those examples: male or female figures engaged in cross-sex activities (a male cooking; a female operating a backhoe). Each researcher takes half the books and proceeds with the analysis—identifying for each figure depicted in both illustrations and text whether the figure is portrayed performing traditional sex-role functions or functions of the opposite sex role. One hundred books are analyzed; the researchers meet and share their findings.

"Why did you categorize Mary as performing a cross-sex function when she was climbing a tree? Girls climb trees," argues Researcher A.

Researcher B similarly questions A's judgments, "You've got the Daddy coded here as a traditional sex-role item, but surely shopping is a traditional female activity so he should be coded as cross-sex."

"Yes, but it's a hardware store," rebuts A.

"OK, but what do we do if we don't know what kind of store it is?" responds Researcher B.

Although these researchers have coded their observations in a detailed and systematic fashion, they have failed to satisfy the basic criterion of objectivity—independent and consistent labeling. Their understanding of what constituted a traditional sex-role activity was subjective or pragmatic. They were including a great deal of speculation (⊚) but had assumed they were at the observational or objective level (⊙), involving a large amount of solid information.

The problem was resolved by simply coding the activity or occupation (reading, sewing, driving, fighting) and by determining whether this activity or occupation was being performed by a male or female figure. With this more objective coding scheme, the two researchers achieved a high level of agreement in their individual assignment of codes. Their observational checkpoints had reduced areas of argument or speculation surrounding their coding; they moved from ⊙ to ⊙ .

Content analysis brings with it a host of concerns. The quality of the information derived from this technique depends on the adequacy of source sampling (Was the sample of children's books a representative sample?), on the appropriateness and relevance of the coding units, and on the reliability of the coding—on its independence and consistency.

PHYSICAL TRACES

Although the term *archival* suggests some form of document (from a music score to sales records), archival research encompasses a broader band of materials, including physical evidence such as garbage, ancient pottery shards, dust, and other remnants from the past. For example, an architect consulted a psychologist, asking where sidewalks should be built on a new campus to accommodate traffic flows. The architect said, "You're an expert on human behavior, tell me where people will walk." The psychologist, having an empirical bent, visited several established campuses and carried out naturalistic observations of traffic flows. He noted that, in addition to the sidewalks, a variety of paths had been worn across the lawns. He consulted the head groundskeeper, who maintained that once a path was established, it was well nigh impossible to discourage its continued use. The psychologist advised the architect to design his sidewalks so they covered the shortest distance between any two entrances; he also advised the architect to save part of his budget to be spent a year later to put in additional sidewalks where the paths indicated natural, but unpredictable, traffic flows existed.

People leave traces indicating behavioral flows everywhere: worn linoleum, dogeared library books, picnic sites. Analyzing garbage, not only of famous people but also of different socioeconomic classes, provides measures of certain aspects of their behavior. Furthermore, a longitudinal study of people's ashtrays can provide crude indices of patterns of stress; such a study could also provide a relatively objective index of the efficacy of New Year's resolutions to give up smoking or the impact of antismoking campaigns.

Let's consider another example of the use of physical evidence as the research datum. Suppose, as the owner of a car rental agency, you wonder about the value of the radio advertising you've commissioned. Do many people actually hear your creative jingle on station OHM? An archival approach might involve maintaining a record of the radio dial position on all cars returned after rental. This provides a measure of the popularity of the various stations, and so you can use the most popular station (ERG) to carry your advertising (adapted from Webb et al., 1966). A moment's reflection, though, raises a question. Don't you want to reach the *potential* car renters rather than, or in addition to, those who actually use your agency? Perhaps the former group listen predominantly to station WATT rather than ERG.

Webb and colleagues (1966) provide many examples of the analysis of physical traces including measuring the food consumption of institutionalized patients by weighing the trucks bringing in food supplies and the trucks carting garbage out; estimating the differential activity level of children by comparing the degree of wear on their shoes; determining the height of individuals in the Middle Ages by measuring the height of suits of armor; and judging the popularity of library texts by measuring the degree of wear and tear on the pages.

STRENGTHS AND WEAKNESSES

Archival research is perhaps one of the least exploited research methods even though it offers some protection against a prime villain, reactivity (the on-stage effect). It is hard to imagine that a student might deliberately deface a text so that the next archival researcher who comes along will judge it to have been well or frequently read. Equally difficult to swallow is the image of a tombstone carver gleefully altering birth dates so as to mislead future generations of scientists. The man whose height is being estimated from his suit of armor can't throw our measurement off by standing on his tiptoes. Nor will the rental car clients fake their radio listening behavior, because they don't know it is being researched. Thus archival research involves the use of unobtrusive or nonreactive measures. Researchers using this method usually need not be concerned that their observations are distorted by subjects' awareness that they are objects of study.

The value of conclusions derived from spoor analysis depends, of course, on how much of the original deposit remains available for analysis. The Nixon tapes offer a classic example of a mammoth attempt to provide a relatively complete verbal record of his office behavior, not all of which record was retained, including the infamous 18-minute erasure. Such records can be incomplete by design or by accident; they can be edited by the crude hand of sloth and decay or by the fine hand of deceit. In either case, running or episodic records provide ingenious social scientists with further fixes on human behavior—with views that go beyond the sheltered laboratory.

While deceit and sloth can affect the amount of information available in written and taped documents, so too can systematic changes in record-keeping procedures. For example, records of crime show that rates shift in some cases as a result of improved record-keeping, while in other cases because of increased detection. In order to differentiate between these two influences, social scientists relying on archival records must be no less sophisticated than when working in the laboratory. They must be *record-wise*. For example, rates of alcoholism in a given region are frequently based on liver cirrhosis death rates. However, such estimates are frequently low because of the stigma surrounding that cause of death appearing on the certificate. Unless investigators become familiar with the practices surrounding the production of archival records, they can be badly misled.

Given the revolution in data storage and retrieval systems through the development and spread of computer facilities, the prognosis for archival research is excellent. How much money did consumers invest in children's toys last December? What's the unemployment rate for university graduates? How many nonnationals are currently employed in the country? Is there a sex difference in the incidence of mental disorders? How much income tax did people in the $60,000-a-year bracket pay last year? Questions such as these may soon be answered with a press of a button—data literally at our fingertips. If you think this is an idle fancy or a futuristic view, listen to a major league baseball broadcast. Every imaginable statistic is available for the pressing.

Although data may be more readily accessible, assessment of the quality of these data is still of concern. We referred earlier to the use by computer programmers of an acronym *gigo* (garbage in, garbage out), which captures the notion that the computer record or memory is only as accurate and detailed as the information that is fed into it. Problems of lost and distorted data still apply. The many film plots depicting the mad, irresponsible, or criminal computer genius who erases information, plants misinformation, or otherwise deliberately distorts the computer record for his or her own ends suggest we must adopt a critical stance. Add to deliberate deception the inaccuracies deriving from carelessness and human error, and the problem is compounded. Yet the seductive computer carries with it an aura of precision and accuracy. At first glance it seems the answer to a researcher's prayer, but let the user beware.

For the imaginative and record-wise researcher, archival records—whether they be laundry lists or Supreme Court rulings, classified advertisements or death certificates—provide rich opportunities to enlarge the validity of our observations and in many instances also provide auxiliary information about the adequacy of such data in terms of biases affecting what was recorded and what was retained.

Perhaps the optimum use of archival research arises when it is employed in combination with other methods. Indeed, to the extent that an observational checkpoint is revealed by more than one of science's methods, our confidence in the validity of the observation is enhanced; it has picked up more "empirical robustness." In this sense all research methods are supplementary. The multimethod bracketing of hypotheses by imaginative and tenacious researchers warrants massive encouragement. A case in point is one student's attempt to study the effects of frustration on eating behavior, in which he extended his laboratory observations of rats to checking the records of the hometown fans' consumption of hot dogs when attending losing, as opposed to winning, football games.

SUMMARY

The archival research method involves an analysis of behavioral remnants—the traces or tracks of past behavior. Such archival traces are frequently subjected to content analysis. A major strength of this method is its nonreactive or unobtrusive character, but it is prey to whatever biases existed in the original deposit conditions, to the subsequent effects of time, or to decay and to deceit.

EXAMPLE

This example was adapted from a report produced by two students. The excerpt describes the use of the archival method as it was employed in the context of a larger study investigating media representations of the desirable or ideal role for women.

MEDIA REPRESENTATIONS OF WOMEN'S ROLES

INTRODUCTION
On the basis of Betty Friedan's thesis (1963), as described in *The Feminine Mystique,* it was predicted that women's magazines in the 1950s and early 1960s would portray a relatively traditional view of the nature and role of the female. As a function of the rebirth of the feminist movement, a more liberal orientation was expected to appear in the late 1960s; however, this shift was anticipated to be minimal for two reasons. First, the magazine selected for study caters to married housewives with families. For the magazine to denigrate the traditional role would be risking some loss of readership. Second, much of the advertising in the magazine is devoted to products oriented toward the home. Producers of these products may well prefer that women maintain a traditional role model, and any attempt by the magazine to encourage alternative role structures might result in a loss of advertising revenue.

METHOD
   Materials.   Magazine X was chosen for study because it is a wide-circulation monthly magazine aimed at the middle-class housewife. Randomly selected issues from 1951 to 1957 were compared with similarly selected issues published in the period 1966–1972.
   Procedure.   Two issues of the magazine were randomly picked from the 12 issues published annually in 1951, 1953, 1955, 1957, 1966, 1968, 1970, and 1972. Each investigator examined one issue from each of the eight years surveyed. A total of 16 issues were reviewed—8 by each investigator. Data for the September 1955 issue were mislaid and so are not included in the results. All but two issues of 1953 were missing from the archives, so a random selection was not possible for this year.
   A cursory scan of two issues selected from 1952 and 1967 revealed that the following themes were evident in the articles: home and family (marriage, love, childcare, divorce, home decorating, sewing, recipes); personal health (exercise, diet), beauty and fashion; human interest; political; travel; general interest (includes any other articles). Each article in the issues selected for study was categorized in terms of these themes.

RESULTS
The percentage of articles of each category type for each time period is presented in Table 5–1.

DISCUSSION
Home and family concerns as well as physical attractiveness are key components of the traditional sex-role model for women. Clearly these issues were central in Magazine X over the period from 1951 to 1957. Of all articles published, 75 percent focused on these themes over the eight-year span. The magazine thus projected a consistently traditional view of the female and her role. The articles revealed a concern with marriage as a stable and sacred institution—with advice on how to keep a marriage intact. Other articles followed the ''efficient homemaker'' motif—budgeting, do-it-yourself, and helpful cleaning hints.

TABLE 5–1   Percentage of Articles by Category

CATEGORY	1951–1957	1966–1972
Home & Family	52	35
Personal Health	6	0
Beauty & Fashion	17	20
Human Interest	16	17
Political	9	18
Travel	0	2
General Interest	0	8

In contrast, only 55 percent of the articles focused on these traditional themes in the late 1960s and early 1970s. A considerably broader coverage of topics is reflected in these more recent issues. Political and social awareness articles doubled in frequency, and items of more general interest began to appear regularly. Thus our prediction that the magazine would reflect a traditional view of women in the 1950s and a more liberal view in the 1960s was supported. Indeed, the change was rather larger than we had anticipated.

One event confounding the interpretation of these results was the replacement of the magazine's editor in 1961. Possibly the new editor was more liberal in her views, and the changes in the magazine were due to her direct influence rather than to a reflection of general liberalization of attitudes regarding women's role in society. Some slight evidence supporting the former interpretation exists in terms of the content and tone of her editorials. Still it may be that this person was hired specifically because her attitudes approximated those becoming prevalent in the society.

REFERENCES
Freidan, B. 1963. *The feminine mystique.* New York: Dell.

INSTRUCTOR'S COMMENTS
To what extent have you effectively ruled out alternative explanations for your results? Or to what extent have you tried to increase your confidence that the results you obtained do in fact accurately represent the changing orientation of this magazine?

Knowing the publication date of the article being coded, combined with your expectation that more recent articles will be more liberal, leaves you open to the possibility that your coding was shaped by your expectation (elastic ruler). This possible source of error could have been reduced or eliminated through the introduction of blind coding.

Your decision to randomly select issues may have introduced a bias. Suppose, for example, that the issues reviewed for the earlier period included (by chance) four December issues, while for the later period no December issues were selected? What implications might this have in terms of the frequency of appearance of the various themes?

The most serious obstacle to confidence in these findings is your failure to demonstrate the objectivity of the category assignment. We have no evidence that the judgments you made were not idiosyncratic. A sample of articles should have been categorized independently by both investigators, and the degree of concordance ascertained. To some extent you have avoided a systematic bias in that each investigator coded an equal number of issues from each time period. Nevertheless, it is possible that the articles categorized by one investigator as political, for example, might be interpreted by the other coder as general interest.

One of the strengths of your study is your use of a pilot run—that is, reviewing two issues not included in your sample in order to establish valid coding categories. Another admirable feature is your awareness of the change in editors (in-the-gap suspect) and your attempt to examine this factor in terms of its implications for your results and conclusions.

chapter 6

Survey Research

One way to increase external validity is to let typical *external* factors or variables into your experiment. Gaining admission to a well-designed laboratory study is like getting in to see the Queen—only a few are called, and even those are expected or coached to leave their "variance" in the lobby—to leave their individuality at home. The Queen would obtain a broader view of human behavior (one of increased external validity) if her footman collected a random sample of people off the street and brought them to her chamber for a chat, drinks, darts, mirror drawing, maze running, and hide-and-seek. While such guests would not behave quite as freely as they would at home, the Queen would nevertheless get a more representative view of her subjects than she typically gets at one of her formal presentations. Similarly, bringing a random collection of people to the laboratory to observe their behavior under a variety of conditions would increase the external validity of our scientific observations. However, we would still be one step removed from "natural" conditions, and we have research questions which cannot be answered in this way. Furthermore, it involves a lot of work!

As a shortcut social scientists have designed the ingenious method of going out to the subjects and asking them how they would behave in a variety of different situations. The asking may be done via some simple, straightforward, paper-and-pencil questionnaire or through in-depth interviewing. The questions may range from voting preferences to measures of stereotypes and prejudice.

Probably you have participated in a survey research project of one type or another. If you haven't been approached by the market researcher in the local shopping plaza on a Saturday afternoon, received a "To the Householder" questionnaire in the mail, or succumbed to the pleas for volunteers delivered to your class by graduate student surveyers, then you may have participated in the national census.

If not familiar with this type of research from a subject's perspective, then perhaps you've conducted some informal surveys of your own. In planning what courses to take this semester, did you ask some students who had already participated in these classes what they thought of the courses? Did you inquire about the type of assignments each professor gave and how leniently these were graded or how interesting his or her lectures were? If so you were employing a rudimentary form of the survey research method. The flexibility of the survey (its multipurpose features) and its deceptively simple technology makes it a popular choice for the novice researcher.

Key components of survey research include (1) the design of the instrument (the questionnaire or interview schedule), (2) the administration procedure (whether the respondent will self-administer the instrument or whether an interviewer will record responses), and (3) the sample selection (who is to be surveyed).

INSTRUMENT DESIGN

Consider the following questionnaire designed to assess attitudes and practices regarding erotic contact between family members.

Erotic Contact with Blood Relatives

Please answer the following questions as honestly and truthfully as you can. Note that this questionnaire is to be completely anonymous. Do not put your name on the form. For the purposes of this questionnaire, please understand erotic contact to mean any behavior intended to arouse or satisfy sexual desire.

Age: _____ Marital Status: _____ Sex: _____
1. Do you have any children related to you by blood?
    Yes _____   No _____
2. Do you believe that erotic contact between parents and their biological children is harmful?

_____	_____	_____	_____	_____
Never	Rarely	Occasionally	Frequently	Always

3. Have you ever engaged in erotic contact with one of your biological parents (excluding sexual intercourse)?

_____	_____	_____	_____	_____
Never	Rarely	Occasionally	Frequently	Very frequently

4. If yes, which parent?
   Mother _____ Father _____ Both _____
5. Who initiated this erotic contact?
   You _____ Parent _____ Not sure _____
6. Have you ever had sexual intercourse with one of your biological parents?

   _____   _____   _____   _____   _____
   Never   Rarely   Occasionally   Frequently   Very frequently
7. If yes, which parent?
   Mother _____ Father _____ Both _____
8. Have you ever engaged in erotic contact with any other relative (excluding parents) related by blood?

   _____   _____   _____   _____   _____
   Never   Rarely   Occasionally   Frequently   Very frequently
9. If you have engaged in erotic contact with another blood relative (excluding parents), please identify the kinship relationship.
   _____ Brother   _____ Sister
   _____ Aunt   _____ Uncle
   _____ Grandfather   _____ Grandmother
   _____ Nephew   _____ Niece
   _____ Female Cousin   _____ Male Cousin
   _____ Daughter   _____ Son

Even though we have indicated to respondents that their replies are anonymous (to encourage truthful reporting), because of the sensitive issues explored in the questionnaire, we may be justifiably suspicious about the veracity of the responses. Biased responding, a problem all survey researchers must face, may be particularly problematic with this questionnaire.

BIASED RESPONDING.   A common form of response bias that occurs in questionnaires, personality tests, attitude measures, and interviews is the *social desirability* bias. Most people want to present themselves in the best possible light, and often this means pretending to conform to cultural ideals—that is, respondents can often determine which option of the alternatives presented is the socially desirable one—the response blessed by society's prescriptions. This option may be selected even though it does not reflect personal views or behavior.

Incestuous relationships are not socially sanctioned, and we might suspect that at least some respondents who selected the first alternative on Item 2 were responding in the socially endorsed direction instead of providing us with their "true" opinion. Indeed, almost every question on our instrument is prey to the operation of this bias.

Surveyers sensitive to this potential source of error sometimes include a scale (a few questions) in their questionnaire packet which is especially designed to measure the extent to which a subject consistently opts for the socially desirable response. Data deriving from high scorers on these particular questions are then discarded on the grounds that the subjects' propensity to endorse socially desirable alternatives may be disguising their "real" views.

"Faking bad," the opposite of the social desirability bias, may occur if there is some advantage for the respondent to appear markedly deviant. Corporal Klinger (Jamie Farr), who appears as a transvestite soldier in the television show *M*A*S*H,* provides a dramatic and humorous example of this form of bias. A respondent, irritated with the invasion of privacy, might be motivated to scuttle the research by faking bad in our questionnaire, or what is more likely, he or she might simply refuse to provide the information. Again, some personality tests include a special set of items designed to assess the strength of the faking bad bias.

Another form of bias, *"nay-saying,"* is identified when the respondent tends to respond consistently to items in a negative direction regardless of their content. *"Yea-saying"* is the exact opposite form of response bias—agreeing with items regardless of the nature of the items.

Some individuals display a *response extremity* bias—that is, they commonly select the most extreme alternative. On Items 2, 6, and 8, of our questionnaire, consistent choices of "Never" or "Very frequently" might be suggestive of such a bias although we would require more items with this response format (and items which are less likely to be responded to with extreme choices) in order to be certain. Items employing dichotomous response alternatives ("Yes" or "No") avoid this problem. Conversely, the tendency to consistently check the middle or neutral category on items providing a range of choices similar to Items 2, 6, and 8 might be termed the *"cop-out"* bias.

Inconsistent responding constitutes a form of response bias as well. If respondents are not motivated to complete the questionnaire in a conscientious fashion, their careless, even capricious, responding may be revealed by contradictory responses. For example, if one of our research participants indicates that he or she has engaged in erotic practices with a son or daughter (Item 9) and also reports that he or she does not have any children (Item 1), we might legitimately be skeptical about the validity of this person's responses.

OTHER ISSUES.   In addition to these more-or-less standard forms of response bias (sometimes called *response sets*), surveyers must guard against the creation of idiosyncratic biases. The manner in which questions are worded can play a big role in shaping the respondent's replies. Suppose, for example, the third question on our questionnaire was worded as follows: "Have you ever been sexually assaulted by one of your biological parents?" This form of the question has a heavier emotional charge, and some subjects may be loath to label their experience in this way. Thus they may select the "Never" alternative when in fact the more accurate response might be "Rarely." Questions of the "When did you stop beating your wife?" variety are similarly avoided. Questionnaire designers attempt to employ terminology which is objective, clear, permits only one interpretation, and is as emotionally neutral (nonevaluative) as possible—an ideal continuously sought and rarely, if ever, achieved.

SAMPLE SELECTION

Every scientist, whether in the lab or in the field, struggles with decisions about sample selection. If researchers could have their "druthers," all their subject samples would be representative of the total population of *Homo sapiens*. Ah, what a dream of glory—to be able to generalize our findings to every single human being on (and off) the planet! But if wishes were horses, beggars would ride. The study based on such a sample has yet to be done, although computers may soon provide the technology to transform this daydream into nightmarish reality.

Meanwhile researchers must compromise by limiting or curtailing the parent population from which they draw their samples. For obvious reasons one of the most popular populations from which samples are selected and studied is the undergraduate university population.[1] However, survey researchers frequently pose questions which necessitate selection from larger, more diverse populations. How will the country vote in the next election? Polling the voting preferences of a sample of university students will not help us predict, with any degree of confidence, which party will capture the majority of seats in the Congress. Thus pollsters and other surveyers interested in predicting or identifying national trends adopt more sophisticated (and more expensive) sampling techniques. First, the total population (all members of the population over voting age) is categorized in terms of certain characteristics believed to be relevant to voting preference (for example, minority group affiliation, religion, age, geographic area, socioeconomic status). Subjects are then selected so that they reflect the proportion of these characteristics in the total population. For example, if 49 percent of the population are male and 51 percent female, then this sex ratio will be maintained in the sample. Similarly, if 10 percent of the total population as defined is unemployed, then 10 percent of the sample will consist of unemployed respondents. This procedure, known as *quota sampling,* is popular with pollsters.

Many other strategies for sample selection have been devised. None are perfect in that none of them can guarantee that the sample is an exact miniature replica of the population. Studies will differ, however, in the extent to which they approximate the population. Before we buy the most recent statistic on the percentage of the population in favor of capital punishment, or the number of dentists recommending toothpaste Y, or the degree of opposition to gun control legislation, we would be well advised to assess the quality of the product. Perhaps the statistic was based on responses to a telephone poll conducted on a one-hour TV talk show last Saturday. Such haphazard sampling is totally inadequate, and we reject the findings out of hand. Maybe the area-sampling approach was employed. Dwellings within each precinct in Des Moines were randomly sampled. We may accept the accuracy of the statistic for those Des Moines residents who were at home when the surveyer called. We may be willing to go further and generalize the findings to those who were not at home. Some of us might even include people

---

[1]For example, in articles published by major psychological journals, Schultz (1969) reports that psychologists rarely, if ever, use subjects taken from the general adult population.

living in comparably sized Midwest cities, but most of us are justifiably reluctant to apply the statistic to natives of New York City.

Next time someone tries to hustle you with a survey statistic, finger it, stretch it, prod it, and sniff it. How was the sample selected, and does this selection procedure offer reasonable assurance that the sample is representative of the target population? Ask two simple questions: (1) Who was left out, and (2) what percentage of the population does this omission represent?

ADMINISTRATION

The most carefully constructed questionnaire or interview schedule, combined with the most sophisticated sampling strategy, may still fail to produce accurate results if the administrative procedures are faulty. Obviously surveys based on interviews are more influenced by interviewer techniques, but the return rate of mailed-out questionnaires can also be affected by the content, and tone, of subject instructions.

Research examining the effects of interviewer characteristics on subject responses has established that the interviewer's sex, social class, age, and race may affect interviewee answers. Further, just as the hypotheses of the experimenter may shape the data he or she collects in the lab, so too may the expectations and attitudes of the interviewer channel the replies obtained from interviewees. Interviewers may unknowingly reinforce the expression of opinions that fit well with their own views—with a nod, a smile, a um hum, or in the extreme, with a spontaneous comment like, "You're absolutely right. I couldn't agree more!" Interview responses obtained by naive interviewers often tell us more about the surveyer than they do about the respondent.

Various techniques may be employed to reduce the impact of interviewer characteristics on the data. An infrequently utilized tactic is to match interviewers with their interviewees on certain demographic characteristics such as age, sex, social class, and race. An alternative strategy (equally rare) requires heterogeneity of interviewers on these variables—that is, equal numbers of male and female interviewers, black and white interviewers, and so on are sent out to the field. Then even though the harvest reaped by each interviewer is biased, we have avoided a systematic bias; we hope to average out our biases.

Careful training of interviewers may help to overcome the problem of the intrusion of the interviewer's personality, expectations, and attitudes into the interview protocol. Training is aimed at standardization. Ideally we would like to rule out the interviewer as a rogue suspect, and so we attempt to train each interviewer to follow a specific uniform procedure. Each interview should begin with the same introductory comments; the questions are asked in a designated order; the wording of each question must be followed exactly; probing techniques are specified and instructions provided as to when to probe. Additionally, interviewers may be taught how to establish and maintain a pleasant relationship with the interviewee—how to develop good rapport. The assumption is that if the respondents feel comfortable and relatively relaxed in the interview they will be more responsive, more open, more cooperative.

The next time you watch an interview on television, try to identify the interviewer's techniques. Try to assess whether this interviewer is likely to elicit accurate responses. Does the interviewer victimize the respondent by employing a brusque, aggressive, nonaccepting stance? Whose views do you learn more about—the interviewer's or the guest's?

STRENGTHS AND WEAKNESSES

The survey method has the advantage of getting the response of large samples of people, even of large random samples, but notice the responses are "lightweight" responses. Your research subjects are "telling you" what they would do—and you know that more often than not there is a world of difference between what people say they would do (or did) in a given situation and what they actually do (or did). In 1949 some 920 Denver residents were asked whether they had made contributions to a charity organization. Of those who replied in the affirmative, 34 percent had not actually done so (Parry & Crossley, cited in Oskamp, 1977).[2] Most of us recognize this inconsistency in ourselves—for example, the parent admonishes little Janey, "Do what I say, not what I do." Nevertheless, our critics, little or big, rarely miss an opportunity to point out this deficit—"I can't hear what you're saying 'cause I'm watching what you're doing." Notice that on a questionnaire we have only to move the pencil a few inches to shift our scores from being a bigot to being a humanitarian. We don't have to move our heavyweight behavior at all. Hanson (1980) has recently reviewed the research investigating the association between attitudes and behavior. Almost half of the studies he examined (20 out of 46) failed to demonstrate a positive relationship between attitudes and behavior.

Thus predicting behavior, even a small, brief behavioral burst, from questionnaires or interviews is tricky. Consider the 1980 presidential election. Almost to the eve of voting day, pollsters predicted a close race; yet Reagan won by a landslide. Although this was a heavyweight decision for the country, each individual voter's contribution was a brief bit of lightweight behavior—an *X* on a ballot. Polling research failed to predict accurately even this tiny behavioral unit until the eleventh hour.

Lack of correspondence between questionnaire responses and behavior may reflect a lack of *internal validity*—our survey procedures were inadequate, and so we did not obtain an accurate picture of the respondents' attitudes. Or the discrepancy between the verbal and behavioral domains may suggest an *external validity* problem in that, like the control group model discussed in Chapter 8, survey research data may not generalize to life outside the laboratory. Still another interpretation is that humans are well able to tolerate such incongruency. One of our colleagues accused of behaving inconsistently replied, quite unabashed, "What's so great about consistency? Who said I have to be consistent?" A fourth possibility is that, in fact, attitudes and behavior agree but are almost continually in a state of flux. At 10:00 A.M., on Saturday, November 1, Mr. Jones responds to

[2]Note that this study provides evidence of the operation of the social desirability response bias.

the interviewer firmly, sincerely, and without a moment's hestitation, "Oh, I intend to vote for President Carter." If the election had taken place before November 6, Mr. Jones would indeed have voted as he indicated; but perhaps his verbal, lightweight response changed after that, and his X on the ballot followed suit.

The use of simple physical evidence can markedly extend the validity of laboratory and questionnaire data. For example, following a campaign to encourage drivers to wear seat belts, a questionnaire study indicated a large increase in drivers' reporting that they had begun to wear belts. Two students supplemented this data by interviewing gas station attendants and by doing spot checks at stoplights and at service stations. Gas station attendants reported little or no shift in percentage of customers wearing belts before and after the campaign, and observational spot checks revealed a much lower percentage of drivers wearing belts than the questionnaire data estimated.

Questionnaire and interview techniques permit us to extend scientific horizons—to go back in time; to go forward into the future; to explore new terrain; to expand our data pool. In so doing they take us out of the lab and into a corner or two of the "real world." As is the case with all the other sieves of science, naive use of the survey approach will allow much that is valid to sift through the mesh and much that is nonsense to remain trapped—looking for all the world like fact, not fancy.

SUMMARY

Survey research offers promise as a strategy to enhance external validity by forcing us out of the hothouse laboratory—by leading us out to "where it's at." As usual though, there is a "kicker"—the elastic ruler comes back to haunt us. Verbal responses can be ephemeral—distorted by bias, blown away by memory loss, twisted by deceit, capriciously fluttering and gently turned upside down by environmental breezes. Much of the elasticity may be removed through careful and sophisticated instrument design, sample selection, and administration.

EXAMPLE

The following is an abbreviated version of an interview study conducted by three undergraduate students.

POLICE OFFICIALS AND PROSTITUTES

INTRODUCTION
The purpose of this study is to determine whether police officials accurately perceive the behavior and attitudes of prostitutes and to investigate the nature of the interactions between prostitutes and police.

METHOD

Subjects. Thirteen subjects were interviewed: eight prostitutes and five police officers. At the time of the interview, the prostitutes, who ranged in age from 18 to 50, were all incarcerated for offenses connected with prostitution. The police officers were all connected with morality work and included two constables, two sergeants, and an inspector. All police subjects were male, and their ages ranged from 30 to 55. Permission to interview a random sample of police officers in the city was sought but not obtained.

Materials. An interview form containing nine questions was designed to provide specific information concerning the behavior and opinions of prostitutes and the nature of their interactions with the police. Similar questions, but appropriately reworded, were administered to the police to determine their perceptions of prostitutes. A copy of the interview form follows.

Interview. We are students working on a project dealing with the relationship between prostitutes and the police. We would like to ask you some questions if you don't mind. If there are any questions you would prefer not to answer, that's fine. We would appreciate any information you would like to give but be assured that you will remain anonymous and your answers will be kept strictly confidential.

1. Do you tend to work a regular area?
   a) yes   b) no

2. How do you get your tricks?
   a) street contacts
   b) bars
   c) pimps
   d) bar or hotel employees
   e) regular customers
   f) police
   g) taxi drivers
   h) telephone

3. Do you get the same amount of money for each trick or does it vary?
   a) same   b) varies

4. Are you friends with other prostitutes?
   a) yes   b) no

5. What is your relationship with the police?
   a) occasionally have a drink with police?
   b) call certain officers by their first name?
   c) discuss personal matters with them?
   d) ask for advice from them?
   e) are sarcastic and/or unfriendly to them?
   f) avoid speaking to them?

6. Do you ever make deals or bargains with the police?
   a) inform the police about criminal acts (pushers, thieves) in return for easy or lenient treatment?
   b) cooperate with the police to get rid of your competition?
   c) turn a trick with a police officer to avoid getting busted?

7. Do you always keep your part of the deal or bargain?
   a) yes   b) no

8. Do you think the police treat you fairly?
   a) yes   b) no

9. Do you think the laws on prostitution should be changed?
   a) made clearer
   b) male prostitution should be illegal
   c) prostitution should be legalized
   d) rehabilitation should be offered instead of fines and jail sentences.

Procedure. The three researchers conducted the interviews together, with one researcher directing the questions and the other two recording the responses. The interviews were approximately one hour in duration. Two of the police interviews were conducted in the home of one of the researchers, and the others were held in the office of the interviewees. All the prostitutes were interviewed in a small room in the jail provided for visiting purposes. At the conclusion of the interview, all subjects were thanked for their time and cooperation.

In an effort to establish rapport before commencing the interview proper, the researchers described the course under which auspices we were conducting the research. We also explored with interviewees some personal history and shared cigarettes.

RESULTS
The percentage of prostitutes and police providing each response alternative is presented in Table 6–1. The greater the disparity between the two percentages, the greater the misperception on the part of the police.

TABLE 6–1   Accuracy of Police Perceptions of Prostitutes

QUESTION	% PROSTITUTES	% POLICE	QUESTION	% PROSTITUTES	% POLICE
1. a)	88	80	c)	0	0
b)	13	20	d)	0	0
2. a)[a]	25	20	e)	38	100
b)	75	80	f)	50	0
c)	13	20	6. a)	0	20
d)	13	40	b)	0	20
e)	0	0	c)	0	0
f)	0	0	7. a)	—	20
g)	13	20	b)	—	20
h)	0	20	8. a)	13	40
3. a)	88	80	b)	88	60
b)	13	20	9. a)[a]	0	20
4. a)	100	100	b)	13	20
b)	0	0	c)	100	20
5. a)[a]	25	0	d)	50	40
b)	13	0			

[a]Percentages total more than 100 because several response alternatives were provided by the interviewees on these questions.

DISCUSSION
To illustrate the experiences and lifestyle of the prostitutes, a typical case is described. At the time of the interview, this prostitute had so many convictions on her record that she could not remember the exact number. She had been "busted" (arrested) seven times within the last 11 months by the same detective. She had been released from jail the previous week but was apprehended again three days later. She reported that she had had the assurance of a job which was to start in three weeks. Given this information the police advised her to plead guilty in the hope of a remand for two weeks. However, she received a sentence of two months. Unable to qualify for legal aid and not able to afford a lawyer, she had little chance of escaping conviction. When she is released, she will have no job and no money and will be forced to return to prostitution in order to support herself. Thus she must risk yet another conviction. In a sense the predictable and repeated chain of events is analogous to being caught in a revolving door.

The results obtained from the interviews suggest that the perceptions of the police with respect to the behavior of prostitutes is reasonably accurate on many points. The most obvious discrepancies occurred in responses about the nature of interactions between the prostitutes and the police. Prostitutes report more friendly or intimate contacts than the police do.

The major weakness of this research is the small size of the samples. As indicated earlier it was not possible to obtain permission to randomly sample police officials. In the case of the prostitutes, permission had been obtained to solicit interviewees in one jail. At the time the interviews were conducted, a total of 14 prostitutes were inmates in the jail, but 4 refused to participate, one was released before she could be interviewed, and one woman who stated that she was a prostitute but had never been arrested for this offense was excluded.

INSTRUCTOR'S COMMENTS

You are to be congratulated for attempting to tackle a significant issue—one that requires the collection of data from groups that are underresearched due to the difficulties in obtaining sufficiently large samples. You made a valiant (albeit unsuccessful) effort to follow "good" research practices with respect to sample selection. Your interview form has several strengths—particularly evident is your attempt to use the vernacular of your interviewees and the effective use of probes. Your sensitivity to the need for good rapport is also noteworthy. How successful do you feel you were in establishing rapport? One concern, which you did not express, relates to the accuracy (truthfulness) of the responses obtained. Apparently you probed for some demographic information (such as number of convictions); perhaps you might have been able to check this information against official records to provide a crude indication of response "slippage." It would have been of interest to have recorded and reported the demographic data.

The use of three interviewers is puzzling. Perhaps you felt intimidated by your interviewees and wanted the moral support of a colleague. Having one person conduct the interview while the other records the responses is also a good strategy. However, an interviewee might well be more circumspect in the presence of *three* interviewers. Since two people were recording, you had an opportunity to assess the reliability of the recording process, yet you do not appear to have compared recorders' responses.

Given the small sample it is inappropriate to generalize beyond your specific samples. While the five police officers may have been reasonably accurate in their perceptions of the eight prostitutes, we cannot assume that this degree of congruence would hold with more representative samples.

chapter 7

Before-and-After Method

In preceding chapters, we described four rather large-holed sieves that science uses to help sort "fact" from "fancy." Each of these four descriptive methods, although relatively imperfect, nevertheless enhances our confidence that the quality of information provided is reasonably precise. Or at least surpasses in accuracy that derived from common sense or shared by Aunt Mabel, or the lottery ticket vendor, or the media advertisers, or the latest science-fiction novel.

The following chapters explore some of the more powerful experimental methods of science, highlighting how such techniques add further precision to our observations and explanations by allowing us to control or rule out certain suspects. But we pay a price for this increased confidence. In attempting to have accuracy, we run the risk of generating hothouse truths—conclusions that prove unreliable, invalid, beyond the protective shelter of laboratory conditions. Thus some of the limitations of laboratory research, principally the issue of external validity (Cook & Campbell, 1979), are elucidated. Research strategies that bridge the gap between laboratory and descriptive studies, preserving some of the rigor of the experiment while incorporating more of the "real world" conditions (longitudinal studies and the field experiment), are described in Chapters 9 and 10.

With the method of naturalistic observation discussed in Chapter 3, the researcher focuses with a wide-angle lens on raw data in their natural surroundings rather than in the library, examining room, or laboratory. The researcher aims at careful semantic description, whether studying the mating behavior of the stickle-back or the fighting behavior of street corner gangs. Researchers in this instance are not primarily concerned with "why" or "how come," although they may suggest theoretical explanations. In contrast, the after-the-fact sieve considered in Chapter 4 focuses on the past rather than the here and now—still using a wide-angle lens, however. The method deals essentially with flotsam and jetsam of prepackaged data scrounged from memories and written records. Also with the after-the-fact method, the researcher wonders "why," whether the why pertains to World War II, an unexpected death, an anxiety state, or a cessation of smoking.

The before-and-after method, to be discussed now, applies to the kinds of questions that start out with a statement such as "I wonder what will happen if. . . ."—that is, you start with O_1, the onset of Susan's rash, and then intro-duce X, a new skin lotion—Hornet Honey. After the prescribed three-month treat-ment, you make another observation (O_2) and report "complexion improved." But did the Hornet Honey help—or was it one or more of the many other X's in the stream of events taking place between O_1 and O_2 that did the trick? Was it one or more of a host of other independent variables?

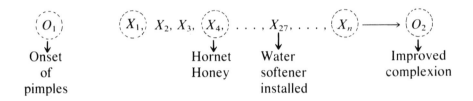

Can you think of some other suspects? In that given period many other suspected reasons could account for the rash's clearing up: She finished exams, started hol-idays, got a new boyfriend, washed her face with water treated in the family's new water softener, stopped eating so much junk between meals, finished some biochemical growing up, got more sunshine, or got used to the rash so that even a small improvement looked great. But Hornet Honey would be only too happy to take credit for the improvement, and probably in such a situation, most of us would be quite content to give the salve a testimonial, even though, as we have just indicated, it is only one of many suspects. Many medical treatments parade as cures, but are likewise one of many suspects. It requires a comprehensive series of experiments of the kind to be discussed shortly to obtain durable information about the adequacy of the supposed treatment.

This before-and-after method pretends to be scientific but would not be re-garded so by most scientists because too many suspects always remain, even after we have ruled out many others. Suspects always remain, so whether a method passes as scientific is a relative question. Four main types of suspects, or rogues, challenge us in our attempts to sort fact from fancy, in our attempts to locate or manufacture stable packages of information (Campbell & Stanley, 1966).

The following medical example helps us identify these four troublemakers.

After exposing them we will consider various tactics we can use to minimize the mischief they do.

FOUR MISLEADING SUSPECTS

A physician has been given the job of evaluating a new drug for treating depressed patients in a hospital. He examines the patients before the treatment (O_1) and after the treatment (O_2). The treatment (X_d) consists of a six-week period during which two of the new pills were taken three times a day. After the treatment period the doctor decides that most of the patients have improved.

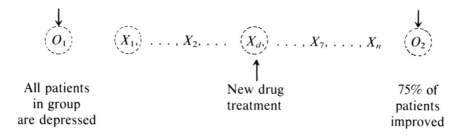

The physician is very pleased and writes an article for a medical journal. A scientist reads the article and writes to the physician, saying there are at least four other explanations why the patients improved, reasons the doctor apparently did not consider, four classes of events that could have accounted for the shift in the dependent variable, in the change from O_1 to O_2. The four suspect types are outlined in Table 7–1.

Historical Suspects (In-the-Gap)

"Were there any changes in ward routine or any ward staff introduced during the treatment period that may have contributed to patient welfare?" A new cook or a new ward supervisor may have been more influential than the drug in bringing about patient improvement. Remember that after careful study many wonder drugs turn out to be duds. Since the physician was looking at the drug and not at other possibilities, the drug gets credit, and other possible suspects go unnoticed.

In other words, the history of the period between O_1 and O_2 is filled with suspects in addition to the drug. Suspects of this class are called historical or *in-the-gap* suspects.

Maturational Suspects (Time-Tied)

The researcher asks another question. "Would 50 percent of the patients have improved in a six-week period even without treatment?" Given time alone some illnesses cure themselves—that is, there are variables such as natural recovery time, in the case we just mentioned, or maturity, in the case of complexion

TABLE 7–1   Common Suspect Types

TYPE		EXAMPLES
Historical (In-the-gap)	(X)	Exam Stock market crash Catching cold Mother dies Hangover
Maturational (Time-tied)	(X^t)	Hungry Tired Older Rested Menstrual period Male midlife crisis
Instrument-decay (Elastic-ruler)	(O_2)	Boredom, fatigue, or mood of researcher Instrument wear or breakdown Bias of researcher, practice
Testing (On-stage)	(O_2)	Recall Putting best foot forward Lying

changes during adolescence. In many instances of the simple before-and-after design, time alone deserves the credit for the improvement rather than the pet treatment of a given investigator. Thus any suspects specifically related to the time between O_1 and O_2 have been called maturational or *time-tied* suspects. Such suspects represent powerful in-the-gap rogues and so they deserve special mention and their own particular label.

Instrument-Decay Suspects (Elastic-Ruler)

The researcher mentions a third explanation apart from the drug—namely, the doctor's ability to measure depression may have changed. We cannot measure depression with a precise ruler; rather we measure it with a person's judgment, which, as we all know, fluctuates from time to time like an elastic ruler. For example, doctors want drugs to work, and this could affect their judgments so that they actually imagine improvement, whereas an unbiased observer would not. Those things that influence the measuring instrument or the person doing the measuring we call instrument-decay or *elastic-ruler* variables or suspects. In other words the elasticity of (O_2) warrants particular attention in the before-and-after design.

Testing Suspects (On-Stage)

Finally, the researcher suggests yet another factor (other than the drug) that could explain the patients' improvement. The very act of interviewing the patients at the beginning to see how sick they were may have influenced them, particularly if they knew what was happening. Some people respond for a while to almost any new treatment. On the second interview they might well want to appear better so as to be able to go home or to help the nice young doctor. Thus in some cases when people know they are being watched or measured, their behavior changes; "they are not themselves." This type of effect we call *on-stage* variables or suspects. Again, the elasticity of O_2 becomes important.

These four types of suspects plague every before-and-after study. Unless we separate out their effects from the effects of the treatment we want to study, we are seldom sure whether the treatment is effective or not. The control-group method, to be examined in the next chapter, goes a long way toward bringing these four rogue suspects under control.

SKILLFUL USE OF THE BEFORE-AND-AFTER SIEVE

The before-and-after model, such as the case of the onset of the rash of pimples, can be used to advantage when (1) the observation under study has remained stable, or not elastic, for a period of time; (2) a quick-acting remedy is being tested; and (3) the number of suspects pouring into the gap between O_1 and O_2 can be carefully controlled. Consider the first instance, the one in which the observation remains the same for an appreciable period of time.

Stable Observations

This can be portrayed as follows:

In this instance O_1 equals O_2 equals O_3. Then after the third observation, we try the new treatment, the Hornet Honey, and find a marked improvement in the rash of pimples—that is, O_3 does not equal O_4. Now we probably have more justification in getting excited about Hornet Honey because the rash has been exposed to a wide variety of other suspects between O_1 and O_3 with no obvious change. Similarly, the other main suspects (in-the-gap, time-tied, and on-stage effects) have had considerable opportunity to work prior to O_4 without any evidence that they are potent agents in this instance. The possibility still remains that there would have been a change in O_4 even if Hornet Honey had not been used—

that is, that the natural course of the rash of pimples had run out (a long time-tied suspect at work) and what we are seeing is a spontaneous recovery that happened to coincide with or follow the administration of the Hornet Honey.

Let us suppose, however, that following O_4 we stop the treatment with the Hornet Honey and that by O_5 the pimples return again. Now we reintroduce Hornet Honey, and at O_6 the pimples disappear. At this point confidence increases that the change is "somehow" connected to taking Hornet Honey. It may well be that the person's anxiety has been reduced, so that had she taken anything in which she had confidence, the same results would be obtained; or it may be directly related to some chemical in the honey. Nevertheless, we have confidence that some part of our treatment ritual is useful. You can probably figure out how to continue the study in order to increase confidence that the improvement depends specifically on Hornet Honey.

Quick-Acting Suspects

The before-and-after method also has considerable power when we feed a quick-acting and powerful suspect, or X, into the gap between O_1 and O_2. For example, it is much easier to detect a cure for depression that takes one day to work than one that takes three months because there are fewer alternative suspects to pour into the 24-hour gap than the 3-month gap (n is much smaller than n^1). There is also less time for time-tied and elastic-ruler factors to operate.

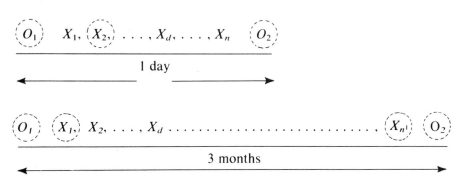

Penicillin is an example of a quick-acting independent variable, the effects of which are relatively easy to detect—that is, with the administration of such an antibiotic, the temperature quickly returns to normal, or the infection very soon shows obvious signs of improvement. Some of the unpleasant side effects, which appear more slowly, however, take longer to tie to the antibiotic. Again, the longer the time interval between X and its effect, the more difficult the research problem. Think, for example, how long it must have taken primitive people to understand the relationship between the birth of a child and the act of procreation.

Slow-acting X's, whether diseases or treatments, confound us. In using the before-and-after method in such instances, we must be prepared for relatively slow progress and a period of trial-and-error treatment with favorite, but often fictional, cures.

Keeping Stray Suspects Out

Obviously if we can greatly reduce the number of stray suspects pouring into the gap between O_1 and O_2, we simplify our task, although controlling the flow of stray suspects into the gap is difficult in economics, political science, sociology, medicine, and psychology. The method gains in power, however, in those investigations in which you can carefully shield the gap between O_1 and O_2 from almost all suspects except the one you wish to study. Furthermore, if you can control for elastic-ruler effects, on-stage effects, and time-tied effects, you have a very powerful investigative method.

Certain observations in physics and chemistry meet these conditions. Let's examine a hypothetical example. A physicist may wish to test the effects of heating a compound on its radioactivity.[1] The physicist places a Geiger counter near the compound, takes the reading, then heats the compound to the desired temperature, takes another reading, and notices that the radiation has decreased.

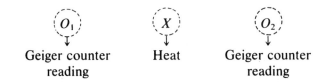

Now you ask the physicist how he or she knows it was the heat and not a reduction in stray sources of radiation from the sun, a wristwatch dial, or dust from bomb-testing fallout that resulted in the reduced readings, since the Geiger counter was exposed to all of these, as well as to the compound under test. Or you suggest that the change in reading is due to an elastic-ruler effect—the batteries in the Geiger counter wearing out between O_1 and O_2.

If the physicist was a careful researcher, this individual would say that he or she placed the compound and the counter in a shielded box so that only the rays from the compound being tested could operate on the counter. The physicist would indicate that he or she had tested the sensitivity of the counter before and after the study and found no change, thus indicating there had been no instrument-decay or elastic-ruler effect of any consequence. Also, there is little concern over time-tied suspects because the natural reduction in radiation of the compound under study is very slow, with appreciable changes taking years, not minutes. Finally, there is no evidence that on-stage effects are operating—that is, that the measuring process itself affects the compound in any way—it does not radiate less at the end of the study just to please the nice young physicist! A critic suggests that the effect was not due to a physical change, but to a chemical change; the heat led to the giving off of radioactive gas, which escaped from the chamber in which the counting was done. However, the student can test this by redesigning the chamber.

---

[1]Actually, heat has very little effect on the radioactivity of a compound, so it requires a carefully controlled experiment to measure such small effects.

While it is true that many studies in the physical sciences require extensive and precise equipment, relatively simple research methods (such as the before-and-after method) are adequate for two reasons, even though this method is more difficult to use in the behavioral sciences. First, as we noted, it is usually easier to control the relevant rogue suspects in physical science. Second, the rogue suspects are usually fewer and better known. Nevertheless, as the physical sciences deal increasingly with less stable materials, researchers must use more complex research methods and statistical procedures.

Alternatively, some behavioral scientists attempt to add precision to their work by restricting their studies to more-or-less stable materials, like white rats, under laboratory conditions where factors such as diet, weight, love life, and the cost of living can either be controlled or assumed to be irrelevant to the rat. In behavioral science situations where the rogue suspects cannot be directly controlled or assumed to be irrelevant, we often require more complex designs, such as the control group method to be discussed in the next chapter.

SUMMARY

The before-and-after method attempts to narrow the number of key suspects down to those occurring in a time gap between two observations. However, four prime suspects still remain, which we label *the four rogues*. Under certain stable or sheltered conditions, the before-and-after method can be a powerful research method, but under usual conditions, the control-group method, to be discussed in the next chapter, is required to "control" the rogues.

Prior to discussing this important method, however, we present a detailed example of applying the before-and-after method taken from a student research project. The example deals with one student's attempt to increase classroom participation. In reading this study you will be able to detect possible influences of the four rogues and become more aware of their confounding impact on your decision making, for you use this before-and-after method regularly in your own life.

EXAMPLE

PROJECT INSTRUCTIONS

Using as a guide Watson and Tharp's (1977) book *Self-directed behavior: Self-modification for personal adjustment,* conduct a study of your own behavior based on a before-and-after design.

pretreatment observa-   treatment   posttreatment
tions or baseline   observation

You will recall that the before-and-after design is weak unless you have a stable pretreatment baseline and also a reasonable posttreatment follow-up, making the improved design look like this:

| pretreatment baseline of two to three weeks' observation and recording | posttreatment observations and recording of four to six weeks |

STEP 1. SOURCES OF DISSATISFACTION OR DESIRED CHANGE
These include wasting a lot of time, skipping classes, smoking heavily, not getting as much out of university academically, recreationally, or socially as hoped; not feeling relaxed or acting naturally on most dates—seem to be acting a part; wanting to get more out of classes and personal relationships.

STEP 2. TARGET BEHAVIORS AND SITUATIONS IN WHICH THEY OCCUR
I have chosen the three following targets behaviors from the preceding list:

A. *Behavior:* Chain-smoking or smoking at an increased rate. Smoking even though I don't enjoy most of the cigarettes—it's automatic and I regret it next day.
    Situations: The situations in which this chain-smoking occurs include bull sessions, beer sessions, dates, tutorials.

B. *Behavior:* Not paying attention and not asking questions or stating opinions in class.
    Situations: I rarely, if ever, ask questions in any class—small or large. In some tutorials I think of questions and ideas but rarely speak. In large classes I sit at the back where it's easy to daydream or read. In tutorials it's hard to do that.

C. *Behavior:* Feeling tense and acting unnatural on dates. I seem to be acting a part, and it's a part I don't know very well, so I suspect neither of us is happy with the performance. I end up talking as if I know everything and also being very critical—not of the girl so much as of everything else. The behavior I would like to increase is talking about things that I know something about and am interested in, and the behavior I would like to decrease is acting like a phony big-time operator.
    Situations: The situations include those where I am on a date and alone with my date. When I'm with a small group, I feel much more relaxed and behave more naturally.

STEP 3. PRINCIPLES OF LEARNING AS THEY RELATE TO ONE OF THE TARGET BEHAVIORS
Not participating in class, for example, can be accounted for by several principles of learning.

A. *Lack of Reinforcement:* I can't remember being reinforced or rewarded for past attempts at participation in high school, so I probably never did build up skills or habits of this kind. At the university very few professors clearly reinforce students who ask questions, so it is unlikely that such responses will be developed at this stage in my education. Therefore the principle that withholding reinforcers will weaken behavior is relevant to my lack of early development of classroom skills.

B. Punishment: My impression is that not only was I not reinforced for participating in class (either asking questions or stating my ideas or opinions), but rather I was usually ignored, punished, or ridiculed. (Some of this may have been imagination on my part, but whether it was or not, it would probably serve as punishment.) Thus the second learning principle appears to be relevant—namely, behavior that is punished will occur less often.

C. *Avoidance Behavior:* A third principle of behavior that appears to be relevant to my lack of class participation is the principle that behavior that is punished not only occurs less often but that punishment leads to escape or avoidance behavior as well. This might account for the fact that not only do I not participate actively but that I also skip classes or "avoid" becoming attentive when I do go to class. Apparently avoidance behavior, once started, is difficult to correct, so that if this principle is operating in my case, I may encounter difficulty in changing my behavior toward more active classroom participation. In one sense I get rewarded by skipping classes and by not asking questions. My reward is that I feel less tense for a while. Then, of course, I feel very tense when exams arrive and I have no lecture notes. Obviously immediate rewards are stronger (reduced tension immediately) than are future punishments (feeling tense at exam time).

STEP 4. SELECTING TARGET BEHAVIOR AND THE SITUATION IN WHICH IT OCCURS.

I decided to select classroom behavior as the behavior to focus on for several reasons: It is important, it is easy to measure changes; I can test out my plan immediately; I can get enough data to meet the course deadline and complete all the steps.

It is difficult to reduce to concrete terms the many ideas, feelings, and behaviors I have developed around classroom situations. In brief, it appears to consist of a general withdrawal of attention, interest, and activity; when I anticipate overtures or pressure to participate, my heart beats rapidly, and my palms sweat. I realize that for the purpose of this project, I must describe a particular target behavior that I wish to increase and also specify the situation or situations in which it is supposed to occur. The target behavior I plan to increase is that of asking questions in class, and there are two situations I will focus on. The first is the small classroom situation or tutorial. If I am successful there, I will then attempt to ask questions in large classes.

Originally I decided to increase the time I paid attention in class as the target behavior. However, it is difficult to keep track of such behavior, since attention ebbs and flows almost imperceptibly, whereas the number of questions I ask is easily counted, and presumably if I am asking questions I am also paying attention, to some degree at least. In brief, my target behavior is asking questions, and the specific situation during which the target behavior is to occur is whenever I am in a classroom.

STEP 5. COLLECTING BASELINE DATA

Once the target behavior and the target situation are clearly defined and before working out a method to improve things, the next step is to determine my current level of performance— that is, to see how frequently I now ask questions so that I have a baseline against which to measure any improvement that might take place following the introduction of a behavioral modification strategy.

In order to keep my record(s) simple and also to make sure I didn't lose them, I simply put a check mark in the upper right-hand corner of my course notebook whenever I asked a question in that particular class. I kept a record for one typical week, so all classes were covered—except one I skipped, which was also typical. Interestingly I asked a question in my first class of the baseline week, which turned out to be the first and last question I did ask that week. So merely collecting baseline data served to get me to ask one question, but that's all. My heart thumped, my palms were sweaty, and my voice broke. All of which suggests that I don't ask questions for pretty obvious reasons—not asking questions lets me avoid all that thumping, dripping, and squeaking.

I think the one-week baseline gave a fair picture of how frequently my target behavior (asking questions in class) typically occurs. In fact, it overestimates my base rate by one— I don't remember having asked even one question in my first eight weeks at the university, the ninth week being my baseline week.

STEP 6. REINFORCERS

According to behavior theory the most effective way to increase the frequency of any behavior is to have it followed as soon as possible by a strong reinforcer or reward.

Surprisingly at first I found it difficult to list what were reinforcers for me. While I won't cover my whole list here, it includes reading mysteries and science fiction; going to rock concerts; horsing around on my guitar; listening to records; beer-bull sessions; necking, etc.; watching football and hockey on TV, or better still, going to the games; having a sauna; going swimming; eating Turtles (the chocolate kind).

Concerning the Premack principle—that is, things I do habitually to which I can tie in a new behavior—I shower every morning, eat three meals a day, and listen to records and read before going to sleep almost every night. I guess one idea might be to use the Premack principle in the following way: I would only listen to records and read if I had asked a question in class that day. However, this seems like punishment, which I gather isn't a good idea to use in attempting to change behavior. Also, since I already do read and listen to records, it couldn't serve as a reinforcer unless I did more of it when I had asked a question. However, as it is, I usually read and listen to records until I fall asleep, so I don't see how I could do more of it. I guess I'm still not too clear on how to use the Premack principle.

STEP 7. DRAWING UP A BEHAVIOR CONTRACT

I had more trouble than I expected drawing up a contract that was clear and that I thought would work. My final contract was as follows:

> On this 17th day of November, 1984 I, John Doe, make the following commitment to myself—namely, that I will attempt to ask at least one question in each small class I attend and that for each question I ask I will immediately reinforce myself with one Turtle and also with a token which is worth ½ hour at the regular afternoon beer-bull session. When I have achieved this goal, I will apply the same contract in large classes.
>
> Signed: _____
John Doe

I feel a little silly about the Turtle reward; it seems childish, but it meets conditions of an immediate reinforcer I can afford and one that represents an overall gain because I don't normally eat them all that often. But I am a little concerned that I may cheat—that is, if I have the candy with me I'll eat it whether or not I ask a question.

Also, I usually go to the regular afternoon beer-bull session, but my contract calls for withholding a strong reinforcer if I fail to carry out the target behavior of asking questions. Therefore granting myself only one half hour at the beer session per question asked turned out to be rough on the days I only asked one question. Once I get there I *stay*. So if I had only earned one token for a half hour, I tried to go to the session late. As tokens I used beer session "tickets" I manufactured immediately after I asked a question. I would scribble on a scrap of paper something different each time, for example: "Admit this great question asker to 30 minutes of Golden Happiness—Molson's Golden, of course." Creating my "tickets" captured some attention that might have better gone to listening to the lecturer. However, I gather that in the beginning of a behavior modification project, one should be grateful for even a very small improvement.

Incidentally, the guys at the beer-bull sessions found out about my project and would demand my "ticket" when I appeared. It would be passed around, and occasionally I would be told my 30 minutes were up and that I had to leave or produce another ticket. This supportive behavior of my friends helped a lot. If they had all got on my back, the way one of them started to do, I would have had to use another reinforcer.

STEP 8. ANTECEDENTS

Learning theory states that much of my behavior is under the control of immediately preceding events or signals called *antecedent stimuli.*

For example, if I happen to run into one of my drinking buddies (antecedent stimulus) between classes, we will likely go for a beer. One beer becomes the antecedent, or triggering, signal for another beer and for a bull session, which becomes the triggering signal for another beer and a wasted afternoon and also, usually, an unproductive evening. Therefore my drinking buddy and I are antecedent signals for each other that start a chain reaction of antecedent, or triggering, signals that control or strongly influence our joint behavior.

Incidentally, running into a drinking buddy is also an antecedent condition for skipping classes that afternoon and also the following morning, because I tend to sleep late due to a combination of fatigue and disgust.

The antecedent conditions that affect my not asking questions in class appear also to constitute a chain reaction, for if a question pops into my head there is a brief period of interest, which triggers nervousness, which triggers a suppression of any question-asking tendency, which, in turn, triggers withdrawal of attention.

It is difficult to list antecedent conditions that favor asking questions, since I don't ask any. However, asking questions should be increased through any reduction in nervousness, plus the "awareness" that I will get something I badly want if I do ask a question. That awareness is an antecedent signal, I guess, if it is conscious. In summary, if my plan to ask questions in class is going to work, I must somehow avoid, or reduce, the potency of certain antecedent triggering conditions, such as

1. Steer clear of drinking buddies in the early afternoon, or learn to replace a "yes" with a "no" response. Come to think of it, sometimes it's me who suggests we go for an early beer, so I am often not under any great pressure from others to go.
2. Reduce the nervousness surrounding the idea of asking a question by practicing relaxation.
3. Increase my awareness during class of the benefits of asking questions, both in terms of short-term reinforcements (candy and bull-session tokens or tickets) and long-term payoffs (learning something).

Relaxation: As noted, I get nervous at the thought of asking a question, which serves to suppress question asking. Learning theory suggests that you can replace one response with another through practice. I practiced replacing my "nervous" response with a "relaxed" response. First I practiced relaxing by

1. Getting comfortable and loosening any tight clothing, and cutting out as many distractions as possible.
2. Taking three very deep and very slow breaths, exhaling very slowly and completely on each breath.
3. Then starting with my feet, I tensed and relaxed each set of muscles in my body, coordinating the relaxation with exhaling. This way I learned to recognize when and where I was tense and worked up from the feet to the legs, to the thighs, to the stomach, chest, arms, shoulders, neck, face, scalp. My neck and shoulders are frequently very tense. I now notice this and can relax them at will.

I practiced for a couple of weeks just before getting up in the morning. Then when I was lying there relaxed, I would imagine asking simple questions in small classes. Also, I then practiced relaxing in class, particularly the neck and shoulders.

It's easy to forget, so I kept a record in my notebook of when I practiced relaxation in class. It's easy to forget to keep a record, so I wrote another contract in which I rewarded

myself by ordering a big pizza on Saturday or Sunday when my record-keeping system was
complete for that week.

STEP 9. BEHAVIOR CHANGE PLAN GOES INTO OPERATION
It is difficult to decide precisely when my behavior-modification plan was put into operation. I guess in one way it started the day I commenced to plan it. In another way it started
when the period of gathering baseline data was over and I started to record progress. In any
case, Table 7–2 summarizes my intervention plan.

Table 7–2 Intervention Plan

Goal:	To increase the frequency with which I ask questions in small and in large classes.
Plan:	1. Draw up a contract specifying target behavior and the situation, and also reinforcements (candy and beer session tokens) to be gained for each behavior unit performed.
	2. Select critical antecedent conditions to be modified in order to increase the likelihood of producing the target behavior. The antecedents to be modified include
	a. Beer-buddies: not accept or propose early afternoon beer sessions.
	b. Nervousness: reduce through relaxation training.
	3. Record results, including a baseline period.

I believe my behavior modification commenced the first day I started to work on this
assignment. Nevertheless, for the purposes of this section of my report, I will say it started
when I put my contract into operation, after the collection of baseline data. Table 7–2
presents an inadequate summary of my intervention plan.

The key elements of the plan from my point of view are avoiding certain antecedents,
reducing the potency of others through relaxation, and using strong reinforcers right after
performing the target behavior. Also, it helped to think of it as a kind of game—a game I
was committed to play but one that included a lot of human interest and humor.

STEP 10. RESULTS
I have summarized the results of my project in Figure 7–1.

It can be seen from an examination of this figure that during the baseline period I only
asked one question, so this behavior is very improbable under ordinary conditions.

For the next three weeks I focused on small classes. I recorded each class day and indicated how many questions I asked. I started off the first week of the intervention plan with
two questions on Monday, followed by two on Tuesday, then dropped down to zero toward
the end of the week. At the commencement of the second week, I was up to four questions
early in the week, dropping to zero at the end of the week. However, by the third week I
seemed to have more or less stabilized, asking questions in small classes at around three or
four questions per day. It is interesting to note how the behavior fell off at the end of weeks
1 and 2. This is not surprising, since Thursdays and Fridays are typically down days, almost
as if one were warming up for the weekend.

Commencing the fourth week I continued to ask questions in small classes but also attempted to start asking questions in large classes. From Figure 7–1 it can be seen that the
small-class behavior change appears to be stabilized, and there is some evidence that I am
learning to ask questions in large classes. However, I don't expect the frequency to reach the
same level in large classes as in small classes, since question asking in large classes should
not be done frivolously, since you are taking an awful lot of other people's time.

Generally speaking I am happy with my progress. I am certainly getting more out of my
small classes. The questions I ask in large classes are still pretty simple, and I am still not
completely relaxed about it.

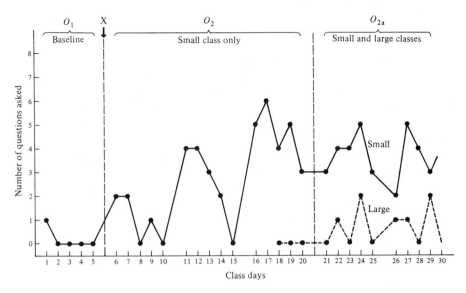

FIGURE 7-1

I plan to continue the same procedure for another two weeks, and if my small-class performance continues as it is, I will let it fly on its own and focus on large classes.

I am still not completely happy about my reinforcements. I have replaced candy with "girl watching," except in one tutorial where I don't seem to need any artificial reinforcements. Also, I use my tokens to buy new records rather than for the beer-bull sessions, which are a mixed blessing. The relaxation training is working relatively well, I feel, except for the odd morning when I sleep late and so don't have time. Sometimes it works too well, and I relax myself right back to sleep. My roommate has agreed to wake me, provided I'm not too cranky.

I am in the process of drawing up a plan and a contract to tackle another one of my dissatisfactions that I listed in Step 1 of this project to see if the system will work again.

In evaluating this before-and-after design, I appreciate the difficulties of deciding just what factors did contribute to my change of behavior. I am satisfied that it was not an elastic-ruler effect. I did ask more questions; even my professor noticed that. But trying to sort out what aspects of my intervention plan—what suspects or combination of suspects—were responsible is very difficult.

For example, I believe the on-stage or testing effects were probably more powerful influences than were the reinforcers. If this had not been a class project and also if my buddies had not become supportive, I don't believe the supposed primary treatment (the contract and the reinforcers) would have had much effect. Time-tied or maturation variables might also contribute—that is, becoming more familiar with my class and the university setting. I don't think so, however, since I have a long history of not asking questions, even in high school.

I can't think of any in-the-gap suspects other than that toward the end of the study my professor congratulated me. But since I had already started asking questions, that is not a prime suspect, although a reinforcing one.

In summary, I think in my view the prime suspects or influences in this study were "testing" (on-stage effects) and examining my own behavior—particularly collecting the baseline data. In other words I think collecting the *O* data motivated me to change more than the so-called reinforcers—Turtles and girl watching. But with this before-and-after design, who knows?

chapter 8

Control-Group Method

In the previous chapter we indicated that the control-group method represents a major breakthrough in helping deal with the four rogues: in-the-gap, time-tied, elastic-ruler, and on-stage. Therefore one of the first questions a consumer of science should ask is whether a control group or groups were used in helping select prime suspects. As we will see, control groups don't guarantee that we will come up with the correct suspect, but they do reduce the risk of error considerably.

Consider what happens if we use two groups of patients instead of one when evaluating a new drug treatment. We split the group of depressed patients in half. One group gets the new wonder pill, and the other group gets a *placebo,* a pill that looks exactly the same but contains only sugar. Some people feel better if they take a pill—any pill. We divide the patients so there is little chance of getting healthier patients in one group than in the other. Ideally, the groups should start out identical in as many respects as possible. To protect yourself from bias in assigning people to groups, pick the names out of a hat; the first name goes to Group 1, the second name to Group 2, the third to Group 1, and so on. Unless you use some such method, you end up with a special collection of patients in one group (for example, staff members attempting to get their patients or relatives into the group that gets the wonder pill).

Having established two comparable groups, we treat them exactly the same way with one exception: One group gets the wonder pill, while the other group gets the sugar pill or placebo.[1]

The procedure now becomes:

Group 1 (O_1) (X_1) (X_2),..., (X_d) ...., (X_n) (O_2)

New Drug

Group 2 (O_{1a}) (X_1) (X_2),..., (X_p) ...., (X_n) (O_{2a})

Sugar Pill

Thus the two groups start out supposedly with the same amount of depression—that is $O_1 = O_{1a}$— or in other words, one group does not have more seriously depressed patients than the other does. Following treatment we see whether O_2 is less than O_{2a}—whether the level of depression is now less for Group 1 than for Group 2.

ROGUE SUSPECTS

Historical Suspects (In-the-Gap)

The main point is to try to run the experiment so that the individuals in the two groups are treated exactly the same, except for one suspect—the drug X_d. Thus we attempt to make sure that the same X's pour into the gap between O_1 and O_2 as between O_{1a} and O_{2a}. To ensure that the nursing staff does not spend more time with the patients in one group than with the patients in the other, the patients in the two groups are mixed up or made indistinguishable as far as anyone who can influence the experiment is concerned. The nurses and other doctors are not told which patients are getting the new wonder drug, X_d and which are getting the sugar pill, X_p. All patients receive pills that look identical.

If both groups are to be open to influence by the same historical or time-tied suspects, then both groups must occupy the same space and time frame—for example, they must occupy the same hospital ward at the same time for the same duration.

Instrument-Decay Suspects (Elastic-Ruler)

If the experiment is run properly, the doctor who measures the depression at the beginning and at the end does not know which patients received X_d and which received X_p, so the physician's biases, or elastic ruler, cannot systemati-

---

[1]In some studies instead of giving a sugar pill, the researcher uses the treatment pill in common use. Thus the researcher can see whether more people improve in the new pill group than in the group receiving the usual treatment.

cally influence the doctor's assessment of one group over the other, either during the study or when deciding which patients have improved and which have not. This *double-blind* procedure, where neither the patients nor the treatment evaluator knows who got what pill, helps protect against elastic-ruler and on-stage effects. Only the researcher knows the code, which is not disclosed until O_2 and O_{2a} are completed.

Testing Suspects (On-Stage)

The on-stage effects of having been interviewed would influence patients in both groups. There will be patients in both groups who want to impress the doctor that they are well enough to go home, as well as some who merely want to "help the nice young doctor." Thus we hope that the resulting influence on O_2 and O_{2a} will be about the same—that is, that both groups will probably show about the same amount of on-stage improvement apart from any effect of the new drug.

Maturational Suspects (Time-Tied)

Furthermore, spontaneous recovery should be about the same for both groups, since the time between O_1 and O_2 is the same as between O_{1a} and O_{2a}. Thus time-tied or natural-recovery suspects should affect each group the same way.

NOW WHAT?

Notice that the control-group method does not eliminate the individual or combined influences of the four rogues; Rather, the control-group design provides the rogues with *equal* access to both groups. Thus O_2 reflects the influence of the four rogues combined with the drug, while O_{2a} reflects the influence of the rogues combined with the sugar pill.

We should not be surprised, therefore, if both groups show some improvement: O_2 shows an improvement over O_1, and O_{2a} shows an improvement over O_{1a}. These changes reflect the effects of such suspects as spontaneous recovery (time-tied), biased doctor (elastic-ruler), nice ward supervisor (in-the-gap), desire to go home (on-stage). If in addition X_d has had an effect greater than X_p, we should have O_2 showing a greater shift than O_{2a}. If the two groups were the same to begin with, the difference between O_2 and O_{2a} provides us with a measure of the effect of X_d over X_p. This is in contrast with the simple before-and-after model where we have X_d effects all mixed up with the effects of the other suspects without being able to untangle them. It was this kind of tangle that led some wit to wisely observe that a good doctor keeps the patient occupied while nature works the cure. It is easier to wait for a natural change when under the illusion that some potion is bringing it about.

When we divide a group in two to make the two sections as identical as possible and then give them the same treatment except for one X, we are using a *control-group* method—a much more precise sieve than the naturalistic observation, after-the-fact, and before-and-after sieves so far discussed. Representing a remarkable leap forward in helping us produce packages of durable information, in one stroke the control-group method permits researchers to assess the effects of their treatment over and above the effects of the four rogues alone.

ELABORATION OF CONTROL-GROUP SIEVE

Suppose that in the example just discussed all depressed patients had been given a stimulant pill each day as part of the regular hospital routine. At the time of the study, Group 1 individuals were given both the new wonder drug as well as their regular pep-me-up pill. Group 2 patients, however, were administered the stimulant drug only.

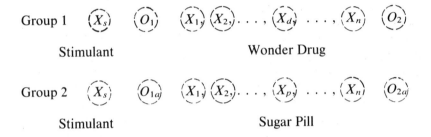

Group 1 (X_s) (O_1) (X_1) (X_2), . . . , (X_d) . . . , (X_n) (O_2)

　　　　　Stimulant　　　　　　　　　Wonder Drug

Group 2 (X_s) (O_{1a}) (X_1) (X_2), . . . , (X_p) . . . , (X_n) (O_{2a})

　　　　　Stimulant　　　　　　　　　Sugar Pill

Can we conclude that if O_2 is different from O_{2a} the difference is due to the wonder drug? One is tempted to answer yes and to argue that, since both groups were given the stimulant, any difference between the groups must be due to the difference between X_d and X_p. It is possible, however, that it was the *combination* or interaction of the stimulant and the wonder drug that led to improvement and that the wonder drug alone may be ineffective. In this instance repeating the study with two other groups of patients while omitting the stimulant pills would inform us what improvement results from the wonder drug alone. Similarly, the effect of making the first observation (O_1) may get mixed or combined with the treatment, and so we may want to know the effect of observing or measuring alone, the effects of treatment alone, and the interaction of the two.[2]

　　Consider another example. Assume we are interested in determining whether providing children with training in physical coordination will improve their intellectual ability, so we design a control-group study to test it. In order to ensure that our two groups are equal in intellectual ability to begin with, we administer an intelligence test to all the children and divide them into two groups with similar numbers of bright, average, and dull children in each group. Group 1 is then given two weeks of training and subsequently both groups are retested.

---

[2]The distinction between O and X can become somewhat vague or arbitrary. In essence an O may be considered as a suspect, or X, when the first O has effects on subsequent observations.

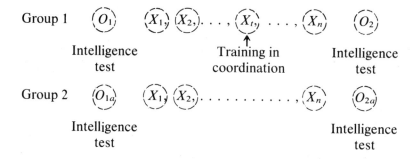

Group 1 O_1 X_1 X_2 . . . , X_t . . . , X_n O_2

Intelligence   Training in   Intelligence
test   coordination   test

Group 2 O_{1a} X_1 X_2 . . . . , X_n O_{2a}

Intelligence   Intelligence
test   test

If the difference between O_2 and O_1 is greater than the difference between O_{2a} and O_{1a}, we may conclude that training in physical skills improves intelligence test scores. But a sophisticated critic argues, "You may have controlled for the four rogues, but you still don't know whether the improvement is due to a combination or interaction of the pretest (O_1) and the training (X_t). Maybe the children in the first group were just more familiar with the experimental setting. The relaxation that comes with familiarity, plus the extra attention during training, may have produced the difference between O_2 and O_{2a}."

How can we answer this critic? One way is to randomly select two extra groups of children from the same classroom. Neither group is given the first intelligence test; but we assume, since they were picked at random from the same classroom, that they would have the same average I.Q. scores as the other groups. In addition, we give training to one of the groups but not the other. The model thus becomes:

Group 1 O_1 X_1 X_2 . . . , X_t . . . , X_n O_2

Test   Training   Test

Group 2 O_{1a} X_1 X_2 . . . . , X_n O_{2a}

Test   Test

Randomly
Group 3   Assigned X_1 X_2 . . . , X_t . . . , X_n O_{1b}

Training

Randomly
Group 4   Assigned X_1 X_2 . . . . , X_n O_{1c}

Assume that we obtain the following results:

$O_1 = 60$ $O_2 = 110$ $O_{1b} = 85$
$O_{1a} = 60$ $O_{2a} = 80$ $O_{1c} = 60$

If we compare O_2 and O_{2a}, we have a measure of the effectiveness of training combined with a pretest—30 units difference. A comparison of O_{1b} with O_{1a} gives an indication of the effect of the treatment alone—25 units difference. The difference between O_{1c} and O_{2a} gives a measure of the pretest effect—20 units difference.

We now conclude that training plus test practice accounted for the greatest improvement. Testing alone and training alone were not as effective as the two combined. Knowing the size of the test effect alone and the training effect alone would not lead to the correct prediction regarding the size of the two effects "interacting" together.

When there is a strong possibility of an interaction between X and O, it is advisable to test the effects of each separately.

By using the control-group design and by assigning subjects at random to groups, we try to reduce the risk of the four rogues or of chance factors influencing one group more than another. Nevertheless, even under such circumstances, the hand of chance may play a hidden part by dealing more quick-healing subjects into the experimental group and letting the new wonder drug receive unwarranted credit; by unpredictable shifts in the sensitivity or bias of the measuring instrument that happens to favor the treatment group; or by mistakes in transcribing or calculating the results.

The best defense against such chance factors leading to faulty conclusions is to consider the conclusions tentative until the study has been repeated and similar results obtained. Chance, being a fickle customer, shouldn't play the same tricks twice in a row. Another defense against chance factors making the independent variable look unwarrantedly good is a so-called crossover design. In this design each group serves as a treatment *and* as a control group—that is, each group is tested under the influence of the independent variable and also tested without its influence, with the order of testing being counterbalanced. For example, to test the effects of threat of shock on errors of addition, we would use the following design:

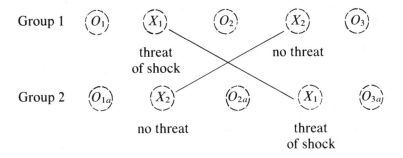

If the performance of *both* is impaired under threat of shock, you have increased confidence that your independent variable is having a predictable influence. It is a form of replication of the study.

The crossover design is particularly appropriate when studying processes

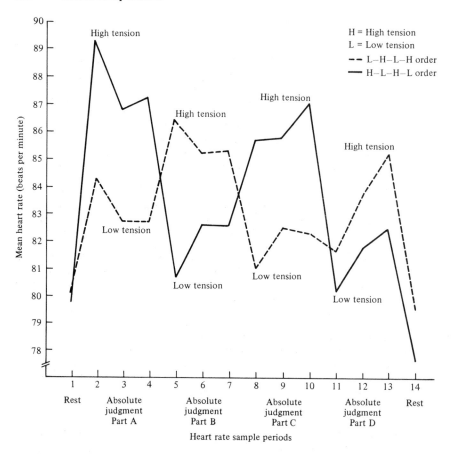

FIGURE 8–1.   Heart Rate (Beats per Minute) Under Strong and Mild Tension and Rest Conditions.

that can readily be reversed. For example, a multiple crossover design (Agnew, Pyke, & Pylyshyn, 1966) employed to investigate the effects of tension on absolute judgment of distance used heart rate as an index of tension. Figure 8–1 provides reassuring evidence that we were not dealing with mere chance fluctuations in heart rate, but rather that our independent variable (brief induced muscle tension) was having a systematic and replicable effect on heart rate.

SUMMARY

The control group adds great power to the research repertoire, permitting us to assess the ''impact'' of the independent or treatment variable over and above the impact of the four rogues. In skilled hands this classic research method untangles scientific and practical knots. Excellent examples of the creative application of research methods to important practical problems are presented by Campbell (1969) in his discussion of social reforms as experiments.

Prior to an overview of the research methods covered so far, we present two examples of applying the control-group method to smoking. The first is part of a student project; the second is taken from published literature.

EXAMPLES

CASE I (STUDENT PROJECT)

Premack (1970) lists increased heart rate from nicotine as one of the intrinsic rewards or consequences of smoking. Therefore one of the reasons why smoking is difficult to give up may be that each time inhalers have a cigarette they give themselves a small "high" from the nicotine and feel refreshed from the increased blood flow.

Not only can smoking pick you up if you feel tired, but it can also calm you down if you're tense. Strange as it may seem, this may also be caused by the nicotine. A stimulant like nicotine can calm you if you're tense by what is called a *paradoxical effect*. Overactive and overtense children are sometimes given stimulants that for some unknown reason calm them down (Black, 1977). Nicotine can work the same way on tense adults; even though it is a stimulant, it may have a calming effect.

Anyway the purpose of our research is to use the control-group method to see if smoking does raise heart rate.

PROCEDURE

Through naturalistic observation we selected 10 heavy smokers from the smoking section of a large introductory psychology class to participate in our study. Two said they were too busy, so we selected two more. We told them that we were studying memory, so they didn't know we were really studying smoking.

We divided them into two groups by drawing their names out of a hat. All subjects were tested individually. The general procedure was as follows:

After they arrived at our laboratory, which was a spare office in the psychology building, they were asked to sit down and were told this was a study to test the effects of relaxation on memory. They read a short passage, were tested for recall, relaxed and had a smoke, then read another passage and were tested for recall again. Group 2 subjects followed the same procedure, but they were *not* allowed to smoke.

To see how well they were relaxing, a pulse meter (San-Ei Pulsemeter, Medical Systems Corp., Great Neck, N.Y.) was used. The pulse meter dial reads out heart beats per minute. The pulse meter is about the size of a pocket calculator. A metal finger sleeve serves as a single slip-on electrode. We used the middle finger of the nonwriting hand, cleaning it first vigorously with alcohol.

After the subjects were hooked up to the pulse meter, they read from the procedure section of a mirror-drawing experiment for three minutes. Meanwhile, one of the experimenters recorded pulse rates every 30 seconds. Following the three-minute reading, subjects were asked to answer a number of standard questions about the passage they had just read. Then members of the experimental group were told to have a smoke and relax for 10 minutes. The members of the control group were told to relax for 10 minutes but were not allowed to smoke. During the 10-minute period, pulse rate was recorded every 60 seconds.

We were supposed to observe to see if the smokers were deep inhalers but forgot to do it for two of them; from memory we concluded that they were, so all members of the experimental group were inhalers.

At the end of 10 minutes, each subject read for three minutes from another standard passage and was questioned, during which time pulse rate was recorded every 30 seconds. The subjects were not told the real purpose of the experiment at this time for fear they would blow our cover; rather they were informed of the real purpose of our study when we reported our results back to their class.

RESULTS

We calculated the average pulse rate for each group at each recording point, but we did not do statistical tests because we had so few subjects.

From the graph in Figure 8–2, you can see that the groups started out approximately the same in the beginning and at the commencement of the 10-minute rest. While both groups showed a decline in pulse rate, the smokers did less so, suggesting some support for the hypothesis that smoking increases heart rate. Also the smokers' pulse rate continued to be somewhat higher during the second reading passage, indicating that the nicotine was still working.

DISCUSSION

Our results support the hypothesis that smoking produces increased heart rate.

However, we should not be too confident of these results for several reasons. We had only five students in each group, so our samples were pretty small.

Also we made a big mistake and tested all the experimental subjects before the control group. Therefore our design looked like this:

Group 1 $\left(O_1 \right)$ $\left(O_2 \; X_1 \right)$ $\left(O_3 \right)$

Reading   Resting   Reading
and
Smoking

Group 2 $\left(O_{1a} \right)$ $\left(O_{2a} \right)$ $\left(O_{3a} \right)$

Reading   Resting   Reading

FIGURE 8–2. Heart Rate Changes as a Function of Smoking

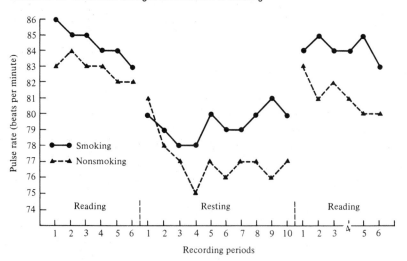

This means that in-the-gap and elastic-ruler suspects could be different for the two groups. For example, a possible in-the-gap suspect operating differently on the two groups could have been experimenter relaxation. By the time we tested the control group, we knew what we were doing and so were more relaxed ourselves and may have had a relaxing effect on them as well.

There is also an obvious elastic-ruler and instrument-decay suspect, for the pulse meter is battery-operated and it could have been losing some of its charge toward the end of the study and so giving lower pulse rate readings for the control group. The graph shows that while they were not a lot lower to start with, they were a bit. Whether this was due merely to chance or to the pulse meter's losing some of its juice, we don't know.

Anyway it was stupid not to test each experimental and control-group subject alternately, for by not doing this we really blew our experiment and failed to take advantage of the strength of the control-group method. Correcting this mistake and having bigger groups would have improved this study a lot. Also we could have used a standardized test for memory and seen whether smoking really did affect memory as well as heart rate.

REFERENCES

Black, W. (1977). Personal communication, November.

Premack, D. (1970). Mechanisms of self-control. In W. Hunt (Ed.). Learning mechanisms in smoking. Hawthorne, N. Y.: Aldine.

CASE II

It is not unusual in applied research to use a combination of independent variables in an attempt to bring about a change.

$$\boxed{O_1} \qquad \overbrace{\boxed{X_t}}^{(X_1 + X_2 + X_3 + X_4)} \qquad \boxed{O_2}$$

Then if this shotgun treatment works, you can, through further research, study the effect of each independent variable singly and in various combinations to determine which are effective.

The research summarized below (Pyke, Agnew, & Kopperud, 1966) studies the combined effect on smoking behavior of (1) behavior monitoring, (2) group discussions, (3) information, and (4) desensitization. Desensitization is a procedure where subjects (1) are taught to relax; (2) draw up a hierarchical list of situations in which smoking takes place, ranging from those where smoking is very frequent to those where it is infrequent; (3) while relaxed, practice imagining themselves not smoking in various situations, starting with the low probability smoking situations and gradually working through the hierarchy to the high probability smoking situations.[3]

Three groups of subjects were used. Group 1 subjects received all treatments: (1) continuous monitoring, (2) group discussion, (3) information, and (4) desensitization. Group 2 subjects received only continuous monitoring; Group 3 subjects were monitored only at the beginning and end of the study. The study design looked like this:

Group 1 O_1 $(X_1 + X_2 + X_3 + X_4)$ O_2 O_3 O_4
Group 2 O_1 X_1 O_2
Group 3 O_1 O_2

[3]Pyke, S., Agnew, N. McK., & Kopperud, J. (1966). Modification of an over-learned maladaptive response through a relearning program: A pilot study on smoking. *Behaviour Research and Therapy*, 1966, *4*, 197–203. (Used with permission of Pergamon Press, Inc.).

Group 1 subjects were monitored for an additional three weeks following the study and for one week four months later.

A summary of the results and discussion of this study follows.

RESULT AND DISCUSSION

Although information concerning amount of smoking is available for most Group 1 subjects over a 13-week period, Group 2 subjects only recorded their smoking for 8 weeks. Therefore the first 8 weeks of the project form the major data for analysis. However, the mean number of cigarettes smoked daily over the course of the project is presented in Table 8–1 to give an overall picture of the results.

TABLE 8–1   Mean Number of Cigarettes Smoked Daily

WEEK	GROUP 1		GROUP 2		GROUP 3	
No.	X	N	X	N	X	N
1	17.4[a]	22	15.5	17	13.78	16
2	10.1	22	13.2	17		
3	6.2	22	13.2	17		
4	4.6	22	12.2	17		
5	4.3	22	11.9	17		
6	5.7	22	11.6	17		
7	4.8[b]	22	11.4	17		
8	5.2[b]	22	11.4	17	10.55	16
9	4.9[b]	16				
10	5.2[c]	15				
Follow-up						
11	9.2	14				
12	10.0	13				
13	11.1	13				
29	13.2	15				

[a]Some subjects (4) did not submit charts for the first few days of the project. These subjects were given the value for the first seven days recorded and this was considered as their first week's total.

[b]One subject did not hand in charts for this week and approximately one week later estimated his consumption from memory.

[c]Two subjects estimated their consumption for this week.

In order to determine whether there was any difference between the enriched treatment group (Group 1) and the control groups over the course of the project, a two-way analysis of variance (Winer, 1962) was performed on the total number of cigarettes smoked during the first and eighth week of the study. The results of this study are summarized in Figure 8–3.

There was a significant decrease for all groups in cigarette consumption from the start of the project to the eighth week. All groups showed a reduction in smoking in the eighth week as compared with the first week; however, this reduction was significantly greater for the enriched treatment group. No significant differences in amount of smoking were obtained among groups on the first week of the project, indicating that the three groups were comparable initially. In the eighth week no significant differences were obtained between the two control groups, indicating that continuous monitoring of smoking is not significantly different from very short periods of monitoring, although the trend favors Group 2. However, Group 1 differs significantly from both control groups, suggesting that all factors or

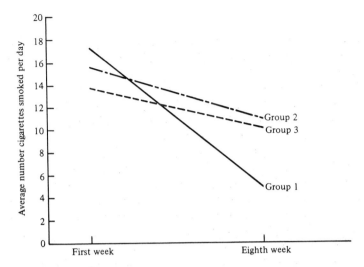

FIGURE 8–3. Average Number Cigarettes Smoked Per Day Per Group in First and Eighth Week of Project.

some combination of the treatment procedures are more effective than monitoring alone for decreasing or eliminating the smoking habit.

The results of the first three-week follow-up can be seen in Table 8–1. This three-week period was fortuitously a time of stress for most subjects, since university examinations were taking place. The results, therefore, provide a most stringent test for the effectiveness of treatment. The gradual increase in the number of cigarettes consumed daily from the first to the third week is perhaps not surprising, since by the final week most subjects were in the midst of their final examinations.

The results of this brief follow-up provide some additional support for the effectiveness of the procedures used in this study. It is obvious that the effects of the treatment were not strong enough to overcome the strains and stresses of examinations for all subjects. However, with the majority of subjects, participation in the project was of benefit in maintaining cigarette consumption at a relatively low level during this period.

A second follow-up was done approximately four months later. The mean number of cigarettes smoked daily at this point was 13.2, as compared with the pretreatment level of the same subjects of 15.9. A statistical test of the difference between these means was not significant. Only two subjects of the 15 who participated in this follow-up were not smoking cigarettes at the time of the follow-up. Five subjects increased their smoking rate over the pretreatment level. The increases were small, with the exception of one subject, who smoked over 100 more cigarettes. Omitting this markedly deviant subject, the pretreatment and follow-up means are 14.7 and 10.8, respectively. A difference of this magnitude approaches statistical significance. We use statistical test methods to help us decide when differences between our experimental and control groups are worth talking about. (We shall discuss statistical methods in Chapter 12.)

In summary, this research indicates that a stated desire to quit smoking is not sufficient motivation for quitting, nor is monitoring plus this desire adequate for most individuals. It further appears that group discussions, feedback, and negative information as utilized in this study do not have a long-lasting effect on cigarette consumption for all subjects, although these techniques were very effective in the initial stages of the project. The problem is therefore not how to reduce or eliminate smoking, but rather how to stabilize or maintain this reduced level of smoking. The results reported by Koenig and Masters (1965) in a study designed to test the effectiveness of three forms of treatment in reducing smoking show a similar pattern. All three of their treatments (desensitization, aversion therapy, and supportive counseling) were effective in reducing the smoking level of subjects during treatment, but six months later, cigarette consumption had increased in the majority of cases.

Both these studies demonstrate the wisdom of extended follow-up observations, in order to gain more reliable estimates of the strength and duration of the treatment effects—estimates less influenced by temporary on-stage and elastic-ruler influences, estimates less influenced by hope, by pretending, by short-term bursts of effort, and by bias.

OVERVIEW OF THE SIEVES OF SCIENCE

Four main types of research are presented schematically as follows:

I. Field Study and Survey Research

$$\left(O_1\right)\ O_2,\ \left(O_3\right)\ O_4,\ \left(O_5\right)\ O_6,\ \dots,\ \left(O_n\right)$$

Number of observations large but can suggest crude classifications and "cause-effect" relationships.

II. After-the-Fact Method and Archival Research

$$\left(X_1\right)\ X_2,\dots\dots\dots\dots\dots\dots,\left(X_n\right)\left(O_1\right)$$

Number of possible suspects large and often difficult to identify or locate—poor memory, data loss or decay.

III. Before-and-After Method

$$\left(O_1\right)\ \dots\ \left(1X_1\right)\ 1X_2,\ \dots,\ \left(X_t\right)\ \dots,\ 1X_n\ \left(O_2\right)$$

Reduces number of suspects but still can't untangle in-the-gap, time-tied, elastic-ruler, and on-stage suspects from treatment or X_t under study.

IV. Control-Group Method

Group 1 $\left(O_1\right)\ \dots\ \left(1X_1\right)\ 1X_2,\ \dots,\left(X_t\right)\dots,\ \left(1X_n\right)\dots\ \left(O_2\right)$

Group 2 $\left(O_{1a}\right)\ \dots\ \left(1X_1\right)\ \left(1X_2\right)\dots\dots\dots\dots\ \left(1X_n\right)\dots\ \left(O_{2a}\right)$

Reduced number of suspects. Major effects of the four rogue suspects should influence Group 1 and Group 2 about the same. So if groups start out the same and end up different, we assume the difference is due to X_t, or X_t in combination with the rogues.

Naturalistic observation is a starting point for science. Distinguished from casual observation, naturalistic observation contributes the following data-collection, storing, and sorting tools: (1) detailed and concentrated observation, (2) accurate recording and record keeping, (3) nonparticipant observation, and (4) identification of patterns or classes among the carefully recorded, detailed observations. All scientific methods rely on these four basic tools.

Even with these tools, however, the four rogue suspects (in-the-gap, time-tied, elastic-ruler, and on-stage) play a part in the data-packaging operation. The after-the-fact method and the before-and-after method can be seen as forms of naturalistic observation, or extensions of it, in which the confounding effects of the four rogue suspects clearly emerge. In those instances where the four rogue suspects can be directly controlled, such as some experiments in physics and chemistry, the before-and-after method has considerable power. The before-and-after model also has impressive power under conditions involving a quick-acting and strong suspect and/or under conditions in which O has remained stable for some time in spite of many varied attempts to modify it.

Otherwise the before-and-after method, being relatively less efficient, should be replaced by the control-group method, where the four rogue suspects, while present, should affect the treatment and nontreatment groups in approximately the same way. Thus if the treatment has an appreciable effect over and above the effects of the four rogues, you have a chance of demonstrating it. However, as we noted, there are instances in which the control-group method is not applicable and in which the case method or the before-and-after method are our only available methods of making decisions (other than relying on the rules of evidence of the armchair, the pub, busy committees, or imperfect memory combined with personal bias). If either the case method or the before-and-after method is to be used, then researchers who apply them and also those who base their decisions on the findings should be aware that they are getting a good mix of bias and perishable data included in the findings. With such awareness we can better decide how much confidence to place in the packages of information these methods produce.

In addition to the four rogues already discussed, three more plague researchers' attempts to untangle the influence of the experimental treatment from that of the rogues, acting singly, or in combination: statistical regression; differential mortality; biased selection.

Statistical Regression

Statistical regression *(drift toward the average)* reflects the fact that, even without treatment, people with extreme scores subsequently score closer to the group average. That is, high scorers, on retest, tend to score relatively lower, and low scorers, on retest, tend to score relatively higher.

Many students find this regression effect difficult to understand. Intuitively, however, you encounter this phenomenon when you do exceptionally well on an exam, when *everything* has worked in your favor—you studied all the right material; didn't have a cold; had a good night's sleep; wrote the exam mid-morning (your best time) etc. etc. In other words, the invisible hand of chance arranged everything in your favor. Thus, the high mark you obtained doesn't necessarily provide a reliable or fair estimate of your ability; rather, it provides an inflated estimate. Therefore, under less ideal conditions, your mark would have been relatively lower, would have been a more typical reflection of your ability, would have been closer to the class average.

Similarly, when you do exceptionally badly on a test, this usually reflects not only that you were poorly prepared academically but also that chance arranged everything against you—by chance you missed a crucial lecture; you had a cold; didn't sleep well; and the bus broke down making you late for the exam, which was held first thing in the morning (your "dumbest" period of the day).

Therefore, statistical regression refers to the fact that extreme scores typically reflect an unusual constellation of forces, unlikely to be repeated on retest. On retest the scores will reflect a more typical constellation of factors, and so produce a less extreme score.

Statistical regression reflects the trend of things to return to "normal" even without treatment. For example, when you're feeling low, or when you've "bottomed out," there's only one direction to go—up. But when you're low, or when things are bad, is also when you're most likely to take "treatment." Thus corrective measures frequently occur when a natural, or spontaneous, return to normal is most likely—and, of course, the treatment gets the credit. This can be seen as a special case of a time-tied suspect (maturation), but also, as a case of statistical regression, in which extreme measurements reflect a floor effect or a ceiling effect, and then move or regress toward the mean, or the average. Thus whenever dealing with extreme values, whether they concern *low* moods, or *high* temperatures, you need a control group to estimate the contribution of statistical regression effects alone.

Differential Mortality

Differential mortality *(biased dropout)* occurs when, during an experiment, you lose subjects from your experimental or control group. For example, the subjects you lose from your experimental group may be, unknown to you, the sickest subjects. Therefore your treatment group improves more than your control group, not because the treatment worked, but because it happened by chance that the most difficult patients dropped out. Differential or biased mortality is difficult to control. Some safeguards include: (1) attempting to use matched pairs of subjects in the experimental and control groups, so if one drops out the other is also excluded from the analysis; (2) carefully reporting the number, and characteristics, of dropouts when you publish your results; (3) viewing your results as tentative until the experiment has been repeated.

Biased Selection

Just as the experimental and control groups may end up different because of biased dropouts, so too they can start out different. No guaranteed method exists for matching the control and experimental groups on all relevant connections—some of which remain unknown. Nevertheless, four safeguards against biased selection include: matching subjects on obvious dimensions; assigning individuals at random to the two groups; using large groups; and having the experiment replicated by an independent investigator.

Finally, while we include *experimenter bias* as a form of elastic ruler, or instrument decay, others assign it a separate category. So if you prefer you can reserve the concept of instrument decay to describe changes in sensitivity of measurement equipment, which can be controlled by the use of the standard control-group design. Experimenter bias, on the other hand, is more difficult to control. You can use "blind" procedures so that the experimenter doesn't know which subjects are in the experimental and which in the control group. However, when blind controls are not possible, the main protection against experimenter bias is having the experiment repeated by an "independent" investigator.

Summarizing, then, we can say that (1) science has no perfect methods for collecting and packaging knowledge or information; (2) scientists use a variety of methods, which differ in precision and cost; (3) a sieve or a scientific method is useful to the extent that it assists a scientist to make decisions by reducing the number of suspects involved; and (4) it is not always possible to use a fine sieve on a problem—a coarse sieve often becomes acceptable if it reduces ignorance even a little bit.

Consumers of science need to be told or to determine for themselves which sieve or sieves of science were used in naming prime suspects, otherwise it is impossible to decide how much confidence to place in the pronouncements of "experts."

chapter 9

Variations of the Control-Group Model

LIMITATIONS OF THE CONTROL-GROUP SIEVE

Moving from the field study to the control-group method provides increasing confidence in our results—for example, even taking into account the influence of the rogues, we find that the new drug did indeed help reduce depression under our particular experimental conditions.

Under our particular experimental conditions? Aye, there's the rub. Although we have high confidence that the drug works with that particular group of patients, on that particular ward, with that particular ward's staff, diet, routines, support therapies, and so forth, we don't know to what extent the drug will work on a different group of depressed patients, chosen by a different doctor, housed on another ward, in another hospital, in another country. As you well know, one person's meat may be another person's poison, and you also know another cook using the same recipe can spoil the broth.

We face a dilemma. In order to be increasingly confident that it was our treatment that did the trick, we try to "control" the possible influence of other factors such as diet, age, sex, duration of illness, physical health, ward atmosphere, and other treatments. We usually control such factors by narrowing them—for example, by limiting the patients who can get into the study to females under 40 with no previous history of depression, with no major physical disability, all living on the same ward with the same nursing and medical staff. In doing so we limit the number of *external* factors that might affect the results. We test the drug under internal "hothouse" conditions.

If we get a difference between our experimental and control groups under such protected hothouse conditions, we can be relatively certain that it was due to our drug and not to chance influences like variations in diet between the two groups. But we buy such confidence at a price, for while busy eliminating external influences to establish the internal hothouse effectiveness, or validity, of our drug, we at the same time narrow the claims we can make about its validity *beyond* the hothouse conditions. Each control we use reduces the generalizations we can make about the drug's effectiveness—reduces our external validity.

Internal validity refers to the confidence you have that the differences you observed between your experimental and control groups arise from the influence of your independent or treatment variable. *External validity* refers to the confidence you have that your treatment effect will prevail, not only under internal hothouse conditions, but also under external field conditions. Such confidence is warranted to the degree that you use a leaky hothouse, to the extent that "reasonable" external influences are allowed into your experiment.

But what are "reasonable" external influences? You don't want your experiment "hailed" out. What become reasonable and what become unreasonable external influences depends on the purpose of your experiment. If you are looking for a treatment of depression that can be used in most state psychiatric institutions, as now constituted, then you should let the characteristics of such institutions into your study. If they provide treatment for male and female patients ranging widely in age, duration of illness, and diet, then such patients should constitute your experimental and control groups. Furthermore, if it is reasonable to expect that in such institutions patients will not always be given, or take, their pills, then such haphazard treatment regimes should be allowed to leak into your study as well.

Notice we are assuming that your purpose is to find a treatment that will "work" under typical psychiatric hospital conditions. If so, then such typical conditions should be allowed into your study—such conditions are "reasonable" influences.

If, however, your purpose is different, if your purpose is to see whether you have a treatment for young, female, first-admission depressions in a university hospital setting with sophisticated staff, controlled diets, and close supervision, then by all means test your treatment under such controlled conditions.

Therefore what are "reasonable" external influences to allow into your study depends on the kind of generalizations you want to make and upon the kind of claims you hope to state concerning the extent to which the results will hold in other situations.

Some researchers seek significant results at almost any cost, and the cost is usually one of reduced external validity; their results can be obtained only under sterile hothouse conditions. While this is hardly an appropriate strategy for applied research, it can be most appropriate for basic research, where research aims at understanding basic processes—for example, in vision, memory, or communication.

Such sophisticated hothouse strategies are also appropriate in applied settings where the cost of error is extremely high, such as in neurosurgery and radiation therapy. In such high-risk areas it is reasonable to assume that resources will be available so that the highly controlled conditions of the experimental setting can be transported to the external treatment settings.

In general, however, we must make tradeoffs between external and internal validity. Every control we introduce to increase the prospect of internal validity reduces the generalizations we can make—reduces external validity. Similarly, every factor we allow to leak into our experiment can mask or wipe out our treatment effect. In choosing what controls are reasonable, we must first decide what generalizations we are prepared to forego. Are we looking for a treatment effect potent enough to prevail under rough-and-tumble field conditions? Or for a tender treatment effect that will only blossom in a carefully controlled conservatory? Your research purpose as well as your particular research style will help decide your overall choice of research strategy, or mix of strategies.

Science is increasing her reach by extensions of her traditional research methods, by extensions of the control-group method, by employment of unobtrusive measures, and by the use of longitudinal studies.

EXTENDING THE CONTROL-GROUP METHOD

There are at least three experimental paradigms, based on the control-group model, which help overcome some of the limits of traditional laboratory research: the natural experiment, the field experiment, and simulation research. Each of these approaches to scientific investigation maintains the manipulative feature of laboratory work but allows for the intrusion of a great many external factors.

The Natural Experiment

The distinguishing feature of the natural experiment is that a manipulation of treatment occurs without the intervention of the researcher. The two principal requirements for a natural experiment are that the treatment must be abruptly introduced and the data, or observations, should be distributed over time. This method makes it possible for the investigator to take advantage of a naturally occurring situation, be it a disaster, such as a hurricane, or a new piece of legislation, such as the Equal Rights Amendment. Sometimes referred to as the *multiple time series design* (Campbell, 1969), it has the further advantage that it can be employed in instances where our question is not amenable to study using the methods we've discussed so far. What has been the effect of integration on the economic and educational status of blacks? For ethical reasons a standard control-group study is inappropriate since this model would require withholding integration for a random sample of blacks. A field study is obviously ruled out, and the other models are inadequate because of the fantastic number of confounding variables.

Campbell (1969) provides us with an elegant example of the use of the natural experiment design. In 1956 Senator Ribicoff of Connecticut instituted a crackdown on speeding as a result of a very high traffic fatality rate the previous year. Was his program effective? Forty fewer deaths occurred in 1956 than in 1955, but if 1956 was an exceptionally dry year, we would expect fewer accidents due to lack of rain or snow. Or perhaps the price of snow tires dropped dramatically, and hundreds of drivers availed themselves of the opportunity to purchase safety at a bargain. Or perhaps the state had invested in a mammoth highway improvement program. These in-the-gap variables confound our interpretation of the simple pre-versus-post model. Public knowledge of the high fatality rate might have produced the reduction in 1956 (on-stage effect), or the accuracy or techniques of recording accidents may have changed concurrently with the crackdown (instrument decay). Traffic fatalities fluctuate yearly, and perhaps the drop after the crackdown merely reflects this normal up-and-down fluctuation. Plotting the number of traffic fatalities for the five-year period preceding, and subsequent to, the crackdown helps to rule out some of the rogue suspects. A control group, consisting of the traffic fatality rates in neighboring states where there was no crackdown, further reduces the number of competing suspects and helps confirm that the crackdown did indeed have a beneficial effect.

The Field Experiment

Experiments are sometimes conducted in natural (nonlaboratory) settings and are superior to laboratory control-group experiments in that they reduce the confounding effects of on-stage suspects and enhance external validity. These advantages are of course counterbalanced by the minimal control that the investigator has over many components of the experimental situation (a reduction of internal validity). Nevertheless, the method has great utility for the study of certain phenomena which are not suitable for laboratory investigation.

One such experiment was reported by Milgram, Bickman and Berkowitz (1969). These researchers arranged for small groups of research confederates to stop in the middle of the sidewalk of a busy thoroughfare and gaze upward at a building across the street. The size of the group of confederates, ranging from one to 15 people, was the treatment (or independent variable)—the manipulation.[1] To what extent would passersby also stop and/or glance up, and would a larger group of confederates be more influential in terms of inducing others to stop and stare? Many more passersby looked up than stopped, and even one research confederate gazing upward was enough to produce imitative behavior in 40 percent of the passersby. A similar percent of passersby were induced to stop when the group of confederates numbered 15.

---

[1] This experiment is analogous to the different treatment approach of the doctor who compares the new wonder drug, not with a placebo (or nontreated control) group, but rather with the "old" treatment.

Simulation Research

Zimbardo and his colleagues have produced perhaps the most dramatic example of simulation research (Haney, Banks & Zimbardo, 1973). In a very realistic mock-up of a prison, university students role-played either prisoners or guards. In a matter of days the guards developed and utilized oppressive and domineering tactics on the prisoners, while the latter degenerated into passive, dependent, pathetic creatures. The experiment was terminated prematurely because of the pathological reactions of both groups.

Again this type of experimental paradigm may be employed to investigate under systematic, controlled conditions events which are otherwise outside the realm of scientific study (for example, international negotiations). Subject awareness, however, has unknown effects on the results obtained, and thus conclusions derived from research of this type are only suggestive.

UNOBTRUSIVE MEASURES

Extensions of the control-group model enhance external validity and so does the use of unobtrusive measures.[2] Such measures may be employed in many types of research paradigms—most common in field studies, they may also be utilized in laboratory experiments.

When we eavesdrop on the conversation of the diners at the next table, watch the stewardess handle the drunken, amorous passenger, or admire the Adonis on the subway, we may well be making unobtrusive observations. A minimum of deception, or feigned indifference, or our studied air of passionate absorption in a newspaper provides us with abundant opportunities to study how people behave when they don't know they are being watched.

For example, one student, curious about what police officers talked about while cruising, adopted an unobtrusive measure by hiding in the back seat of a cruiser. In so doing he obtained a radically different picture of the content and style of police officer conversations than he had obtained through questionnaires, interviews, and archival research. However, when the officers stopped for coffee and our researcher tried to leave the cruiser as unobtrusively as he had entered, he learned to his dismay that in the back seat of police cruisers there were no handles on the inside doors. He was therefore apprehended, and only after careful examination of his person and his credentials and after repeated assurances that it was only a college prank was our trembling novice researcher sent on his humble way. While laboratory studies protect you from many facets of the question under study, unobtrusive probes, if discovered, can teach you more than you bargained for.

The Watergate goof remains a classic example of a politically motivated unobtrusive probe that not only failed, but shook a nation in the process. The ethical implications of applying unobtrusive measures are serious and complex,

---

[2]The classical reference on this topic is Webb, Campbell, Schwartz, and Sechrest (1966).

and any student would be well advised to consult several faculty advisors before launching into this important—but risky—extension of research methodology.

You are already somewhat familiar with some unobtrusive techniques as they have been applied in field studies and field experiments. Some are reminiscent of nineteenth-century naturalistic observation. Instead of studying the migratory behavior of caribou herds from cover, unobtrusively we study the migratory behavior of crowds leaving a rock festival. But when we extend the method from studying the mating behavior of the confused fruit fly to bugging our parents' bedroom, we cross a dangerous line—ethically dangerous, physically dangerous. A discussion of some of the ethical implications of social science research appears in Chapter 14.

While we stress the risks involved, we don't completely discourage the use of selected unobtrusive measures. If behavioral research is to be more than hothouse and lightweight, we must find ways of extending the validity of our conclusions beyond the laboratory and the questionnaire. Stretching before us are vast regions of rich speculative space that can be strategically sprinkled with observational checkpoints gleaned from unobtrusive measures that require no gross intrusions into the bedrooms or the backrooms of the nation. What we propose is creative triangulation rather than dirty tricks.

A colleague, curious about how much of the space around people they consider to be theirs, first carried out laboratory studies where he would approach closer and closer until the person signaled that he had "entered" their space. Then he moved his research out of the laboratory—to meetings, cocktail parties, elevators—moving closer and closer to people until they backed off or commented. Here he was seeing to what extent his measures of personal space obtained in the laboratory setting held up in a variety of external everyday settings and to what extent differences existed between these settings. At some risk to himself he even extended his studies to men's washrooms. In such a milieu one might predict a bimodal distribution, with some individuals protecting a large region of personal space and with others welcoming intrusions. Apart from his washroom studies, our colleague ran no risks, and in no case did he raise thorny ethical issues; yet he did extend the validity of his findings well beyond the laboratory.

Other researchers (Byrne, Ervin & Lamberth, 1970) interested in the extent to which similarity in values influences attraction arranged coffee dates for their research participants. In some instances the paired daters held many values and attitudes in common (as determined by a previously administered questionnaire). Other pairs were quite dissimilar in their values and attitudes. After the date each participant completed a questionnaire designed to assess the degree of attraction (liking) the person felt for his or her partner. Then one of the researchers asked the two people to come to his office and chatted with them briefly and informally. Unobtrusively he measured the distance between the subjects as they stood facing him across the desk. This information provided an unobtrusive measure of attraction.

Such ingeniously simple uses of multimethod research are rare. Perhaps we give too much publicity to those particular unobtrusive methods relying on elaborate hardware or dramatically staged accidents. In any case we should not lose sight of the prime purpose of unobtrusive research, which is to carefully observe human behavior under conditions in which the subjects are unaware that they are being studied, be they in the field or in the laboratory. The purpose of such measures is to supplement, but not replace, other forms of research in which the on-stage effect influences reactive measures and in which the setting of the study unduly shapes behavior.

SUMMARY

Just as the behavior of bodies in a vacuum is different from their behavior under "normal" conditions of pressure and gravity, so phenomena studied in the rarified atmosphere of the laboratory are not necessarily isomorphic with the appearance of the same phenomena occurring in the hustle and bustle of "real" environments. The concept of external validity refers to the extent to which events (data) garnered under "pure" laboratory conditions can be exported, or carried over, to the impure world in which we live. Research strategies such as natural and field experiments, simulations, and unobtrusive measures, in addition to providing opportunities to investigate issues not amenable to laboratory study, also inject a few (or many) impurities into the science stew and so improve external validity.

EXAMPLE

The following is an example of a field experiment entitled "Is chivalry dead?" conducted by a psychology student.

IS CHIVALRY DEAD?

To what extent will bystanders intervene in a violent argument when the protagonists are a man and a woman? Latané and Darley (1968) describe the phenomenon of bystander apathy in emergency or crisis situations. Essentially they report that bystanders are less likely to offer assistance if a *group* of people witness the event than if a *solitary* person witnesses it. An acrimonious argument involving shouting, swearing, and shoving is *not clearly* an emergency—no one is actually hurt. I am attempting to determine whether the group effect found in emergency situations will similarly occur in this type of situation. Since Latané and Rodin (1969) found that help is more likely to be forthcoming from a group of friends than from strangers, this variable will also be examined. I was also interested in finding out whether people would be more likely to intervene if a woman was being hassled by a man than vice versa.

METHOD

Subjects. The subjects for this study were young white male shoppers at a small indoor plaza in a metropolitan area.

Procedure. Two friends of the experimenter, a male and a female of approximately equal height and weight, both in their early twenties, staged an argument in the plaza. The argument progressed by stages from loud shouting (15 secs.) to shouting and swearing (10 secs.) to shoving (5 secs.). The argument was structured so that one confederate was the aggressor while the other played a passive or conciliatory role. They alternated roles from trial to trial. The fight was staged (1) when a solitary male shopper was advancing toward the fight location and (2) when two male shoppers, obviously friends, were advancing. One of the low traffic exit hallways was eventually selected, after trial-and-error disasters in heavy traffic parts of the mall.

RESULTS AND DISCUSSION

The results in terms of the number of people who intervened are presented in Table 9–1.

TABLE 9–1.   Frequency of Intervention

	ALONE		WITH FRIEND	
	Intervened	*Didn't Intervene*	*Intervened*	*Didn't Intervene*
Man aggressing	1	2	0	6
Woman aggressing	0	3	1	5
Total	1	5	1	11

These results suggest that chivalry is dead. The only solitary shopper to intervene in the argument was almost forced to do so because the female confederate, when shoved, stumbled into him. The fellow (with friend) who intervened when the woman was aggressing seemed to regard the scene as funny. He commented, "Hey, man, who wears the pants in your family?"

REFERENCES

Latané, B., & Darley, J. M. (1968). Group inhibition of bystander intervention in emergencies. *Journal of Personality and Social Psychology, 10,* 215–221.

Latané, B., & Rodin, J. (1969). A lady in distress: Inhibiting effects of friends and strangers on bystander intervention. *Journal of Experimental Social Psychology, 5,* 189–202.

INSTRUCTOR'S COMMENTS

Your question is an interesting one, and you generated a creative technique to try to answer the question. You have also linked your research to a broader issue—bystander helping. The most serious criticism of your paper involves errors of omission rather than commission. You have neglected to describe your procedures in sufficient detail to permit replication. For example, what was the dialogue between the sparring partners; how much preliminary training did they have; were you the only observer; how did you determine whether or not an intervention had occurred? Since you were aware of the subject's condition (alone or with a friend) and the previous research, perhaps your observations are biased. What might you have done to control this? How do you know if the subjects were fooled by the fake argument; did you talk to them afterwards in an attempt to determine whether they had decoded the situation as a staged event? Apparently there were 12 trials (fights), 6 with a male aggressor and 6 with a female aggressor. Did your confederates change their performance in any significant way from trial to trial? Perhaps they became more convincing with practice; perhaps less convincing as they became bored. Were these changes, if they occurred, equally distributed across the two subject groups (solitary versus with friend)?

Problems such as those mentioned and the small and restricted sample prevent us from drawing any firm conclusion with respect to chivalry. Another issue concerns the ethicality of research of this type. Did you debrief your subjects—explain to them that the events were staged? Do you see this research as an invasion of privacy?

chapter 10

Developmental and Longitudinal Studies

The only thing you can be sure about is that things will change: babies grow up, then grow old; organizations move in fits and starts, many of them false starts.

In this chapter we review some ways of mapping change in individuals and organizations. If we plan to map change, whether individual or organizational, we must have some idea ahead of time about what routes that change might take. We can't cover all possible routes; we can afford to stake out only a few. What then are some of the popular routes that change can follow?

FIGURE 10–1. Up-and-Down Curve.

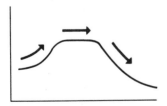

Notice that these simple up-and-down maps of change can differ in several respects: They can differ in the rate of growth and decline, in the level they reach,

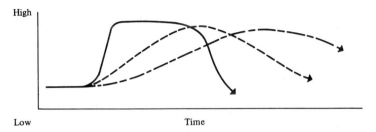

FIGURE 10–2. Rates of Change.

and in the duration of such plateaus. Therefore for comparative purposes we need to elaborate the basic up-and-down curve so that we can focus on *rates* and *levels* of change.

RATE OF CHANGE

Individuals or organizations frequently differ in how slowly or rapidly they change, how rapidly they reach a certain state or level of performance (see Figure 10–2).

　　All children learn a variety of skills but at different rates of acquisition: toilet training, walking, talking. Similarly, adults lose their capacities but at different rates of decline—some losing their memory, eyesight, or coordination much faster than others do. Organizations also differ in the rate that they reach certain organizational states: the rate at which they reach a certain size, degree of specialization, rate of return on investment, or market penetration.

　　Important developmental and longitudinal research questions focus on such rates of growth and decline and on possible factors that may hasten or retard them—genetic, nutritional, maturational, technological, political, or market factors.

UPPER LIMITS OF CHANGE

Not only do individuals and organizations differ in their rates of change on selected measures but they differ also in the levels they reach (see Figure 10–3).

　　For example, children differ not only in the rate of growth, but they differ also in the height they reach. Why is that? What combination of genetic, nutritional, and maturational factors help establish such *ceiling* effects? We observe such apparent ceilings, or limits, in individual measures of intelligence and in organizational measures such as span of control—the number of people or operations that an executive can manage.

　　Thus we see change take many routes: The common up-and-down route can vary in terms of its rate of growth or decline, the ceiling or limits it reaches, and the duration of such limits or plateaus.

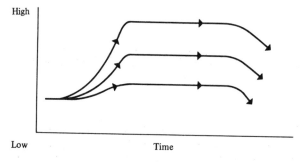

FIGURE 10–3. Levels of Change.

In some cases one relatively simple up-and-down curve can describe the growth and decline of certain individual or organizational characteristics. Usually, however, we string a series of such curves together to describe the repeated and uneven up-and-down route that change follows (see Figure 10–4).

Such a *time series* may describe the health of an individual or the productivity of an organization. The overall growth and decline of such a curve may in the case of the individual reflect the growth and aging process and in the case of an organization reflect an increasing then decreasing share of the market.

The smaller up-and-down blips may in the case of the individual represent genetic releasers (puberty), stress (failure at school), or chance (financial inheritance). In the case of organizations, such blips may reflect the influence of temporary shifts in the market, temporary increases in productivity attributable to the new incentive system, new competition, or government write-offs.

Thus the up-and-down map of change, while descriptive of many familiar processes, may follow a given course for a combination of reasons—which makes researching it complicated, but challenging.

Now that we have seen how change may take various routes at variable rates to different levels, we need to examine how we can stake out and at least partially map the zigzag courses of change. We rely mainly on three research strategies to provide observational checkpoints: (1) cross-sectional studies, (2) retrospective (after-the-fact) studies; and (3) longitudinal studies.

FIGURE 10–4. Time Series.

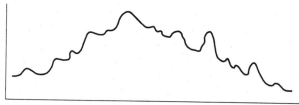

Time

CROSS-SECTIONAL STUDIES

This method provides most of the observational checkpoints in developmental psy-chology—with this method we map, from birth to death, the growth rates, ceiling effects, and declines in physical and psychological characteristics.

Called *cross-sectional* because it takes age slices, this method enables a researcher to measure a given characteristic—say, height—in samples of people of different ages at the same time (for example, July 1981), compute an average for each age, and then draw a curve or map of how average height changes with age (see Figure 10–5).

The cross-sectional method allows you to map such curves without taking 70 or 80 years to follow *one* large sample from birth to death. It is a relatively quick method to get average trends—that is the advantage of it. For curves that are strongly determined by age alone, the method is adequate.

Where age is only one of several strong factors influencing the rate of change, the cross-sectional method can be misleading. If some samples used to represent the height of a certain age group have benefited or been hampered by other strong factors, then that sample is not typical and so should not be compared with other points on the curve.

For example, it is assumed that height, which reaches its ceiling or limit in early adulthood, starts to decline when people reach their fifties or sixties, but there is some evidence that this "decline" may be an artifact of cross-sectional data because our current 20-year-olds are taller than their fathers and grandfathers. Thus it may not be that fathers are shrinking; rather their sons, who are large, produce sons who are even larger, thus providing an inappropriately taller baseline against which the fathers are compared (Damon, 1965).

Briefly, the cross-sectional method provides an average curve for age-related characteristics, but given points on the curve may be pushed up or down by other strong factors not related to age, but rather to nutrition or social factors. Such

FIGURE 10–5. Cross-Sectional Research.

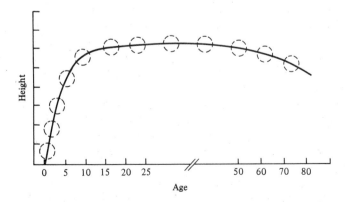

atypical points on the curve, supposedly comparable to all other points, are not and so invisibly distort the age curve.

Therefore when using the cross-sectional method, you must be cautious and must continuously ask yourself the question, "In what other important ways, beside age, do my samples differ?"

It is a safe bet the samples do differ in various ways, and so rather than using a fine line curve, you would do well to at least visualize a curve surrounded by a region of uncertainty (see Figure 10–6).

Visualizing it in this way you acknowledge that cross-sectional curves represent crude estimates that may deviate significantly from a curve that is based on following and measuring the *same* individual through time (longitudinal method). Maps of change based on cross-sectional studies should be updated frequently and compared with earlier cross-sectional curves for evidence of atypical bulges or dips so that particular points of uncertainty are highlighted and used with caution.

The obvious way to increase the comparability of points on the curve is to avoid cross-sectional studies, to go to longitudinal investigations where you study the same people over time rather than a cross-section of people at the same time. Alternatively, we can obtain cheap and crude estimates using retrospective studies.

RETROSPECTIVE STUDIES

Rather than trying to determine whether 60- or 70-year-olds are shrinking by comparing them with 20-year-olds (cross-sectional studies), we can compare their current height with a *recalled* height at age 20 or in early adulthood. This solves one problem—you are now comparing a person against him/herself rather than against a 20-year-old stand-in. However, you run smack into another problem—namely, the unreliability of recalled data—the problem of the fallibility of human memory.

When recalled data are compared with data recorded at the time of the event, we find ample evidence of distortions in memory, not just random distortions, but also on-stage, rose-colored distortions.

For example, mothers are unreliable sources of recalled information con-

FIGURE 10–6. Uncertainty Band.

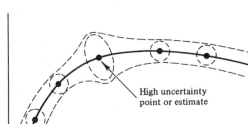

High uncertainty
point or estimate

cerning the length of labor, their health during pregnancy or their baby's weight and health; mothers may also provide "favorable" distortions concerning the age at which their child's toilet training and weaning occurred.

In brief, beware of recalled data as a means of charting age curves for any characteristics, unless you are using it only in a supplementary manner: (1) to help check cross-sectional data, (2) with some archival data to back it up,[1] or (3) to fill in gaps in a longitudinal study.

In any case, enclose such recalled estimates within a large uncertainty circle.

LONGITUDINAL STUDIES

In order to avoid the unreliability of recall that affects many retrospective studies and to avoid the confounding fact that the different samples used in cross-sectional studies differ in more ways than age, we should, whenever possible, use a proper longitudinal study to map the curves of change.

The longitudinal study differs from the cross-sectional study by observing the *same* subjects repeatedly over the time period under investigation; it differs from the retrospective study in that it relies on current observations rather than on recalled or archival data. Furthermore, longitudinal studies provide a way of mapping, not only general group trends in the growth and decline of various physical and psychological characteristics (that is, boys versus girls, identical twins versus fraternal twins), but also information about individual differences in rate of change, level achieved, duration of plateau, and onset and rate of decline.

Although the longitudinal method represents a major improvement over the cross-sectional and retrospective study, it too poses problems including the following: (1) sample shrinkage—subjects disappear because of change in residence, illness, boredom, death; (2) testing effects—repeatedly measuring the same people with the same yardsticks can lead to instrument decay (see Chapter 7), boredom and loss of motivation—that is, to systematic on-stage effects; (3) external validity limits—the conditions under which this sample grew up (nutritional, social, educational) may shift so that this sample's developmental curve no longer provides a valid picture, or map, of the curve that would emerge with a new sample of people under current environmental conditions.

Hence, longitudinal studies require large samples to counteract the effects of sample shrinkage; such studies also require nonreactive, or alternate form, measures to help counteract the effects of boredom and practice; finally, these studies must be periodically updated by contemporary longitudinal studies using new samples to reflect the influence of shifting environmental conditions on developmental curves.

Nevertheless, in spite of these reservations, the longitudinal study represents an important research tool, not only in psychology, education, and organizational

---

[1]When you have adequate archival data (see Chapter 5), retrospective research deserves increased confidence.

behavior but also in anthropology and sociology (historical method) and in economics (time series). Because of its many applications we now examine some of its variations.

In considering the following research designs, remember that, like any designs, they can't tell the whole story of "what leads to what"—the best that any research design can do is to help reduce the number of suspects. Furthermore, because longitudinal studies are usually conducted outside the laboratory, large numbers of uncontrolled influences can affect the results and raise serious questions about their internal validity. Donald Campbell (1969) and Cook and Campbell (1979) have provided models of a variety of "quasi-experimental" longitudinal designs.

Interrupted Time Series

This design involves a series of observations or measurements before and after the particular "treatment" or event occurs (see Figure 10–7).

Which of the seven time series mapped in Figure 10–7 would you choose as good bets for demonstrating a treatment effect—an effect over and above that

FIGURE 10–7.   Interrupted Time Series.

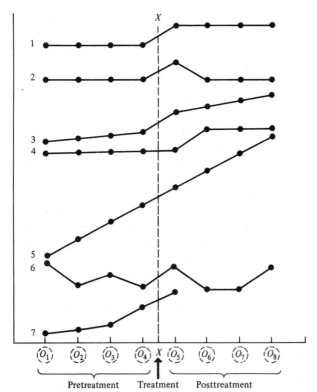

of the various rogues? Time Series 1 and 2 look like reasonable bets; Series 3 and 4, possible bets; and Series 5, 6, and 7, warranting no bets at all. Series 6 deserves particular attention because it presents the typical course of change of many of life's important processes: health, mood, energy level, productivity. Because of the zigzag pretreatment and posttreatment course of this series, we can usually have little confidence in any study of such a time series unless we have major shifts in behavior or a control group is employed.

Notice that the time series is a variation of the before-and-after design discussed in Chapter 7 and is subject to the same limitations. It gains in power to the degree that the pretreatment observations are stable and precise so that posttreatment changes stand out. It also gains in power to the degree that the treatment is potent and quick-acting; otherwise historical and maturational suspects can produce changes in the treatment group that are wrongly attributed to the treatment.

This design is also at the mercy of instrument-decay effects, as is any repeat measurement design. It is particularly vulnerable to experimenter bias, to the degree that the observations are unreliable or subjective—that is, to the degree that the observations are surrounded by large areas of uncertainty.

A repeated interrupted time series, where feasible, provides increased confidence in the treatment—that is, if the introduction of the treatment leads to a significant shift from pretreatment baseline, and then a withdrawal of the treatment results in a return to pretreatment baseline.

Repeated interrupted time series and treatment reversal designs enable ingenious researchers to help manage the rogues. One of the popular variations is the *A B A B* design portrayed in Figure 10–8.

The *A B A B,* or *O X O X,* design depicted in Figure 10–8 maps the percentage of time a young student spent out of his seat under two conditions of teaching—a lecture method (baseline) and a game method.

Even when mapping the behavior of one subject and even when the behavior is variable, some treatments are strong enough to show their effects repeatedly. Reversal designs include the following: *A B A*—two baseline periods interrupted by one treatment period; *B A B*—two treatment periods interrupted by one baseline

FIGURE 10–8. *A B A B* Reversal Design.

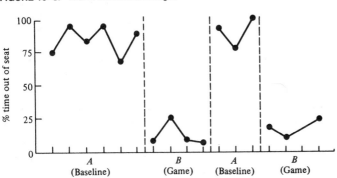

period; *A B B A*—baseline and treatment periods repeated; *B C B*—two treatment periods interrupted by a different treatment. Researchers argue over which statistics, if any, to use in analyzing time series designs. Many researchers simply rely on graphing results and placing confidence in those treatments that show little or no overlap with baseline—such as those in Figure 10–8. Other researchers prefer statistical tests, such as an integrated moving average, which assigns heavy weightings to those observational checkpoints near the treatment period. We strongly recommend graphing your data in order to get a picture of its variability; then whether you do statistical tests or not, you are in a better position to decide how much confidence your treatment results warrant.

In addition to repeat time series and reversal designs, increased confidence in treatment effects can, of course, be obtained by using control groups where feasible.

MANAGEMENT TRAINING—AN EXAMPLE

As an example of a question that lends itself to longitudinal research, consider the introduction of a management training program into an organization—how are such programs typically evaluated?

The desired map of change probably will look like that in Figure 10–9:

FIGURE 10–9.   Desired Curve of Change.

This curve, representing management skills, portrays a multitude of characteristics: delegation of responsibility, clarity of communication, effective use of time, morale building—in brief, a multifaceted curve.

Typically in most management training a pretreatment baseline is rarely measured; if at all, it is estimated by retrospective methods—that is, by supervisors or trainees *recalling* how they performed before treatment. We recognize this is a notoriously unreliable method of establishing observational checkpoints, so we should enclose the pretreatment curve within a large band of uncertainty.

Now we come to the treatment that is usually a stew of treatments (audiovisual displays, lectures, handouts, discussion groups, workshops, individual assignments, parties). Probably neither the people paying for the training program nor the people providing it have any precise idea about rate or levels of change beyond the crude picture in Figure 10–9.

However, from an outsider's viewpoint it would be reasonable to assume that if the training program has any effect at all there will be individual differences in rate, level, and dimension of change. On any given dimension (for instance, more efficient use of work time), we might have at least the following curves reflecting individual differences in rate and level of change (see Figure 10–10).

In Figure 10–10, Trainee A shows a *rapid* rate and *high* level of change; Trainee B, a lower rate and a lower level; and Trainee C, little change at all. On the basis of a posttraining questionnaire (O_4) we find most trainees reporting a Type A curve—that is, they're using a *recalled* pretreatment baseline and *reporting,* after training, a rapid rate and significant level of improvement.

So, using a self-report measure, we obtain a rosy picture of rate and level of change. The personnel department that sponsored the training program is happy, the president is happy, and consultants who put on the program are happy with their extended contract to train more managers. But what kind of questions might you raise about the results? (1) A recalled pretreatment baseline is probably highly unreliable; (2) on-stage and instrument-decay effects strongly influence how individuals respond to ratings and questionnaires (for instance, the training seminars sure beat working; can you really admit you learned little or nothing; you had a good time and would like to go next year); (3) you've only got one real observation (O_4) to estimate rate, level, and duration of change, and that's a self-report measure, notoriously open to bias.

Now a new president takes over the firm and is concerned about the costs (time away from work, consultant fees) of all this training. Furthermore, the president is not convinced that it does all that much good, in spite of the posttraining questionnaire results. The president hires you to help evaluate the "real" effects

FIGURE 10–10. Individual Rates of Change.

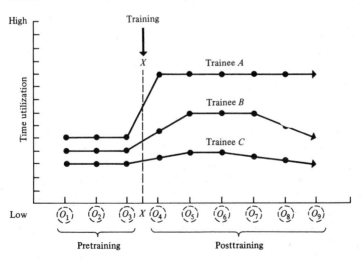

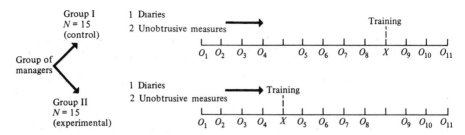

FIGURE 10–11.   Time Series Control-Group Design.

of training. What might you do? The following are examples of how you might improve the evaluation procedure:

1.   Increase the reliability and duration of the pretraining and posttraining observations—that is, have trainees keep pretraining and posttraining diaries of how they utilize their time. Furthermore, supplement these estimates with unobtrusive pre- and posttraining observations in order to provide a check on diary accuracy.

2.   Delay training for a random half of the subjects, and use them as a no-training control—that is, a *multiple time series control-group design* such as that in Figure 10–11.

The inclusion of this "equivalent" control group permits you to estimate the effect of keeping a diary on time utilization and also allows other historical and maturational suspects to influence the control group as they would the experimental group.

Now you return to the president with the following results (see Figure 10–12):

FIGURE 10–12.   Efficiency of Time Utilization.

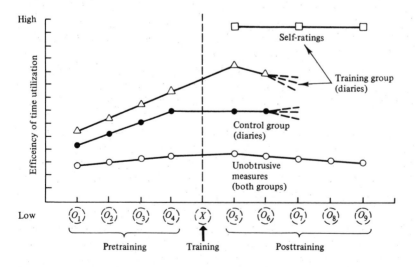

On the basis of these results, you report that

1.   Diary reports of efficient time utilization show marked increases *before* training for both experimental and control groups; here we have evidence of a testing or on-stage effect—that is, merely keeping track of how you spend your time leads to "reporting" more efficient time utilization.

2.   Unobtrusive time-sampling surveillance of a random sample of both experimental and control-group members before training reflects only small increases in efficiency of time utilization (testing or on-stage effects—no differences between groups).

3.   Following training the experimental-group diary reports continue to claim increased time utilization efficiency; however marked individual differences soon start to appear, and quality and number of diary reports diminishes markedly—sample shrinkage and data mortality.

4.   The no-training, control-group diary reports do not show the posttraining "booster" effect shown by the experimental group—but soon show similar sample shrinkage and data loss.

5.   The unobtrusive measure has settled back to the pretreatment, pretesting baseline for both experimental and control groups, except for one member *in each group* who continues to maintain pretreatment gains—that is, subject by treatment interaction (for instance, while most subjects fail to show significant or stable unobtrusive measure gains resulting from diary keeping or training, one manager from each group, *for unknown reasons,* did show such gains. Further study of these two may provide productive hypotheses for further research.

6.   Self-report questionnaire ratings of the overall value of training by trainees remain high for 3, 6, and 12 months following training.

Summarizing, if we base our conclusions on unobtrusive measure data, we conclude that diary keeping alone or in combination with training has little enduring effect on efficient time utilization. If we rely on diary reports, we conclude that diary keeping and training increase *reported,* but not necessarily actual, efficiency of time utilization before training and for a short time after training. If we rely on general rating by trainees following training, we conclude the training leads to rapid and significant improvements on a variety of dimensions.

While acknowledging that you are measuring only one dimension of managerial skill (time utilization), the new president places most confidence in the unobtrusive measure and decides such workshops may build morale but probably are an ineffective means of training—at least concerning the dimension of more efficient time utilization.

Notice that even if an equivalent control group, as was used in this study, is impossible, a *nonequivalent* control group can be useful in obtaining estimates of the role of testing or time in shaping the curve of change. For example, you could have probably obtained a fair estimate of the effect of keeping diaries even if the control group had been run at a different time from the experimental group or in a different plant. Certainly it's not as powerful a control, but it's better than no control. Notice in this study the greatest increase in *reported* time efficiency and unobtrusive estimates of time efficiency occurred *before* the training.

Also observe that if you want to map precisely the rate of increase or decline of a characteristic you require multiple measures over the relevant time period. The diaries recorded time utilization for every 15-minute period during the working day for four weeks before the training and supposedly for three months following. Thus the diary method is designed to provide a fine-grained measure of change—15-minute units over a 16-week time span. The fact that these 15-minute units were filled with rose-colored data indicates that you can also end up with fine-grained *distortions* of the rate of change.

The unobtrusive measure likewise sampled 15-minute units but only one per morning and one per afternoon for each subject, taken more or less at random, and then compared with the same time period in diary reports. As noted the unobtrusive measure data not only differ markedly from diary data but also reflect a much deflated rate and level of change for comparable time periods. Unobtrusive measures also picked up interesting, "casual" comments: "I'm three days behind in my diary; I've got to get caught up by Friday" (thus the diaries in some cases will reflect *recalled* data); "What kind of things are they looking for in these damned diaries anyway?" (This person seems to be asking what kind of on-stage performance one should give); "We better get together on our diaries; we don't want to turn in conflicting information."

Not only do these comments raise important questions regarding the reliability of the diary reports, but they also place grave ethical responsibilities on the researchers—people's jobs and careers could be placed in jeopardy as a result of identifying their source. Research ethics are discussed in Chapter 14.

We've indicated the importance of having relatively fine-grained and objective estimates to map rates of change. The same requirements apply in order to map the duration of change. Failure to conduct fine-grained, objective, posttreatment follow-ups probably constitutes the most single glaring weakness in studies of change; consider, for example, the famous Hawthorne effect.

The Hawthorne Effect

The basic up-and-down curve of change is a powerful model for describing many time-related phenomena including charting the course of problem-solving intelligence from birth to old age, mapping the "melt rate" of New Year's resolutions from December 27 to January 27, or plotting the course of management skills from before training to a few weeks after (see Figure 10–13).

Among the most famous investigations of organizational change are the Hawthorne studies (Roethlisberger & Dickson, 1947). From this research has emerged a phenomenon known as the *Hawthorne effect,* which describes temporary changes that are due mainly to on-stage or testing effects or to the effects of novelty. For example, in the Hawthorne studies it was found that when illumination levels were raised production in the factory increased; but it was also found that when illumination levels were lowered production also increased. The impor-

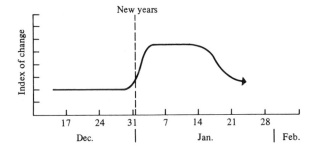

FIGURE 10–13. New Year's Resolution Meltdown → A Classic Hawthorne Effect.

tant point to note is that *novelty,* like New Year's resolutions, can produce change, but not necessarily enduring change.

In evaluating longitudinal studies, consumers of science must ask one critical question: "How do I decide how much of the ups and downs of human or organizational behavior to assign to chance (that is, to the rogues) and how much to specific "treatments"?

In brief, you decide by obtaining some estimate of the range of variation in the behavior without the influence of some selected treatment or intervention. Then you add your "treatment" and determine whether the behavior (1) obviously shifts to new range—higher or lower, (2) maintains the new range (longer than a New Year's resolution), and (3) is maintained when using observations that are not readily open to on-stage and elastic-ruler effects. Science is in the business of mapping heavyweight changes in behavior over significant periods.

You can analyze shifts in behavior by plotting the maps of change and making eyeball assessments of whether there has been an "impressive" shift. If a neutral observer agrees with you, then your conclusions warrant increased confidence. If a hostile observer agrees with you—one who doesn't believe in your treatment—your discovery is astonishing.

With the advent of computers and complicated statistical models, science relies less on eyeball analysis; rather, we compare statistical estimates of day-to-day variability and statistical estimates of whether the shift is larger following an experimental intervention than can "reasonably" be expected by chance, larger than the four rogues usually manage on their own. The four rogues, singly and in combination, can engineer some remarkable shifts in the ranges of human behavior. Therefore it is wise to use a control group, equivalent or otherwise, wherever possible or, lacking a control group, to use extended baseline and follow-up observations involving nonreactive measures and treatment reversal designs.

SUMMARY

In conducting longitudinal studies keep the following recommendations in mind:

1. Cross-sectional studies and retrospective studies provide very crude maps of the curves of change.

2. Interrupted time series gain in power:
   a. when control groups—equivalent or nonequivalent—are used or when treatment reversals are feasible,
   b. when at least some of the observations or measures are robust—are relatively resistant to on-stage and elastic-ruler effects;
   c. such robust measures are continued long enough to determine whether you have a change over and above a New Year's resolution meltdown or a Hawthorne effect.

EXAMPLE

The following is adapted from a student project on testimonials in relation to interrupted time series.

THE TESTIMONIAL

INTRODUCTION

Testimonials arise from something the subject consumed or did which they claim improved their condition. However, since such claims are typically based on after-the-fact or uncontrolled time series observations, testimonials remain highly suspect.

Testimonials usually arise from informal time series "studies" conducted by the subject on themselves. Besides the fact that recalled data is very open to bias, these people fail to take into account the usual ups and downs of whatever symptoms or behavior they're looking at, even when it is not treated at all.

In class we discussed three types of time series: (1) unstable, (b) reactive, and (3) process. These three types are graphed in Figure 10–14.

The main thing to notice about these time series is that while they show different overall trends, they all contain temporary ups and downs in addition to their different trends. The *unstable* time series shows large variability without any overall up-or-down trend. The *reactive* time series shows variability but also shows a stable baseline to start with, a drop for a while, then a return to baseline level. The *process* time series shows variability plus an overall downward trend; an upward trend could still be called a process series.

The point to remember is that without adequate controls (control groups, treatment reversal designs) the average person will likely credit, or blame, any natural up-or-down trend on a favorite suspect. The average person fails to appreciate that the rogues can manufacture all kinds of variability and even shifts in trend.

To obtain a rough estimate of which suspects receive testimonials, I conducted an informal survey of eight of my fellow students in residence. I asked them: "What things have you recently taken, or done, that helped you feel better or that you heard helped someone feel better?" The following is a list of some of the more popular responses:

honey	more sex
distilled water	less sex
no liquor	positive thinking
liquor	additive-free foods
jogging	yogurt
no jogging	skim milk yogurt
tranquilizer	yogurt, plus yoga, plus jogging

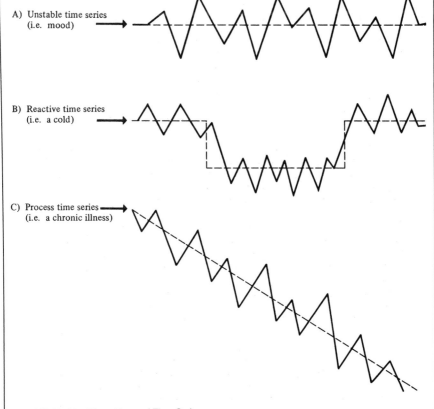

A) Unstable time series
   (i.e. mood)

B) Reactive time series
   (i.e. a cold)

C) Process time series
   (i.e. a chronic illness)

FIGURE 10–14.   Three Types of Time Series.

stimulant	Interferon
herbal tea	bee stings
hard work	prayer
less work	smoking pot
Gestalt therapy	stopped smoking pot
stopped Gestalt therapy	olive oil, honey, and ginseng root
broke up with boyfriend or girlfriend	seeing a counselor
got new boyfriend or girlfriend	stopped seeing a counselor
stopped drinking milk	

My purpose is not to knock any of the preceding "cures" but to give a sample of the kinds of things receiving testimonials. I also want to suggest that probably *any* nonlethal "treatment," no matter what it contained or required you to do, would receive some testimonials. Because of the hidden work of the rogues, any entrepreneur, peddling almost any treatment, will accumulate some satisfied customers, who in turn, by word of mouth will further advertise the innocuous product.

Why should this be so?

Fact 1: Any human characteristic goes up and down—mood, health, energy, aches and pains, weight—even without any specific treatment or planned intervention.

Fact 2: Most of us are bound to try some "treatment" when we're feeling low.

Fact 3: Even without treatment, in the vast majority of cases, you would eventually feel better. You will credit any improvement to the treatment you took. You won't credit it to chance factors; you won't credit it to one or more of the rogues (for example, statistical regression).

Fact 4: You tend to take treatments when a characteristic has reached its high point (e.g., fever) or at a low point (e.g., mood). At these points the characteristic has probably already reached the ceiling, or floor, level and so usually has only one direction to go— toward improvement. Therefore any treatment, even completely ineffective ones, will appear to have had an early beneficial effect.

Fact 5: If the treatment does not have an *immediate* effect, it can be claimed to be a delayed-action treatment and so still gets credit when your inevitable return to normal occurs (for instance, in a reactive time series).

Fact 6: Even in down-trend *process* time series, dud treatments will get credit for periodic upturns.

Fact 7: Innocuous cures, with any kind of advertising, will invariably make money since they capitalize on (1) the natural variability in human characteristics and (2) the failure to recognize the potency of the rogues working singly or in combination.

My general conclusion is that testimonials will flow to ineffective treatments while nature (maturational factors and statistical regression) effects a cure. As doctors like to say: "Without treatment a cold lasts two weeks; with treatment it only lasts fourteen days."

chapter 11

The Number Game

In science we aim to make our observations (O's) and suspects (X's) clear to make our dependent and independent variables open to public inspection. Science and measurement go together. To understand science you must understand the simple rules of measurement.

Language consists of a set of symbols, sounds, or written squiggles and a set of rules for combining them. In English the symbols are words, and the rules are our grammar.

Measurement is a language, too; its symbols are numerals. In this section we talk about tying numerals to objects and events to help us describe and order our world. Numbers condense or package data into memorable chunks.

Not only do we use numbers to label the sweaters of football players and to count poker chips but we also use them to tell how we measure up in height, school grades, and income. We use numbers to describe things we can't see, like temperature, anxiety, and the national debt. Furthermore, we use numbers to help us move from small bits or samples of information to generalizations, such as predicting the number of cases of cancer in the whole population on the basis of the number we find in a sample of the population.

In the following chapters we describe the major rules of the number game and show how breaking the rules—wittingly or unwittingly—fouls the game.

Almost everyone knows that measurement and numbers belong together. In fact, *measurement can be defined as tying numbers to objects and events according to certain rules,* in the same sense that words are tied to objects and events.

In the case of measurement, instead of tying *word* labels to shareable objects or events, we tie *number* labels to them. Measurement also involves logical rules for combining numbers, which are translated into concrete operations. For example, the logical symbol + (plus) can be concretely expressed by pouring water from one beaker and *adding* it to the whisky in another beaker.

BLACK MAGIC?

Measurement, we have said, can be defined as tying numbers to objects and events according to certain rules. Although not able to explain the rules in detail, most of us recognize when a rule has been broken, particularly when a child breaks the rules as in the following dialogue:

YOU: How old are you, Kim?
KIM: I am five years old, and I am seven years old.

While you don't know the name of the rule, you know that Kim has broken some rule about tying numbers to objects. After some discussion you convince Kim that one age number is enough for anyone, and she finally agrees that she is five years old and that her brother is seven years old. You then continue your discussion:

YOU: Who is older, Kim, you or your brother? Which age number is bigger?
KIM: I am older; my number is bigger.

Once again, even though you may not know the name of the rule, you know that Kim has broken it. Five doesn't come after seven; five goes before seven—anybody knows that—well, anybody who's learned the rule.

On Being Number-Numb

We laugh when children break rules in tying number words to objects and events. When researchers do it, it is not so obvious, and it can be disastrous.

Have you noticed how otherwise very competent people are number-numb? A faculty member is a case in point. He speaks of numbers as "those ugly little squiggles that are the constituents of a black art." When the abolition of child labor in mine and factory freed children from punishing physical work, he claims the evil powers rushed in with arithmetic, algebra, trigonometry, and statistics as new forms of child torture.

MEASUREMENT SCALES AND RULES

Those of you who major in psychology or become social scientists will encounter different types of measurement scales ranging from crude to precise. An appropriate measurement scale will help you locate an important phenomenon, or discover a subtle change in behavior, that a crude or inappropriate scale will miss. Since the scientific method rests on systematic observation, and since measurement is the fundamental tool of observation, you need to know how to select and evaluate (perhaps even construct) these vital tools.

The four major types of scale encountered in social science are: (1) nominal, (2) ordinal, (3) interval, and (4) ratio scales. To understand the construction and application of these scales and to appreciate their relative power to detect differences in human behavior, you should know the different rules upon which each one rests.

At this point we could list and describe some of the logical rules for combining number symbols, such as the nominal rule, the ordinal rule, and the interval rule. An alternative procedure is to attempt to discover the logical operations by examining a concrete example of their application.

We have noted that *measurement* can be defined as rules for tying numbers to objects and events. At the concrete level a measuring instrument is a good example of tying numbers to an object according to certain rules. Therefore let's examine a common measuring tool to discover some of the rules that went into its construction. An ordinary one-foot ruler provides an excellent example.

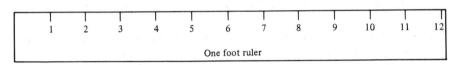

One foot ruler

In the case of the ruler, someone has assigned numbers to this flat piece of wood. What rules were followed? Examine the ruler for a moment; notice the symbols; observe how they are placed. If you examine another school ruler, even one made by a different manufacturer, you will find many similarities. While the color of the wood or the paint may differ, the two rulers will have several characteristics in common—the placement of the numerals in both cases has followed the same rules.

Nominal Rule

Notice first that different symbols are used to label different points on the piece of wood. If this were not the case we could be faced with a ruler of the following type:

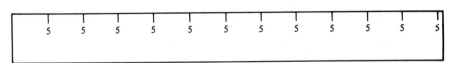

The nominal rule—the naming or labeling rule—demands that you apply different, agreed-upon labels (names, numbers, symbols) to different objects or events.

This first rule—the nominal rule—is considered by some not to be a form of measurement. They point out that it is merely a labeling operation, useful for identification purposes, but in no way does it tell us anything about "more than" or "less than" relationships. Nevertheless, since counting is a form of measurement and since it is based on the assumption that we have met the requirements of the nominal rule, it is important to include this rule as one of the rules of measurement. In other words, since the nominal rule is fundamental to all other measuring rules, it should be included. There are many examples, like that facing the psychiatrist attempting to make a diagnosis, in which we fail to meet the conditions of the nominal rule. Nevertheless, we go merrily along counting objects and reporting the results in numbers, when the results are, at worst, meaningless and, at best, highly perishable or personal.

When different investigators end up with different counts, what are we to assume? Since counting itself is fairly simple, the safest assumption is that the nominal rule has been broken—that is, there is no agreed-upon way of assigning labels to the members of the various populations being counted, and so the counting operation itself becomes a counting of ghosts. Since all other rules of measurement assume that the nominal rule has been met and since there is ample evidence that the nominal rule is often ignored, we conclude that this important rule must be included among the rules of measurement.

Ordinal Rule

Not only are different numbers assigned to different objects and events, but the numbers have a reserved place in the number series—this is the ordinal rule. If it were otherwise, we would encounter such rulers as the following, where different rulers have their numbers in different orders.

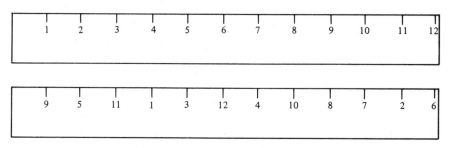

An object measured by the first ruler might be assigned the number 2, but when measured by the second ruler, it would be assigned the number 5. If numbers on a ruler, or in the number series generally, were permitted to play musical chairs, we couldn't use the numbers to talk about order or to indicate where in the series a given object or event occurs. Think of the problems involved in a simple example:

    YOU: How did Sally make out in the 100-meter freestyle?
    PAUL: She came in second.
    GEORGE: She came in fifth.

In an effort to resolve the conflicting answers, you ask Ringo. He replies, "Sally came in *B*." Ringo doesn't like numbers and will use them only when no alternative method is available. The three foregoing systems for describing order are outlined as follows:

PAUL: 1, 2, 3, 4, 5, 6, 7, etc.
GEORGE: 9, 5, 11, 1, 3, 12, 4, etc.
RINGO: A, B, C, D, E, F, G, etc.

It is important to remember that the symbols we use and where they appear in the series are mere customs. As long as Paul, George, and Ringo use the same rules consistently, they are playing the game. Paul's number series has the advantage of being in common use: large-group rules; it is blessed by custom. Notice, however, that when George's number series, individual rules, is put next to Paul's there is no contradiction in their replies to our question. In both instances Sally was assigned the position right after the beginning position—that is, Position *B* in Ringo's terms. If George wants to persist in having his own individual ordinal scale and he uses it consistently, we can learn to translate it into our own terms. He plays by the shareable rules of language, and anyone who wants to learn his system can do so. If, however, the positions of the numbers change, if George haphazardly changes them from day to day, then this would be an unstable system, and George would be breaking the "reserved-place" ordinal rule.

It should be noted that in these examples the nominal rule is also violated. You will recall that we stated that in the case of the nominal rule different agreed-upon labels are assigned to different objects or events. In our examples although different labels are applied to differing objects or events, they are not agreed upon—that is, there does not appear to be consensus as to the label for second place. In one case it's 2, in another 5, and in Ringo's system it is *B*. Each of the rules builds on preceding ones, so that in order to develop an ordinal scale, you must first satisfy the assumptions of the nominal rule.

So far we have considered two rules of the number system: Rule 1—by custom, different objects and events are assigned different symbols or numerals; Rule 2—by custom, the symbols or numerals are assigned a reserved position in the series of numerals. Notice that the alphabet, as well as the whole number system, fulfills these two rules. Thus if you want to label events or simply talk about their order, the alphabet will do as well as the number system, providing you don't have to talk about more than 26 objects or events. While the alphabet is a useful system for labeling events and describing their order and while it can be used to describe relations such as "earlier than" and "bigger than," is it really of much use if we want to talk about "how much bigger" one object is than another?

The Interval Rule

Returning to our standard 12-inch ruler, notice that the symbols are placed equal distances apart. A ruler is divided into a series of equal-sized units. But how far apart are the letters of the alphabet? One alph? You see that the order rule makes no assumptions about how far apart the symbols are. All of the following scales meet the ordinal rule:

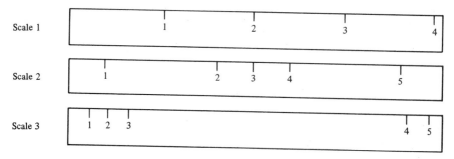

YOU: How did our team make out in the 100-meter free style?
REPLY: We placed first, second, and third.

Does that mean by Scale 1, Scale 2, or Scale 3? Usually when we ask such a question, we are not concerned about how big an interval separates the swimmers but only about the order they came in, regardless of interval. If we want to know the swimmers' times or the distances separating the best jumps of three pole-vaulters, however, can we handle the problem with only an ordinal scale? Suppose Elvis vaulted 13'9", Blane vaulted 14'0", and Turk vaulted 14'6". How do we communicate this information with only an ordinal scale? We could say Blane beat Elvis by a bit and Turk beat Blane by more than that. So we have communicated more than just "order" information.

We have communicated some distance or interval information as well. How did we do it? By selecting a standard that we called "a bit" (the distance separating Elvis and Blane) and comparing it to the distance separating Turk and Blane, we decided that the latter distance was bigger than "a bit."

The important point, of course, is that to talk about "more than" and "less than," we need to know what a "than" is; if we want to talk about "more than a bit" and "less than a bit," we need to know what a "bit" is.

Selecting a standard, or a basic unit, is an arbitrary decision. When faced with this problem, you look around for a readily available standard and make that your "bit." People's feet were usually readily available, and so "one foot" became an early unit for measuring distance. Using people's real feet for measuring distances must have led to certain inequalities as well as inconveniences. When good old Dad's farm was divided, the son with the biggest "foot" did better.

Eventually someone with small feet recommended that they should have one special foot to avoid arguments; everyone agreed, and, of course, they decided to use the king's foot. Now a king doesn't go traipsing all over the countryside just to measure things with his foot, so they had to cut off one of his feet, to be sent around for measuring. This left the king with only one foot, hence the origin of the term *one-foot ruler*.[1]

The point is that if we want to talk about how much more than or less than one object is in relation to another, we need a unit—a standard interval that is easy to apply. It often takes years to develop such a unit and to sell others on using our particular interval, whether it is a second, a bushel, a micro-mercury, a megaton, an ounce, a degree of temperature, a unit of anxiety, intelligence, depression, or a foot.

In summary, if all we want to do is to label or identify objects or packages of data by using numbers, we follow the nominal rule (different objects get different numbers). We can do this as long as we can tell the objects or the qualities of objects apart. If we also want to describe order relationships among objects by using numbers, we must include the ordinal rule. We can do this as long as we can order the objects (from earliest to latest, or smallest to biggest); then we assign the first number, 1, in the number series to the first object in the ordered series and the second number, 2, to the second object in the ordered series, and so on. If, in addition to labeling and ordering, we want to describe with numbers the interval separating objects, then we must use the interval rule and select or develop a measuring instrument that is divided into equal units.

There is one more characteristic about our one-foot ruler that deserves comment. Notice that it has a zero point. This is so obvious that its importance is often overlooked.

The Ratio Rule

Unless a measuring instrument has a zero point, it is impossible to say anything about how many times bigger or smaller one object or quantity is than another. Without assuming that there is such a thing as zero age, we would not be able to say that Harry is twice as old as Mary. Consider an example. In a test of knowledge of French nouns, we have the following results:

Vladimir knew none of the words.
Hamish knew 5.
George knew 10.
Gloria knew 15.

We can portray the results in the following way:

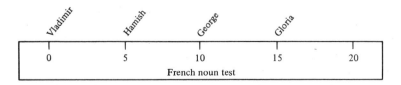

[1]There may be the odd scholar who has some reservations about the complete historical authenticity of this interpretation.

Thus our test of French nouns is a measuring instrument that appears to have all the characteristics of an ordinary ruler—that is, it appears to meet the nominal, ordinal, interval, and absolute-zero rules. If this is so, then we can say that George knows twice as many French nouns as Hamish knows, and that Gloria knows three times as many as Hamish knows. We can do so only if we are able to agree on where zero belongs on the scale. As you can guess, certain very simple French nouns weren't included on the test the teacher gave—words like *l'amour* and *la bouche*. Therefore it is quite likely that there are at least five French nouns that even Vladimir knows that, if included on the test, everyone would get correct. This would involve moving the zero point on our scale five points to the left. Now look at the old scale alongside the new, and see how this affects what we can say about how many more nouns Gloria knows than Hamish or Vladimir knows. In the case of the first scale, we had concluded that George knew twice as many French nouns as Hamish knew, but with the new zero point, this is no longer the case. Similarly, on the original scale Gloria knew three times as many French nouns as Hamish knew, whereas on the new scale, she knows only twice as many.

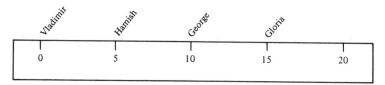

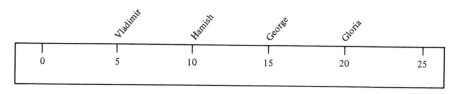

It is apparent, then, that if we want to talk about how many times greater or smaller one object is in relation to another, we must have a way of deciding where absolute zero is on the scale. In many cases, such as most test scores (arithmetic, French, intelligence, anxiety, beauty, musical talent), we use an arbitrary zero. In those cases where we are not sure where zero lies, we should not (1) attempt to say how many times bigger or smaller one score is than another or (2) attempt to use any statistical procedures that involve multiplying or dividing the scores.

Arbitrary Zero

You may say that one way around the problem is simply to report that, in the case of our original French test, George knew twice as many of the words as Hamish did on *that particular test*. In this way you are making no claim about whether George knows twice as many of all French nouns but only twice as many of the ones on that particular test. And, of course, you would be perfectly right in doing so. However, most tests are designed to estimate amount of knowledge in a given field, with the test questions representing only a small sample of all possible questions in that area. Thus while it is relatively easy to say whether someone gets a score of zero on the particular sample of the questions selected, it is extremely difficult to decide whether that person would get zero if all possible questions dealing with the topic had been asked.

Most students who succeed in getting poor marks on tests know what we are talking about. When they say the test was unfair, they are saying that it was a bad sample of questions, and by poor luck the teacher just happened to select the only questions the student didn't know. Thus in your friend's eyes, your score of 80 and his score of 10 certainly does not indicate that you know eight times more about the field than he does. In fact, by the time he finishes complaining, he implies that he could answer hundreds of questions about the topic, whereas you were able to answer only the eight particular questions the teacher selected. So he goes away mumbling and concluding that he knows more about the field than you do but that the educational people seem almost diabolical in their ability to select those few questions for which he has no answers.

Actually this is a critical problem facing educators, particularly with the present knowledge explosion. No longer can we expect professors of physics to know everything about physics or professors of psychology to know everything about psychology. The professors solve this dilemma by becoming more and more specialized, by carving out smaller and smaller areas or data pools within their own discipline within which they attempt to become very knowledgeable, and then they dump all that knowledge in the student's lap. How is the student to face the dilemma of information overload at exam time? The naive student attempts to learn all the material that the professor presents, as well as to cover the outside readings. Wise students know how to study strategically. They have learned to spend more time on some parts of the course material than on others. They have learned to identify the professor's preferences. The students do this on the basis of how much time the professor spends on different topics, by noting what topics appear to excite the professor, by seeing what sorts of questions the professor traditionally asks, by looking over the professor's exam papers for the past years, and by talking to former students. This strategic approach to learning may appear to be unscholarly. Certainly some students carry it to the extreme, devoting almost all their time to attempting to predict the few questions that will be asked, and then applying their very limited energy to studying these few questions. This is, of course, a self-defeating approach to learning. Nevertheless, serious students, facing the impossible task of preparing for all possible questions, rely not only on their own particular interests but also on the biases of the professor in guiding them on what aspects of the topic require more concentrated work than others.

This discussion is not merely a diversionary bit of advice on the strategy of getting through university. The scientific way to estimate a student's knowledge of a given area would be to have all competent professors in that area write out a list of all conceivable questions. These questions would then be put into huge drums grouped into classes from most important to least important. On a given examination a sample of 10, 15, or 100 questions would be drawn out of each drum and would constitute the exam—the number of questions to be drawn depending on the amount of time available for the examination. Such a list of questions would constitute a random sample of hard, average, and easy questions. Under the present circumstances in which a given professor decides which questions to ask, we have a biased sample of questions covering the field. If a student repeatedly does well on the series of exams based on the random sample procedure, we would conclude that the student knows the topic well. When a student does well for a given professor, we are not sure whether he or she knows the topic well or *knows the professor well.*

Similarly, when you read the results of a poll concerning who will be the next president of the United States or concerning premarital sexual relations, are you getting the answers from a cross-section of the population in the country, or are you getting the answers from the friends and colleagues of the person who carried out the poll? In other words, are you learning about the topic, or are you learning more about the biases of the person who conducted the poll? *Absolute zeros* refer to topics and total populations. *Arbitrary zeros* refer to samples and biased groups of one kind or another.

In the example of our test of French nouns, we were not talking about how many of all (population) French nouns the student knew but only about how many of those selected for the test (sample). Thus we were using an arbitrary zero, so it is impossible to talk about whether Gloria knows 2 times or 20 times as many French nouns as Hamish does. If we wanted to be able to make such statements with confidence, we would have to test the students on all French nouns. If we wanted to make an approximation, we could test them on several samples of French nouns picked at random from a data pool of all French nouns.

Before discussing how science and measurement go together, we shall summarize measurement rules. Nominal scales are used when we compare objects or data clusters and can decide which ones are the same and which ones are different. After this we can count how many objects fall into each category. Ordinal scales enable us to talk about relations such as "more than" or "less than," or "earlier than" or "later than." As long as independent observers can rank-order objects or events on some less-to-more dimension, they have an ordinal scale.

In some cases we want to know more than who came first and second. We also want to know by how much one swimmer beat the other. In instances where we want to describe by how much objects or events differ, we use an interval scale. Finally, absolute-zero scales are used when we want to compare one event, not merely with another person or sample, but with an absolute-zero or population value (knowledge of *all* French nouns). Each of the four scales, then, has a different purpose, but each succeeding scale assumes that the rules of the preceding scales have been met. If an ordinal scale is to be used, it is assumed that the nominal rule has been met. If an interval scale is to be used, it is assumed that, in addition to the interval rule, the nominal and ordinal rules have also been met.

In primitive disciplines like social and medical sciences, remember that nominal and ordinal scales can be of invaluable assistance in describing or packaging data. Just as a crude thermometer is better than no thermometer, so initially crude measures of anxiety, or management ability, or patient improvement are better than no measure, are better than casual observation. Furthermore, what may start out to be crude measures are, with experience, gradually refined and transformed into more sensitive measures that can detect smaller and smaller differences and changes.

In the section to follow, we will have an opportunity to examine some of the challenges involved in constructing simple nominal and ordinal data-packaging methods.

SCIENCE AND MEASUREMENT GO TOGETHER

Everyone knows that science and measurement go together, but not everyone appreciates the importance of the relationship. You now have some familiarity with the sieves of science:

field study	natural experiments
after-the-fact	field experiments
archival research	simulation methods
survey research	unobtrusive measures
before-and-after	developmental and longitudinal methods
control-group method	

and you are also familiar with the measurement scales:

nominal
ordinal
interval
ratio (absolute zero)

used to clearly describe suspects (X's) and observations (O's). Scientists technically refer to suspects as *independent* variables and to observations as *dependent* variables. They are variables in the sense that they can take different values, and the changes in the dependent variable are assumed to *depend* on changes in the independent variable.

Just as moving from the after-the-fact sieve to the control group sieve increases confidence in your findings, so too moving up from nominal scales to ordinal, interval, and ratio scales increases the precision of your measurement.

Recall the control group study in Chapter 8 of treating depressed patients with a new drug. This study can be conducted at different levels of precision, depending on the precision used in manipulating the independent variable (the drug) and the degree of precision used in measuring the dependent variable (the degree of depression). At the crudest level we could manipulate the independent variable on a nominal scale (Drug *A* versus Drug *B*) and measure the dependent variable also at a crude nominal scale level (depressed versus nondepressed).[2] The following figure displays the research design as well as the results of the study:

	(O_1)	(X)	(O_2)
Group 1 (N = 10)	10 depressed 0 not depressed	Drug *A*	8 depressed 2 not depressed
Group 2 (N = 10)	10 depressed 0 not depressed	Drug *B*	9 depressed 1 not depressed

Not very encouraging results. But is it that the drugs have similar effects or that the scale is too crude to detect the differences? Note that the dependent variable can only take two values—depressed versus nondepressed. There is no provision for shifts in degree of depression; it may well be that Drug *A* helps relieve the depression of significantly more patients than does Drug *B*, but this result cannot show up in this study since, for example, there is no category for mild depression.

Now look what happens to our results when we increase the degree of precision by using a four-category ordinal scale instead of a two-unit nominal scale for assessing depression.

	(O_1)	(X)	(O_2)
Group 1 (N = 20)	10 severe 10 marked 0 moderate 0 mild	Drug *A*	2 severe 6 marked 7 moderate 5 mild
Group 2 (N = 20)	10 severe 10 marked 0 moderate 0 mild	Drug *B*	7 severe 12 marked 1 moderate 0 mild

Following treatment with Drug *A*, 12 out of 20 patients are well enough to go home, having shifted down to mild or moderate depression, whereas only one patient was well enough to go home following Drug *B* treatment.

Had Drug *A* been a miracle drug, a drug capable of shifting most patients from a seriously depressed state to a state of *no* depression, then we could detect its effect with a crude two-category nominal scale. However, although not a miracle drug, it is significantly better than Drug *B*, being capable of shifting severely depressed patients to a state of only moderate or mild depression. With a four-

[2]You can think of this as a two-point ordinal scale rather than the two-category nominal scale, if you prefer.

point ordinal scale, we detect this important new information; with only a crude two-point nominal scale, we missed it.

Therefore remember that the cruder the measuring scale used to detect shifts in your dependent variable, the stronger must be the effects of your independent variable.

Notice we still don't know anything about the effects of different amounts of our independent variable (Drug *A*), since previously we used only one dosage level. In certain amounts it may prove to be a miracle drug. To find out about the effects of different amounts, we conduct a study in which we manipulate the independent variable on a milligram scale (a ratio scale with an absolute zero and equal units). The results of this study follow:

	O_1	X	O_2
Group 1 ($N = 20$)	10 severe 10 marked 0 moderate 0 mild	Drug *A* 150 milligrams	1 severe 3 marked 8 moderate 8 mild
Group 2 ($N = 20$)	10 severe 10 marked 0 moderate 0 mild	Drug *A* 100 milligrams	2 severe 6 marked 7 moderate 5 mild
Group 3 ($N = 20$)	10 severe 10 marked 0 moderate 0 mild	Drug *A* 50 milligrams	4 severe 8 marked 5 moderate 3 mild

Notice as the dosage becomes larger, the number of patients helped also increases. Also notice that we don't know what a larger dosage than we have tried would do; it might be even more effective, or it might start causing negative side effects—obvious ones like hives and drowsiness that can be detected by casual observation involving crude nominal and ordinal scales or subtle ones like subsequent difficulties in carrying a baby to full term, which may take years to link to the drug.

By combining the control-group method with increased precision in the measuring scales used both to measure our dependent variables and to manipulate our independent variables, we are able to get a clearer picture of nature's rhythms. For example, Agnew and Ernest (1971), using human subjects, compared the effects over time of three dosage levels of a sedative drug and three levels of a stimulant drug with a placebo on a variety of measurement scales. The results obtained from one of the self-rating mood scales used are given in Figure 11–1.

In this large study the effects of all three independent variables (type of drug, dosage, and time since drug taken) all show up clearly on a variety of rating

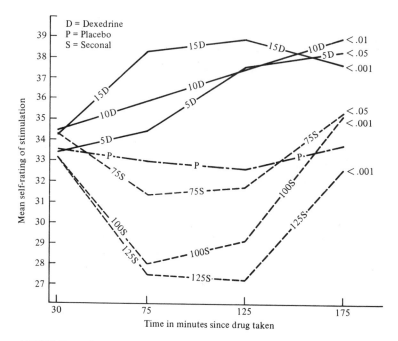

FIGURE 11–1. The Influence of a Sedative and of a Stimulant on Mood.

scales but not on certain perceptual and cognitive tests. Thus not only is it appropriate to have sufficient degrees of precision in your measuring scales, it is also important to select scales that measure relevant aspects of the behavior under study. This selection is influenced both by past experience and by theoretical hunch.

It is clear that science and measurement go hand in hand. If you believe your independent variable has a strong effect on your dependent variable, you can probably detect such an effect with a crude nominal or interval scale. If, however, you suspect only a mild or moderate effect, you should use a more precise measuring scale—one with small units able to detect small differences. If you are not sure what aspect of behavior will be affected, you had better use several different scales.

Most wise researchers carry out naturalistic observations or conduct pilot studies to get a "feel" for the strength and rhythm of the relationship between the dependent and independent variable before launching into elaborate research projects. You would probably be wise to do the same.

What to Look for in Pilot Studies

A pilot study familiarizes you with some of the characteristics of your independent and dependent variables. What appeared under casual observation to be clear suspects and observations, on closer examination turned out to be fuzzy categories—the drug changes color from day to day and the patients' degrees of depression are highly variable.

Indeed, as well as giving some crude estimates of the potency of your independent variable, a pilot study helps you decide how you should scale your independent and dependent variables. Whether you need few or many categories for each and whether those categories lend themselves to nominal, ordinal, interval, or ratio scaling becomes more obvious. Whether or not observations lend themselves to one scale or another can be determined by asking certain key questions—for example, we need to know how many categories we would require to describe the independent variable and its range of impact upon the dependent variable. If we use too few categories, we lose valuable information—as was the case when we used only two nominal categories to detect the effect of our drug on depression in the previously discussed drug study. On the other hand, if we use too many categories, we raise the cost of our study and probably overtax the ability of our observers to make fine discriminations.

Many factors affect our decisions, including theoretical assumptions, past experience (our own and that described in the literature), and the availability of resources and measuring instruments.

For example, once you have satisfied yourself, on the basis of a pilot study, that you are working with an ordinal scale, the next key question is: How many categories do you need? Too few categories in an ordinal scale can cause trouble, but so can too many. A psychiatrist is interested in evaluating the effectiveness of a new treatment for neurosis. She sets up a five-point ordinal scale as follows:

Markedly worse	Moderately worse	No change	Moderately improved	Markedly improved
1	2	3	4	5

Improvement scale

Category 3 is to be assigned to patients who demonstrate no change; Category 4 is to be assigned to those showing moderate improvement; Category 5 to those showing marked improvement; Category 2 to those who seem to be moderately worse following treatment; and Category 1 to those who seem to be markedly worse after treatment.

Our researcher examines the patients before and following treatment and assigns each to one of the five categories. She has a colleague independently follow the same procedure. You will recall from our discussion of nominal scales that one of the ways of determining whether you have clear categories is to see if different observers can independently label the objects or events the same way. We are essentially following the same procedure here with ordinal scales.

The worst that can happen with the ratings of our two observers is almost no agreement between them in assigning patients to categories—that is, had the patients been assigned their categories by drawing the numbers out of two hats rather than having them assigned by psychiatrists, the results would have been similar. Or perhaps there may be large disagreements between the two—that is, Psychiatrist B has assigned some patients to Category 5, and Psychiatrist A has assigned some of the same patients to Category 1, and vice versa. Under either of the preceding conditions, it is apparent that (1) the scale is inadequate, (2) at least one of the psychiatrists has a very personal or pragmatic view of improvement. However, if the differences occur around scale points 2, 3, and 4, she will recognize that Categories 2 and 4 are fuzzy, that they contain large areas of uncertainty, and so she collapses them into one category by combining them with Category 3:

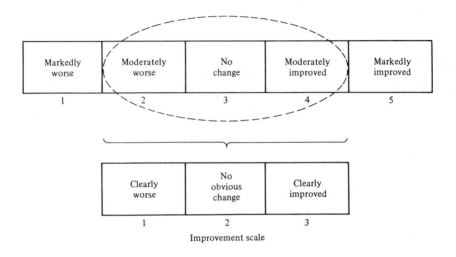

Improvement scale

If this is the case, she has an ordinal scale that will detect the results of treatments that have a large effect—that shift a significant number of patients into new Category 3. Even a crude scale like this is preferable to no scale at all or, in other words, to individual bias.

But she may decide she wants to develop a scale that will be sensitive not only to strong treatments but also to moderate treatments. If so, she devotes time to attempting to clarify the distinction between Category 3 (no appreciable change) and Category 4 (moderate improvement) of her original five-point scale. She can attempt to make these categories more distinctive by giving examples of what she considers to be moderate improvement: "patient may still have severe nightmares but not as frequently"; "patient still experiences strong anxiety in presenting class paper but is attending class more regularly." After attempting to clarify distinctions between the middle categories, she tests this scale again to see if she is now getting more agreement among independent judges in the use of the middle categories. If so, she has reduced the region of uncertainty in her original Category 4, and she has increased the sensitivity of her scale in detecting moderate, as well as marked, changes.

SUMMARY

Naturalistic observations and pilot studies can help you decide what kinds of measurement scale to use in manipulating your independent variable and in describing your results. Using a common one-foot ruler as an example, we described four types of measurement scales: (1) nominal; (2) ordinal; (3) interval; and (4) ratio, or absolute zero.

The results you report depend not only on the type and precision of your measurement scales but also on the kind of analysis you perform. Statistics play a large role in shaping the results of science. Among other valuable functions, statistics serve to summarize the results of applying your measurement scales. The next chapter describes some of the vital descriptive and predictive functions that statistics perform in the service of science.

chapter 12

Statistical Foundations

There are two kinds of statistics: one called *descriptive statistics,* which helps to package data into neat bundles, and a second kind called *inferential statistics,* which helps us make educated guesses on the basis of small samples of data.

DESCRIPTIVE STATISTICS

One death is a tragedy.
One million deaths is a statistic.

This chilling quotation illustrates that statistics not only condense information but in so doing also deprive it of some of its meaning. You are already familiar with the use of statistics to package or summarize information. The "average" American earns $528.54 per week, comes from a family of 2.3 members, has completed 12.2 years of education, and before dying at age 68.4 has consumed 538.5 hamburgers and 608.4 Alka-Seltzers.

Like any summary such statistics tell you something about everyone in general and nothing about anyone in particular. Nevertheless, such numerical summaries simplify communication when large quantities of information must be transferred. For example, listen in on the following dialogue between two professors:

PROFESSOR BLENDER: You have a large introductory psychology class this year—over 400 students, I believe.

PROFESSOR MAKAN: It's a pain teaching such a mob. What can they learn?

BLENDER: How did they do on their exam?

MAKAN: Sit down and I'll tell you. Aaron got 67.5, Abbott got 73.5, Agnew got 34.2, . . .

BLENDER: I don't want to know what each individual student got. Don't you know the class average?

MAKAN: Of course; it was 78. But what does that tell you?

BLENDER: It tells me that your class average is higher than anyone else's. You must have smart students.

MAKAN: From the average you can tell that? How do you know I'm not just an easy marker? One student got 97, but I've got some real dummies, too. Another student only got 18.

From this brief dialogue you appreciate that an average doesn't really tell you a lot by itself. Even when you also know that the scores ranged from 18 to 97, you still don't know whether most students scored below the class average of 78, with a few very smart ones scoring high enough to pull the average up, or whether approximately half scored above and half scored below. It is the purpose of descriptive statistics not only to summarize data but to do so with a minimum loss of important information.

There are two major kinds of descriptive statistics. One deals with descriptions of central values like *averages,* and the second deals with descriptions of variability like *ranges.*

Central Values

There are three main ways of describing the center of gravity of a data pile or distribution:

THE MEAN.   This is the average score obtained by adding all the scores and dividing by the number of scores. For the scores in Column A of Table 12–1,

$$\text{The Mean} = \frac{\Sigma\, x}{N} = \frac{300}{15} = 20$$

This mean represents the arithmetic center of gravity in interval and ratio-scale distributions.

THE MEDIAN.   This is the middle score, on either side of which lie the low half of the scores and the high half of the scores. For the scores in Column A of Table 12–1,

$$\text{The Median} = 19$$

TABLE 12–1   Descriptive Statistics

PATIENT		ANXIETY SCORE X	DEVIATION FROM MEAN x	SQUARED DEVIATION x^2
Hamish		27	+7	49
Irv		25	+5	25
Vera		25	+5	25
Bob		24	+4	16
Jane		23	+3	9
Norm	Mean	20	0	0
Joan		20	0	0
Laura	Median	19	−1	1
Dave		18	−2	4
Igor		18	−2	4
Anne		17	−3	9
Lucy	Mode	17	−3	9
Mary		17	−3	9
Charlie		16	−4	16
Neil		14	−6	36
		300	0	212
		Col. A	Col. B	Col. C

There are seven scores higher than 19 and seven scores lower than 19. This is the *middle* score, rather than the average score, and is a particularly useful description of central position when dealing with ordinal scale data.

THE MODE.   This is the commonest or most frequently occurring score or category. For the scores in Column A of Table 12–1,

The Mode = 17

Three students obtained the score of 17. The mode doesn't tell you how well they did relative to other students; it merely identifies the score that the largest number of students achieved. The mode is generally useful for describing concentrations of people or events in nominal categories.

Each of these measures alone tells us something about the center of gravity of a set of scores: The mean describes the arithmetic balance point; the median describes the frequency or middle balance point; and the mode describes the frequency concentration point or heaviest category. Taken individually none of these measures tells us anything about the shape of the distribution of scores, but taken together they give us some hints. For example, we have a balanced or symmetrical distribution if all three of these indices lie on the same score.

Although knowing all three measures of central tendency for a given distribution tells you more than knowing only one, you still know relatively little about the *differences* between the scores in the set. To describe such score differences—

that is, to tell you how spread out the scores are around the mean—three further descriptive statistics are used: the range, the variance, and the standard deviation.

THE RANGE.   This statistic describes the difference between the highest and the lowest scores. In Column A of Table 12–1, the range = 13. The range tells you what range of possible scores your particular distribution covers. For example, in the psychology quiz we discussed earlier, the mean was 78 and the range was 18 to 97, indicating large differences among individual students. While the range indicates the extremes of the distribution of scores, it is based on only two scores and may therefore give a false impression of variability. For example, the student scoring 18 may have been the only failure in the class, and without him the range may have been 58 to 97. Therefore although the range adds to your information about individual differences in performance, it is not a very representative measure because it is based on only two scores. The next statistic is much more representative because it is based on *every* score.

THE VARIANCE (σ^2).   This important statistic, applicable to measures on interval and ratio scales, is the average of the squared deviations from the mean. For example, in Column B of Table 12–1 we listed how much each individual score deviates from the mean—a plus sign indicating how much a given score is above the mean and a minus sign how much a given score is below the mean. To get rid of these signs, we squared these deviations (as in Column C) and added them to get a so-called sum of squares.

$$\Sigma\, x^2 = 212$$

To get the variance, we divide the sum of squares by N—that is, by the number of scores:

$$\text{Variance} = \sigma^2 = \frac{\Sigma x^2}{N} = \frac{212}{15} = 14.13$$

But having squared the deviation scores to get rid of the signs leaves us with an average of *squared* deviations, which gives a misleadingly large number. We need an average of deviations regardless of signs. The next statistic does just that.

THE STANDARD DEVIATION (σ).   This most widely used measure of variability is merely the square root of the variance:

$$\text{Standard Deviation} = \sigma = \sqrt{\frac{\Sigma x^2}{N}} = \sqrt{\frac{212}{15}} = 3.8$$

Now we have a measure of variability that (1) is based on the deviation of *all* scores from the mean; (2) treats negative and positive deviations the same; (3)

is expressed in the same units of measurement as those from which it was derived, rather than on their squares.

We claim that measures of variability help describe individual differences in a group. The standard deviation is of particular value in that it provides a standard unit for such comparisons—one that can be used on any interval or ratio scale. Suppose your class takes two tests—one in psychology and one in physics—and that you score 78 in psychology and 68 in physics. In which test did you do better? In psychology? Maybe, but that assumes it is as easy to get one grade point in psychology as it is in physics. Maybe each grade point in psychology is easier to get than a grade point in physics. We can then ask, "How well did you do relative to the rest of your group?" The group's average in physics was 53, and in psychology it was 63. This suggests that it may be easier to get a point in psychology than in physics, even though you are 15 marks above the group average in each. Does *that* mean you did equally well in both? Well, that depends on how much the marks vary around the mean—and that's why we use the standard deviation. We note that the psychology scores are much more variable than

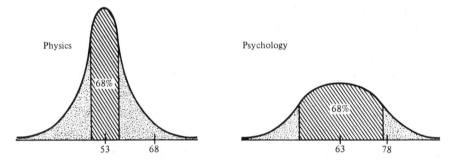

are the scores in physics. Notice that, although you are 15 points from the mean in both distributions, you were much closer to the top of the distribution in physics with a score of 68 than in psychology with a score of 78. In fact, when we calculate the standard deviations (σ) for each distribution, we find that you are 2.6 standard deviation units above the mean in physics and only 1.2 standard deviations above the mean in psychology. Thus relative to your classmates, you did better in physics than you did in psychology.

In addition to helping describe and compare individual differences in performance, the standard deviation helps us describe and analyze different data piles or distributions. Although it isn't particularly useful in describing misshapen or skewed distributions like the following skewed curve, the standard deviation is very useful in describing symmetrical distributions called normal or bell curves.

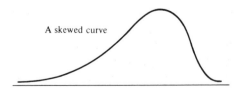

A skewed curve

The normal curve has approximately 34 percent of its area lying between the mean and $+1$ standard deviation, 14 percent of its area between $+1$ and $+2$ standard deviations, and 2 percent lying between $+2$ and $+3$ standard deviation units. Notice, too, that since the normal curve is symmetrical, the mean, median, and mode all lie at the same point.

A useful statistic is one that summarizes data with a minimum loss of information. The standard deviation in combination with the normal curve is such a statistic. Notice how little information I acquire from merely knowing that your

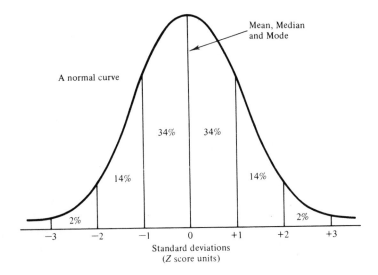

score on a given test is 72. I have no idea whether you did relatively well or very poorly. Notice, however, how much more I learn about your performance if I am informed that in a normal distribution you scored 2 standard deviation units below the mean. Now I know that only 2 percent of the class obtained lower scores than you did. If, in addition, I am told that your actual score is 72 and that the standard deviation is equal to 4, I can estimate the mean to be 80 (your score of 72 plus 2 standard deviations). I can estimate the highest score to be 92 (your score plus 5 standard deviations).

You can see that the standard deviation (or *Z score*, as it is frequently called) combined with the normal curve becomes a powerful descriptive statistic. Knowing where your score lies in Z score units tells where your score lies in relation to all other scores in that distribution. Furthermore, because the Z score describes your relative position in a set of scores, it can be used to *compare* your relative position in two or more score sets. For example, if I say you scored 21 in Anxiety and 104 in ESP, I tell you very little. But if I say your Z score in Anxiety was $+2$ and your Z score in ESP was zero, you know you scored relatively high in Anxiety and only average (at the mean) in ESP. Furthermore, if I tell you that your Z score for time spent in the pub is $+3$ and your Z score in math is -3, it reveals that you lead your group in pub time and trail your group in math grades; some people might even wonder if the two Z scores are tied together in some way.

CORRELATION

To say that two variables are *related* indicates they are somehow tied together—like pub time and math grades. For example, two variables may be negatively related; as one score goes up, the other score goes down:

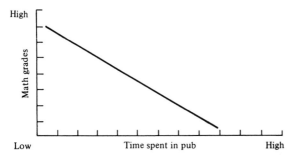

Or the two variables may be positively related; as one score goes up, so too does the other one. If hours of study and math grades were *perfectly* correlated, we would expect that each pair of scores would occupy the same relative position on their respective distributions—that your hours-of-study score and your math score would each lie the same distance, in Z score units, from their respective means. If, for your group, your study-time score was $+2$ Z scores above the group mean, then we would expect your math grade to also lie $+2$ Z scores above the group mean in math, as indicated in Figure 12–1. Notice that in the case of a perfect correlation, when you plot score pairs for each individual in the group the plots lie along a straight line.

However, rarely, if ever, are two variables perfectly correlated, particularly human variables. There are always a few people who study very little and still get

FIGURE 12–1. Perfect Positive Correlation.

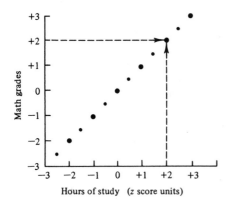

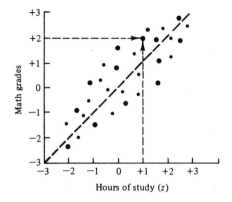

FIGURE 12–2. Strong Positive Correlation.

good math grades, and other unfortunates who study a great deal and persist in getting low grades. Thus when we plot score pairs for two human characteristics, we don't expect to see them lie neatly on the straight line of a perfect correlation; rather we expect to see them marching fairly closely around such an imaginary line, as in Figure 12–2, or, in the case of unrelated variables, to be scattered all over the place, as in Figure 12–3.

By an "eyeball" analysis of these figures, you can *see* different degrees of correlation: perfect correlation in Figure 12–1, strong positive correlation in Figure 12–2, and no obvious correlation in Figure 12–3. One way for you to determine degree of correlation is to plot the score pairs—in raw, or in Z score units— and see to what degree the plots cluster around a positive or negative diagonal. This *scattergram* provides an excellent way to get a feel for your data, for its variability, and we strongly recommend you make such plots.

If you require a more precise and shorthand measure of the degree of relationship, you can calculate a *correlation coefficient*. This is nothing more than a statistical means of describing the differences between pairs of Z scores. In brief,

FIGURE 12–3. No Correlation.

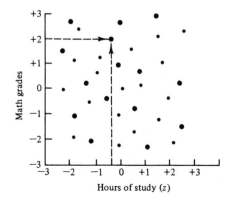

if a pair of scores have similar positions (in Z score units) in their respective distributions, their correlation approaches one, or a perfect positive relationship. However, if any given pair of scores occupy very different or unpredictable relative positions (have very different Z scores), then their correlation approaches zero. Notice that if you calculate a correlation coefficient greater than 1.0 you have made an error—numerically 1.0 is as high as correlations go. Notice also if you discover a correlation higher than 0.90 when using human variables, check your calculations and increase your sample size—such a correlation is suspiciously high. Using a small sample of the data from Figure 12-2, we show in Table 12-2 how to calculate a Pearson product-moment correlation:

TABLE 12-2   Pearson Correlation Coefficient

	RAW DATA						
Ss	HOURS OF STUDY X	MATH GRADES Y	DEVIATIONS FROM MEANS x	y	xy	x^2	y^2
A.B.	27	88	11	28	308	121	784
B.J	23	78	7	18	126	49	324
C.W	22	69	6	9	54	36	81
D.N	10	50	-6	-10	60	36	100
E.R	8	30	-8	-30	240	64	900
F.G	6	45	-10	-15	150	100	225

Sum: $\Sigma X = 96$ $\Sigma Y = 360$ $\Sigma xy = 938$ $\Sigma x^2 = 406$ $\Sigma y^2 = 2414$
Mean: $\bar{X} = 16$ $\bar{Y} = 60$

Standard Deviations (σ)

$$\sigma x = \sqrt{\frac{\Sigma x^2}{N}} = \sqrt{\frac{406}{6}} = 8.22$$

$$\sigma y = \sqrt{\frac{\Sigma y^2}{N}} = \sqrt{\frac{2414}{6}} = 20.06$$

Correlation (γ)

$$r = \frac{\Sigma xy}{N\sigma x \sigma y} = \frac{938}{6(8.23)\ (20.06)} = \frac{938}{6(165.09)} = \frac{938}{990.54}$$

$r = .947$

Note: if you have a large number of subjects, you can calculate correlations using *raw* score data on a small computer or desk calculator—consult the machine handbook for the simple procedure:
i.e.,

$$r = \frac{\Sigma XY - \frac{(\Sigma X)\ (\Sigma Y)}{N}}{\sqrt{\left[\Sigma X^2 - \frac{(\Sigma X)^2}{N}\right]\left[\Sigma Y^2 - \frac{(\Sigma Y)^2}{N}\right]}}$$

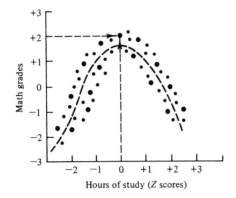

FIGURE 12–4. Curvilinear Correlation.

In the case of the relationship between hours of study and math grades just discussed (Figure 12–2), how much confidence do you have in the very high correlation (.94) that we reported? First notice that we used a small sample of subjects, or observational checkpoints—only six. There is no magic sample size, but we recommend at least 100 subjects to estimate degree of correlation.

Nevertheless, apart from sample size, on the basis of your own experience how much confidence would you place on such a high correlation? What other variable, or characteristic, probably influences math grades besides hours of study? Mathematical aptitude and background are obvious additional suspects. Therefore you might anticipate a curved relationship between hours of study and math grades—the highest grade coming from people with mathematical aptitude who study a medium amount, low grades from people who don't study, and medium and low grades from people without math aptitude who study a lot, but to little avail. Perhaps the relationship might resemble that mapped in Figure 12–4.

The Pearson product-moment correlation is designed to measure straight-line relations (linear), not curvilinear as shown in Figure 12–4. Psychology majors like to experiment by proposing variables which, on the basis of casual observation, should be highly correlated (for example, having the same subjects repeat an intelligence test one week later) or by proposing other variables that are probably not correlated at all (people's heights and their score in mathematics exams). Great arguments ensue, and some even lead to worthy research speculations.

What Does a Correlation Tell You?

Although it is simple to calculate a correlation coefficient, it is not so simple to decide what to conclude from a high coefficient.

While a high correlation tells you that score pairs occupy similar relative positions on the two distributions, it does not tell you if they are tied together intimately like Siamese twins—when one moves, the other must move—or only related casually like two strangers on a subway—when the subway moves, they both move, but they don't necessarily move together for, unlike Siamese twins, one can move to another car without the other, and furthermore one can leave the train or the "relationship" without the other. It is each one's relation to the subway that is the key relationship, not their relationship to each other.

Don't leap to the conclusion that, because one variable appears to be moving with another, the first one "causes" the other. Many supposed relationships turn out to be pseudorelationships, like the young lady traveling by train from New York to San Francisco who reported to the conductor that a strange man was following her. Indeed he was; his seat was two seats behind hers! But it was the train to which he was related, not the young lady—except in her imagination. There are many instances where two variables appear to be related, but are really only incidentally related to each other through a third variable (the train, in this instance). For example, there is a strong positive correlation between the purchase of bathing suits and the sale of ice cream, but you don't conclude that buying bathing suits makes you eat ice cream; rather you say a third variable, temperature, is the independent variable to which ice cream consumption and bathing suit purchases are related.

Whenever you are tempted to conclude that a variable is dependent upon, or moves with, another, stop and think, "Does it make sense on the basis of logic and experience?" Moreover, always look for a third variable to which the two may be tied—as in the preceding cases of temperature and trains.

Beware of Correlations

You probably wouldn't be surprised to learn of a negative correlation between being a Boy Scout and getting into trouble with the law—that is, relatively few Boy Scouts end up formally charged and convicted of crimes. Also, it would not surprise you to learn about a positive correlation between university education and above-average income.

It is, however, quite possible that both of these relationships "ride" on a third *hidden* variable—namely, socioeconomic status. Notice that most Boy Scouts *happen* to be middle- and upper-class kids, and middle-class kids rarely get booked or convicted—whether they are Boy Scouts or not. Similarly, if you took a sample of middle- and upper-class people who hadn't graduated from a university, you would probably find their subsequent incomes were comparable with those of university graduates—the implication being that it is not so much the university education that is related to subsequent income as it is middle- and upper-class contacts and opportunities—the "old boy" network, if you will.

You may disagree with these speculations. Good! Such disagreements stimulate further research. How would you go about testing either of these hypotheses linking criminal conviction negatively and income positively to socioeconomic status of parents?

We now move from descriptive statistics to inferential (or predictive) statistics.

INFERENTIAL STATISTICS

Most social science experiments compare differences among two or more means or averages. For example, suppose we study the effects of two methods of teaching mathematics—one employing a text using programmed instruction à la B. F. Skinner and another based on the same material but written in a traditional manner. We divide our class at random into two groups:

Group 1 X_1 O_1
Group 2 X_2 O_2

One group studies from the programmed text (X_1), and the other studies from the traditional text (X_2). Then both groups write the same exam, and we calculate the means:

$$O_1 = 80$$
$$O_2 = 75$$

We obtained a difference. So what? Even if we had used the same text with both groups, we probably would have obtained a difference. Groups rarely yield precisely the same means even when treated identically, because we never control the operation of all chance factors. The question is not, "Did we get a difference?" but rather, "Did we get a difference worth talking about?" In statistical language we want to know whether we got a *significant difference*.

At least four common factors produce a significant difference:

1. The operation of chance. By luck we ended up with more bright students in Group 1 than in Group 2, even though we drew the names out of a hat.
2. The operation of the chosen independent variable. The programmed text was a more effective teaching aid, and so Group 1 students did better on the exam.
3. The operation of error. A mistake was made in scoring the tests that favored Group 1.
4. The operation of fraud. The researcher fraudulently manipulated the data in favor of Group 1 to accommodate the professor's bias.

Therefore while statistical tests help you decide whether you obtained a reliable or significant difference between your two group means, such tests do not tell you whether such differences arise from the operation of your independent variable, from errors in calculation, or from fraud. Such tests don't even completely rule out the possibility of chance, but such tests do help you identify differences that do not occur frequently by chance alone.

So when you conduct a statistical test on your data and obtain a significant result, you have some confidence that such a large difference is not likely due to chance—although such large differences may occur five times in a hundred due to chance alone. However, you choose to decide that, rather than an unusual chance event, the difference was "caused" by something else. Having done your statistical test to control for the operation of obvious chance factors and having found a significant difference, you then puzzle over the alternatives of whether the significant difference results from the impact of your independent variable, or error, or even fraud.

Parenthetically, notice that while fraud appears as a viable alternative in fringe research areas like ESP, it is rarely so listed in traditional research areas or in research design courses—perhaps because researchers are less fraudulently inclined that are other segments of the population or perhaps because fraud represents an alternative too threatening to the research enterprise to be contemplated openly. (A discussion of instances of possible fraud perpetrated by a famous psychologist appears at the end of Chapter 14.)

Maps of Chance

To determine whether our differences arise from chance factors, we compare our results with what we would expect by chance; we compare our results with maps or models of chance. You already know about such maps. If I flip a coin producing 10 heads in a row, you say, "Hey, wait a minute." Why? Because my results deviate significantly from your map of chance—my results were surprising. Your map of chance for tossing coins is 50–50. The further my results deviate from a 50–50 distribution of heads and tails, the more willingly you entertain the possibility of the operation of "something" in addition to chance. Like what? Like an independent variable: like a biased coin or a biased tosser—*something* more than chance.

If you keep this example in mind, you need have no fear of inferential statistics, for such statistics are merely maps of chance against which you can compare your findings and decide whether your results (your experimental tosses) have gone beyond the limits of what you willingly accept as mere chance happenings. Inferential statistics provide a model against which to compare your results. If nothing else but chance is influencing your results, inferential statistics provide you with the distribution of differences you should expect. When you get a difference that occurs rarely by chance, you have two choices open: You can either decide you obtained one of those rare, large, but unreliable, differences delivered by chance, or you can decide to credit the difference, not to capricious chance, but to the operation of your independent variable.

By using inferential statistics you never rule out the operation of chance, but you do make it a less likely explanation. Ten heads in a row *could* happen by chance, but not ruddy likely!

Sampling Theory

Inferential statistics rest on sampling theory, and you already have a solid background in this theory, even though you may not know it. Sampling theory deals with the relationship between "samples" of experience and "total" experience.

For example, that sample of 10 heads in a row went against your total experience of coin tossing; that sample didn't belong to your population of coin-tossing experience. It was a sample that seemed to belong to another population of experience—to experiences characteristic of fraud and trickery.

Similarly, a host of samples make up your total experience (population of experience) concerning friendship. When a friend acts unfriendly once or twice, you take it in your stride as part of the chance ups and downs of friendship. But if the unfriendliness continues, the time arrives when you say, "No, this is too far out from friendship." These samples of behavior come from another population of experiences—an unfriendly population. That person is no longer classed as "cranky friend" but is now classed as "new enemy."

Sampling theory is a statistical means of deciding to which population a given sample belongs when such a sample may be found in both populations; unfriendly samples or bits of behavior emerge from cranky friends as well as from enemies. Similarly, friendly samples of behavior emerge from friends and also from con artists. To which population does the person producing this particular sample belong? Five heads in a row can result from tossing a legal coin and also from tossing a biased coin; from which population does this particular coin come? Ordinarily you decide such questions by getting more samples—by continuing to toss the coin or by continuing to closely observe your "friend." If in the *long run* heads or unfriendliness continue, you conclude these are not normal chance variations but rather that the coin is biased toward heads and that the person is biased toward unfriendliness.

But often we must make such judgments without the benefit of long-run experience. We must make judgments on the basis of short-run experience, on the basis of *samples*. Inferential statistics and sampling theory provide help in comparing short-term sample results with the results to be expected by chance in the long run.

Sampling Error Theory

We have just indicated how the information contained in short-run samples of experience can differ from the information contained in long-run populations of experience. Research in the social sciences involves sampling; it involves conducting observations on a few individuals—on a sample—to provide estimates about the total group or population that sample represents. When we observe the impact of a new drug on a sample of depressed patients or the impact of a new teaching technique on a sample of students, we don't merely want to know how it affected that small sample of people; we want to estimate, from the sample results, what the impact of our independent variable will be on depressed patients in general or on students in general.

But because the members of a population differ from one another—some very depressed, some less depressed—and because chance factors invariably play a part in determining which individuals end up in a given sample—the patients in our treatment group may be less depressed than most—because of these factors, the mean or standard deviation obtained from a sample is sure to differ from the mean or standard deviation obtained from observing *all* members of the population—all depressed patients. Therefore sample "facts" remain crude estimates of population "facts."

How reliable are such estimates? This is the question sampling theory addresses. To appreciate the simple logic involved, consider the following example. Suppose you wish to know the mean height of American females. Measuring the height of millions of females is prohibitive, so you take a sample. Your sample consists of the first 10 females who enter the lobby of a large hotel. You determine their average height to be 5 feet 2 inches. How good an estimate is this of the average height of all American females? You decide two estimates are better than one. Just as you are about to take a second sample, much to your surprise you see some Japanese women entering the hotel. What luck! Now you can compare the height of American women and Japanese women. You measure and average the heights of the cooperative Oriental ladies and find it to be 5 feet 8 inches. What's going on? Japanese are supposed to be shorter than Americans, not taller.

After a little inquiry you discover that the hotel is housing athletes attending an international athletic event. *By chance* you measured 10 members of the American women's gymnastic team and 10 members of the Japanese women's basketball team—hardly typical or representative samples of their respective populations in either case.

From this example we learn three points about the reliability of estimates of population values based on sample values. These three points can be framed into questions you should ask about any sample:

1. How representative is the sample of the population I want to talk about? Was it a *random* sample—that is, did every member of the population have an equal chance of getting into the sample? To the extent that this is so, you have increased the likelihood that your sample fact will provide a reliable estimate of your population fact.
2. Does this sample "feel" representative? Before you get too far into your study, try to decide on the basis of your previous experience whether you have drawn a typical sample. For example, in your sample of American females, you may have noticed that they all smoke, or that most of them are young, or that they all carry basketballs. Your past experience can frequently guide you in assessing the representativeness, and so the reliability, of your sample data.
3. Have you a large enough sample to obtain a reliable estimate? Intuitively you are familiar with this question. Intuitively you know that large samples of experience give more reliable estimates than small samples, whether we are estimating friendship or height. In estimating the height of American women, the means of several small samples will vary more (will prove less reliable) than the means of several large samples. The *sampling error*, or variability, of the means of small samples is larger than the sampling error of the means of large samples.

It is this third point in particular that inferential statistics address—the issue of how much confidence we can afford to have in comparing the mean of the experimental group with that of the control group when we know that small sample means are unreliable. The haunting question remains: "Is the difference we find between the two means due to our treatment or merely due to the fact that small sample means bounce around even without treatment?" We remain caught on the horns of a dilemma: On the one hand we can't afford to measure very large numbers of subjects in order to determine the *population* mean accurately; yet on the other hand we know the means of small samples provide unreliable estimates of the populations they are supposed to represent.

We need some rational way of helping us decide when sample means are reasonably accurate estimates of their respective population means—methods of deciding when sample "facts" are reliable estimates of population "facts." The rational solution we rely upon is called *sampling theory*. A detailed examination of this topic lies beyond the scope of our discussion; nevertheless if you keep the following principles in mind, you are less likely to be hoodwinked by chance playing tricks with sample means:

1. Sample means become an increasingly accurate estimate of their population means as you increase the size of your samples. We recommend that you use sample sizes of 30 or more per group when you want to compare an experimental sample with a control sample.
2. When deciding whether you have obtained a significant difference between your experimental and control groups, you must take into account:
   a. the size of the difference between their means, *and*
   b. the variability (i.e., standard deviation) of the two samples—the size of the variability in each sample and the similarity of the variability in each sample, *and*
   c. how much the two samples overlap each other.

Particularly when you're getting started on social science research, it is wise to obtain this information by plotting your results. Notice in the following three figures how the two means remain the same, but the variability and the degree of overlap differ; particularly notice how such differences suggest very different conclusions.

The three figures present three different versions of an experiment to test whether students using a program instruction text (Group 1) perform better on a math exam than students using a standard instruction manual (Group 2). As noted in all three examples, the experimental group scores five points higher than does the control group on the math exam. But notice in Figure 12–5 how the samples show wide variability and large overlap—such differences as this between samples occur frequently by chance. Therefore we conclude since such differences occur relatively frequently in random sampling we can have little or no confidence that the program text is responsible—that is, we can frequently expect such differences even in two samples receiving identical treatments—using the same text.

In Figure 12–6 the difference between the means remains the same (5), but the sample variability is less and so is the degree of overlap. Although such differences between samples occur by chance, more frequently than 5 times in 100

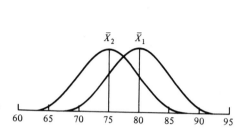

Math grades	
Group 1	Group 2
X_1	X_2
93	87
86	82
82	76
77	72
73	68
69	65
$\Sigma x_1 = 480$	$\Sigma x_2 = 450$
$\bar{X}_1 = 80$	$\bar{X}_2 = 75$
$\sigma x_1 = 8.80$	$\sigma x_2 = 8.39$
$N_1 = 6$	$N_2 = 6$

FIGURE 12-5

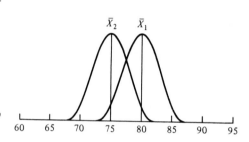

Math grades	
Group 1	Group 2
X_1	X_2
86	81
82	78
81	76
80	73
77	72
74	70
$\Sigma x_1 = 480$	$\Sigma x_2 = 450$
$\bar{X}_1 = 80$	$\bar{X}_2 = 75$
$\sigma x_1 = 4.14$	$\sigma x_2 = 4.09$
$N_1 = 6$	$N_2 = 6$

FIGURE 12-6

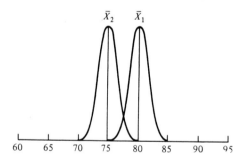

Math grades	
Group 1	Group 2
X_1	X_2
84	79
82	78
81	75
79	74
78	73
76	71
$\Sigma x_1 = 480$	$\Sigma x_2 = 450$
$\bar{X}_1 = 80$	$\bar{X}_2 = 75$
$\sigma x_1 = 2.89$	$\sigma x_2 = 3.03$
$N_1 = 6$	$N_2 = 6$

FIGURE 12-7

sample pairs, the result is promising and warrants increasing the sample sizes to see if the differences hold.

In the third case we can be relatively certain we have a difference "worth talking about"—the sample variance and overlap is relatively small, while the difference between the means remains at 5.

While eyeball examination increases our confidence in the results presented in Figure 12-7 over those in Figures 12-5 and 12-6, we can gain additional confidence by performing a statistical test (a *t* test). This test is designed to measure the "significance" of a difference between independent samples by comparing the difference you obtained with the difference chance alone can deal an experimenter. The procedure outlined in the following table uses data reflecting the differences we observed in Figure 12–7.

If we go to an appropriate map of chance (*t* table), we discover that for samples of this size this particular *t* value would occur rarely by chance alone—that is, if 100 such comparisons were made between *control* groups of this size, we would expect such a large *t* value to occur less than 5 times in 100 trials. So we can decide, on the one hand, that we have stumbled on one of these rare tricks of chance or decide, on the other hand, that it was not the work of chance but the influence of our treatment (the programmed text) that "pushed" the samples apart.

Samples of raw data for the other two cases are listed in the figures, so for those who wish to examine the likelihood of obtaining these sample differences by chance alone, one can compare the resulting *t* values with those provided in

TABLE 12–3   *t* Test for Small Independent Samples

MATH GRADES		DEVIATIONS			
GROUP 1[a] X_1	GROUP 2[b] X_2	x_1	x_2	x_1^2	x_2^2
84	79	4	4	16	16
82	78	2	3	4	9
81	75	1	0	1	0
79	74	−1	−1	1	1
78	73	−2	−2	4	4
76	71	−4	−4	16	16

$$\Sigma X_1 = 480 \quad \Sigma X_2 = 450 \qquad\qquad \Sigma x_1^2 = 42 \quad \Sigma x_2^2 = 46$$
$$\bar{X}_1 = 80 \quad \bar{X}_2 = 75$$
$$N_1 = 6 \quad N_2 = 6$$

$$t = \frac{\bar{X}_1 - \bar{X}_2}{\sqrt{\dfrac{\Sigma x_1^2 + \Sigma x_2^2}{N_1 + N_2 - 2}\left(\dfrac{N_1 + N_2}{N_1 \cdot N_2}\right)}}$$

$$t = \frac{80 - 75}{\sqrt{\dfrac{42 + 46}{6 + 6 - 2}\left(\dfrac{6 + 6}{6 \cdot 6}\right)}} = \frac{5}{\sqrt{\dfrac{88}{10}\left(\dfrac{12}{36}\right)}}$$

$$t = \frac{5}{\sqrt{2.93}} = 2.92$$

For *df* = 10 *p* < .05[c]

[a]Group 1 studied from programmed text (Experimental).
[b]Group 2 studied from standard text (Control).
[c]For degrees of freedom = 10 ($N_1 + N_2 - 2$) probability (*p*) of obtaining *t* = 2.92 by chance is less than 5 in 100.

the *t* tables of any standard statistical text (for degrees of freedom = 10, or $N_1 + N_2 - 2$).

ANALYSIS OF VARIANCE (ANOVA)

Just as a *t* test can help you decide whether your experimental and control groups differ by more than the hand of chance usually arranges, an *F* test, analysis of variance (ANOVA), helps you decide whether your experimental group and several comparison groups are separated by differences greater than you would expect by chance alone.

One-Way Analysis of Variance (One Independent Variable)

For example, you may be studying the effects of alcohol (independent variable) on coordination (dependent variable) using a control group, group 1 (12 ounces of Coke); and three experimental groups: group 2 (12 ounces of Coke plus 1 ounce of alcohol); group 3 (12 ounces of Coke plus 2 ounces of alcohol); group 4 (12 ounces of Coke plus 3 ounces of alcohol). You speculate that as alcohol consumption increases, so too will errors in coordination, but when you plot your results (Figure 12–8) it doesn't look that way—group 3 has the lowest, not the second highest, error rate as predicted.

The question is, are these more than chance differences? An analysis of variance (*F* test) helps you decide whether two or more of these groups differ by more than chance expectancy. An *F* test is based on the differences between the means, in relation to the variability and the size of the groups. A significant *F* test, in this alcohol experiment, tells us that two or more of the groups differ by more than expected by the usual tricks of chance.

Having obtained a significant *F* we can now use eyeball analysis and *t* tests to decide which particular pairs of groups differ. We find that group 4 differs significantly from all of the groups; that groups 1 and 2 did not differ, nor did groups 1 and 3, but groups 2 and 3 did. On the basis of *this* study and this sample we conclude that 3 ounces of alcohol disrupts coordination, and tentatively decide that 2 ounces *may* facilitate coordination.

FIGURE 12–8. Effect of Alcohol on Errors of Coordination.

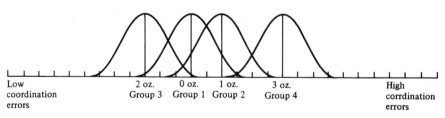

| Low coordination errors | 2 oz. Group 3 | 0 oz. Group 1 | 1 oz. Group 2 | 3 oz. Group 4 | High corrdination errors |

You are probably wondering why bother doing an analysis of variance at all since you end up doing *t* tests anyway. There are two reasons. First, if you fail to get a significant *F* test this tells you the differences you observe are likely due to chance, and so you stop the analysis right there, saving yourself the bother of doing a series of *t* tests (six in our example). Second, when comparing several groups an initial *F* test provides more protection against flukes of chance than you get by starting with a series of *t* tests.

But ANOVA has another great advantage; it enables researchers to measure the combined effects of two or more treatment variables; it enables us to measure what are called *interaction* effects.

Two-Way Analysis of Variance (Two Independent Variables)

In the foregoing example we studied the effect on coordination of *one* treatment variable (alcohol—a one-way analysis of variance). But suppose we wanted to add another treatment variable, such as drinking history. We now have two independent or treatment variables. This involves a *two-way* analysis of variance, the columns representing the one treatment variable (four levels of alcohol) and the rows representing the other treatment variable (two levels of drinking history).

	Alcohol			
	0 OZ.	1 OZ.	2 OZ.	3 OZ.
Novice drinkers	Group 1	Group 2	Group 3	Group 4
Practiced drinkers	Group 5	Group 6	Group 7	Group 8

The *F* tests in a 2 × 4 analysis of variance can measure quantitatively what we observe in Figure 12–9b.

FIGURE 12–9.   Effects of Alcohol and Drinking History on Errors of Coordination.

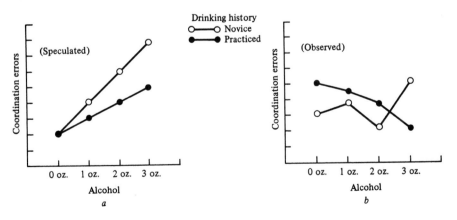

From these observed results (Figure 12–9b) we can't say that more alcohol leads to significantly more errors in coordination—you *can't* make any across-the-board generalization about the effects of alcohol in this study. In addition, you can't, for example, say that being a novice drinker leads to significantly fewer errors—you *can't* make any across-the-board generalizations about drinking history. However, you *can* say "It all depends," it depends on special combinations of amount of alcohol *and* of drinking history—that's an interaction effect.

We usually hope for straightforward simple effects like those in Figure 12–9a. In this tidy speculation, errors of coordination increase with amount of alcohol consumed. They increase for both novice and for practiced drinkers, but more so for novice drinkers. Now these are results that make sense, results that are simple enough to remember.

Instead of such simple results, however, we frequently obtain results like those plotted in Figure 12–9b; we obtain effects where factors combine in "funny" ways: Novice drinkers show fewest errors on 2 ounces of alcohol and the greatest number of errors on 3 ounces of alcohol, while practiced drinkers show fewest number of errors at 3 ounces of alcohol. Analyses of variance enable researchers to measure the statistical significance of complex effects of various treatment combinations using two-way, three-way, or four-way ANOVA designs.

When examining social science research, look for interaction effects, and expect some treatments and some people to combine in surprising ways. Look for interaction effects in the graphs, in the statistical analyses, and in the discussion. How does alcohol affect coordination? It all depends on amount of alcohol, *and* on drinking history, *and* on ?

Summarizing, we now have the scattergram to help us decide *visually* how closely two measures (taken on the same individuals) are related and the correlation coefficient to help us decide *quantitatively* the degree of relationship. We can also map sample distributions to help us decide *visually* how two or more samples compare in terms of their means, variability, and overlap, and we have the *t* test to help us decide *quantitatively* the statistical significance of the differences between 2 groups, and analysis of variance to help us decide quantitatively the statistical significance of the difference between more than 2 groups.

Chi Square

Another popular and useful statistical tool—the chi square test—helps us decide whether the distribution, particularly of nominal scale data, deviates significantly from chance. For example, one student proposed the provocative hypothesis that women are both more softhearted and softheaded than are men. He also speculated that, since Republicans are more hardheaded and practical than are Democrats, women would tend to support the Democratic party.

To test his hypothesis he drew two samples at random of 60 women and 60 men from a large introductory psychology class. He then had each individual indicate his or her political preference for one of the two main parties. He got usable data from 50 males and 50 females (that is, after refusals and after eliminating those choosing other parties—for example, the Communist party).

He reported the following results:

	Female	Male
REPUBLICANS	10	30
DEMOCRATS	40	20

Based on visual inspection he concluded his hypothesis was supported. On being challenged to provide evidence that such a difference was not merely due to chance (to sampling error), he performed a chi square test—very simply as follows:

TABLE 12–4   Chi Square Test

---

1. General Chi Square (X^2) Formula:

$$X^2 = \sum_{r=1}^{r} \sum_{c=1}^{c} \frac{(fo - fe)^2}{fe}$$

where: fo = Observed frequency in a given cell.
   fe = Expected frequency in that cell.
The Chi Square is obtained by adding the differences between fo and fe (according to the formula) over all cells—the cells in the rows (r), and columns (c) of the table.

2. Example of Chi Square for 2 by 2 contingency table:

	WOMEN		MEN	
	$fe =$ 20		20	
Republican	$fo =$ 10		30	40
		30		30
Democrat	40		20	60
	50		50	100

$$X^2 = \frac{(10 - 20)^2}{20} + \frac{(30 - 20)^2}{20} + \frac{(40 - 30)^2}{30} + \frac{(20 - 30)^2}{30}$$
$$= 5 + 5 + 3.3 + 3.3$$
$$= 16.6. \quad df = 1 \quad p < .001^a$$

---

[a]For degrees of freedom = 1 (number of rows − 1) (number of columns − 1), probability of X^2 = 16.6 less than one chance in 1000.
Experts disagree over the need for a Yate's correction for small cell frequencies and for all tables with degrees of freedom less than 2. Our practice is to use the correction if a cell frequency is less than 10, or if the chi square level of significance is borderline around the 0.05 level. We follow Guilford (1956, p. 237): "The correction is particularly important when chi square turns out to be near a point of division between critical regions." With the correction, the chi square formula becomes:

$$x^2 = \sum_{r=1}^{r} \sum_{c=1}^{c} \frac{([fo - fe] - .5)^2}{fe}$$

Notice that in Table 12–4 the expected cell frequencies appear in the small boxes within each cell. If you have a complex table, consult a standard statistics text for help in computing these expected frequencies. In our table we simply went to the row totals and assumed an *expected frequency* of 50–50—half women, half men.

For 2-by-2 tables a raw score formula allows you to avoid calculating expected frequencies by merely using the observed frequencies in each cell *(A, B, C, D)*:

A	*B*
C	*D*

	Female	Male	
REPUBLICAN	*A* 10	*B* 30	40
DEMOCRAT	*C* 40	*D* 20	60
	50	50	100 (*N*)

$$X^2 = \frac{N(AD - BC)^2}{(A + B)(C + D)(A + C)(B + D)}$$

$$X^2 = \frac{100(10 \times 20 - 30 \times 40)^2}{(10 + 30)(40 + 20)(10 + 40)(30 + 20)} = 16.6^{[1]}$$

$$d.f. = 1 \qquad p < .001$$

Having demonstrated that such a combination of cell frequencies is likely to occur less than one time in 1000 by chance, the student expresses greater confidence in his hypothesis. An unconvinced student repeats the study, and she obtains less dramatic but still significant results:

	Women	Men
REPUBLICANS	18	28
DEMOCRATS	32	22

$$X^2 = 4.03 \qquad p < .05$$

The student decides that there is some evidence that women do indeed tend to support the Democrats, not because they are softhearted and softheaded, but rather because "intelligent" people tend to support the Democratic party, whereas

[1]X^2 for raw score formula will closely approximate that found by calculating differences between observed and expected frequencies.

simple-minded people support the Republicans. She then did a study showing that Democrats have higher grade-point averages than Republicans do:

Academic Performance

	ABOVE MEDIAN	BELOW MEDIAN	
REPUBLICAN	19 [23]	27 [23]	46
DEMOCRAT	31 [27]	23 [27]	54
	50	50	100

$$X^2 = 2.58, \qquad d.f.\ 1, \qquad p < .20$$

In this study the researcher drew a random sample of 100 students from another introductory psychology class and obtained the results tabulated in the preceding contingency table. It turned out, by chance, that there were 46 Republicans in her sample, and so if there was no relationship between political affiliation and academic performance, you would expect, by chance, a 50–50 split—expected frequencies (*fe*) of 23 above the whole group median and 23 below. Similarly, for the Democrats a 50–50 split would lead to expected frequencies of 27 above and 27 below the median academic performance.

On the basis of eyeball analysis the researcher is pleased with the results—more Democrats than Republicans scored above the academic median, quite a few more. Of course there were more Democrats in the sample, so that is why it is important to figure out the expected frequencies for each cell; that is why it is important to do an appropriate statistical test—like a chi square. The researcher finds, to her disappointment, that a chi square of 2.58 (*d.f.* = 1) can occur by chance close to 20 times in 100 random trials. Therefore she hasn't obtained a *statistically* significant result—which by custom is set at less than 5 times in 100 random trials. Nevertheless, it is an *emotionally* significant result, and she argues that her findings represent a strong trend supporting her hypothesis—she will increase her sample size and prove her hypothesis next semester. Others, who disagree with her hypothesis (quite a few Republicans, for example), accuse her of trying to read her own bias into the results, rather than accepting the quantitative judgment of her own statistical test.

As you can imagine, the argument continues and will continue. The chi square provides a simple and useful tool to help wage this kind of war *quantitatively* and provides a simple map of chance against which to compare your research results.

But notice when you establish chi square categories or cells (a contingency table), you provide opportunities to test how fuzzy the categories are—to test how large a region of uncertainty they contain: (O)

For example, arguments about whether someone belongs to the male or female category rarely arise, apart from the female Olympics. However, whether to categorize someone as a Republican or a Democrat can become tricky. Do you accept as reliable evidence the fact that they put a pencil mark after Republican or after Democrat on one question on a questionnaire? Or do you ask for evidence of party membership? Or do you ask for evidence of active party support for at least three years? Until such issues are resolved, the various categories or cells of our first chi square table should perhaps be drawn as follows:

	Female	Male	?
REPUBLICAN	10	30	40
DEMOCRAT	40	20	60
	50	50	100

Therefore keep a weather eye open for the fuzziness of the categories of all scales, but particularly with nominal scale data of the type used in the cells of chi square contingency tables. When you find such fuzziness—independent observers can't agree on who goes into which cell—take the results with a grain of salt.

WHICH TEST?

Consumers as well as practitioners of science must learn to "read" graphic and quantitative descriptions of the degree of relationship between observational samples (scattergrams and correlations) and the differences between observational samples (distribution plots, contingency tables, *t* tests, analysis of variance, chi squares).

You will encounter a host of statistical tools. Some, called *parametric statistics,* are based on the assumption that your samples have been drawn from populations that are *normally* distributed and have the *same variability.* Other statistical tests, called *nonparametric,* do not assume normalcy, or variance equivalence (homogeneity) in populations, and so can be applied to a wide range of observations. Arguments among experts continue over when to use a given statistical test—some preferring to use nonparametric statistics when sample data suggest the parent populations are nonnormal (skewed) and/or the experimental and control populations have markedly different variances. Other experts believe that, since parametric tests are more powerful—detect finer differences—and are not all that sensitive to violations of the normalcy and variance assumptions, the parametric test should ordinarily be used. Our bias is to examine the data from several angles: Plot it and examine it visually; do parametric tests where possible; do nonparametric tests when in doubt or when parametric tests aren't available.

The following brief list of nonparametric and parametric statistical tests are more or less matched in terms of the kind of relationships, or differences, they are designed to measure:

NONPARAMETRIC	PARAMETRIC

Spearman rank-order correlation . . . . .Pearson product-moment correlation

Sign test $\Big\}$ . . . .—*t* test for related samples (e.g., two
Wilcoxon test measures on the same subjects)

Mann-Whitney U test $\Big\}$ . . . .—*t* test for independent samples
Median test

Kurskall Wallis one-way
   link test $\Big\}$ . . . . .One-way analysis of variance
Median test

Freedman two-way ranks test . . . . .One-way analysis of variance with repeat
measures

Chi square test . . . . .No comparable parametric test

The detailed procedure for doing these tests can be found not only in statistical texts but also increasingly in the instruction manuals for desk calculators and microcomputers.

However, if in doubt, plot your data or a random sample of it. If you are a consumer, keep a weather eye out for information that lets you do rough plots in your mind's eye of sample sizes, variances, and overlap and also watch for fuzzy categories or scales as well.

The preceding lists represent different statistical ways of helping you to quantitatively describe your observations—nominal scale observations, ordinal scale observations, or interval and ratio scale observations. Each method lends itself to certain scales, and each method also provides a suitable map of chance so you can determine how often the differences, or changes, you observed would likely occur by chance alone—would occur between a series of two groups receiving no treatment or between a series of groups receiving the same treatment.

Statistical tests help to identify which of the many observations you make are worth talking about—worth talking about in the sense that they are statistically improbable. By *custom* social scientists consider differences that occur less than 5 times in 100 by chance alone as *statistically improbable*. So when you read, "A finding is significant at the .05 level of confidence," or "*p* is less than .05," it simply means that the researcher is reporting that such a difference between the experimental and control groups would probably occur less than 5 times in 100 if they had been drawn from the same population—that is, if there is no *real* difference.

But if the .05 level (5 times in 100 trials) is merely set by custom as the arbitrary boundary line of statistically improbable events, wouldn't it be safer to set an even more stringent boundary line? For example, why not define a statistically improbable event as one that occurs only once in 100 trials or once in 1000 trials? Then if you turned up such a rare event in your experiment, you could be almost certain it wasn't due to chance playing a trick on you. Well, the reason is that by reducing the risk of being hoodwinked by chance you increase the risk of throwing the baby out with the bathwater. By reducing the risk of one kind of error, you increase the risk of another.

Type I and Type II Errors

As noted, maps of chance provide no ironclad protection against error—particularly against two types of error. For example, in deciding whether a coin is biased, if you're "trigger happy" you can accuse the tosser of using a biased coin too soon, after perhaps five heads in a row. By rejecting the possible role of chance, you commit a *Type I error*.

On the other hand you can be too cautious and not decide to accuse the tosser of using a biased coin until 12 or 15 heads in a row have been tossed. By rejecting the possible influence of bias you commit a *Type II error*.

Technically we are talking about accepting or rejecting the *null hypothesis*. The null hypothesis states that there is no real difference between the pretest and posttest or between the experimental and control group. It presumes that whatever differences do exist are due to random chance fluctuations.

A Type I error occurs when you erroneously reject the null hypothesis—when you mistake a chance difference for a treatment difference, when you mistake a chance grimace for a hostile look, when you mistake a useless drug for a curative one, when you mistake a true coin for a biased one.

But just as you can be too trigger happy—seeing real differences where only chance differences exist—you can also be overly cautious—refusing to recognize real differences. When you go on betting tails after the tosser has thrown 15 heads in a row, well, you're making a mistake, and that kind of mistake is called a *Type II error*.

Someone who cries, "Wolf," when a spring breeze rustles the leaves commits a Type I error, someone who says, "Nice puppy," as the wolf snaps at his hand commits a Type II error.

The likelihood of committing one or the other of these types of errors may be related to personality characteristics—like the tendency to take or avoid risks. However, another way of thinking about the likelihood of making a Type I error is in terms of the maps of chance you use to decide whether you've got a difference worth talking about. If you wish to reduce the risk of Type I errors, you only accept differences, or results, that occur very rarely by chance—that is, once in 100 trials or once in 1000 trials. On the other hand, if you wish to reduce the risk of making Type II errors, you move in the other direction by accepting experimental results that could occur by chance 5 times, 10 times, or even 20 times out of 100 random trials.

As you can see reducing the risk of one kind of error increases the risk of making the other. Therefore it is not merely a question of trying to avoid making an error; it becomes a question of avoiding a high-cost error. If you're betting pennies on whether a given coin is biased or not, the cost of making a Type I or a Type II error is probably no more than 25¢—so who cares. But if you're betting your life on a new surgical treatment for your brain tumor, you care; your family and friends care; the surgeons care.

In such a situation you look at the results to date: Out of 10 patients with your kind of tumor who have had the new surgery, the results are 3 dead, 7 living and somewhat improved. Is it really 7 out of 10—70 percent chance of success?

Or is it really 50–50 or 30–70? Only more trials will decide! Should you wait for the results of more "experiments" or accept surgery now? You can decide surgery works (is better than 50–50), elect surgery, risk a Type I error, and maybe die under the knife. Or you can decide to wait for more data, risk a Type II error, and die from an enlarged, inoperable tumor.

Therefore Type I and Type II errors represent more than esoteric statistical phrases; rather, they represent a rational approach to analyzing the risks involved in making decisions under uncertain and sometimes critical conditions.

Fortunately most decisions don't present us with such pressing, high-risk situations. Under more mundane circumstances how should you, a consumer of science, respond to a statistically improbable research result—one that in your opinion balances the risks of Type I and Type II errors? What questions might an informed consumer of science ask? You might consider the following:

1. "Yes, I understand your finding is statistically improbable, but it could still be due to chance. Therefore before I assign it a high level of personal confidence, I would like to see some independent researcher repeat the study and obtain similar results."
2. "Granted you obtained a statistically improbable result, but it could be due, not to your treatment, but to some other shaping influence:
   a. to an unusual trick of chance;
   b. to error in data recording or calculating;
   c. to, I hesitate to say it, fraud.
   Therefore before I assign it a high level of personal confidence, I'd like to see some independent researcher repeat the study and obtain similar results with larger samples of people than you used."

Independent and consistent labeling are the hallmarks of objective language, as we discussed in a previous chapter. Independent and consistent replication of observations are the hallmark of objective science. Statistically significant results from one-shot experiments are no substitute for independent and consistent replication of experiments. While statistical tools are helpful, they remain just that—tools. In skilled hands they help us explore a multilayered reality. In unskilled or irresponsible hands they help foul the media and the scientific literature with false claims and numerical noise.

n = 1 RESEARCH (STUDYING ONE PERSON)

We have stressed the need for large experimental and control group samples if we want to obtain reliable estimates of the target populations they represent. How then can we hope to have any confidence in very small sample research, in research involving only one subject? Recent publications (see Robinson & Foster, 1979) explore this question in detail, and we presented an example of an n-of-1 study in Chapter 10 (longitudinal methods).

Here we merely want to point out that if the population of behavior you want to describe or predict is not human behavior in general, but rather the behavior of a *particular individual* being studied, then n-of-1 research can be powerful research.

However, such research is relatively rare in psychology because we lack familiar statistical tests to help us decide whether the changes we see in our single subject's behavior are due to our antecedent treatment—the antidepressant drug—or mainly, or totally, due to the tricks of chance—to one or more of the rogues. Nevertheless, you can increase your confidence in your findings by: (1) repeating the treatment on the same subject; or if this is impossible, (2) repeating the treatment on the same "type" of subject—another subject similar in degree and duration of depression, someone drawn from the group of subjects you wish to generalize to.

This *n*-of-1-at-a-time research is common in animal studies and typically involves no statistical tests of significance. Confidence in their findings is based on: (1) knowing their subjects well enough to recognize a change warranting further investigation; (2) using subjects of the same type—similar heredity, age, sex, early experience; and (3) aborting studies in which they "see" the rogues running wild.

Thus there is a solid tradition in science for $n = 1$ studies, with confidence based not on statistical tests, but on high familiarity with the subject matter, and familiarity too with known rogues who haunt the network under investigation. Like any research method it carries with it regions of uncertainty; nevertheless, it remains a potentially powerful but neglected mode of study—notice most mothers, and many family physicians, are skilled $n = 1$ investigators who learn to differentiate between significant changes in physical and psychological dimensions on the one hand, and mild, random fluctuations and malingering on the other.

Remember that in group comparisons—comparing an experimental group with a control group—we noted that reliable differences depend on (1) the difference between the means of the two samples; (2) the size of the variability within the two samples; and (3) the degree of overlap between the two samples.

Exactly the same principles apply in *n*-of-1 research except instead of measuring a group of individuals under control conditions and another group of individuals under experimental conditions, in *n*-of-1 research, in its simplest form, we take repeat measurements of the same individual under control conditions, then repeat measurements under experimental conditions. Following this we compare the means and variances of those two observational samples. If by eyeball inspection the means differ "quite a bit" *and* there is little or no overlap between the two samples—the control and experimental samples—of behavior of that individual, then we seriously entertain the possibility that our treatment "worked" for that individual, at that time. If you want to see if it will work again for that subject, you use a treatment reversal design (Chapter 10).

If you want to see if a treatment will work on somebody else, choose another individual, *at random,* from the target population and try your treatment again.

If you keep these principles in mind, *n*-of-1 research becomes a powerful method of investigation. As in group research, plot your results to get a "feel" for your data. To reach conclusions about the power of their treatment, most researchers rely on visual inspection of stable baseline (control observations) and significant follow-up observations (treatment and posttreatment). Some n-of-1 researchers apply statistical tests suitable for intrasubject, rather than intersubject, comparisons.

If you're interested in n-of-1 studies, start by using yourself as a subject. The example at the end of Chapter 7 might give you some ideas.

SUMMARY

In the toolbox of social science, statistical devices abound. Descriptive statistics help package observations into mind-sized bites. Inferential statistics help us defend ourselves from being perpetually hoodwinked by capricious chance.

But remember that *statistically significant* findings represent a beginning, not a research climax. A statistically significant finding encourages further investigation but does not bestow a label of truth on your results. After having obtained an "improbable" research finding, you write up your research project (as outlined in Chapter 15) and submit it to a journal. Your manuscript is then critically examined by several reviewers familiar with your research area, and they decide whether your experimental procedure, your maps of chance, and your calculations seem appropriate and also whether your conclusions appear reasonable. Only if you pass all these tests is your manuscript then published. Then, other investigators can check your findings on new samples of people, perhaps controlling more carefully against the rogues, taking longer baseline measurements, or using larger samples.

In brief, although statistical tests (like t tests and chi squares) help you decide whether you have obtained a statistically significant result, it still requires experience, critical judgment, and continued research to determine whether you have obtained a result of scientific import or social consequence. Research requires not only tenacity but also courage. The researchers' code might well be taken from the famous poem "Invictus" by W. E. Henley:

Under the bludgeonings of chance my head is bloody, but unbowed.

chapter 13

Validity—The Reach of Research

In the preceding chapters we have discussed the language of science, the sieves of science, the measuring scales of science, and the statistics of science—these are the tools we use to explore and map multilayered reality. But how accurate are the maps we produce—how *valid* are they?

INTERNAL AND EXTERNAL VALIDITY

Campbell and Stanley (1966) provided the key concepts of *internal* and *external* validity which we, like a host of other writers, use to analyze research validity.

When you do obtain a significant difference between pretreatment and post-treatment observations or between experimental and control groups, you must still decide whether or not that difference was due to your favorite suspect—that is, to your "treatment." Or was the difference due to the four rogues (history, maturation, testing, instrument decay) acting singly or in combination; to data "mortality" (selective data loss) or to data "drift" (technically called *regression toward the mean);* to fraud; or to data error (mistakes in data recording or calculation). These questions all concern internal validity—internal in the sense that they can all influence the results *within* the time-space frame of your specific experiment.

The following are some of the ways these internal validity threats can be reduced: by using control and experimental groups to which subjects have been assigned at random; by using reverse treatment designs; by obtaining stable baseline and long-term follow-up observations; by plotting our data; by using statistical tests; by using nonreactive measures; and, most importantly, by *independent* replication of the experiment.

By skillful use of these methods we confront questions of internal validity— we help assure ourselves and skeptical others that our *specific* treatment conducted by specific experimenters, or observers, does indeed lead to significant differences between our specific samples of subjects, on our specific measures; in our specific experimental context; at that specific time; using that specific statistical test. No mean accomplishment, but . . . surely not the prime purpose of research.

The purpose of using a specific sample of subjects was to *represent* a larger parent population. The purpose of using a specific treatment was to represent a class of treatments; the purpose of using a specific researcher was to represent a class of researchers; and so on. How representative the specific subjects, treatments, measures, or researchers are of their parent populations determine the extent of their *external validity*—determine how far our results, obtained inside the experimental space-time frame (*internally valid* results), reach beyond, or generalize, to a larger space-time frame— that is, how well a specific drug treatment in a given setting generalizes to similar drugs, administered by other trained researchers, in other settings.

In brief, whether or not a specific mix of the treatment procedure worked on the specific subjects inside the particular experimental context involves questions of internal validity. Whether the specific treatment mix will generalize to a useful class of treatments, a larger class of subjects, a larger class of experimenters, or a larger class of measures outside, or external to, a specific experimental context involves questions of external validity.

Issues of internal validity refer to *observed* subjects, to observed treatment procedures, and to observed experimental contexts. Questions of external validity refer to the generalization of these observations to classes of subjects, classes of treatments, and classes of experimental contexts not yet observed but which the sample of specific observations represents!

The following tables summarize the rogue sources of variance that can threaten internal and external validity:

THREATS TO INTERNAL VALIDITY

1. History—in-the-gap suspects.
2. Maturation—time-tied suspects.
3. Testing—on-stage suspects.
4. Instrument decay—elastic-ruler suspects.

5. Statistical regression—extreme data points drift toward the mean.

6. Subject selection—pretreatment differences between experimental and control samples.

7. Mortality or data loss—a biased "drop out" of subjects or data from either the experimental or control group.

8. Interactions—any of the above may combine with the treatment (that is, prime it, magnify it, depress it).

THREATS TO EXTERNAL VALIDITY

1. Sample restrictions—The people studied, or observed, are not a representative sample of the target population—of the people you really want to study.

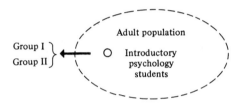

2. Measurement restrictions—The specific observations you make are not a representative sample of the target behavior—of the behavior you really want to study and understand.

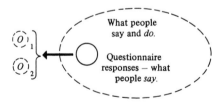

3. Treatment restrictions—The specific treatment you apply is not a representative sample of the target treatment—the type of treatment you really want to study and evaluate.

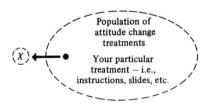

4. Research context restrictions—Your specific research context is not a representative sample of target contexts—your "hothouse" conditions place restrictions on how far you can generalize to field conditions.

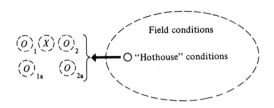

SAMPLING RESTRICTIONS

In considering threats to external validity, remember that researchers may not be able, or willing, to select a representative sample of subjects from their target populations; they may end up, for convenience, studying attitude change in undergraduate psychology students (accessible population). No problem—if you recognize the resulting sampling restriction, if you recognize the limitations this restricted sampling places on the generalizations you subsequently make.

Your results obviously cannot be generalized to adult Americans, but only to introductory psychology students. To all introductory psychology students? No, only to those who have a chance of getting into your sample—the ones on a given campus. Yes, if you put the names of all first-year psychology students on that campus into a hat and then draw your sample at random. But that is rarely done. More commonly, researchers use students from Professor X's introductory class because it's readily accessible (that is, he's interested in your research topic, or he's happy to give up an hour's lecture time). You can now generalize to all introductory psychology students in Professor X's class. Or can you? You can if you put all the names in a hat and draw your sample at random—or included the whole class in your study. But you may have had to settle for volunteers. So you put their names in a hat and select your experimental and control group samples—now you can generalize to volunteer introductory psychology students in Professor X's first semester 1986 psychology class.[1]

This represents a drastic shrinkage from the adult American target population—a drastic shrinkage even from the general population of introductory psychology students. As a practitioner or a consumer of science, you can see how important it is that you identify the actual population the experimental sample represents—it includes only the people whose names had an equal chance of getting into the hat. If they were a random sample of volunteers from Professor X's psychology class, then you can generalize the results you obtained from the sample of volunteers to the hatful of volunteers from which you drew that sample.

But surely that's being unduly cautious. Why not generalize to Professor X's whole class? In fact why not generalize to psychology students on that campus or to all introductory psychology students?

Such generalizations are unwarranted for a variety of reasons: because vol-

---

[1]If you had been measuring height or weight, would you be less cautious about generalizing? No? Maybe volunteers are oral gratifiers and eat more.

unteers frequently respond differently from nonvolunteers; because Professor X lectures long and loud on the evils of prejudice and so has probably primed his students; because this particular university has very high entrance standards and so the students are not intellectually or academically representative of psychology students on many other campuses. In brief, sampling restrictions usually place strong limitations on the external validity, or generalizability, of social science research.

MEASUREMENT RESTRICTIONS

Just as the samples you select may underrepresent the people you wish to study, so too the measure or dependent variable you select may be a limited measure of the behavior you wish to study. Just as the limited sample of people you select restricts the generalizations you can make about people, so also the specific measuring scales you select and apply further restrict your generalizations to the behavior accessible through that measuring scale or that method of observation.

Therefore if we select a questionnaire to study attitude change and use only volunteers from Professor X's class, our generalizations are doubly restricted: First, we can only generalize to the hatful of volunteers from which we drew our research sample; and second, we can only generalize to changes in *questionnaire* behavior. We may legitimately claim that following treatment our subjects can indeed "talk" a better game, but we can't claim that they can play a better game—not unless we also employ unobtrusive follow-up observations in our sample of dependent measures.

How far you can generalize from what people *say* they will do to what they *actually* do concerns a growing number of social scientists. While the details of the debate lie beyond this discussion, consumers of science should be aware that the strong relationship assumed to exist between attitudes and behavior appears to be much more flimsy than we once supposed (Ajzen & Fishbein, 1980). Yes, wise consumers of science will be cautious about generalizing too far from observations obtained by questionnaires, ratings, and interviews because people appear to talk a better game than they play—whether the target behavior is bridge, tennis, or tolerance for minorities.

Before considering the validity of tests and questionnaires, recall that measuring scales should be reliable as well as valid. A clock is reliable if it keeps *consistent* time. The clock is valid if it keeps the *correct* time. If your clock is consistently two hours behind the official time, it is nevertheless a reliable clock—it measures time consistently, but it is not a valid measure of the time in your zone. Therefore you can have a measure that is reliable but invalid; however, to be valid, a measure must also be reasonably reliable.

Since so much social science and educational research employs tests and questionnaires, the validity of such instruments deserves special mention.

Types of Test Validity

When you complete a test or questionnaire you usually want to know (1) what your score is and (2) what that score means. There are at least four related kinds of larger meaning or validity associated with a test: (1) content validity, (2) predictive validity, (3) concurrent validity, and (4) construct validity.

If we critically examine the items on a test—say a mathematical aptitude test—and determine that they include a representative sample of simple, average, and difficult questions drawn from each of the domains of arithmetic, algebra, trigonometry, and calculus, we conclude that the test has reasonable *content validity*—that is, it represents well the population of mathematical questions.

Next, to the degree your score on one test helps estimate your current score on a different test, then the first test shows *concurrent validity* with the second. For example, if by knowing you scored two standard deviations above the mean in a mathematical ability test, we can then accurately estimate your *current* score on a mechanical aptitude test to be one to two standard deviations above the mean—we have evidence of concurrent validity.

Furthermore, if on the basis of your high score on mathematical ability we can make a better-than-chance prediction that in two years you will graduate in the top half of your class in electrical engineering, we have evidence of *predictive validity*—predictive validity involves a significant interval of time between the two measurements or observations.

Now we come to *construct validity* which, while important, is also difficult to explain. A construct is a complex speculative dimension (for instance, anxiety, intelligence, sociability) that represents a network of relationships. No single test or study defines a construct. In fact, a given test may be related to several constructs—for example, observed performance on a mathematical test may help infer (1) mathematical ability, (2) intelligence level, (3) anxiety level, (4) vocational interest.

Estimating the validity of a construct—intelligence, for example—is an ongoing research activity and involves exploring the emerging network of concurrent and predictive relationships through which "intelligence" appears to run.

The value of a construct lies not only in helping you organize and simplify a network of current knowledge but also in enabling you to make valid and surprising predictions.

While these four types of validity typically apply to tests and questionnaires, the principles on which they are based apply to almost all forms of measurement—a measure lacks generalizability to the extent that it lacks content, concurrent, predictive, and construct validity.

TREATMENT RESTRICTIONS

Just as the specific sample of people and the specific measures you select may both underrepresent your target populations, so too may your specific treatment underrepresent the general treatments (or treatment construct) you wish to study.

For example, your hypothesis may be that attitudes change toward minority group members following an emotionally involving experience in which the experimental group members witness a majority group member helping a minority group member out of a crisis. It's your belief that the experience of witnessing the rescue scene should be as realistic as possible. Since such scenes are difficult to engineer, you settle for a movie scene—you restrict your population of treatments to film simulations. In order to get your experimental subjects emotionally involved (to identify with the ''hero'' and the ''victim''), you want them to watch the whole movie. However, you can only have 50 minutes of Professor X's class time for everything: pretest $(O)_1$, film (treatment (X)), and posttest $(O)_2$. Therefore you have to settle for a film clip—further restricting your treatment population to accessible film clips.

As if that wasn't bad enough, the sound on the film clip is poor at times, and you're not sure whether it ''broke the mood'' of those who were emotionally involved.

Thus you drastically and successively reduce the size of the population of treatments you started with. Nevertheless, you did get a shift in questionnaire responses in the predicted direction. What kind of generalizations can you make? Well, you can make them only to Professor X's volunteers, tested on that questionnaire, before and after that film clip.

Next time you decide you'll prescreen a series of appropriate film clips and draw one at random—then you can generalize to all the treatments (all the film clips) you've chosen, as well as to all the students who volunteered. If you draw your questionnaire at random from a hatful of appropriate questionnaires, you can generalize to those as well—keeping in mind the tricks that chance plays with small samples.

RESEARCH CONTEXT RESTRICTIONS

Just as the specific sample of people, *and* the particular measures, *and* the specific treatment all underrepresent your target populations of people, measures, and treatments, so too does the specific experimental context in which you do your study underrepresent the population of contexts you'd like to study and generalize to.

A host of features of the research context come to mind: The room was hot; the study was conducted between four and five in the afternoon; Professor X made a long introduction, not only making you rush your testing, but also he actually hinted at the purpose of the study.

So research context includes rogues that idiosyncratically can shape your results so as to reduce the generalizations you can make and, in turn, reduce your external validity. Major rogues to be watched for include (1) in-the-gap suspects combining with your treatment (hot room, darkness, sleepy); (2) time-tied suspects combining with a treatment (late in day, tired, cranky); (3) pretest or posttest priming (Professor X's hints at the purpose of the study); (4) Hawthorne effects (easy to change your prejudice for half an hour or so); and (5) experimenter effects (Oh yes, we forgot to mention the experimenter in the study was black—maybe the subjects changed their "attitudes" (questionnaire responses) because they sympathized with him, not with the "victim" in the film. What if a white experimenter were to replicate this study? Any guesses about the results?

Surely we're not now going to suggest that to increase generalizability a researcher should describe various and relevant research contexts, place them in a hat, draw one at random, and then use that one to guide a particular piece of research. Theoretically not a bad idea, and practically not so farfetched as it seems.

In a curious way science practices what we've been preaching—in a haphazard, semirandom way different researchers dip into these various hats drawing out this sample of subjects, that dependent variable, this independent variable, that research context. Taken one study at a time the external validity of any given study remains highly circumscribed, drastically restricted. But taken together the many researches add up to . . . to what? To just one hat dipper after another? No, to a host of loosely coordinated explorers, driven by curiosity, probing every currently accessible nook and cranny of multilayered reality.

Loosely coordinated explorers? What forces coordinate them? The scientific culture coordinates them: The language and logic of science help coordinate them; the currently popular dependent and independent variables help coordinate them. For example, psychologists draw samples of introductory psychology students from a subject pool hat and subject them to an array of measures— O's—drawn from dependent variable hats, before and after subjecting them to an array of treatments— X's—drawn from independent variable hats and conduct their studies in an array of classroom and laboratory contexts drawn from the research context hat.

But couldn't all this be done in a more coordinated manner? Yes, but to the extent that you coordinate, you also control the size and content of the hats; you place restrictions on the explorations of multilayered nature. The creative scientist is one who draws from a larger or different hat, or who draws out a powerful new construct, or who builds a new dependent or independent variable. Creative scientists frequently work on the fringes of their discipline—too much coordination shrinks their work space, crowds them—crowds out some error but also crowds out precious creativity.

Nevertheless, one creative person or promising idea can provide an opportunity for coordinated explorations by many others. Coordinated or programmatic research leads to a systematic investigation of a given population (for instance, autistic children) using a sample of measures representing a given dependent variable (social interaction) or a sample of treatments representing a given independent variable (reinforcement) within a sample of research contexts (schools, hospitals, and private homes.)

Such studies represent one small segment of a much larger series of studies focusing on *reinforcement* as an important independent variable—as *the* most important independent variable according to B. F. Skinner.[2] Thus an independent variable can become the focus for coordinating the research of thousands of researchers. This array of researchers draw samples from many population hats, draw sample measures from many dependent variable hats, draw a variety of treatments from many reinforcement hats, and conduct their studies in a variety of research contexts. Surely then we now have a reasonable example of external validity as applied to reinforcement. Yes, this is so, except the follow-up time of many operant conditioning studies on humans has been nonexistent or brief. Thus we are restricted in the generalizations we can make concerning the durability of many of the changes brought about through selective reinforcement—is it in some instances a Hawthorne effect, lasting no longer than a New Year's resolution? Time will tell!

Notice that external validity issues are never settled; external validity refers to the expanding reach of research in the exploration of multilayered shifting nature. External validity, like the future, always lies around the corner.

SUMMARY

In this chapter we discussed validity, how far research results generalize, and how far they reach beyond a particular study.

1. Threats to *internal validity* include rogue suspects (uncontrolled or chance variables), other than the treatment (independent variable), operating within the particular research context that may account for the differences you observe between your pretest and posttest observations or between your experimental and control group.
2. Threats to *external validity* include a series of restrictions on generalizations you can make beyond your particular research setting:
   a. Sampling restrictions.
   b. Measurement (dependent variable) restrictions.
   c. Treatment (independent variable) restrictions.
   d. Research context restrictions.

While the degree of generalization or the degree of external validity of a particular research study may be severely restricted, researchers investigating a given topic usually (1) sample from a variety of populations and so extend the sampling validity; (2) employ different variations of popular dependent variables and so extend measurement validity; (3) experiment with different versions and amounts of popular independent variables and so extend treatment validity; and (4) conduct their studies in a variety of research settings and so extend the context validity.

Most researchers, while having an eye on external validity, probably focus their energies on establishing the internal validity of their study. Other research-

---

[2]B. F. Skinner, a famous psychologist, has challenged many popular assumptions. His speculations and experiments led him to conclude that behavior, far from being free, is shaped and controlled by reinforcements and rewards.

ers, engaged in programmatic research, are balancing their attention between ensuring internal validity as best they can, while at the same time systematically designing and conducting a series of studies so as to extend the external validity of their findings. But it is perhaps the theorist reviewing a wide array of individual research studies who focuses most on the issues of external validity.

The expanding production of individual research studies and the endless extension of the external validity of such studies consumes the scientific enterprise in its compulsive exploration of our expanding multilayered experience.

RESEARCH CHECKLIST

The following checklist may help you decide how much confidence to place in a given research finding:

1. Does the investigator demonstrate that he or she has made a careful attempt to control the four rogue suspects?   Yes _____   No _____
    For example, you would have more confidence if a control group design had been used than if a before-and-after design had been used.

2. If two or more groups were used, was there a reasonable attempt made to ensure that they were equal to begin with (randomization)?
    Yes _____   No _____

3. Did the investigator use enough people in each group to make you feel that the samples adequately represented the target population the investigator wanted to end up talking about (kids of different ages and from different socioeconomic backgrounds)?   Yes _____   No _____

4. Does the particular dependent variable represent a reliable and valid means of measuring the target behavior under study?
    Yes _____   No _____

5. What prior evidence is presented to justify the selection of the particular treatment, to assume it is strong enough to influence the target behavior significantly?

6. How representative is the research context of target research or treatment settings?

7. Did the investigator publish or make available raw data so you could check the investigator's calculations or data packaging procedures?
    Yes _____   No _____

8. Did the investigator repeat the study and get similar results?
    Yes _____   No _____

9. Is the investigator an established one whose work has usually proved to be durable in the past?   Yes _____   No _____

10. Has another investigator repeated this study and published similar findings?
    Yes _____   No _____

11. If so, was the second investigator independent of the first investigator (not his or her graduate student or employee)?
    Yes ————————— No —————————

12. Do the findings make sense in terms of other durable findings in the same field?
    Yes ————————— No —————————[3]

In summary, all that statistical procedures do are to identify any trend in the data that the investigator chooses to include in his or her analysis. This trend may be there because of Treatment X or because of how the investigator, wittingly or otherwise, built it into the data. It is only through an examination of the research methods employed that you can decide how much confidence you have that the data pattern or trend is related to Treatment X.

[3]Too much reliance on item 12 will reduce the possibility of introducing new and startling information into the literature. Therefore if most of the other questions are answered positively, item 12 should not be used as a basis either for denying the investigator his or her right to publish or for denying the speculative their right to explore new ideas.

chapter 14

On Ethics

In this section we devote one chapter to research report writing and another to ethics.

Writing so clearly that other researchers can readily repeat your scientific recipe remains the cornerstone of empirical science. Although scientific prose seldom provides rollicking reading, its quiet power reshapes our world.

While the horrors of Hiroshima and the specters of germ warfare tie the physical sciences in ethical knots, it is only recently that the social sciences are being lassoed by ethical loops as well. No less a moral authority than Ralph Nader chided American psychologists at their 1976 annual convention for intruding into the lives of those who won't fuss too much, while avoiding the more professionally hazardous study of powerful groups.

At the same meeting, two past presidents of the American Psychological Association noted the increasing danger that psychotherapy was going only to the rich, raising the thorny issue of ethics tied to affluence—the poor and the weak be damned.

Finally, arguments rage back and forth about whether a famous psychologist diddled his data, and, if he did, whether it makes any difference.

How would you describe a scientist? What traits or characteristics come to mind when you think about scientists in general? Although each of us might generate a unique total list, at least some of us would no doubt agree on certain adjectives, including perhaps intelligent, creative, well-educated, absent-minded, analytical, objective, rational, honest, impartial, fair, trustworthy. The last four descriptors speak to the ethicality/morality of the scientist. Certainly, science is based on the assumption that the ethical integrity of its disciples is of the highest order. Were we not to make this assumption, the game of science would be a farce, a scam, an endeavor suitable only for fools, dilettantes, and con artists.

Suppose this were the case and some researchers "diddled their data"—made it do what they wanted it to. Scientific literature would then be filled with contradictory findings. To illustrate, some investigators would have clear documentation that democratic leadership style is the most productive; another dissenting clutch of scientists would present equally clear data that autocratic forms of leadership reign supreme; still others would espouse a laissez-faire model; and perhaps a smaller group would present evidence that leadership style has no relationship to productivity. Thus replicability, a key concept in scientific research, becomes meaningless if data are invented and observations are not public and shareable. Obviously the utility of research findings beomes minimal under such conditions.

This assumption of ethicality is so crucial to the practice of science that it may be seen as the pivotal point on which the science seesaw teeters. Social science practitioners today are increasingly sensitive to questions of ethics, morality, humanism, civil rights. Over the last decade increased time and energy have gravitated around ethical issues; ethics committees abound within disciplines, within universities, within research organizations. Nevertheless, the view of the inherently high level of moral judgment and ethicality of scientists served to retard the development of formal ethics codes. For example, it was not until 1966 that the American Psychological Association recognized the need for the establishment of a set of ethical standards in psychological research (American Psychological Association, 1982).

RELATIVITY OF ETHICS

Rules of ethics reflect the value substrata of a culture. Just as values and other cultural components (technology) vary from society to society, so too will ethical standards. For example, while the Navahos, in common with our own and many other cultures, have prohibitions against lying, stealing, cheating, murder, and rape, the most serious crimes are those of incest and witchcraft (Kluckhohn & Leighton, 1949). Among the Saulteaux of the Berens River, violence of any form (including verbal aggression) is strenuously avoided (Hallowell, 1940); yet among the Hopi, who also eschew physical aggression, verbal warfare is an ever-present feature of communal life (Eggan, 1943). Both cultures regard competition as being in extremely bad taste and revere cooperation, in contrast to our own society where merit is selectively attached to both traits. Ethical concerns related to the expression of sexuality show great cross-cultural variability. For the Keraki males in New Guinea, a period of passive, then active, homosexuality is a necessary prerequisite to normal heterosexual developments (Benedict, 1938).

In addition to cross-cultural variation, ethical standards change over time. As one moves from one historical period to another, rather dramatic alterations in

costume fashions are accompanied by (albeit mostly unrelated to) equally astonishing modifications in laws and ethical concerns. Throughout much of recorded
history, women were regarded as chattels or inferior beings, a view reflected in
the "rule of thumb" of nineteenth-century English common law, which legalized
a husband's right to chastise his wife with a rod not thicker than his thumb. Such
practices created no ethical conflict or burden for the perpetrators of this code of
ethics. Only recently are women gradually acquiring the same rights, privileges,
and responsibilities as those of the opposite sex (Brown & Seitz, 1970).

Even within a single culture and given time period, considerable variance in
the ethical principles accepted and practiced by various subgroups may be observed. Attitudes among members of the Pentagon toward the ethicality and le-
gality of a particular military policy are likely to be incongruent with the attitudes
of their wives (Ellsberg, 1973). And certainly the ethical stance of some Nazi
researchers who used Jewish prisoners as experimental subjects was divergent
from that of the German "man-in-the-street."

The relationship between science and ethics has been fraught with minor
spats, hurt silences, martyred expressions, and vicious, acrimonious disputes. At
times scientific investigations were severely hindered by ethical concerns stemming from theological teachings. Consider, for example, how progress in medicine was retarded by the religious strictures against mutilation of the dead body.
White (1955) has provided us with an inventory of illustrations that highlight the
uneasy association of science and religion.

During a brief halcyon period in the history of science, the primary injunc-
tion to scientists was to search for the truth "no matter what." Admonitions to
seek knowledge for its own sake were the norm; if unscrupulous minds used such
knowledge in an unethical fashion, this was in no way the responsibility of the
scientist. If research on methods to reduce prejudice uncovers effective techniques
for producing attitude change which then are subsequently employed to manipulate prisoners of war as part of a brainwashing program, it's not the scientist's
fault. The more contemporary view, however, recognizes that "the double-edged
potentiality of scientific knowledge poses ethical problems for all scientists"
(American Psychological Association, 1982, p. 16); that scientists have some responsibility for the monster they have spawned. This modern stance, combined
with a general evolution in standards of humanitarianism and respect for human
beings, has forced the scientist out of the ivory tower and into the more philosophical, religious, and political arenas where ethical issues are debated.

The moral of the story (to make a bad pun) is that principles of ethics and
moral precepts are not self-evident or absolute. Being culture-bound and time-
tied, ethics can only be understood in the context of the culture that espouses
them. Our amazement at the atrocities of Genghis Khan, at the horrors of the
Crusades, at the child abuse during the Industrial Revolution, at the tortures of
the Spanish inquisitors, at the heartless behavior of GIs in Vietnam reflects only
our own provincial natures and our inability to divest ourselves of our own cultural trappings and, chameleonlike, to take on the coloration of another. In the
same way, future generations may well register disgust over many of our current
"ethical" practices.

Ethics and the Social Scientist

As social scientists whose subject matter is (1) animate, (2) reactive, and (3) often human, we are perhaps more sensitized to ethical concerns than is the physicist measuring the aurora borealis from photographs, or the geologist mapping rock types on the basis of drill core, or the chemist analyzing the molecular structure of a complex protein. The onion root tip does not object to nor change its appearance because it is being examined under a microscope; yet how would we react to detailed scrutiny of our behavior in the intimacy of our own homes? Investigations related to altruism, child-rearing patterns, lynch mob behavior, leadership, authority, fiscal policy, population growth, cancer, cloning, the treatment of schizophrenia, penal reform—all cry out for attention to ethical principles. A code of ethics, after all, is really meant to guide our behavior so as to protect (not contravene) the rights, privileges, and general expectations of others.

Why Have a Code of Ethics?

A key reason for designing and encouraging the adoption of a code of ethics is to inflict or impose our current sense of values on our colleagues. Secondly, the more-or-less uniform acceptance of rules of conduct helps to establish the "old boy's club"—to guarantee some sense of familiarity and comfort in interacting with other members of one's discipline. Thus some concerns dressed in ethical costume reflect protectionism or elitism or isolationism, rather than any general worry about the public weal. To police the science, identify and weed out the incompetent, the insincere, or the unworthy, and thus maintain the purity of the profession is yet another function of a common code of ethics. Such a code helps protect the public from charlatans (those lacking the training specified for membership in the discipline) and from deviants (those adequately trained but practicing in unethical ways).

To protect the individual practitioner from pangs of conscience, gnawing doubts, and perhaps even financial ruin through legal suits is another, but less publicized, value of an ethics code. How can scientists be faulted if their research project seems to lead to negative outcomes for their subjects, when they scrupulously followed the rites and rituals (including ethical prohibitions) accepted by their discipline? In some sense a code of ethics serves somewhat the same function in a science as do quality control procedures in a factory.

ETHICS QUIZ

Before commencing an in-depth examination of specific statements of ethics, it may be useful to sensitize yourself to some of the issues by completing the following quiz.[1] In each case decide if the key figure has behaved ethically or not.

---

[1]Items for this quiz are based on principles selected from the *Ethical Principles of Psychologists* (American Psychological Association, 1981) and the *Ethical Principles in the Conduct of Research with Human Participants* (American Psychological Association, 1982).

1. Professor C.S., as part of his responsibilities as a faculty member in Fly-By-Night U, acts as a supervisor of the research work for a number of graduate students. Typically, this involves several discussions prior to the beginning of the study (perhaps five hours total), some discussion concerning the analysis of obtained results, and reading one or two thesis drafts. Professor C.S. and his students almost always jointly publish these studies, and C.S. is invariably senior author.

   Ethical _____   Unethical _____

2. One of the assignments in a fourth-year sociology course on research methods requires that students maintain a personal journal or diary on family interactions to which a structural analysis (network approach) is subsequently applied. One of the students expresses reluctance (on personal grounds) about carrying out this assignment. The course director, convinced the research procedures are acceptable and, sensitive to the pedagogical benefits of the assignment, urges the student to conduct the study.

   Ethical _____   Unethical _____

3. A professor of physical education, P.T., designed a study on the "second wind" phenomenon, which required that research participants engage in grueling and arduous feats of muscular stamina and strength. The proposed project, after compulsory review by the university's Research Ethics Committee, is given a clean bill of health. P.T., much relieved at obtaining ethical clearance, proceeds to conduct the research without further independent assessment of the ethical issues involved.

   Ethical _____   Unethical _____

4. Psychologist T.I. is employed by the inner city school system to administer intelligence tests to children who do not perform at an acceptable level. Very conscientiously, T.I. reports back to the teacher the following information: each tested child's I.Q. score, those items on which the child did poorly, those items or subtests completed at a satisfactory level, and the child's demeanor in the test situation.

   Ethical _____   Unethical _____

5. Deception was employed in a study assessing the relationship between gender-role orientation and self-esteem. Research subjects, prior to participation, were informed of the requirements and purpose of the experiment to the extent possible given the deception component. Freedom to withdraw from the study, at any time, was emphasized. Following an assessment of gender-role orientation, all female subjects, irrespective of their actual performance, were told their scores revealed a masculine orientation, and male subjects were informed their scores reflected a feminine orientation. Measures of self-esteem were then administered. Immediately on completion, subjects were thanked for their participation and promised a detailed report of the study. Two months later subjects received the report, which fully described the deception.

   Ethical _____   Unethical _____

6. A Skinnerian disciple, S.B., appeared in a recent television commercial advocating that parents of children doing poorly in school consider the purchase of an Apex teaching machine.
    Ethical _____ Unethical _____

7. Neuropsychologist Dr. Rabid is conducting research on the cortical changes in dogs that accompany or result from repeated severe physical pain as induced by whipping.
    Ethical _____ Unethical _____

8. Social psychologist F.A. is researching the organizational structure of certain voluntary groups. Inasmuch as there is a friendly rivalry among these groups, F.A. is frequently asked by a club how they compare with other groups under study. F.A. would not reveal any budgetary information but was willing to describe organizational hierarchy and style.
    Ethical _____ Unethical _____

9. Researcher A.B. has been extremely fortunate in obtaining financial and other support for his research endeavors. He has consistently obtained large grants from the Firm Foundation, and his employing organization is heavily committed to his research in terms of purchase of equipment, administrative support, and so forth. A.B. has been scrupulous in his publications to acknowledge the support of Firm Foundation, since their financial contributions made the implementation of the research program possible.
    Ethical _____ Unethical _____

10. The associate director of a research unit is aware that one of the scientists in the agency is behaving in a seriously unethical fashion. Although he has brought this individual to task several times for his violation of ethical standards, the behavior persists.
    Ethical _____ Unethical _____

11. Part of the course requirement for an introductory psychology course is participation as a subject in an experiment. Professor W.J. is using some of these students for her research on the effects of high arousal (induced by applying shocks to the fingers) on memory. One student, when informed of the nature of the research, was reluctant to serve as a subject. The experimenter waved aside objections by reminding the student that participation was a course requirement.
    Ethical _____ Unethical _____

12. J.L., a specialist in child development, acted as a consultant to a toy manufacturer. Her job involved testing toys in free-play situations. The manufacturer wished to use the results of the testing in his Christmas advertising and asked J.L. for permission to use her name in this context. This was not to be an endorsement of any particular toy, but only a statement that J.L. had tested the toys. J.L. agreed to allow her name to be used in this way.
    Ethical _____ Unethical _____

13. A team of researchers obtained measures of achievement motivation, creativity, and liking for teacher from children selected from several private

nursery schools. The directors of some of these schools requested copies of all the test scores for each child. Since the researchers felt dependent on the good will of the school administrators for subjects, they provided the information requested.

Ethical ——————— Unethical ———————

14. Researcher R.P. has employed a graduate student to run the subjects through his experiment on sensory deprivation. Subjects were obtained through an advertisement in the college paper, which stated that $25 would be paid to individuals who wanted to participate in some research on "peace and quiet." No further information was provided by the graduate student when the subject came to the lab.

Ethical ——————— Unethical ———————

15. As co-investigators for a large grant-supported study concerned with the cultural adjustment problems of new immigrants, X.Y. and X.X. employed a number of assistants to conduct structured interviews with a representative sample of immigrants. Prior to contacting any research participant, these assistants were given extensive instruction by X.X. concerning ethical issues relevant to the research. Nevertheless, it comes to their attention that one of the assistants has implied to interviewees that their participation in the research will reflect favorably on their applications for work permits. Who bears responsibility for this breach of ethics?

a. X.Y.
b. The assistant
c. X.X.
d. The assistant, X.X., and X.Y. are all fully responsible

While the list of such quiz items could go on and on, the 15 items provided are probably sufficient to illuminate the complexity and breadth of ethical concerns. According to principles accepted by the American Psychological Association, *all* of the foregoing are unethical. Therefore to score the quiz, give yourself one point for each scenario in which you decided the key figure had behaved or was behaving unethically. The correct answer for item 15 is alternative *d*. Those readers who obtained the maximum score of 15 are highly sensitized to ethical issues.

For those of us who achieved a less than perfect score, the following explains the relevant principle breached in each vignette (American Psychological Association, 1981; 1982).[2]

1. "Publication credit is assigned to all those who have contributed to a publication in proportion to their contribution" (p. 7). In the example it would appear that Professor C.S. did not play as major a role in the research as the graduate student (Principle 7f).

———————

[2]Principles from the 1981 publication are identified by a number, while those from the 1982 report are labeled with letters.

2. Ethical concerns regarding the decision about whether to conduct a particular research study are covered by Principles A, B, and C. The explication of these principles indicates that professor-researchers should respect a moral reluctance on the part of their students "to carry out a research procedure" and "should not pressure them to perform the procedure" (1982, p. 30).

3. An investigator must carefully evaluate the ethical acceptability of a planned study. Given the nature of the study in this example, the investigator has a "serious obligation to seek ethical advice" (Principle A, p. 26). The approval of a review committee does not absolve the researcher from soliciting other independent assessments of the ethical issues involved (1982, p. 29). The study may also be a breach of Principle G, which requires that the researcher protect subjects from physical discomfort.

4. and 13.   This form of reporting is unethical, since there is no indication of any limitations on the information in terms of reliability or validity nor was there an attempt to ensure that the information would not be misused (Principle 8c).

5. Although the investigator was sensitive to certain ethical issues, the study as described illustrates contravention of Principles H and I. There was no attempt on the part of the investigator to detect and remove any damaging consequences for the individual participants occurring as a result of the deception. Anger or resentment of subjects on discovery of the deception was not monitored.

6. and 12.   Psychologists do not participate in commercials recommending to the general public the purchase or use of a specific product (Principle 4f).

7. The procedures employed by Dr. Rabid contravene principles related to the humane treatment of research animals (Principle 10).

8. F.A. has contravened the obligation to safeguard the confidentiality of information obtained about these organizations in the course of this research (Principle 5 and Principle J).

9. In this example the support of the host institution has not been properly acknowledged in the publications (Principle 7e).

10. The associate director failed to bring these unethical activities to the attention of the appropriate committees on ethical standards and practices for the discipline (Principle 7g).

11. "The investigator respects the individual's freedom to decline to participate in or to withdraw from research at any time" (p. 9, Principle 9f and Principle F).

14. R.P. did not adequately disclose aspects of the research, which might have influenced the subject's willingness to participate. Also, R.P.'s assistant similarly did not explain the nature of the research and R.P. is responsible for ensuring the ethical treatment of subjects by his employee (Principles 9c and 9d and Principles C and D).

15. In instances where several investigators and research assistants are working

on a project, all parties involved are fully responsible for protecting the well-being of the participants (Principle C). Further, this example illustrates the unethical use of coercion to participate in the research (Principle F).

ILLUSTRATIVE CASE STUDIES

In order to probe the intricacies of ethical concerns in more depth, three studies conducted by psychologists will be explored here in detail. The first study, reported by Milgram (1963), involved deception. A paid volunteer subject was told that the purpose of the experiment was to evaluate the effectiveness of punishment on learning. Through a further deception, the volunteer subject was to function as "teacher," and another subject (actually a stooge in the employ of the experimenter) was to act as "learner." Each time the learner made a mistake in the designated task, the teacher was to administer an electric shock, increasing the intensity of the shock with each failure. The final deception was that the stooge, communicating by intercom with the teacher, complained of a heart condition, warned that he couldn't continue, and emitted sounds of pain when shocks were applied. Subjects expressing concern about the condition of the learner were instructed by the experimenter to continue the experiment. The crucial question was the extent to which subjects would obey this directive in the face of the learner's rather dramatic pleas to desist. At the conclusion of the experiment, subjects were debriefed—that is, the deception was explained, and they were reassured that the learner was in the best of health and had not, in fact, been subjected to any shocks. Milgram states, "A friendly reconciliation was arranged between the subject and the victim, and an effort was made to reduce any tensions that arose as a result of the experiment" (Milgram, 1963, p. 374).

Was this an ethical study? Baumrind (1964) questions the ethicality of Milgram's research on several grounds. First, the conditions of the experiment contravene the subjects' expectations to be treated with respect and not be embarrassed or humiliated. Second, subjects have the right to assume that their security, self-esteem, and dignity will be protected. In Baumrind's view the experience could well act to alter a subject's self-image. The very fact that subjects believed the deception makes them fools and thus damages their self-image. Further, they realize what they have done, that they are the type of person who could deliberately inflict considerable pain on a stranger. What harm this knowledge does to self-perceptions is unknown, but clearly the potential is there. Debriefing does not alleviate these harmful effects, since the subjects know that they would have shocked the learner had the current been turned on. Finally, involvement in a study of this type could reduce a participant's ability to trust authority in the future. Milgram (1965) disagrees, of course, with Baumrind's analysis, and the interested reader should refer to his rebuttal.

As a technique to avoid the ethical problems attendant on research involving deception, naturalistic experimentation (subjects are unaware that their behavior is being studied) has increased in popularity. Piliavin and Piliavin (1972) provide us with a typical example of this type of research. In their study the experimenter's confederate, walking with the aid of a cane, collapses in a subway car. What appears to be blood trickles from his mouth. If someone offers assistance, the confederate allows himself to be helped to his feet. If no one intervenes before the train slows to a stop, the experimenter, posing as a passenger, helps the stooge, and they both leave the train.

Over 45 percent of a sample of randomly selected subjects regarded this particular study as unethical (Wilson & Donnerstein, 1976). More general concerns about this genre of research have been expressed by other authors (cited in Wilson & Donnerstein, 1976, and Wiesenthal, 1974) and include the following: (1) There is no informed consent on the part of subjects who participate, (2) there is no attempt at debriefing, (3) invasion of privacy is an issue if the individuals in field settings do not normally expect to be observed, and (4) awareness of the prevalence of such research could lead to a reactive subject pool in public situations.

Another investigator, A. R. Jensen (1969a), aroused the vigilance and vitriol of the scientific community with his thesis that black-white I.Q. differences reflected genetic differences. On the basis of a series of studies conducted by other researchers, he reported that white children seemed to be better at associative and rote learning. Jensen noted that the I.Q. difference persists even when socioeconomic status is controlled and, further, that the gap between whites and American Indians (despite poor schooling) is less pronounced than that between whites and blacks. One additional piece of supporting documentation was the failure of remedial education programs. Essentially Jensen's conclusion was that, while environmental factors are relevant, genetic factors may be the principal causative agent underlying the alleged lower educational potential of blacks.

The Council for the Society for the Psychological Study of Social Issues (SPSSI) was quick to respond to this heresy (1969) in what has been labeled "a dogmatic and emotional" fashion (Hebb, 1970). The SPSSI spanked Jensen for espousing a socially dangerous view, presented some legitimate criticism of his article, and publicly washed its hands, in Pontius Pilate style, of any sympathy for his position. Their principal ethical concern was

> We are concerned with establishing high standards of scientific inquiry and of scientific responsibility. Included in these standards must be careful interpretation of research findings, with rigorous attention to alternative explanations. In no area of science are these principles more important than in the study of human behavior, where a variety of social factors may have large and far-reaching effects. When research has a bearing on social issues and public policy, the scientist must examine the competing explanations for his findings and must exercise the greatest care in his interpretation (pp. 1039–1040).

Jensen, of course, argues (1969b) that he has, in fact, maintained high standards of scientific inquiry and scientific responsibility and suggests that his critics have not. He refers to their rebuttal as "sheer propaganda."

What can we conclude from these three case studies? Clearly in addition to the characteristics described earlier, we lack uniformity in our judgment of what constitutes a breach of ethics except in extreme cases. Agreeement on general principles can be obtained, but when we attempt to apply the principles to the concrete instance, we encounter acrimonious dispute and any decision is a subjective call. Why should this be so? Because questions of ethics resemble the Gordian knot; they are inextricably interwoven with personal, subgroup, and cultural values, attitudes, and beliefs. They are, in fact, the antithesis of the first rule of science—objectivity. Currently, controversy rages over the ethicality and morality of abortion, mercy killing, sterilization of the retarded, and the like. Even the most casual review of these debates reveals the heavy value-ridden, emotionally laden tone of the arguments both pro and con.

THE ANIMAL CONTROVERSY

Among the more volatile and acrimonious debates ripping through the scientific world today is one involving animal lovers versus animal researchers. Yet, concern for the care and use of animals in research is not a recent phenomenon in the scientific community. The Animal Welfare Act, first enacted in 1966 and amended by Congress in 1976, regulates the transportation, housing, and care of laboratory animals. Granting agencies such as the National Institutes of Health have adopted guidelines governing the use of research animals, which must be adhered to by grant recipients. Many scientific organizations have similarly tackled the issue of ensuring appropriate use of animals in research. The American Psychological Association, for example, first established a committee to address the ethics of animal experimentation in 1925. Current guidelines, approved in 1979, specify the following: that the researcher comply with all government laws and regulations; that a scientist trained and experienced in the use of laboratory animals should supervise and be responsible for their humane treatment; that researchers must minimize discomfort, illness, and pain to the animals; pain, stress, or privation may only be used if alternative procedures are not possible and if the research is justified by its prospective value; that researchers should consult with the committee; that the principles should be posted in every facility where animals are used; that apparent violations of the principles should be reported to the supervisor and if unresolved should be referred to the committee.

Such efforts, however laudatory, have not silenced those concerned about animal rights. Most vociferous among the critics is the Mobilization for Animals Coalition, an international network of hundreds of animal-protectionist organizations (King, 1984). This group has accused experimental psychologists of subjecting animals to such things as: repeated, inescapable, painful electric shocks; starvation and dehydration; mutilation; crushing forces which smash bones and rupture organs; pain and stress designed to make healthy animals psychotic (Coile & Miller, 1984; King, 1984). Nor are all members of the scientific community convinced that all animal research meets appropriate ethical standards (Bowd, cited in Carroll, Schneider & Wesley, 1985).

FROM PRINCIPLE TO PRACTICE

To what extent do the mechanisms created by scientific organizations ensure that research practices are ethical? Somewhat reassuring is the report by Coile and Miller (1984) that none of the allegations of the Mobilization for Animals group were found to be true in a survey of 608 published articles involving research with animals. Less reassuring is Bowd's observation that a significant proportion of the published research involving painful animal experimentation is unnecessary in that the research did not contribute new knowledge (cited in Carroll, Schneider & Wesley, 1985). However, the American Psychological Association committee charged with responsibility for adjudicating complaints of ethical malpractice reports only one case of a failure to ensure the welfare of animal research subjects in a three-year period from 1981 to 1983 (Hall & Hare-Mustin, 1983; Mills, 1984). The most frequent type of ethical complaint concerned authorship controversies.

Adair, Dushenko, and Lindsay (1985) have examined the extent to which the development of ethical codes and practices has influenced the conduct of published social psychological research. Their survey of 284 empirical studies indicates that researchers rarely state that informed consent was obtained from their subjects or that subjects were aware of their right or freedom to withdraw from the experiment. Although the research as actually conducted may have attended to these ethical issues, the failure to report them leaves the question open.

The principle of informed consent implies that research participants must not be misled about the experiment. Nevertheless, deception is permitted under certain special conditions. Given the concern about deception, the finding of Adair and colleagues that experiments involving deception are increasing is surprising although there is more reporting of the use of debriefing procedures. Baumrind (1985) similarly reports that the ethical standards implemented by the American Psychological Association in 1973 have not decreased the incidence or magnitude of the use of deception in social psychological research and she suggests employment of alternative research strategies.

Adair et al. also highlight a number of methodological problems created by stringent application of current ethical standards. For example, it appears that when conditions of informed consent are instituted, fewer subjects agree to participate. Those who do agree constitute a biased sample. The debriefing procedure required in cases of deception may contaminate subsequent results obtained with later subjects because research participants sworn to secrecy have been found to disclose the nature of the experiment to others.

Maintaining an appropriate balance between the benefits of research and the costs to participants while at the same time ensuring methodological purity will tax the creativity and ingenuity of the researcher for some time to come.

Cost-Benefit Ratio

By and large the legal profession accepts the principle that it is better to let 100 guilty go free than to convict one innocent person. The costs (damages or harm) attendant on erroneous convictions are deemed to be greater than the benefits of utilizing more stringent procedures, which would ensure a higher conviction rate of the guilty but would also entrap some innocent persons. Similarly, many issues in science reflect various mixes of costs and benefits. Some unpleasant and even dangerous subjects would not be pursued except that the possible gain to society is great. Milgram's (1963) study[3] is a case in point. Did it alert us to a potential social danger that ought to cause us some concern? What about the cost-benefit ratio of brain study? Although some benefits of understanding the operation of the brain are obvious, what about the dangers of a little knowledge, as sensationalized by Michael Crichton in the book *The Terminal Man?* Implanting devices to help someone see or hear is surely beneficial, but what if the appliance ultimately fosters even more serious deterioration in the nervous system? Investigations of the physical and psychological effects of starvation are meritorious, important, and useful, but how much should one try to persuade a volunteer to stay with such a study after nine months when the subject shows an inclination to drop out (Keyes, Brozek, Henschel, Mickelsen & Taylor, 1950)?

Increasingly, the needs of society influence the nature of the questions attacked by science. Each society has a need to defend itself, so we have research on the development of more deadly (more efficient) weaponry and ever more virulent strains of bacteria. Each society has a need to feed itself, so we have research on undersea farms and new frost-resistant varieties of wheat going hand-in-hand with the development of safer and more effective population control techniques—including abortion. Society has a need for more energy, so researchers strive to locate and discover new sources of energy and to use existing sources more efficiently, even though this may result in oil spills and other forms of pollution that conservationists deplore.

Are the disadvantages (costs) of such research outweighed by the advantages—the greater good for the greater number? Calculation of the total cost-benefit ratio for any of the preceding is a complex, subjective, and incomplete process—never definitive, only suggestive—and the resultant ratio figure may well differ from one calculator to another. Consensus of judgments of the ethicality of a particular piece of research is understandably hard to achieve.

AND NOW

It may be that the heyday of the ethics seeker is over. Confronted with essentially unresolvable disputes, social scientists appear to be stepping smartly along in the footprints of the physicians as they search for clarification, not of the moral or ethical basis of their research, but of its legal ramifications and possible liability (Nash, 1975; Silverman, 1975).

Increasing public sophistication regarding the impurities of science and heightened awareness of the feet of clay of most scientists have produced a public attitude of skepticism or cynicism about scientific ideals. Scientific pronouncements are not being accepted as gospel as they were in the good old days, and the

[3]The authors are indebted to Dr. J. Jenkins for his contributions to the analysis of this issue.

scientist no longer sits at the right hand of God. So there is much less reluctance to bring the scientist to task (through legal suits) for infringement of civil liberties, damages resulting from negligence, and so on. Indeed, there may even be an element of punitiveness as a reaction to the sense of having been duped by science. Some ethical concerns may well have moved over into the legal arena (breach of confidentiality, deceit, invasion of privacy) so that the policing of scientific research is being taken out of the hands of the scientists and delegated to the legal system. So scientist beware—the freedoms of the past are slipping away.

SUMMARY

What is considered to be ethical behavior varies from culture to culture and from time to time. Although a given group may be able to agree on a set of ethical principles, it is much more difficult to agree on whether a given principle has been breached in a particular case. Increasingly, formal legal criteria are supplementing less formal ethical criteria in judging the appropriateness of the behavior of scientists.

EXAMPLE

THE BURT AFFAIR: FRAUD IN SCIENTIFIC RESEARCH

Research findings may be attributed mainly to chance or mainly to the influence of an independent variable, but rarely are they attributed to fraud or to data-diddling. Trust in the honesty of research colleagues remains a cornerstone of science. To be tricked by capricious chance is frustrating enough; to be tricked by a sneaky colleague is intolerable.

Recently, evidence has surfaced suggesting that a famous British psychologist, Sir Cyril Burt, fabricated data linking I.Q. to heredity (Eysenck, 1979; Kamin, 1981). Burt estimated that intelligence level was determined 80 percent by heredity and only 20 percent by environment.

The evidence of fraud is indicated on two counts. First, Burt reported data from sources that now appear to be imaginary or nonexistent—nonexistent theses and research reports. Second, Burt reported identical correlations for supposedly different pieces of research. Since identical results rarely arise from different samples, it would appear that Burt didn't bother calculating new correlation coefficients on the basis of new data but merely used correlations computed on earlier data.

Currently, the debate rages hot and heavy as to whether the evidence proves fraud or is merely an indication of sloppiness and aging on Burt's part. Regardless of the debate's eventual outcome, it raises two important issues for us. In the first place the intensity of the debate provides a current example of how sensitive scientists are to charges of fraud against one of their own number, of how such charges threaten the integrity of science. But in the second place this debate also provides an example of how scientists, in protecting themselves against chance, also defend themselves against fraud. You will recall that the best way to increase confidence that your findings are reliable is to use large samples and to publish your procedures and findings so that others can check your results.

Fortunately, the hypothesis that intelligence has a large genetic component does not rest on Burt's work alone. A variety of studies by other investigators also supports the hypothesis that I.Q. and inheritance are significantly related (Rimland & Munsinger, 1977). Had such independently arrived at data not been available, the current debate would be even more acrimonious.

In conclusion, while fraud and chance remain real alternative explanations for significant results, we rarely entertain the alternative of fraud seriously—perhaps because the implications are too threatening. Besides, we already have our hands full attempting to protect ourselves against the innocent tricks that chance plays on us without worrying about dirty tricks from colleagues. While chance and cheating each constitute formidable adversaries in science, our best defense against both remains replication of results by independent investigators.

chapter 15

Research Report Writing

One should always gear one's writing to fit the audience. Dr. Figmund Sreud's article in *Psychology Today* is very different from the paper he published in the *Journal of Experimental Psychology,* because the former is intended for a lay audience, while the latter is designed to inform or impress fellow researchers. The rules for popular writing about the social sciences are probably not unlike the rules for accurate journalism, and indeed most of the interpretations of scientific data for the public is relegated by default to the nonscientist. Taken in the aggregate, scientists are appallingly bad writers—technically unimpeachable but about as interesting as watching paint dry. A typical scientist has an unerring ability to take the most fascinating discovery and milk the intrigue and wonder out of it, leaving an empty husk. Notable exceptions exist, of course, such as Isaac Asimov, B. F. Skinner, J. B. Watson, Margaret Mead and a few others. Caution, pedantry, and the demands for objectivity, once ingrained, are difficult to shed.

The following report form is based in part on the specifications laid down in 1983 by the American Psychological Association for papers submitted to its journals.[1] These specifications may appear compulsive and arbitrary—and they are. Their nuisance value, however, is undoubtedly outweighed by the advantages

---

[1] Other sources which the novice report writer may find useful include: Alsip and Chezik (1974), Anderson (1966), and Lester (1976).

accruing from uniformity. It is much easier to extract information from a report whose organization follows a set pattern; such organization, moreover, expedites evaluation of the reports by an editor or professor. Furthermore, in a literature search one can determine the relevance of a piece of research to one's particular interest much more rapidly and locate desired information more quickly in papers that are organized the same way and written in a similar style.

STYLE

A crude autopsy performed on the corpus—research report—reveals that the cause of death is style, not structure; so let us deal with that agent first. The main characteristics of scientific writing style are precision, terseness, and impersonality—all of which combine to produce unambiguous prose. A statement is precise if its implications are eminently clear—if it says one thing and no other. To report that the subjects in the study were relatives of the experimenter is not only bad methodology but is also vague. Are they siblings, parents, cousins, great-aunts, or what? Many statements that pass by unnoticed in the course of normal conversation would be unacceptable in a scientific paper because they are open to a variety of interpretations. Consider your responses and those of a sample of your friends to the following statements and related questions:

> "Uncle Fred is a moderate smoker." How many cigarettes does he smoke in a day?
> "Senator Fogbound won his seat in the recent election by an overwhelming majority." What percentage of the vote did he get?
> "Ms. Simon is a middle-aged woman." How old is she?
> "Aryn read several books last summer." How many books did Aryn read?

It is apparent that the words *moderate, overwhelming, middle-aged,* and *several* mean different things to different people. Researchers try to avoid ambiguity in their report writing; otherwise their research is not public and shareable, and the scientists find themselves operating at the pragmatic level of language.

A statement is terse if it is economical, if it does not waste words. The aim is to be pithy, to maximize the amount of information per word, and to avoid the kind of redundancy exemplified in this sentence. Since scientists do not have to entertain, but aim only to educate or inform, the need for flowery descriptions is reduced; it is compensated for, to some extent, by the demands of caution. Rarely can researchers make a definitive statement in unequivocal terms about the implications of their findings. The world is filled with reasonable alternative explanations for the same set of data, and even with the admonition to be brief, some of those alternatives must be presented for the reader's consideration.

To achieve impersonality avoid the first person *(I* or *we)*—even at the expense of cumbersome circumlocutions. For example, it is proper to say, "It is the opinion of the investigators that . . . ," whereas only the uninitiated would write instead, "We thought that . . . ."

STRUCTURE

In addition to stylistic qualities there are structural features shared by most scientific writing. In psychology the typical research paper consists of the following sections appearing in the order listed: title, author's name and institutional affiliation, *abstract, introduction, method, results, discussion, references,* and when appropriate, an *appendix.* Each of the main content sections is described in more detail below. Other disciplines may employ a slightly different format, which can be revealed by a quick look through a few recent periodicals.

Abstract

The abstract is written mainly for the benefit of the researcher who is scanning the literature in search of information germane to the researcher's own work, and it is most helpful, therefore, if the abstract is brief and summarizes the study accurately. Resemblance of the abstract to the main text is essential, not coincidental; the abstract is a faithful summary of the report, so it should not include any new material.

The abstract should describe the hypothesis, together with a brief description of the variables under investigation. The apparatus or measurement devices should be alluded to, and the procedure should be described in general terms. The results and their evaluation should be summarized briefly, while the conclusions based upon them should be listed in more detail.

Introduction

The introduction should outline the purpose of the research and describe in general terms the nature of the problem under study. A few closely related previous experiments should be cited, and any findings directly pertinent to the study should be described. Any expectations or biases (predictions) you have about how the study will turn out (derived from past research, a theory, or a personal hunch) should be specified and a rationale (theoretical background) provided.

Method

The method portion of a research paper is typically subdivided into three units: (1) subjects, (2) apparatus and/or materials, and (3) procedure. This section is analogous to recipe instructions and clearly describes what was done and how it was done. It is the empirical cornerstone of your work.

SUBJECTS. This label does not refer to the issues covered by your study, but rather to the people or animals or organizations who participated—who provided you with the information to answer (it is hoped) your initial question. To bake this research cake, the following ingredients in varying amounts are required:

1. How many subjects are in your sample?
2. What are the characteristics of your sample on relevant variables ? (Sex, age, socioeconomic class, diagnosis, education)

3. How did you obtain your sample? (Ask for volunteers, conscript friends, or what?)
4. If you divided your subjects into groups, on what basis was this done? (At random, by age, or how?)
5. How many subjects are in each group?
6. How many potential subjects were contacted in total?
7. How many refused to participate?

APPARATUS AND/OR MATERIALS. A brief description of each piece of apparatus employed should be presented; but if the apparatus has been described in the literature, a reference to this description will suffice. If you have specially constructed apparatus, use a labeled diagram or photograph. Include a brief description of each kind of material employed (questionnaires, tests, inventories, tasks, drawings, photographs). The identification of those tests or tasks constitutes the operational definition of the dependent measure. If you are measuring the anxiety level of your subjects, you may operationalize the concept *anxiety* by employing a commonly used test such as the Taylor Manifest Anxiety Scale (Taylor, 1953). For certain kinds of reports (theses, but not manuscripts), a copy or example of each type of material should be presented in an appendix. To continue the cookbook analogy, this section refers to the designated oven heat, kind of cake pan, and so on.

PROCEDURE. In this unit of the report, instructions are provided for the treatment of the ingredients (fold in the egg whites; boil the syrup mixture till it forms a hard ball; mix at medium speed for two minutes on a portable mixer). Describe what you did with your subjects in sufficient detail that your study could be duplicated exactly by someone unfamiliar with the research area. One approach is to describe what happened chronologically as the typical subjects performed in the study.

Everything that was done that might *reasonably* have had a bearing on the outcome of a study should be mentioned. While it is probably unnecessary to inform the reader of the experimenter's items of apparel, other unprogrammed events may be quite relevant. Consider, for example, the following project. A study was being conducted to determine the effects of arousal (administration of shock) on speed of recognition of unfamiliar words. In order to ensure that the subjects were actually aroused, heart rate was continuously monitored. To obtain heart rate recordings, electrodes were strapped to each leg. As the male subjects entered the laboratory, they were instructed by a glamorous female experimenter to "Please roll up your pants and pull down your socks," so as to ready the legs for electrode placement. After about 150 repetitions of these instructions, the experimenter flubbed thoughtlessly by saying, "Roll up your socks and pull down your pants, please." Experimenter and subjects alike were of little research value for the next few minutes. This event could well have influenced the performance of this particular group of subjects. Subject instructions should be paraphrased in the procedure and quoted verbatim in an appendix, if an appendix is allowed.

Results

Describe how you scored or coded and analyzed your data. Present the results of your significant analyses in clearly labeled tables or figures. Describe each result verbally, but do not repeat information that is already provided in tables or graphs. Analyses that do not yield statistically significant results should be mentioned, but tables illustrating such nonsignificant findings are typically omitted or placed in an appendix.

Discussion

Here the results are interpreted in relation to the problem under investigation. Some reference should be made to their reliability, and their limitations should be explained. Aspects of the procedure that might profitably be changed if the study were repeated should be mentioned. Uncontrolled and/or confounded variables should be identified if possible, and ways of avoiding them on subsequent occasions should be suggested. Something should be said about the extent to which the results jibe with expectations or predictions and about their agreement or disagreement with the results of previous similar experiments, as well as about their integration with relevant theory. Finally, indicate what conclusions you can draw on the basis of your study and what the practical implications of your results are.

References

In order to report your references correctly, you need to be a trifle compulsive because the rules and rituals associated with this component of scientific writing tend to be "nit-picky." References are listed alphabetically according to the author's surname. The year of publication (in brackets), and the title of the article, chapter, or book follows the author's or authors' names; then the source of the item (periodical name and volume number) is provided. For the appropriate detailed format in listing references, refer to the *Publication Manual* of the American Psychological Association (1983). References cited in the body of the report require only author identification and year of publication at the point in the text where the reference is made. To illustrate, "Anderson (1980) found that . . . ," or, "It was found that . . . (Anderson, 1980)."

Appendix

As a crude rule of thumb, include in an appendix any materials which, while important, are not crucial to a general understanding of the study and which, if included in the main body of the report, would be distracting to the reader. Students conducting a research project to fulfill thesis requirements are typically encouraged to err on the side of overinclusion and to provide copies of all tests, questionnaires, exercises, and the like, as well as tables of mean scores for every measure; in extreme cases a supervisor may even request the incorporation of raw data. Manuscripts prepared for publication in a journal, on the other hand, rarely include an appendix.

CONTEMPORARY CONCERNS

Like the spread of the dandelions, the social science literature proliferates at an alarming rate. The pressure to publish, as a means of attaining job security, status, or even a form of immortality, plagues us all. To cope with the burgeoning mass of articles, new journals are spawned, and into their hungry maws pour tons of tasty manuscripts. To illustrate the point: Almost 1000 journals publishing material related to psychology are reviewed by *Psychological Abstracts*. As a conservative estimate perhaps another 500 periodicals exist that also contain articles of psychological content. If each journal contains about 35 articles per volume, over 50,000 psychology articles are published annually. And we haven't even mentioned the book or thesis markets.

Under such conditions quality control becomes a critical problem. Journal editors, far from infallible, are ill equipped to deal with the multitude of papers that flood in daily. Most sophisticated researchers are aware that a negative judgment about publication from one journal needn't mean automatic rejection from others. A rejected manuscript is typically shipped off, often without revision, to the next most prestigious periodical, until the goal of publication is attained.

From the point of view of the reader, this cancerous body of literature is overwhelming. What a puerile hope to keep abreast of new developments in the field! What an idyllic fancy to assume that key studies, the classic papers, will be easy to identify! Naturally mechanisms to assist the harassed researcher have emerged. Special journals provide summaries of articles *(Psychological Abstracts, Dissertation Abstracts)*, reviews of current research *(Annual Review of Psychology)*, reviews of recent texts *(Contemporary Psychology)*, theme articles that review the literature on a given topic *(Psychological Review, Psychological Bulletin)*. In addition, computer programs now permit extremely rapid search of selected literature for specific content areas and spew out abstracts of all articles caught in the scan. As a function of the information overload, scientists must rely increasingly on summaries of research and on secondary sources.

How are we to manage this information overload? Perhaps we should propose a kind of eugenics program urging voluntary sterilization (no publication) on 50 percent of the social science labor force—selected at random, of course. Or maybe a technological device would be more effective—every second article self-destructs after five years. Or only a random sample of submitted acceptable manuscripts would be published. More realistically, but smacking of censorship, a central clearinghouse coordinating all publication vehicles might prevent the shopping around for acceptance by the repeatedly rejected manuscripts described earlier. But under such a radical scheme, we might have missed the contributions of Einstein and Skinner. In the absence of any of these radical procedures, you might pause and consider before adding your personal building blocks to the tower of Babel and then add only your "best" blocks.

SUMMARY

Like a recipe, a research report rests on clarity of procedure and reliability of results. The cornerstone of the research report is the METHOD section where the researcher describes in unambiguous terms; subjects; apparatus or materials; procedure.

The acid test becomes: "Are my instructions so clear that another investigator can duplicate my procedure?"

Did you ask a "significant" question? Did you obtain "important" results? Only time will tell.

EXAMPLE

We provide here a sample of student report writing to illustrate the procedures outlined in this chapter. The topic is "ESP Ability Among Believers and Nonbelievers."

ABSTRACT

Using Zener cards extrasensory ability was compared between five couples who believed they possessed extrasensory powers and five couples who did not. While there was no clear difference between believers and nonbelievers, there was a trend favoring believers, some of which was due to cheating.

INTRODUCTION

This pilot study was designed to explore the hypothesis that people who believe they possess extrasensory ability obtain a higher number of "hits" in a standard ESP test situation than do nonbelievers.

Rhine and Pratt (1957) report some evidence that believers (sheep) perform better than nonbelievers (goats). However, there are major problems with much of the evidence supporting the reality of extrasensory perception.

First, much of the evidence is anecdotal and based on "after-the-fact" information and so open to the usual criticisms aimed at this primitive research method. For example, a person will hear that a relative died and then recall that they had dreamed about that person the night before. Such evidence is open to serious question because believers are probably more likely to report such incidents than nonbelievers and perhaps may even be inclined, unwittingly, to create or modify memories designed to support the cause for ESP. Also such after-the-fact data fails to include the "false positives"—that is, the number of occasions when you dreamed a relative was ill and in fact was not.

Finally, much of the evidence or data is vague enough to be interpreted several ways. For example, if you dream there is "something wrong" with a relative and then check to see if he or she is having trouble, you can usually find that he or she is, because everybody always has some trouble.

In view of the many difficulties involved in interpreting after-the-fact data about ESP, this study uses the more powerful control-group model to compare ESP performance among believers and nonbelievers.

METHOD

Subjects. The subjects of this study were volunteers from an introductory psychology class, 10 of whom claimed to be believers in ESP because of personal experience with it and 10 of whom claimed to be nonbelievers with no personal ESP experience. The members of each group were organized into pairs, one member of each pair designated at random as the sender and the other as the receiver.

Materials. The test materials were standard Zener cards used at Duke University specifically for ESP research. Each card has one of five geometric figures printed on it; the deck consists of 25 cards, with each figure appearing five times in random order.

Procedure. Each pair of believers and each pair of nonbelievers completed 50 ESP trials. Believer and nonbeliever pairs were tested alternately so that the four rogue suspects (Agnew & Pyke, 1982) would not favor one group over another. The procedure for each pair of subjects was as follows:

1. The sender was seated in one room and the receiver in an adjoining room with an experimenter present in each room.

2. The experimenter in the sender room shuffled the deck of Zener cards and without looking at it handed the top card to the sender, who concentrated on the geometric figure appearing on it for 15 seconds. The end of this period was signaled by a bell.

3. At the sound of the bell, the receiver indicated on the report sheet which of the five symbols he or she believed was being sent. The card was returned to the experimenter who recorded it on the record sheet, then reinserted it into the deck and reshuffled the deck. This procedure was repeated until 50 such trials had been completed, after which the number of hits was calculated, the subjects informed of the results, and all were thanked for their cooperation. During the trials there was no visual contact between the sender and the receiver; experimenters were on the lookout for any sound signal codes the sender might be using. The sender was instructed not to speak during the trials.

RESULTS

Table 15–1 represents the number of hits out of the 50 trials obtained by each pair of believers and by each pair of nonbelievers.

Since each receiver has one-fifth chance of being right on any given guess by chance alone, we would expect the average receiver, without ESP ability, to make approximately 10 hits. According to Guilford (1965), 16 or more hits would rarely occur by lucky guessing—would occur only 5 times in 100 tests like ours. As can be seen, only Pair 3 among the believers reached this significant level of performance; they achieved 19 hits. Pair 5 among the nonbelievers approached this significant level with 14 hits.

TABLE 15–1 Number of Hits Out of 50 Trials for Believing and Nonbelieving Pairs in an ESP Study

	Believers	Nonbelievers
Pair 1	11	8
Pair 2	9	10
Pair 3	19	7
Pair 4	12	11
Pair 5	11	14
TOTAL	62	50

Overall, the believers achieved more hits than the nonbelievers did.

DISCUSSION

While this pilot study provided no conclusive evidence in support of the hypothesis that believers possess more ESP ability than do nonbelievers, it *appeared* to provide a bit of encouraging evidence. One pair of believers did perform significantly better than we would expect by chance alone, and the overall trend favored the believers.

In ESP studies questions concerning unwitting sensory signaling arise, as do questions of cheating. During the experiment no evidence of either was detected.

However, after the experiment was completed, it was disclosed that the high scoring pair of subjects had, in fact, cheated, with the help of one of the instructors. The cheating pair used a disarmingly simple plan based on the sender arriving at the experiment coughing and blowing his nose. Therefore the experimenters were not suspicious when he coughed and blew his nose periodically during the experiment. By prior agreement when a particular geometric figure appeared, he would merely cough, thus signaling to the receiver that the figure was before him. Consequently, the receiver got all appearances of that card correct, plus another 9 hits by lucky guessing, giving him an unusually large and significant score. While this deception led to some bitterness, it served to underline the care that must be taken in interpreting experimental results, particularly when the experimenters themselves are believers.

REFERENCES

Agnes, N. McK., & Pyke, S. W. (1982). *The science game: An introduction to research in the behavioral sciences* (3d ed.). Englewood Cliffs, N.J.: Prentice-Hall.

Guilford, J. P. (1965). *Fundamental statistics in psychology and education.* New York: McGraw-Hill.

Rhine, J. G., & Pratt, J. G. (1957). *Para-psychology.* Springfield, IL.: Chas. C Thomas.

INSTRUCTOR'S COMMENTS

This is an interesting pilot study in which you introduced yourselves to the topic of ESP and gained a feel for some of the problems and possibilities involved in testing for ESP effects.

Some of the terms used in the introduction require more detailed elaboration. For example, what is the definition of a "hit" and why are believers called "sheep" and nonbelievers, "goats"? There seems to be an assumption in the introduction that there is no question about the existence of ESP. You should have indicated that this is still an open question and you should have cited additional references.

Your experimental procedures suggest that ESP can be turned on and off like a tap in 15-second spurts. Is that how you conceive of it? Was it significant that the experimenter did not know which symbol was being sent? Why?

Learn not to waste data-gathering opportunities. You could have had sender and receiver reverse roles for another 50 trials without appreciably increasing your experimental workload but resulting in doubling your data base and also allowing individual differences among senders and receivers to express themselves.

Your bitterness over "cheating" by two of your subjects is understandable. Deception of subjects by experimenters is commonplace, and we can probably expect increasing incidents of counterdeception by subjects. Either way deception raises important methodological and ethical issues, as you have discovered firsthand. The cheating subjects should have been replaced, and their data omitted from your table and only mentioned in a footnote.

chapter 16

Sex and Science

To newborn infants the world probably appears as a buzzing confusion. With experience they discover order, manufacture it, or impose it upon multilayered nature filled with vague shifting patterns. Similarly, adults when confronted with new situations experience a buzzing confusion—a lack of pattern. They, too, in time discover order or impose it on the unfamiliar city, the foreign language, the strange customs, or the complicated equipment. Recall the confusion you felt the first time you arrived in a large unfamiliar city, or looked under the hood of a car, or saw the insides of a TV set or computer—random visual stimulation with few patterns emerging and no sense of understanding. However, with the help of signposts, instructions, and experience, patterns slowly emerge out of the "noise."

Gradually we develop simple maps inside our heads. The more complex the situation, the more we must rely on these oversimplified maps or theories of what leads to what. Such theories must be oversimplified because we can't begin to attend to or remember the multifaceted world and its myriad of shifting parts.

Not only are theories or models useful means of summarizing and bringing order into what has happened or what is happening, but they also help us make predictions that allow us to walk into the future with some degree of confidence, however ill-founded that confidence may be.

In this final section we discuss how citizens and scientists wend their zigzag way through multilayered reality, with the aid of necessarily simple theories, maps, and models. An example of an organizing principle or oversimplified map familiar to most of us is a stereotype—widely shared beliefs about the characteristics of a particular group. In this chapter we describe how stereotypes about females emerging from a patriarchal ideology (another oversimplified map) have shaped the course of science. The necessity for and seductive quality of theorizing is outlined in Chapter 17 along with advice on theory evaluation. Future perspectives are presented in the final chapter.

SCIENCE AND SYMBOLISM

At first blush, science seems to be one of the few human enterprises relatively devoid of sexual connotations. After all, science is touted as the objective search for truth (with a capital T). Scientists, as neutral, dispassionate observers, have no truck with the ardor, passion, romanticism, and political polemics permeating other less lofty human pursuits. Yet from another perspective, scientists do not so much discover truth as they construct it. Constructed truths are manufactured from the values and ideologies of the host society. And, given that our society has been guided by a patriarchal ideology for the past 6000 years, perhaps we should not be too surprised to learn that the influence of sex on science has been more ubiquitous and invidious than anyone would have supposed.

Science studies nature—physical nature, human nature—and there has always been a sexual dimension in human thought about nature. In conventional mythology, nature is typically identified as female (Merchant, 1980). Remember the margarine advertisement—"It's not nice to fool mother nature." Beyond the simple sex label, science eroticizes nature by conceptualizing her as being hidden, enclosed, and having secrets. The role of science, then, is to denude nature, to rip away her veils, to disclose her secrets. In this sense, science appears both voyeuristic and exploitative.

Linnaeus' (1707–1778) classification scheme for plants reflects the eroticization of nature in science. Of the myriad characteristics of plants that might be employed to develop a taxonomy, which did Linnaeus choose?—the stamens and pistils, the sexual parts of plants. Lascivious descriptions of Linnaeus' system appeared in the scientific literature of the day—a pansy described as a loose woman with petals gaping wantonly and pollen, titillating dust. Some scientists even attributed deviant sexual desires to women who were interested in botany.

In addition to science's erotic symbolism of nature, science also seeks to control her for she is unpredictable, wild, tumultuous, and potentially destructive. The parallel with the patriarchal view of the need to control females is obvious.

SCIENCE AND OBJECTIVITY

Just as the examples of symbolism in science reflect a prevailing cultural value (patriarchy), so too does that cherished hallmark of science—objectivity. The scientific method and its various refinements attempt to free us from the bugaboos of irrationality, emotionality, and subjectivity. Patriarchal values assert that male minds are uniquely capable of the logical, rational, objective thought required for scientific pursuits. Above all, emotional detachment is the quintessential element in scientific pursuits, and, therefore, the stereotype of women as emotionally labile fosters their exclusion from the center stage of science.

The ideology of objectivity requires the notion of a distinction between subject (the scientist) and object (that which is studied—nature). The investigator is an active agent, whereas the object is passive. Here again we pick up the scent of science as a masculine endeavor.

Finally, the objectivity principle implies an immunity and/or protection from the social/political/economic influences of society. The scientist—by virtue of natural inclinations or talents (rational mind), training (in habits of thought, critical analysis, and so forth), and appropriate use of scientific methods, techniques, and strategies—presumably can produce research free from the distorting influence of cultural values, mores, stereotypes, and similar factors. Such research should yield "pure" or absolute truth: truth uncontaminated by the cultural biases of the scientist or the scientist's society. However, Fee (1976, 1981) argues that society generates the type of scientific knowledge that best fulfills its social, economic, and political needs. Kuhn (1970) similarly suggests that our values and biases shape our knowledge of nature more than our objective observations or our rationality. Shields (1975), in a scathing indictment, contends that scientific empiricism does little more than provide a justification for prevailing social values. In a similar vein, Pyke (1982) implies that prevailing ideologies produce supporting empiricism. Bleir (1984) summarizes this position: "Science is *not* the neutral, dispassionate, value-free pursuit of Truth; . . . scientists are not objective, disinterested, or culturally disengaged from the questions they ask of nature or the methods they use to frame their answers. It is, furthermore, impossible for science or scientists to be otherwise, since science is a social activity and a cultural product created by persons who live in the world of science as well as in the societies that bred them" (Bleir, 1984, p. 193). Can it be that a society gets the kind of science it deserves, the kind it can tolerate?

WOMEN'S ROLE IN SCIENCE

If the reader is prepared to accept (or even entertain) the assertions above that (1) the common form of social structure for humans in modern history is patriarchy; (2) ideologies vis-à-vis women and men in patriarchal social systems postulate a subordinate position for women; and (3) the processes and products of science are heavily influenced by these ideologies, then the fringe participation of women in science is easily understood.

Until recently, females have not been welcomed into science, into what was seen as an appropriately male activity. Consequently, relatively few great women appear in mainstream science. However, women are clearly visible on the periphery. For example, women frequently served as helpmates to scientist husbands, or fathers, or brothers. Carl Linnaeus' wife, Prudence, played an essential role in furthering his career by editing his work and handling his voluminous correspondence. Women also served on the fringes of science as popularizers (that is, writing science books for children) and as illustrators. Many women were active amateur scientists, particularly in the fields of botany, geology, and astronomy. And, of course, some women practiced medicine both as midwives and as local experts with specialized knowledge of the medicinal properties of plants.

Historically, however, women were excluded from institutionalized science. As science professionalized itself (through the use of Latin and the demand for particular education credentials), it became increasingly difficult for women to gain a foothold in this prestigious occupation. It was not until after World War II that the Royal Society was prepared to admit female members. White (1975) offers a more contemporary perspective, suggesting that variables such as the decreased likelihood of sponsorship, lack of role models, atypical (interrupted) career paths, and exclusion from the "old boys' network" all operate to dissuade women from careers in science.

SEX BIAS IN SCIENCE

Social scientists are trained to develop certain habits of mind (critical analysis skills) and are equipped with research technologies designed to enhance the probability that social science research will reflect the principles of objectivity and impartiality. However, certain ingrained beliefs, ideas, orientations, attitudes, and habits serve as "hidden hands" molding the researcher's work. This unwitting shaping of research is certainly true of issues related to sex and gender. Indeed, the vast bulk of research and theory in social science rests on the implicit patriarchal ideology that: (1) females are different from males on most variables, (2) these differences have a biological origin, and (3) the position males hold on a variable is superior (Pyke, 1982). This androcentric bias has had an enormous impact on the production of scientific truth.

Historical Examples

Sir Francis Galton (1822–1911), considered the father of the modern study of sex differences, was firmly wedded to the view that females were inferior to (not just different from) males, not only in terms of physical traits such as strength, but also in terms of their powers of discrimination. Because he believed that sensory discriminatory ability was a valid indicator of intelligence, females were judged to be deficient in mental capacity (Buss, 1976). Galton did not confine himself to passing judgment on alleged sex differences in the physical, sensory, and ability realms; he also made some pungent remarks about personality differences. He regarded women as coy, capricious, and less straightforward than men, subject to petty deceits and allied weaknesses. As might be expected, Galton was a member of the British Anti-Suffrage Society.

Stephanie Shields (1975) provided another example of how the scientific establishment was influenced by the accepted doctrine of female inferiority. Sex differences in the localization of functions in the brain seemed a promising avenue of research. Initially, the frontal lobes were believed to be the seat of the higher functions (for example, abstract reasoning), and it was "discovered" that males had larger frontal areas whereas in females it was the parietal areas that were larger. Later, when the parietal region was thought to play a significant role in the higher functions, science reversed itself. It was then "discovered" that males had larger parietal areas whereas females had larger frontal areas. Here we have an instance of empirical findings tracking dominant social values.

Content

Bias may also be reflected in the questions asked or research topics studied. Doherty (1973) commented on the relative dearth of empirical work on nurturance, and until quite recently, relatively little research existed on achievement motivation in women. Denmark (cited in Grady, 1981) reports that topics such as maternity, pregnancy, and sexuality are underresearched. These topics, because they pertain especially to women, are not regarded as important as are topics relevant to men. Until very recently, the subjects of sex and gender roles were ignored by most social scientists (Gray, 1977; Woolsey, 1977). Percival (1984), however, reported that the most frequently used introductory psychology texts in Canadian universities in 1981 were relatively free of sex bias.

Subject Selection

Preference for male subjects in social science research has been well documented (Carlson, 1971; Carlson & Carlson, 1960; Greenglass & Stewart, 1973; Pyke, Ricks, Stewart & Neely, 1975).

This neglect of female research participants means that we are relatively ignorant about how females would perform under these various research conditions. However, the problem is even more serious because, as Greenglass and Stewart (1973) have demonstrated, studies employing all male samples are more likely to generalize to the opposite sex than those utilizing all female subjects. Thus the scientific literature not only lacks information about women but actually perpetrates erroneous information based on the overgeneralizations from research involving men.

Theory Bias

Observations heaped on a huge table—like a bargain-basement sale—don't make a science. We rely on theories to help us select observations from the heap, link them into a pattern, and explain them. In one sense, then, a theory functions like a bias. To illustrate the biasing effects of the sorting and interpreting screens of theories, let's examine a provocative new theory—sociobiology.

Although sociobiology had many precursors—among them, Tiger's *Men in Groups* (1969), Morris' *The Naked Ape* (1967), and Ardrey's *The Social Contract* (1970)—it was E. O. Wilson who, in 1975, established sociobiology as a comprehensive and coherent theoretical position that attracted both admiration and admonition in the scientific community. In creating sociobiology—which is defined as "the systematic study of the biological basis of all forms of social behavior" (Wilson, 1975, p. 4)—Wilson claimed that this new science subsumed or cannibalized many of the social sciences (for instance, psychology, ethology, sociology, anthropology). Parenthetically, it should be noted that Wilson, by this means, addresses the problem of the arbitrary boundaries between disciplines.

Essentially, "the basic premise of Sociobiology is that human behaviors and certain aspects of social organization have evolved, like our bodies, through adaptations based on Darwinian natural selection" (Bleir, 1984, p. 16). According to evolutionary doctrine, organisms are basically in the business of reproduction. Those organisms that survive to leave the maximum number of offspring (or other genetically related kin) are the most fit in the sense that their genetic packages remain (are well represented) in the population gene pool. These gene packages are adaptive because they are associated with maximum fitness (that is, reproductive success). *Natural selection* refers to the process whereby certain genes are progressively eliminated from the gene pool because their hosts are less fit (leave fewer progeny who carry the gene). Conversely, the representation of other genes in subsequent generations is gradually increased as a function of the reproductive success of their carriers.

From this evolutionary hub, Wilson and his colleagues extrude streamers of theoretical propositions offering genetically based explanations for (1) male sexual promiscuity, (2) altruism, (3) incest taboos, (4) warfare and aggression, (5) homosexuality, (6) ethics and morality, (7) cooperative behavior, (8) hypergamy (female tendency to marry males of higher status), (9) female infanticide, (10) smiling, (11) phobias, (12) the human sense of free will, (13) the disappearance of slavery, (14) the sexual division of labor, (15) female subordination, (16) selected religious practices, (17) private property, (18) patriarchy, (19) the family as a social structure, (20) the disappearance of the estrous cycle in females, and so forth. The handling of altruism is especially intriguing since self-sacrifice genes should have disappeared long ago from the gene pool, assuming that "self-sacrifice results in fewer descendants" (Wilson, 1978, p. 152). Wilson, observing the altruistic behavior in ants, bees, wasps, and termites, notes that the self-sacrifice evident among these social insects has the effect of protecting the other genetically related members of the colony. Hence, the genes (including those relevant to altruism) of the suicidal stinging bee are preserved in its relatives. Thus "natural selection has been broadened to include kin selection" (Wilson, 1978, p. 153).

For consumers of science, sociobiology has a seductive quality. Its comprehensiveness, its relative simplicity in terms of the reduction of complex, mystifying forms of social behavior into a fistful of basic propositions, and the personal immediacy or relevance of the phenomena under consideration, all of these features combine to produce a scientific best seller. Yet for every reader of Wilson's two volumes (1975, 1978) or Dawkins' *The Selfish Gene* (1976), how many have read the scathing but somewhat pedantic and tedious critiques offered in Montagu (1980)? How many enthusiastic consumers have been exposed to alternate interpretations of the same evidence? Is Wilson's main appeal simplicity, buttressed with catchy anecdotal sketches of the behavior of subhuman species, or does he provide a valid and powerful insight into complex human behavior?

To dramatize the potent influence of a theoretical orientation on the selection and interpretation of observations, consider the following two excerpts from Wilson (1978) and Mackie (1983), respectively. They are both discussing the work of Money and Ehrhardt (1972). These latter authors studied 25 genetic females (XX) who were exposed prenatally to heavy doses of androgen (masculinizing hormones), which resulted in a hermaphroditic (adrenogenital syndrome) condition. Corrective genital surgery was performed and the infants were raised as females. Money and Ehrhardt compared this clinical group with a matched control group. Wilson describes this research:

> Did the girls show behavioral changes connected with their hormonal anatomical masculinization? As John Money and Anke Ehrhardt discovered, the changes were both quite marked and correlated with the physical changes. Compared with unaffected girls of otherwise similar social backgrounds, the hormonally altered girls were more commonly regarded as tomboys while they were growing up. They had a greater interest in athletic skills, were readier to play with boys, preferred slacks to dresses and toy guns to dolls. The group with the adrenogenital syndrome was more likely to show dissatisfaction with being assigned to a female role . . . .
>
> So at birth the twig is already bent a little bit—what are we to make of that? It suggests that the universal existence of sexual division of labor is not entirely an accident of cultural evolution. (Wilson, 1978, p. 132)

Mackie (1983) in summarizing the same research reports:

> The researchers found that the fetally androgenized females were more interested in masculine clothing, games and toys. Although they regarded themselves as female, they were considered by their mothers and themselves to be tomboys. In comparison with the control group, these subjects were less interested in baby-sitting and future marriage as opposed to careers. Interestingly, no greater incidence of physical aggression was reported. Money and Ehrhardt concluded that the male sex hormone had had a masculinizing effect. However, critics point out that their behavior is within the normal range for females in our society and further, that female gender identity is not seriously disrupted by the presence of prenatal androgens. (Mackie, 1983, pp. 78–79)

In the first account of this research the meager empirical observations with their fuzzy surround region of doubt or area of uncertainty (see Chapter 1) are linked into an interpretive pattern supporting a genetic biological determinist position. Mackie weaves the same empirical bits into a cultural determinist tapestry. Who's right? Probably both—as a colleague remarked, "Much can be said for both sides." The point we are making is that most subsets of empirical checkpoints, given their scarcity and ambiguity, can be successfully employed to support even diametrically opposed theoretical models. Thus reliance on secondary sources is risky business indeed because the empirical data are painted (or tainted) with hues from the theoretical spectrum.

Studies reporting sex differences trigger a bias toward interpreting such differences as biological in origin (the sociobiological position) rather than as environmentally determined. Sex, after all, is a biological variable and therefore (as the reasoning goes) any observed difference between the sexes must have a biological base. Again, this bias appears in nonhuman primate studies where the tendency to ignore habitat influences on social structure and social behavior is even more pronounced (Lancaster, 1976).

Another characteristic of the androcentric bias in theory involves utilization of the male condition as the prototype. The position of males is the norm, or the natural estate, or the right condition, with women fitted into the theory later as a footnote (Leonard & Collins, 1979). As Weyant (1979) notes, behavioral scientists have often seemed incapable of viewing women except in relation to a male model.

Evaluation

There are some areas where females consistently outperform males (obtain higher scores or show higher levels of functioning). This is contrary to the androcentric bias stemming from the patriarchal ideology. Hence, in order to keep intact the overall frame of reference of male superiority, some social scientists have adopted a position that devalues the superior skills of females. In essence, whatever males are better at (visuospatial tasks, for example) is better than what females are better at (for instance, linguistic tasks).

Favreau (1977) provides a prime example of the operation of a bias in evaluation, taken from the work of Broverman, Klaiber, Kobayashi, and Vogel (1968). These authors developed a theory that led them to predict that females should excel only on simple tasks. How can they accommodate this view to the fact that women are superior linguistically? They argue that because verbal skills require extensive prior practice, only minimal involvement of the higher cognitive processes is necessary. Hence, language, perhaps the most distinctive accomplishment of human evolution, is alleged to require only minimal cognitive involvement, in order to maintain the patriarchal ideology that females are inferior (Favreau, 1977; Pyke, 1982).

Inference Bias

Bias may enter in when researchers interpret and generalize their research findings from the experimental situation to the real world. Garai and Scheinfield (cited in Favreau, 1977) report that females excel in perception of detail in tasks that require frequent shifts of attention, and females also show greater verbal fluency. Generalizing from these findings, the investigators note that these facilities make females better equipped than males for almost all secretarial skills. They fail to mention other occupations such as law, writing, teaching, and broadcasting for which women should be equally well suited on the basis of these two skills (Favreau, 1977).

Language Bias

Consider the form of the following pairs of statements:

A. Color blindness occurs more frequently in males than in females.

vs.

B. Girls are more passive than boys.

A. Learning disabilities are more frequent among males than among females.

vs.

B. Girls are more dependent than boys.

A. Hyperactivity occurs more frequently in boys than in girls.

vs.

B. Girls are more verbally facile than boys.

Obviously the paired statements are not linguistically parallel forms. If we were to rephrase the first *A* statement above to a form analogous to its partner, we would say: "Males have poorer color vision than females." Similarly, the second *A* statement would be reworded as, "Males do not learn as well as females."

There is an inherent inaccuracy in the *B* statements because they seem to suggest that *all* females are more whatever than *all* males. This implication is not evident in the *A* constructions. Of particular interest is that the inaccurate *B*-type assertions are typically applied only to one sex—females.

Other forms of language bias abound in the scientific literature. Lionel Tiger provides a blatant type of labeling bias. Describing a pattern of bonding among male baboons, Tiger cites the work of DeVore and Hall who indicate that bonded males ". . . tended to support each other in aggressive interaction with other males" (Tiger, 1969, p. 27). On the very next page, in describing comparable aggression in female baboons, Tiger says, "Two or more females commonly 'gang-up' to threaten or attack another female." (Tiger, 1969, p. 28). Thus if males exhibit this behavior, it's "cooperative bonding" and if females do it, it's "ganging-up."

More recently, some social scientists have studied the connotations of allegedly generically neutral terms such as *he, his, man*. Such terms, if the context is appropriate, are presumed to apply to both sexes. Moulton, Robinson, and Elias (1978) demonstrated that even in a neutral context such terms are typically interpreted as gender-specific—that is, to refer to males only. Thus many journal editors and text publishers have adopted a policy of using the forms *he/she* or *his/her* to indicate clearly that the statement is meant to include both sexes.

Selection and Distortion of Evidence

Many people have read or heard or believe that the following statements are scientifically validated facts:

1. Girls are more social than boys.
2. Girls are more suggestible than boys.

3. Girls have lower self-esteem than boys.
4. Boys are more analytic than girls.
5. Girls lack achievement motivation.

On the basis of a review of 1600 studies on sex differences published between 1966 and 1973, Maccoby and Jacklin (1974) conclude that these statements are unfounded. The accumulated available research evidence does not, in fact, support them, yet such conclusions continue to appear in the scientific literature and elsewhere. Thus even scientists selectively recycle subsamples of unfounded research findings that support cultural stereotypes.

In some instances actual distortion of evidence may exist. Favreau (1977) cites an article by Hutt in which Hutt reports that three studies support the claim of male superiority on a particular task. One of these three studies does not support Hutt's position.

Statistical Bias

Many scientists use statistical techniques to help decide if their observations are worth getting excited about, or worth sharing with their colleagues. Suppose a scientist compares the performance of females and males on a perceptual restructuring task such as identifying a simple figure hidden in a more complex pattern. The scientist's pet theory about the relationship between sex and cognitive/perceptual abilities leads him or her to suspect that the males will be superior on this task. Males obtain an average score of 15, whereas the average for females is 10. To help determine whether this difference is a "true" difference—one worth shouting about, one that supports the pet theory—the researcher submits the data to a statistical test. Statistical convention requires that the scientist start off with an assumption that the two groups do not differ—the null hypothesis. Then, statistical maneuvers are applied that provide information on the probability that the difference of 5 units is a random or chance finding. A probability level of 0.01 obtains, which means that there is one chance in 100 that this difference of 5 units is due to sampling error or some other uncontrolled or unknown factor. Our scientist then rejects the null hypothesis and concludes that a real, authentic, true, significant difference does exist between males and females on this task. Note that the scientist could be wrong because there is still that one chance in 100 that the observed difference is artifactual.

What if the investigator had found, after application of a statistical test, a probability value of 0.15? Then our investigator knows that there are 15 chances in 100 that this difference of 5 units is due to chance. Again, by convention, this probability is regarded as too high, too risky, to permit a conclusion of a real or significant difference in performance between males and females. However, by the rules of statistics, the scientist cannot confirm the null hypothesis and conclude that he or she has discovered that males and females have similar perceptual restructuring abilities. Hence, a failure to obtain a real difference (defined as a probability of 0.05 or less) equals an ambiguous result. Returning to our discussion of sex and science, the implication is that one can never statistically "prove" that the sexes are similar, that they do not differ. Our main decision aid in science fails to help us make decisions about similarities.

Favreau (1977) describes another biasing effect of the use of statistical procedures. On a test of mathematical ability, the average score for boys was 40.39; for girls, 35.81. This difference proved to be significant at the 0.01 probability level. The conclusion that boys have significantly superior mathematical ability is tempting and implies that all boys perform better than all girls. Yet, as illustrated in Figure 16–1, the lowest scores in the group of boys are as low as those of the lowest girls, and the scores of the best-performing girls are as high as those of the highest boys. In essence, the use of the statistical procedure disguised the extensive overlap between the sexes on this measure of mathematical ability.

Publication Bias

Because of the ambiguity of results that do not permit the investigator to reject the null hypothesis, many scientific journals have an explicit or implicit policy that only studies reporting statistically significant differences will be published. Consequently, many studies appear in the literature reporting "real" sex differences when in actuality the difference reflects that one chance in 100 that the difference is artifactual. The other 99 studies that failed to show a sex difference didn't get published. This publication bias then leads us to assume differences between the sexes where in fact no such differences exist.

Journal policies may also be biased against publishing reports of sex differences that are contrary to established, accepted findings. There also seems to be an avoidance of the publication of replications—studies that try to duplicate the procedures of previously published work. Both of these factors tend to augment or exacerbate the problem of accepting as authentic those findings that are really attributable to chance. Finally, as Grady (1981) notes, journals may eschew certain research topics or content areas, regarding them as trivial or overresearched. This may be particularly the case for topics related to women's issues.

FIGURE 16–1   Mathematical Ability Score

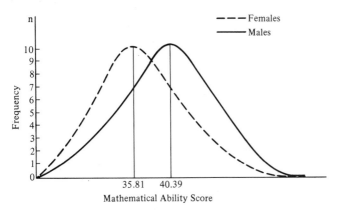

Design Sources of Bias

In a fascinating program of research, Rosenthal (1963) and his colleagues demonstrated that a researcher's knowledge of the hypotheses or predictions associated with a piece of research may actually shape results in keeping with the hypotheses. In other words, the experimenter's expectation about how the study will turn out works like a self-fulfilling prophecy. Recalling our earlier discussion, that ideology produces the supporting empiricism (Pyke, 1982), Weyant (1979) has argued that experimenter expectancy effects serve to enhance the possibility of revealing a sex difference.

The demand characteristics of an experiment (Orne, 1962) are a potential source of bias for any study. Essentially, an experimenter may inadvertently structure an experiment so that the probability of obtaining certain results increases. For example, the researcher's demeanor in interacting with the research participants will obviously have an impact on the behavior of the participants.

More specifically, the particular task that the investigator assigns to the participants may bias the findings. Weyant (1979) provides an example of the operation of this type of bias in research on sex differences. A consistent sex difference cited in the psychological literature has been the greater social conformity of females as compared with males, leading to the conclusion that females were more susceptible than males to group pressure or influence. However, the tasks employed in these conformity studies were typically of the spatial/perceptual variety—a selection that favored males. When the tasks used were of roughly equal familiarity for both sexes, the sex difference in conformity disappeared. The view that women are conformists has a long history. In the fifteenth century, two Dominican priests believed that more witches were female because females were more susceptible to Satanic pressure and enticements.

Grady (1981), reviewing studies of aggression, identified a similar source of bias in both the experimental condition utilized and the type of response option available to the research participants. In studies involving female participants, aggression is typically induced by requiring the subjects to read a story presumed to arouse aggression; to measure the amount of aggression so induced, subjects complete some sort of questionnaire. When male subjects are used, aggression is more actively and directly induced through threat or hostile treatment and the effect is assessed in terms of the administration of shocks to a victim. These demand characteristics could well yield experimental findings supporting a conclusion that males are more aggressive than females.

ALTERNATIVES AND REFORMS

Although the section above is slanted in terms of a selection of examples revealing forms of biases that result from adoption of a patriarchal ideology, it should be remembered that a feminist ideology can function similarly. For example, Jeanne Block (1976) has identified several sources of bias evident in the review of the sex difference literature done by Maccoby and Jacklin (1974) mentioned earlier.

Perhaps one test that might be applied before accepting the validity of any phenomenon is that it be studied by adherents of different ideological orientations. If a finding withstands scrutiny from opposing ideological perspectives, our confidence in the "reality," truth, or authenticity of the findings is even greater.

As Fee (1976) suggests, the biological determinism so prevalent in theories about sex differences during the Victorian era gradually gave way to environmental or cultural conditioning theories in part because of the influx of women scientists. Ensuring a heterogeneous population of scientists almost guarantees that a smorgasbord of world views or ideologies will prevail; and thus our chances of locating robust effects are increased and opportunities for falling prey to an artifactual effect accordingly diminished.

The heightened sensitivity (or raised consciousness) of the social science disciplines to sex bias promotes increasingly objective research. Although insight or awareness may not necessarily produce change, the exposé tone of the feminist assault on the foundations of science has no doubt led some researchers to exert greater care in the design, analysis, and reporting of their work.

And on a variety of fronts, scientists are being exhorted by granting agencies, journal editors, and their professional associations to "clean up their act." To illustrate, Stark-Adamec and Kimball (1984) present a comprehensive description of the many avenues by which sex bias may enter research and they develop guidelines to aid researchers in their efforts to generate nonsexist research. These guidelines have been adopted and endorsed by the Canadian Psychological Association.

The Stark-Adamec and Kimball (1984) article, as well as most of the others cited in this chapter, encourage moving scientific practice closer to its advertised claims of impartiality and objectivity. Other social scientists, and these are fewer in number, while certainly not prepared to jettison much of the scientific armamentarium, are arguing in favor of extending the list of "legitimate" research strategies. Their recommended additions carry a "feminine" connotation, which, if adopted, would counterbalance the masculine orientation of hierarchy, domination, power, and control evident in traditional experimental science. Qualitative methodologies and descriptive research, commonly termed *soft methods,* are among those being proposed, along with an increased recognition of the validity of a phenomenological approach and the relevance of personal experience (Wallston, 1981). Wallston also urges researchers "to place more emphasis on situational variables and their interaction with person variables" instead of relying on a "solely intra-psychic approach" (Wallston, 1981, p. 608). Parlee (1981) presents an interesting analysis of the control group paradigm in research and describes how feminist researchers can capitalize on broadening the narrow conceptualization of control groups to promote more rigorous research.

At a more philosophical level, Ruth Bleir (1984) reminds us that nature does not exist prepackaged in the structures, taxonomies, classifications, and processes identified and labeled by science. These forms are artificial creations of human thought designed to order our experience. As Bleir comments, "We tend to mistake our cognitive techniques to comprehend the universe for the universe itself"

(Bleir, 1984, p. 197). Bleir, like Wallston, advocates a new approach in science with an emphasis on contextuality, interaction, process, and change, as opposed to or in addition to the cause-and-effect paradigm with its emphasis on control. Bleir's model implies an awareness "that there can be no single 'correct' explanation, no simple dramatic 'cause.' Rather, there will be an array of factors, some more important than others, each factor having its own historical course of development and its own situational specificities, interacting with other such factors over time and eventually leading to the phenomenon under scrutiny" (Bleir, 1984, p. 203).

Historically, the social sciences reflect the operation of nomothetic methods—directing energy toward the search for general laws, modelling the "pure" sciences of chemistry and physics. This tradition assumes people are more alike than they are different, that events follow a unidirectional, linear, rational pattern. In contrast, Bleir and other feminist scholars urge adoption of a more idiographic approach to understanding nature. This world view promotes a conception of events as nonlinear, multidirectional, and of people as more dissimilar than alike (Marceil, 1977). Full recognition is accorded to the idiosyncratic complex concatenation of factors derived from a unique biology and articulated by a unique environment, which are relevant to the production of any behavior, any event, any belief (Pyke, 1982).

SUMMARY

This chapter highlights the sensitivity of science to belief systems, values, ideologies, the "taken for granted" implicit world view of the scientist. Although focusing on one particular theme—namely, the conception of females inherent in patriarchal thought—other ideological perspectives, although less ubiquitous, would have served as well. Recognition of the imperfections and vulnerabilities of the scientific enterprise remains vital for the production of better-quality science and important for all of us if we are to be sophisticated consumers of science's products.

EXAMPLE

The following is an historical example of the impact of ideology on empiricism (Fee, 1976).

A small brain = a small mind.

Physical anthropologists of the Victorian era eagerly embraced Darwin's theory of evolution, published in 1859. Within the patriarchal structure of Victorian society, women were regarded as inferior and subordinate to men. Applying evolutionary theory, many scientists of that period concluded that females represented an earlier stage of evolutionary development. This then explained the lower status of females—socially, economically, politically. Because they had not climbed as high up the evolutionary ladder as men, women therefore could not be expected to function as creatively, intelligently, and productively as their male counterparts.

A related part of the argument, which helped to explain why in some "primitive" cultures women held considerable power and status, was that as one proceeded up the evolutionary scale the sexes became more and more divergent or differentiated. Hence, the great distinctions between males and females in Victorian England were justified because the Victorian upper class obviously represented the epitome of civilization—the acme of evolutionary progress.

Interest in developing a measure of intelligence led some scientists to resort to the use of brain size as a possible indicator, and so the science of craniology was born. The following predictions regarding brain size might be generated from the propositions outlined above:

1. Females would have smaller brains than males.

2. The difference between male and female brains in primitive cultures would be less than that observed in more advanced cultures.

3. Within more advanced cultures, the difference between male and female brains would be less in lower socioeconomic classes than in higher classes.

As expected, the predictions were confirmed. Women were simply not equipped, as a result of their evolutionary history, to function on a par with men. It seemed they were destined to be always subordinate to men. As George J. Romanes (1887) put it, "It must take many centuries for heredity to produce the missing five ounces of the female brain" (cited in Fee, 1976).

As science moved into the twentieth century, patriarchal ideology remained, but changing economic conditions required some adjustment to the evolution paradigm of the Victorian era. Science itself changed its complexion with the trend toward increasing precision and experimentation. At the turn of the present century, Karl Pearson, a statistician of some renown, expressed his disgust with the quality of Victorian evolutionary theorizing and set about to demonstrate the absence of any correlation linking brain size, cranial measurement, and intelligence. Pearson's assault proved fatal to the "science" of craniology, which disappeared from the scientific scene.

Somewhat reminiscent of the craniology debate is the recent controversy on brain laterality (the extent to which functions or abilities are localized in the right or left hemisphere of the brain). Many researchers assume that being lateralized is preferable to lack of lateralization primarily because children with various learning problems exhibit ambiguous cerebral dominance. Because the incidence of learning problems in young males is higher than the frequency of these difficulties in young females, and because females are more lateralized for verbal functions than males, it has been hypothesized that males are less lateralized than females. On the other hand, females appear to be less lateralized than males because they show less impairment following damage to either brain hemisphere than do males with a comparable degree of cerebral assault. In some sense then, females have the best of both worlds. These incongruent findings have led some researchers to conclude that the female brain specializes, that is, lateralizes, *too* early and is thus not able to "advance" further (Pyke, 1982; Unger, 1979). Thus after a hundred years, the Victorian view of female evolution is reborn, albeit in a more sophisticated and elegant guise.

chapter 17

Theories, Maps, and Models

A theory, a map, or a model is an abstraction, and abstractions involve representing the part of the world under examination by a model of *similar,* but *simpler,* structure. The important point is that theories are simpler than the data they are designed to represent. Theories are built (1) by squeezing some parts of experience together—all blacks, all women, or all Republicans and (2) by ignoring or omitting some information, such as the differences that exist among blacks, among women, among different Republicans.

WHY BOTHER WITH THEORIES?

There are at least five reasons why theories are critically important in science.

1. No Other Choice

The most important reason for relying upon theories is that we have no alternative. We would have an alternative if, like some magic computer, we saw, heard, and felt everything, if we had a massive and unlimited memory file storing each bit of information separately and permanently, and if we could draw at will from this memory file any information and experience we wished for examination. Obviously we're not like this. We listen, look, and feel *selectively.* We also forget, condense, and distort the information we do have. We tie bits of information together in our heads that are not necessarily tied together in the world around us. We are, in fact, information screening, condensing, and relating machines. The end result of this process are theories, or mental maps, of what goes together, of what leads to what. If it were otherwise, we would go crazy from the great avalanche of detailed bits of information and experience to which we are exposed both from the outside and the inside.

Herbert Simon (1979) recently received the Nobel Prize for demonstrating that we—like bears with small brains—must face *boundless* problems with very *bounded* rationality. You will recall that when burdened by after-the-fact observations the psychiatrist, faced with too much information or too many alternative suspects, develops biases or theories of what to look at and what to ignore. Some psychiatrists focus on biochemical information, some on early training. The important point is that by focusing on certain kinds of information, by developing biases, and by forgetting, we reduce the avalanche of information and experience to manageable size—to a size that fits our bounded mental capacity.

Like the psychiatrist, the scientist and the citizen increasingly face information and opinion *overload*. Like the psychiatrist, we too develop simplified pictures, stories, models, or theories of what goes together and what leads to what in fast-moving, multilayered experience.

Thus through experience, training, and bias, we group together certain people, objects, or events—at the same time ignoring many differences. We may group all blacks together. Even if we do it on the basis of color, we must ignore the fact that many nonblacks are as dark as many blacks. We may go beyond simple classification and, on the basis of selective experience, bias, or training, conclude that blacks and low intelligence or laziness go together, without considering the question of how many exceptions there are to this simplified theory or picture. Others may say that low intelligence and laziness are strongly tied to early environment, ignoring the role that inheritance may play. We develop theories about women, men, Communists, Democrats, Jews, Wasps, the Irish, the rich, the foreign, teachers, elections, liquor, inflation, and LSD. To the extent that we omit critical information, the results of our oversight or error come home to roost, causing us varying degrees of trouble. To the extent that we can screen out information contrary to our theory or bias, we continue blithely on our way.

We rely so heavily on biases, general theories, superstitions, and maps—those simplified pictures or stories of our worlds—because with our limited information-processing and storage equipment we have no other choice.

2. Simplified Decision Making

With the aid of bias, ignorance, and superstition, we drastically reduce the size and complexity of the problems we face. Nevertheless, even within this drastically reduced problem space, the complexity still remains overwhelming, so we need mini-theories, hypotheses, and hunches to help focus our limited attention, our limited energy, our limited mental capacity—to help simplify our decision making.

For example, crude superstition may help us focus on witches as the cause of disease, but even then we need mini-theories and hunches to guide us in deciding how to identify a witch, how to protect ourselves against their spells. Similarly, in a more enlightened era a general theory may help us focus on germs as the cause of illness. Nevertheless, we still need mini-theories, hypotheses, and hunches to help us focus our attention on given samples of subjects or given dependent and independent variables. Therefore we need general theories—or biases—to help us focus on a given problem space and then mini-theories and hunches to help us explore within that problem space.

Within such problem spaces many of our day-to-day decisions are based, not on hard evidence, but on hunches, points of view, biases, or theories—major theories or mini-theories. Some of us have the ability to formulate a point of view very quickly, particularly if we have little information about the issue. It's much easier to develop a theory if you are relatively ignorant about the area in question. As one national leader replied to a reporter, "I would have a ready solution if I didn't know so much about it."

In any case, theories or biases[1] do simplify decision making by providing us with decision guidelines. These guidelines generally reduce the amount and kind of information we consider and also reduce the number of possible alternative decisions we might formulate. In other words, the 1001 potential decisions we might make on any question are reduced to 1, 2, or 3—merely because we have a theory that channels our thinking along certain lines and not others.

Working with a colleague who can't choose from the menu of scientific alternatives is like dining day after day with someone who can't decide what to "try" on the restaurant menu—integrative theoretical and methodological biases help coordinate the work of scientific colleagues.

3. Theories Are Fascinating

Thirdly, we promote theories because they intrigue us, regardless of whether the theory concerns why Reagan beat Mondale; why Cathy and Bill split up; why the stock market took an unpredicted and downward trend just after we made our plunge; or whether there's life on other planets. Most of us, when faced with an unexpected event, must "explain" why it happened. As with a puzzle we worry away at it until some explanation emerges that satisfies us—for the time being. It's particularly gratifying if our theory presents some dramatic new map of reality and if others feel compelled to "buy" our map.

4. Predicting the Future

A fourth reason for relying on theories is our need to predict the future. We need to predict what will lead to what, even when we lack necessary information. The predictions may range from attempting to decide which of three job

---

[1]The major difference between a theory and a bias is perhaps who holds it—if you or a friend hold it, then it's a theory; if a stranger or your theoretical critic holds it, it's a bias!

offers is likely to give you the best chance of promotion and development to predicting the future effect of continued drinking, smoking, air pollution, or inflation.

Scientists and nonscientists act on predictions. We use the weather forecaster's predictions to help us decide what to wear and whether to leave earlier because of predicted snow or sleet. We predict that the car will start; when this prediction, much to our dismay, is not confirmed, we predict that the public transportation system will be operating, that the driver is sober, that the brakes are sound. We predict that the water supply is pure, the cook is clean, the judge is honest, and that our mate is trustworthy. We predict that in our absence our roommates will not die, and in some cities, we even predict that our apartment won't be burglarized. We're constantly operating on the basis of a variety of predictions of varying probability, often without recognizing it.

5. Rewards from the Scientific Community

Finally, theories are important for scientists because the academic and scientific communities offer their highest awards to those who build and test stronger theories. The eminent people of science, those to whom the accolades flow, are the theory builders.

In the final section of this chapter, we shall develop some crude yardsticks that can be used to help us evaluate the adequacy of a theory. Before doing that, however, we shall briefly examine one way in which science can be viewed—as a love affair.

BUILDING MODELS

Theory-building becomes a game of building models or pictures of the world. Some models are based on how we see the world through our own eyes; other models are based on how we see the world through an ordinary microscope. There are also models based on how we see the world through an electron microscope and models based on how we see the world through a telescope, or how the world looks through the eyes of a Protestant biochemist, or how it looks through the eyes of a Catholic gynecologist. Once theorists and researchers have stabilized a map or model, it usually requires a great deal of time, data, argument, and valiant attempts at propping and patching before they reluctantly go about radically changing its superstructure. In other words, if the data coming in through their or others' research do not fit the map or model, they are more likely to question the adequacy of the data or the competence of the researcher than they are to question the adequacy of the theory.

Eventually if "significant" observational checkpoints persistently appear off the path of the theory (map), the "believer" will stretch the theory—or modify the map—to accommodate resilient data and will continue to do so until the theory becomes shapeless—the map a hopeless mess of criss-crossing corrections.

A Love Affair

Because any experiment is open to criticism, the theorist always has a way out in rejecting unwelcome data. The rejection of a theory once accepted is like the rejection of a woman once loved—it takes more than a bit of negative evidence. In fact, the rest of the community can shake their collective heads in amazement at your blindness, your utter failure to recognize the glaring array of differences between your picture of the world or the woman on one hand and the data on the other.

You will perhaps find it easier to understand some of the excitement and despair in the world of science if you view research as a love affair between the investigators and their pet hypothesis. During the initial courting stage, researchers are open to certain kinds of information; but as they invest more time, energy, and money in the courtship, they become hostile to any information threatening the relationship. Perhaps as the data come in, they have private moments of uneasiness which they share with no one. As they analyze the data, they may have moments of agony, but it takes more than one or two lovers' quarrels to break up a love affair, which is just as well. If it were otherwise, there would be almost no marriages, just as there would be very few, if any, worthwhile results from research. Fly-by-night relationships in almost any field yield little that is memorable or of lasting value.

We suspect there are those who would disagree violently with this love-affair model of research. They will say that researchers must be completely dedicated to objectivity, that their only interest is the truth. Perhaps researchers like that exist. We haven't met enough to fill a phone booth. We have, however, met many researchers who can be brutally objective about someone else's research project, or someone else's beloved, but not about their own.

But you are no doubt wondering what happens after a while. Does the love-affair model shift to the marriage model? Yes, we believe so. After working with a project, we gain some objectivity and can accept some of the limitations and restrictions of our model. Many of us will still keep serious family quarrels to ourselves. The very senior and established researchers can afford to joke in public about the possible limitations of their models and speak philosophically about the relativity of truth in science. But if you are wise and humane, you'll no more join them in making fun of their theories than you would join them in their very personal games of making pseudo-fun of themselves, their spouses, or their dogs. As you know, making fun of something you love or cherish is one thing; having someone else do it is quite another.

THEORY EVALUATION

We proposed earlier that we rely heavily on theories for a variety of reasons: (1) we have no choice in that we are theory-manufacturing or information-condensing organisms; (2) theories make decision making simpler; (3) theories are fascinating; (4) theories help us make predictions about the future; and (5) theory production and testing are rewarded by the academic and scientific establishments.

Therefore a variety of reasons abound for bothering with theories. But how are we to decide the superiority of one theory over another? Generally speaking, we choose those theories that provide us with acceptable information in a shorthand or economical way, that assist us in making decisions and approaching our goals, or that at least appear to help us avoid frequent high-cost errors. Scientists ask the following questions when evaluating theories:

1. Which theory is the simplest to learn and use?
2. Which theory is more readily open to test?
3. Which theory provides us with sufficiently relevant and precise information at each step in our decision making in dealing with the question at hand?
4. Which theory provides us with unique and original information or allows us to predict the most new facts or solutions?
5. Which theory best fits with other accepted facts or theories?
6. Which theory is internally consistent—that is, doesn't contradict itself?

Simplicity

We like simple theories because they are easy to remember and to apply. Scotsmen are stingy, Englishmen are cold, blacks are lazy, Jews are pushy, WASPs are self-righteous, spare the rod and spoil the child, GM products are better than Ford products. While these theories or condensations are simple, they are obviously very imprecise; nevertheless, some are widely held. So right or wrong, simplicity is important. This is particularly so when, even though the theory is wrong, we personally don't suffer from its application.

If, on the other hand, the application of an imprecise theory leads to our immediate discomfort, we then examine its relevance or its precision. Thus parents come to a psychologist complaining, "Even though I've whaled the daylights out of him, he still misbehaves. In fact, he seems to be getting worse." Such people are then ready for a more precise and more complex theory, such as, "On some occasions, some children respond better to reward than to punishment." For a more detailed background of this theory, we might even be prepared to invest in and study a book on child-rearing. Or if the problem at hand is buying a new car, we may, through bitter experience, be forced to subscribe to the theory that only on certain years are some GM models better than Ford models and acquaint ourselves with the theories or condensations in such publications as *Consumer Reports*. Notice that increased precision is purchased at the price of increased complexity in our theories. The general rule is: The more accurate we want to be, the more complex the theory, and the more information we need in reaching our conclusion.

You can usually spot a simple theory by its emphasis on one or two bits of information: Behavior depends essentially on race, *or* behavior depends essentially on early training, *or* behavior depends essentially on biochemical factors, *or* behavior depends essentially on punishment, *or* behavior depends essentially on the institution that you are working for. While any one of these *one-cylinder* theories may have some validity, the more precision we want in our solution, the more likely we will need to combine these one-cylinder theories into multicylinder theories: Behavior depends on intelligence, *and* on early training, *and* on genetics, *and* on biochemistry, *and* on work situation.

So we face the problem of reaching a balance between simplicity and precision. If we want to predict the developing behavior of a child, we have to combine a series of one-cylinder theories. If, however, we merely want to predict the behavior of a particular bus driver (when he or she will come to our stop), we will usually be sufficiently accurate if we consult the bus schedule published by the institution that employs the driver. In such cases we usually don't care about the driver's intelligence, early training, genetics, or biochemistry.

Therefore it is not a question of simplicity versus complexity; it is a question of whether a theory or condensation includes enough information to meet our needs or help us make the decision at hand.

If you want to understand or predict complex human behavior, then your theories, of necessity, must be fairly complex because (1) people differ, (2) they learn, (3) their behavior changes from one situation to another, and (4) they change with age. Therefore any time you encounter a theory about human behavior based on the assumption of stability, you will realize that such a theory leaves out a great deal of information. Examples include theories about introverts and extroverts, depressives and nondepressives, laziness and activity, responsibility and irresponsibility, and so forth.

The reason why these theories have some appeal is (1) they are simple, and (2) there are a few people who fit them. But these theories do not include most people. Most people are sometimes extroverted and sometimes introverted, sometimes lazy and sometimes active, sometimes responsible and sometimes irresponsible, sometimes security-seeking and other times risk-taking. Therefore the next time you hear a speaker describing a theory about human behavior that divides people into a few simple classifications, you can bet that a great deal more is left out than is included and that the major appeal of the theory is on the basis of simplicity.

Testability

While simplicity and personal appeal are important yardsticks in theory evaluation, the yardstick of testability counts high in science.

Think, for example, how would you test the theory that blacks are less intelligent than whites. It would be a relatively simple matter if we wanted to test the theory that blacks are taller than whites. We merely obtain a nonelastic ruler and measure a large, random sample of blacks and a large, random sample of whites. But intelligence tests are elastic rulers. The scores depend on (1) how the tests are administered and by whom and (2) whether the people being tested and compared have been exposed to similar educational opportunities. Perhaps eventually some researchers will develop an acceptable test of intelligence that is as nonelastic as a tape measure or at least not as elastic as the tests we now have, but until better tests are available, the theory is relatively immune to test.

Similarly, if we wanted to test whether GM products are better than Ford products, we need a series of nonelastic yardsticks of what we mean by *better*, and then we need to measure a large number of different cars manufactured by the two companies. Reasons that make some theories difficult to test or evaluate include the following: (1) elastic yardsticks; (2) disagreement over which of the available yardsticks to use; (3) inability to measure a large, representative sample of the population we are theorizing about; and (4) refusal of citizens and scientists to change their minds, even in the face of new information. With some theories it is difficult to agree how they should be tested, and with others we are not prepared to invest the resources necessary to test them.

Karl Popper (1969, 1972), a highly respected philosopher of science, proposes that while testability is necessary in theory evaluation, we should increasingly direct our efforts toward highly critical tests—tests in which we play devil's advocate against our pet theory.

Popper points out that our common practice of conducting empirical tests of a theory, and accumulating positive instances, is a relatively weak form of theory evaluation, akin to scientific rationalization—for example, only publishing positive results that fit popular theories of the time. His point is particularly applicable to social science research where predictions that fail the test rarely get into print, so we lack a balanced perspective on the predictive power of a theory.

Overstating Popper's argument to make the point, we flaunt our successful predictions and rationalize or bury our unsuccessful ones—like doctors who claim the operation was a success—but the patient died!

Popper's plea that we focus more on negative than positive instances, and that theorists and researchers become their own severest critics, is highly rational, which is both its strength and its weakness.

On the one hand, it is a rational defense against: (1) the tricks of chance on a positive role (rolling seven sevens, or making several successful predictions in a row—which can generate "true believers" not only in gamblers but also in researchers); (2) rationalizing through highlighting positive instances and discounting negative ones; (3) rewarding only positive instances through publication, grants, and awards. On the other hand, practically and emotionally it takes unusual theorists or researchers to criticize their own brainchild, to prove it a phony, a false or flimsy creation.

While we cannot argue with the logic of Popper's proposal, we suspect that devil's advocate tests of a theory will continue to come mainly from its opponents, rather than its proponents, whose main resources will continue to gravitate around the task of generating and publicizing positive results.

Novelty

Theories that lead to surprising or novel information are highly valued. Thus Theory A raises few eyebrows with the statement, "Students will get higher marks if they do one hour's study a day for 10 days than if they do 10 hours a day for one day." Eyebrows shoot high, however, if the theory states, "Students will get higher marks by listening to a tape recording of lecture notes for one hour a night while they sleep for 10 nights than by spending one hour a day for 10 days studying the same material."

Naturally, theories that lead to novel or surprising information are not necessarily readily accepted. Unless such theories produce an overwhelming amount of evidence, or permit a large number of researchers to test them readily and obtain the same results, or help provide some structure to a shapeless theory, or fill in an obvious gap, then, without such strong results, these additional maps of reality typically languish for years in obscure journals until more and more evidence accumulates or until the biases and attitudes of a sufficiently large number of the population change so that the new information becomes acceptable.

Goodness of Fit with Other Facts and Theories

As we noted at the outset, a few new facts do not change a well-established theory or lead to the acceptance of a new theory. This is so, not merely because some scientists are biased, but rather because we all use familiar theories to evaluate new information—to help us in our decision making. If we gave every new bit of information or theory careful consideration, we would be overloaded with work in 10 seconds. For example, drug companies put hundreds of new drugs on the market each year, and only a few can be adequately evaluated, merely because of the time and effort required. Furthermore, thousands of research studies are published annually, but only relatively few are repeated by other investigators. Most investigators spend their time preparing to publish their own research.

No simple solutions exist, other than using our own personally accepted theories or small modifications of them as guidelines in helping us decide what we will read and examine carefully.

Sometimes learning a new theory is as difficult as learning a new language. Apparently not only laypersons but many physicists as well just couldn't learn Einstein's theory of relativity—they couldn't fit it into the well-worn tracks of their minds.

Internal Consistency

Another way of classifying or evaluating a theory is to assess its internal consistency—a minimum condition a theory must fulfill to be seriously considered. A theory that contradicts itself proves embarrassing at times, even though each part is acceptable taken separately. Consider the following examples: (1) He who hesitates is lost, and fools rush in where wise men fear to tread; (2) "Colonel Cathcart was conceited because he was a full colonel with a combat command at the age of only thirty-six; and Colonel Cathcart was dejected because, although he was already thirty-six he was still only a full colonel" (Heller, 1961, p. 192).[2]

[2]Heller, J. *Catch-22*, p. 192. New York: Simon & Schuster, 1961. Copyright © 1961 by Joseph Heller. Reprinted by permission of Simon & Schuster.

There are contradictions in the preceding examples, and with such contradictions, a theory provides no overall guidelines to aid us in predicting or in making decisions. According to Theory 1, we should both buy and not buy the speculative stock, and according to Theory 2, we really can't decide whether Colonel Cathcart is happy or dejected. Until we have more information about the conditions surrounding lost opportunity because of hesitation, we can't use Theory 1 effectively.

As a rule, scientific or philosophical theories rarely display such gross inconsistencies; however, scientific inconsistencies exist and are fair game for long arguments. For example, modern physics wrestles with the unpredictability of individual subatomic particles, which leads to predictable events—a case of the unpredictable leading to the predictable. Similarly, while insurance companies can't predict which specific 55-year-old males will die this year, they can accurately predict how many 55-year-old males will die.

Understanding and Prediction

You see that theories help us both to *understand* certain parts of our world and to make *predictions* leading to new information and new solutions.

Understanding is a difficult term to define. Perhaps one of the most common meanings of the term *understanding* is that we develop a more satisfying picture of some part of the world. For example, we may ask, "What's college like?" The reply may be, "College is like high school, except no one cares if you come to class, and in most classes you don't get any comments on the work you hand in." Or you may ask, "Why is Harry so cranky?" And you may get the reply, "He had a fight with his girlfriend." Typically, you will respond, "Oh, I understand." You understand because you can now combine some bits of information that you already had in a new way; you now feel you have a better picture. Our point is that understanding may give you a more acceptable picture about a part of the world, but nevertheless that picture may be quite erroneous. Unfortunately, you can walk away feeling you understand after a wide variety of different replies to the same question. It is proposed, then, that the term *understand* implies a personally acceptable picture of what goes together or what leads to what but need not imply an *accurate* picture. The accuracy is subsequently, if at all, determined by more direct personal experience or by more accurate additional data from another source.

On the other hand, the term *prediction,* if stated in testable form, is a more scientifically useful concept. Theories that enable us to understand are personally useful, while theories that enable us to predict are both personally *and* scientifically useful.

This does not mean that the term *understand* cannot be redefined to include tests of the adequacy of the information; it is merely that the term, as commonly used, does not usually imply such tests, whereas the term *predict* more frequently does. Therefore theories that predict new information should be ranked more highly than those that lead to understanding, as defined above.

We have stressed the importance of the testability of a theory. Testing a theory can be done in several ways. A theoretician may state a prediction in a testable form, which we then subsequently test and support or refute; or the theoretician can perform an experiment based on a prediction of the theory, and we can attempt to repeat the experiment. Replication in science is probably the foundation of testability.

However, theories typically cover a large speculative space, one in which the density of observational checkpoints will, of necessity, be relatively low. Therefore a strong theory is one that accommodates other strong theories *and* popular facts.

As noted in Chapter 1, in their attempts to understand we increasingly see theorists straddling traditional boundaries or levels, such as the social biologists who speculate that human behavior can be ''seen'' as separate traits, as general as aggression, as elusive as creativity, as atypical as homosexuality, and including xenophobia, spite, altruism, conformity, and upward mobility—each with its own genetic origin and evolutionary justification.

Thus sociobiological theorists are focusing their search for the antecedents of such human behavior at the level of the gene, whereas, traditionally, social scientists have ''seen'' the relevant antecedents for such behavior arising at the level of the family, the institution, and the culture. This means war—theoretical war—with both sides seeking and publicizing speculative and logical arguments, and of course assembling positive instances to support their case.

Apart from the details of the argument, one can expect such heated disputes whenever theorists or researchers seek for the antecedents of a given type of behavior and ''see''—via the combined efforts of external eye and the mind's eye—relevant antecedents mainly residing at one level rather than another, in the infinite network of possible relations. At the end of this chapter you will find a brief excerpt from the writings of a strong critic of sociobiological theory who points out the error of these researchers' theoretical ways—that they seek and ''see'' at an inappropriate level.

But no matter which side of the debate you examine—as Popper's devil's advocate—you will usually find a large speculative space sparsely dotted with strategically selected observational outcroppings. In other words, a given theory serves not as an objective answer, but as a decision aid for theorists and researchers in managing the high uncertainty embedded in the complex interplay of potential antecedents, consequences, and chance factors—hundreds of them. As one side or the other become more self-righteous, if you listen carefully you can hear it—the laughter of the gods!

SUMMARY

We are inclined to view theories as decision-making aids, perhaps not as whimsical as the toss of a coin nor as crude as a race tout's tip, but decision aids nonetheless. Forced to act in the face of ignorance, we build theories—those simplified and crudely drawn maps of the past, present, and future—that give us some semblance of confidence as we race or stagger through life's maze of alternatives.

Are theories true or false? No one knows, since most theories are designed to cover mammoth areas or massive populations, and we can usually explore in detail only a tiny corner or a few instances. Thus whether a theory is true or false is anybody's guess; whereas everybody knows that a decision aid is worthwhile if it helps you make even one decision that is not immediately followed by a disaster.

EXAMPLE

THEORETICAL DISPUTE

Disputes center around the theoretical assumptions of sociobiology—particularly concerning the relative importance to be assigned genetic and cultural antecedents of complex human behavior such as aggression, altruism, homosexuality, and so forth.

The following comments are by Stephen J. Gould, who "sees" sociobiologists assigning genes too specific and powerful an influence to such complex behavior. Thus this theoretical dispute concerns the levels at which antecedents are sought and the weighting assigned to each antecedent when it is acknowledged that multiple levels are involved.

"Biological potentiality vs. biological determinism. Humans are animals, and everything we do is constrained, in some sense, by our biology. Some constraints are so integral to our being that we rarely even recognize them, for we never imagine that life might proceed in another way. Consider our narrow range of average adult size and the consequences of living in the gravitational world of large organisms, not the world of surface forces inhabited by insects . . . . Or the fact that we are born helpless (many animals are not), that we mature slowly, that we must sleep for a large part of the day, that we do not photosynthesize, that we can digest both meat and plants, that we age and die. These are all results of our genetic construction, and all are important influences upon human nature and society.

These biological boundaries are so evident that they have never engendered controversy. The contentious subjects are specific behaviors that distress us and that we struggle with difficulty to change (or enjoy and fear to abandon): aggression, xenophobia, male dominance, for example. Sociobiologists are not genetic determinists in the old eugenical sense of postulating single genes for such complex behaviors. All biologists know that there is no gene "for" aggression, any more than for your lower-left wisdom tooth. We all recognize that genetic influence can be spread diffusely among many genes and that genes set limits to ranges; they do not provide blueprints for exact replicas. In one sense, the debate between sociobiologists and their critics is an argument about the breadth of ranges. For sociobiologists, ranges are narrow enough to program a specific behavior as the predictable result of possessing certain genes. Critics argue that the ranges permitted by these genetic factors are wide enough to include all behaviors that sociobiologists atomize into distinct traits coded by separate genes.

But in another sense, my dispute with human sociobiology is not just a quantitative debate about the extent of ranges. It will not be settled amicably at some golden midpoint, with critics admitting more constraint, sociobiologists more slop. Advocates of narrow and broad ranges do not simply occupy different positions on a smooth continuum; they hold two qualitatively different theories about the biological nature of human behavior. If ranges are narrow, then genes do code for specific traits and natural selection can create and maintain individual items of behavior separately. If ranges are characteristically broad, then selection may set some deeply recessed generating rules; but specific behaviors are epiphe-nomena of the rules, not objects of Darwinian attention in their own right.

I believe that human sociobiologists have made a fundamental mistake in categories. They are seeking the genetic basis of human behavior at the wrong level. They are search-ing among the specific products of generating rules—Joe's homosexuality, Martha's fear of strangers—while the rules themselves are the genetic deep structures of human behavior. For example, E. O. Wilson (1978, p. 99) writes: "Are human beings innately aggressive? This is a favorite question of college seminars and cocktail party conversations, and one that raises emotion in political ideologues of all stripes. The answer to it is yes." As evidence, Wilson cites the prevalence of warfare in history and then discounts any current disinclination to fight: "The most peaceable tribes of today were often the ravagers of yesteryear and will probably again produce soldiers and murderers in the future." But if some peoples are peaceable now, then aggression itself cannot be coded in our genes, only the potential for it. If innate only means possible, or even likely in certain environments, then everything we do is innate and the word has no meaning. Aggression is one expression of a generating rule that anticipates peacefulness in other common environments. The range of specific behaviors engendered by the rule is impressive and a fine testimony to flexibility as the hallmark of human behavior. This flexibility should not be obscured by the linguistic error of branding some common expressions of the rule as "innate" because we can predict their occurrence in certain environments.

Sociobiologists work as if Galileo had really mounted the Leaning Tower (apparently he did not), dropped a set of diverse objects over the side, and sought a separate explanation for each behavior—the plunge of the cannonball as a result of something in the nature of cannonballness; the gentle descent of the feather as intrinsic to featherness. We know, instead, that the wide range of different falling behaviors arises from an interaction between two physical rules—gravity and frictional resistance. This interaction can generate a thou-sand different styles of descent. If we focus on the objects and seek an explanation for the behavior of each in its own terms, we are lost. The search among specific behaviors for the genetic basis of human nature is an example of *biological determinism*. The quest for un-derlying generating rules expresses a concept of *biological potentiality*. The question is not biological nature vs. nonbiological nurture. Determinism and potentiality are both *biologi-cal* theories—but they seek the genetic basis of human nature at fundamentally different levels."[3]

[3]Selection is reprinted from *The Mismeasure of Man* by Stephen Jay Gould by per-mission of W.W. Norton & Co., Inc., pp 328–30. Copyright © 1981 by Stephen Jay Gould.

chapter 18

The Truth Spinners

Last chapters furnish authors with a final opportunity to elaborate cherished biases, to play with controversial topics, to peek into the future.

FITTING SPECULATIVE MAPS TO OBSERVATIONAL CHECKPOINTS

Our view of science combines "discovery" and "invention" models. Think of science as a set of ever-expanding maps describing what leads to what—how much of drug A leads to how much improvement in symptom B.

In new fields of research we encounter highly inventive or speculative maps with few observational checkpoints available. In some established research areas, we encounter well-documented maps of selected space-time samples, documented in the sense that various researchers have "been there" with similar sensory instruments and agree that the map is "accurate," the discoveries are open to inspection. Yes, but any research space is infinite—not only speculatively infinite but observationally infinite as well. In other words, you can always add more observations in a given speculative space; you can always modify the amount or form of delivery of your independent variable—the new drug—or combine it with other drugs or treatments. Furthermore, the precision and range of your dependent variables—of your observations—can always be expanded: a more precise yardstick of depression; checking the drug effects on additional symptoms or on new diseases, on different age-groups, with different durations of illness, with different temperaments, with different expectations or diets, with different auxiliary therapies or previous treatments, and so on forever.

In science no one can say, "I've been there; I know all about it." The best anyone can say is, "I visited a tiny part; I have some rough sketches." Relative to the complexity of nature, our instruments are crude; relative to the shifting complexity of experience, our categories are fragile.

By recognizing the infinity of research space, we recognize, too, the inevitability of unanswered questions; we recognize that we don't know what we will find if we increase the range of our independent variable or if we increase the range and precision of our observations.

For example, observational checkpoints constitute an infinitesimal portion of the speculative space covered by most theories. In other words, a speculative map or theory covers much more space than can usually be explored; consequently, researchers can do no more than sparsely sprinkle a speculative space with observational checkpoints. The density of such checkpoints provides a crude index of the theory's empirical foundations.

Practical considerations limit the number of observational checkpoints. With limited resources researchers must choose between establishing a high density of checkpoints in a small speculative space (thoroughly explore a small speculation), or establishing a low density of checkpoints in a large speculative space (superficially explore a large speculation).

Digging and Fishing for Truth

You obtain a crude sense of the dilemma by putting yourself in the position of a geologist looking for a mine. Each hole you drill constitutes an expensive experiment. Guided by your speculative map of where the gold lies, you must decide not only where to drill, but how deep to drill—the deeper the hole, the higher the cost.

You wonder, should you concentrate your holes in one area and at one depth and, so, thoroughly test a small speculation but perhaps miss a major body of ore several hundred feet to the west or only a few feet deeper? Or should you spread your few holes over a wider space—a wider speculation?

Fishermen face a similar problem but with the added complexity that their body of ore (school of fish) moves around. How should they conduct their experiments? Should they concentrate on one small corner of the ocean or try different spots for a short time each?

Social scientists, dealing as they do with a vast set of mobile phenomena like feelings, opinions, and behavior rhythms, face problems similar to those of fishermen, for even if they have thoroughly experimented in a small speculative space (fished a given spot), that is not to say that another researcher on another day may not make a catch.

If you keep the analogy of the fisherman in mind, you will better appreciate the challenge facing the theorist and the researcher; the theorist speculates where the best holes are; the researcher tries them out. You will also understand why a research hole is never "fished out"—why different researchers fishing at a different time or using a different lure may get a strike in your "fished-out" hole.

So even for small speculations, the typical density of observational checkpoints remains relatively low. Some expensive research strategies involve simultaneously putting down many lines at different depths, but even then a host of questions remain unanswered: What would have happened if we had used different lures? at different times of the day? and jigged them at a different rate? and what if it had been cooler or raining?

The Density of Observational Checkpoints

Perhaps now you sense the infinity of theoretical space and the practical impossibility of exploring it all. You appreciate, too, the practical necessity of settling for low-density sprinklings of observational checkpoints—fragile, isolated, empirical outposts in ever-expanding speculative space.

Take, for example, a relatively small speculation. Speculate about the relation between hours of study and marks in math; as your hours of study increase, so too should your grades. How might it look?

We show that the proposed positive correlation is a straight-line graph supported by balloons—speculative balloons—for, so far, speculation is all we have holding up the relationship, since we have conducted no experiments; we have no "formal" observational checkpoints.

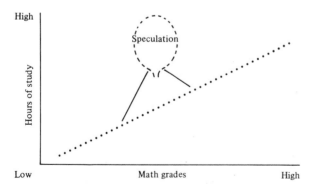

Next we check the "goodness of fit" of our speculative map—our speculative graph—with some observational checkpoints. Where should we start? We invest in two sets of observations: one of a group that studies, on the average, 15 minutes per night; and another of a group that studies, on the average, 45 minutes per night. We then calculate the *average* math grades of the two groups and plot the results:

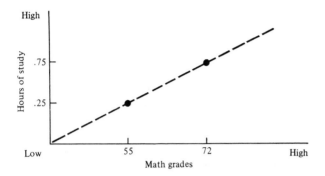

Our observational checkpoints fit our speculation concerning a positive relationship, but the density of our observational checkpoints (two points) relative to the speculative space (the whole line, constituting thousands of points) is low. We can demonstrate how low by plotting the curve not with a starched line, as we have done, but with a flexible line, a line made of pieces of black, wet spaghetti:

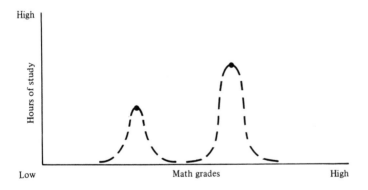

If we plotted all our graphs in this way, we would better appreciate how much of a curve is supported by theoretical starch and how much by observational checkpoints.

How reliable are our checkpoints? Do they represent two solid empirical outcroppings? No, they represent two averages—an average is a corset for holding data together. Look what happens when we take the averaging corset off our two checkpoints:

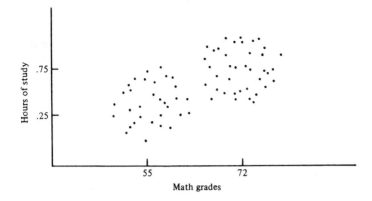

Now we have two loose clusters of data, with each dot representing a student. How stable are these checkpoints? We don't know until we observe the same students again or observe another sample. Suppose we do and add their data to the graph:

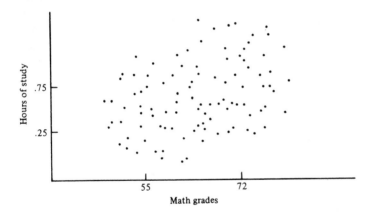

Now you can see how important averages and other data-packaging concepts are in protecting us from the buzzing confusion of raw data, of unpackaged or unbiased data. In the first graph we packaged a speculation. In the second we packaged some observational checkpoints. In each graph we "create" a semblance of order in a tiny portion of the network. In the fifth graph we move in the direction of a "raw" data world and can appreciate how the data swarm approaches a buzzing confusion, just as the graph approaches visual noise without the aid of speculative bias or an observational corset to give it order. You can see how useful averages can be, but you can also appreciate now that testing the goodness of fit of speculative maps to observational checkpoints is no simple matter. Both speculative space and observational space are infinite.

TRAPPED INSIDE A CHINESE PUZZLE BOX

Emerging from the previous chapters is a theme of a multilayered, moving reality, an analogy of science trapped inside an infinite maze of Chinese puzzle boxes.

We encounter this multilayered puzzle box theme in physics—the endless search for the *smallest* particle *and* the endless search for the *edge* of the universe; we also encounter this nest of puzzle boxes in biology—unknown "somethings" nesting in proteins, which nest in genes, which nest in chromosomes, which nest in cells, which nest in organs, which nest in living organisms, which nest in ecologies, and so on; we encountered a puzzle box theme in psychology—the mysteries of the gene, which nests in the nervous systems, which nest in early and subsequent experience of the developing individual, who is laughing on the outside and crying on the inside; and we encounter the puzzle box theme as well in sociology—individuals nesting in groups, which nest in institutions, which nest in cultures. Furthermore, all of these surfaces seem, somehow, to influence each other.

This puzzle box theme presents science in a dynamic vein and the image of science shifts from noun to verb—shifts from science as a collection of facts, to sciencing as an ongoing series of explorations, as a moving picture of changing images or new perspectives from *within* a puzzle box stretching to infinity in all directions—toward the invisibly small on the one hand and toward the invisibly distant on the other.

Such a puzzle box theme requires revised scientific methods and revised scientific concepts as well—some of which already populate the scientific horizon, others remaining vague targets of speculation. What methodological and conceptual trends can we see?

METHODOLOGICAL TRENDS

Two methodological trends appear to be emerging: (1) an increased reliance on multidimensional time series studies and (2) creative developments in "triangulation" methods (Campbell, 1975b), both of which address a multiple layer, or multiple surface, model of science.

Multimethod Time Series

We discussed the time series when examining developmental and longitudinal research methods. This multimethod tactic employs more than one dependent measure, as in our example (Chapter 10) when we collected time series data via (1) diary, (2) unobtrusive measures, (3) questionnaires.

The multimethod time series enables you to simultaneously monitor, through time, several layers of multilayered reality—that is, what people say *and* what they do. The multimethod time series helps you to extend the external validity of your explorations, not only through tracking several dependent variables, but also by tracking long enough to help you identify spurious Hawthorne or on-stage effects.

We anticipate seeing more multimethod time series of attitude, personality, training, therapy, and selection. Although multimethod studies extend external validity, they extend research costs as well. Furthermore, in some instances they encounter high data "mortality" because people (subjects and experimenters) move or lose interest.

Triangulation Research

Triangulation research has probably been the unofficial method of choice of most researchers. In general, triangulation involves locating "something" by viewing it from different angles.

We can view something (that is, how someone spends his or her time) from the viewpoint of diaries, unobtrusive measures, questionnaires, reports from friends and family members. In this sense triangulation research is a form of multilayered research. However, it offers a means of helping researchers explore the external validity of their work without necessarily getting involved in a costly multimethod time series. For example, if you wanted to get several fixes on whether students significantly change the way they allocate their study time as a result of a study skills training course you could: (1) have them complete a questionnaire—knowing it to be a crude fix, knowing it to be an estimate surrounded by a large region of uncertainty— (o) —but not completely devoid of information; (2) ask a family member or friend who has the opportunity to observe the individual in question—again, not a precise estimate, but *another* estimate; (3) finally you could probably afford to do a sample of unobtrusive measures on a sample of the students—cruising the residence and libraries, for example. Now you have three fixes on a given behavioral space and, with them, a multilayered view of the target behavior—yet problems still remain. In some instances all three fixes will agree, in others only two will agree, and in some all three fixes will diverge so you are left to weigh one fix over the others or throw that group into your "don't know" category—that is, beyond the reach of your study.

This kind of multimethod triangulation offers the novice investigator an affordable opportunity to engage a research problem without merely resorting to the common practice of giving yet another questionnaire, to yet another captive group of introductory psychology students, and then going through the ritual of doing chi squares, correlations, or *t* tests regurgitated by some canned program the student researcher doesn't understand.

Triangulation research can have a broader significance than providing rough multimethod estimates. Triangulation can involve three fixes: (1) a fix based on *prior* experience with the target behavior; (2) a fix based on a theoretical perspective which runs, to some degree, *counter* to your prior experience; and (3) a fix based on additional, disciplined observations—an experiment.

Surely this describes the traditional research procedure—a literature review to document prior experience; hypotheses to reflect your theory; an empirical test of the hypotheses to add new disciplined observations.

So what's new? Perhaps the perspective of the researcher? If investigators adopt the traditional perspective that their job is to discover facts on the surface of reality, then nothing is new. If, however, researchers adopt the perspective that they're exploring dynamic, nested, puzzle boxes (with Karl Popper leaning over their shoulders admonishing them to take critically formulated multiple fixes[1]), then triangulation takes on a new dimension. Then the powerful roles of prior belief and current theory become clear, the given experiment becomes one tiny observational fix and is so placed in perspective. The importance of disciplined observational checkpoints is not diminished; rather, the challenge is increased because the researcher is tracking a multilayered dynamic reality—surfaces within surfaces within surfaces. While we await the emergence of well-documented multiple surface time series pictures, we recognize that prior belief and current theory play dominating roles, roles which we learn to acknowledge formally, rather than in passing as is now the case.

Triangulation, to the degree that it reflects this multilayered dynamic perspective, will extend the external validity of a given study by placing it in an extended empirical, rational, and nonrational context.[2]

Action Research

Action research, a term coined during the forties (Lewin, 1946; Chein, Cook & Harding, 1948) to describe disciplined, multimethod, multisource data collection and evaluation, remains a useful designation for systematic explorations of a complex problem space by investigators and policy makers who bring different perspectives but share common concerns. As social science research increasingly addresses complex social issues, this method as well as extensions to it (Campbell, 1975b; Frohman, Sashkin, & Kananagh, 1976) will become more popular.

Such approaches emphasize a multilayered and shifting model of reality, acknowledging the need for repeated "triangulations," or multiple perspective "fixes," as useful means of managing uncertainty. Figure 18–1 provides a simple visual model of the iterative, multiple-method process of data collection, interpretation, and action.

An action research cycle commences when a question or data base triggers a decision (State 0) in a key player to: (1) collect data, (2) and/or involve other key players with different perspectives but shared, salient concerns in a puzzle, resulting in a "triangulated" investigation.

---

[1]For a lucid presentation of Popper's position, see Campbell (1974b). Also see Popper (1972; 1973).

[2]See Tversky (1977) and Howard (1978) for an elegant blending of empirical, rational, and nonrational influences as they apply in a given investigation. Such studies may become "exemplars" for future social scientists.

CYCLES OF PLANNED CHANGE – AN ACTION-RESEARCH APPROACH

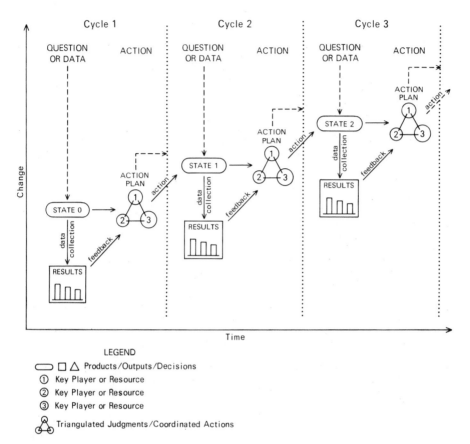

FIGURE 18-1   Cycles of Planned Change—An Action-Research Approach

The degree to which the "vested interests" of a key player supersede common interests across players determines the centrality or marginality of that individual's participation. Indeed, the role of some key players may become adversarial, but if a "solution" requires their support, then their methodological and speculative perspective, and their biases, become relevant "sources of variance" to be addressed by action researchers in their research designs and data collection. The degree of centrality/marginality of key players evolves across cycles, thus influencing the degree to which the project becomes action as opposed to research oriented, and also influencing which particular antecedents and consequences are focused upon, and which research methods are applied.

While overlapping common concerns—a shared driving curiosity—provide initial and continuing motivation that energizes the iterative process, the steering should be data driven. It is this latter commitment to disciplined data collection and interpretation—as policy guides—that enables this iterative, multiple-perspective research process to make its unique contribution.

In action or policy research, researchers collaborate with policy makers and problem "owners"—those plagued with the problem and those vested with the responsibility of ameliorating it. In this partnership researchers can play various roles. They can:

1. Help clarify the question and identify main assumptions;
2. Conduct critical evaluation of current theory and research; identify major gaps, and affordable opportunities for basic, applied, or pilot project research;
3. Help translate key questions into research relevant form, without trivializing them; help identify potentially powerful, and researchable antecedents; and recommend feasible research methods;
4. Conduct selected research: data collection; analysis; and feedback for multiple-perspective interpretation;
5. Participate in repeat cycles of the above—repeat cycle sciencing.

Like $n = 1$ research, action research is an unfamiliar but potentially powerful extension of common-sense problem solving.

For example, a university counseling service—whose members, although representing different schools of thought, were all disenchanted with their results—applied an action research approach to the question of how they could improve their "treatment" of low moods and depression. In the process, they of course identified popular antecedents: heredity (unknown gene combinations); stress (a major loss, or a "run" of disappointments); and so forth. But in addition, a new member of the team—who specialized in seeking behavioral antecedents at the *physiological level*—contributed three neglected or hidden but potentially powerful antecedents: certain foods; reduced sunlight; and disruptions of master internal "clocks" that coordinate physiological functions.

For a variety of reasons this different perspective generated persistent curiosity from team members unfamiliar with, or even biased against, physiological antecedents and explanations. The probable reasons include: (1) shared and strong dissatisfaction with their own and popular treatment methods (various forms of one-to-one and group counseling, and drugs); (2) some basic research supporting the probable linkage of diet, sunlight, and master physiological clocks to mood level and swings; and (3) the fact that these antecedents are open to manipulation and therefore to research and treatment trials—particularly dietary antecedents.

This latter reason gains in significance as one contemplates the profound difficulty of managing the popular antecedents in the network, such as attempting to shield people from their genes, or from the stresses of living and the dirty tricks of chance. And while it is important to identify the major antecedents in a network, it is particularly important to identify those most open to modification, for this is the basis of both experimental science and practical application.

Therefore, while basic research and theory swings more of its curiosity, experimentation, and speculation toward the role of physiological antecedents that affect mood, applied centers like the counseling center concentrate some of its resources in the same region of the network using *n*-of-1 and action research methods. These combined efforts represent a multimethod, multilevel exploration of one region of the Chinese puzzle box we call reality.

Action research represents an attempt to bring multiple perspectives to bear on a given problem, and to do so in a disciplined manner that capitalizes on the strengths of various forms of scientific and common-sense problem solving. In so doing, it extends our scientific as well as our individual and social capacity to manage uncertainty.

CONCEPTUAL TRENDS

Uncertainty in Science

Certainty rests precariously upon three foundations: (1) observations (the empirical foundation); (2) logic (the rational foundation); and (3) faith or bias or values (the nonrational foundation).

In science, certainty rests heavily on the observational, or empirical, base, buttressed by rationality—by logical and mathematical supports:

> The development of the method of experimental science is possibly the most significant intellectual contribution of western civilization. . . . in this flowering something of undeniable importance took place: the incorporation of mathematics and experimentation within a single method. Previously they had functioned as rival methods: mathematics is one way to get knowledge of nature, and experimental observation is another (Morris, 1955, p. 63)

Conversely, in religion, certainty stands on a foundation of faith, on a non-rational cornerstone buttressed by archival miracles and hope:

> Faith is to believe, . . . what we do not see, and its reward is to see and enjoy what we believe. (St. Augustine—On the Gospel of St. John, 1972, p. 340)

However, these contrasting models of science and religion, while scoring high on the yardstick of simplicity, fail to present a fair picture of how much science also rests on nonrational foundations and how the "science versus religion" debate is warming up again. Arguments between the empirical-rational school of thought versus the nonrational schools will rage. Already the creationists (those who believe in the biblical account of the origin of the universe) are demanding equal time in the public school curriculum with the Darwinians (those who support the evolutionary view). Furthermore, prominent members of the scientific community [for instance, Einstein & Infeld (1966); Kuhn (1970)] acknowledge the strong nonrational foundations of science.

In the midst of such debate we adopt a compromise position; we see knowledge resting on a three-legged foundation: one leg representing empiricism (observational checkpoints); one leg representing rationalism (logical and mathematical relations); and one leg representing the nonrational (such as speculation, values, bias, faith).

This three-legged model of knowledge rests on one main assumption:

> The human senses and human mind draw tiny finite samples from an infinite multi-layered, expanding reality. Therefore what lies beyond the reach of our current senses (and their extensions) and beyond the reach, too, of our current logic we must sketch, or map, with the aid of speculation and imagination—with the aid of non-empirical, nonrational structures—with the aid of faith, bias, hunch, and theory.

An articulate spokesman for the critical role that nonrational forces such as values play in shaping the structure of knowledge is Thomas Kuhn (1970) who portrays scientific disciplines as somewhat akin to modern primitive tribes, in that their research rituals and products are strongly determined by the beliefs and values of that particular scientific tribe. For Kuhn it is such values and biases that shape our "knowledge of nature" more than do our objective observations or our rationality. In brief, it is the "tribal" values of the scientists that determine where they focus their observational checkpoints and their logic, where they focus their increasingly sophisticated puzzle-solving skills. Kuhn would presumably entertain St. Augustine's statement that we believe in order that we may understand as an appropriate description of science, particularly on the basis of historical evidence. Here he is pointing to the history of the revolutions in scientific belief systems, which in turn radically reshape our "knowledge." From this perspective we can anticipate that future generations will look on our theories (germ theory, child-rearing theories, cancer treatment theories) as being as primitive from their enlightened point of view as we view earlier demoniacal theories of disease. Remember, however, that Kuhn's historical method (the after-the-fact method) is open to many alternative interpretations, and so Kuhn's interpretation remains one among many. Accordingly, his own theory would constitute one of the alternative tribal beliefs or myths.

Nevertheless, a Kuhnian view of science would suggest that just as a robin's "knowledge" of the world is tiny and naive, so too is our current scientific knowledge tiny and naive when compared with what "ultimately" may be known or even compared with what will be considered "knowledge" 100 years from now. From this perspective our tiny samples of observation and our tiny samples of explanations (our logic, mathematical models, laws) provide a trivial basis for generalizing to an infinite multilayered reality.

You may adopt a skeptical viewpoint and treat the products of science as you would the artifacts of an aboriginal tribe, guided by an endless parade of primitive superstitions—each one more sophisticated than the last, but not necessarily any more accurate concerning the "true nature of things." As Kuhn observes:

> There is, I think, no theory-independent way to reconstruct phrases like "really there"; the notion of a match between the ontology of a theory and its "real" counterpart in nature now seems to me illusive in principle. Besides, as a historian I am impressed with the implausibility of the view. (Kuhn, 1970, p. 206)

Or while you may agree that in some respects the scientific tribe replaces one set of superstitions with another, nevertheless you may also believe that in an uneven, trial-and-error way, each new superstition captures a less distorted reflection of some facet of multilayered nature. In other words, while modern science remains a long way from having the whole picture of multilayered reality, it is nevertheless gradually obtaining a less distorted picture of certain facets or certain regions or levels of that reality.

It is to such a view that Donald Campbell and Karl Popper seem to subscribe—to the view that, although laced with human bias, modern knowledge reflects *more than* current superstition and that our knowledge also reflects, to some degree, the complex editing of the hidden hand of "nature."

But whether one adopts Kuhn's haunting skepticism or Campbell and Popper's sophisticated realism, we are presented with a view of science exploring a relatively small corner of multilayered nature. We are presented with a picture of any given scientific discipline as relying on tiny samples of observations that grossly underestimate the population values they represent and also relying on tiny samples of hypotheses that also drastically underrepresent the possible and plausible hypotheses, or the models, to be drawn from a universal hat. This view presents science as an empirical-rational exploration of a highly bounded space-time frame—bounded by bias, values, theory, assumptions, and speculations—by the blinders of our modern scientific "tribe."

Once inside this protective corral of value or bias, then science can afford to practice rational-empiricism, to practice its impressive puzzle-solving skills, then it can afford to start sampling. Researchers can take tiny samples of subjects, or tiny samples of dependent variables drawn from the dependent variable hat, or one version of a treatment drawn from a popular independent variable hat, or one research context drawn from a hatful of possible contexts—all the while designing their studies, logically, to help control the various rogue suspects, and then comparing their results with selective maps of chance, in an effort to protect against the tricks of random sampling.

Thus science can be viewed as a series of disciplines, each focusing on a relatively tiny aspect of multilayered moving networks we call reality.

What we are seeing, then, is an increasing awareness of issues of external validity, an awareness of how our samples of observations underrepresent the population of observations, of how our samples of maps of reality underrepresent the population of possible maps, and how we must rely on nonrational assumptions, or on superstitions, or on values, to shrink the problem spaces we investigate to human size—to help wall out the infinite expanses of ignorance and to help fill in the gaps between our sparsely scattered observational checkpoints.

We need a new unit of analysis for science—the "fact" is no longer adequate. The fact fails to do justice to the tentative quality of sample observations and their elastic interrelationships. We need a unit of analysis that reflects the semistable quality of modern science, that reflects its trial-and-error, successive approximations of limited slices of shifting multilayered nature; we require a unit that reflects the provisional quality of knowledge, a unit different from *the Fact!*

FROM FACTS TO SURFACES

If asked to choose which one word best characterizes science, most of us would probably choose the word *facts*—''science is built on facts''; ''facts are the steppingstones of science.'' But is *fact* on its way out as the byword of science? Probably.

And yet, objective language remains a basic language of sciencing, and such language demands independent and consistent labeling of objects and events (Chapter 2)—that sounds like we're talking about facts! Furthermore, independent replication of experiments remains a cornerstone of science—that also sounds like we're talking about facts.

On the other hand, we noted that sciencing involves a low density sampling of observational checkpoints in a large problem space—theoretically at least in an infinite space-time frame. We noted, too, that any observational checkpoint—even your own weight—is surrounded by a region of uncertainty— $\bigcirc$. Yes, but it is a relatively small region of uncertainty, so let's call such observations ''factlike.'' But what about observations concerning the ''smallest'' particle; the ''edge'' of the universe; attitudes toward minorities, intelligence, mood, laughing on the outside? These appear factlike (at times independent observers agree), and yet we recognize them, somehow, as surface observations—as the detection of surfaces, as elastic, or as temporary surfaces in a moving nested array of Chinese puzzle boxes.

Furthermore, what surface we detect depends on which measure we use (which dependent variable) and which experimenter we use, at which time, in which experimental context. Thus finding stable observational checkpoints—stable facts or surfaces—becomes an exciting challenge. In keeping with our theme of multilayered reality—the dynamic puzzle box model—let's focus for the moment not on facts but upon surfaces and upon their detection.

When physicists face the problem of detecting and mapping invisible, vague surfaces—subatomic ''somethings''—they aim tiny radioactive tracers in the suspected direction and then track the deflection of the tracers: ''If you are firing machine gun bullets at a pile of raisin buns and some of the bullets bounce nearly backwards, you will infer that the buns contain something harder than raisins'' (Walker, 1963, p. 25).

The key principle to remember in the preceding example is that a surface is defined as something that *kicks back*. Similarly, imagine yourself being given a bagful of baseballs, placed in a pitch black room, and told to throw the baseballs in order to determine the size, shape, and contents of the room. You do so and report on the basis of what you hear and feel the following discoveries: a window—now broken—on your right; no wall, or a very distant wall, straight ahead; a sick or groaning person on the floor; a piano on your left; a high ceiling with a now broken chandelier. Oh yes, and *you* were also in the room—you've got a lump on your head to prove it—you located yourself as well.

Next you are given a bagful of photons to throw (that is, given a flashlight) and sent back into the same ''room.'' You discover, not a room, but a cave containing stalactites and stalagmites as well as strange plants and mosses; there's also a woozy Bengal tiger with a huge lump on its head lying on the cave floor; and gentle snowflakes are wafting down through a distant hole in the cave roof.

So it is obvious you detect some different surfaces by throwing photons than by throwing baseballs. Furthermore, someone with less acute vision than yours would detect less when they throw the photons, just as someone with less acute hearing than yours would detect less when they throw baseballs. Therefore it's *not only* what you throw, and *not only* what surfaces are there that can kick back, but also which of the kickbacks you can detect.

Next you're given a bag of beta particles and sent into a different space. You throw them around and get no kickbacks whatsoever; you locate no surfaces. But you were tricked; it was the same cave, except that most surfaces can't kick back beta particles, such particles pass right through. Furthermore, even when they are kicked back, they pass right through you, undetected. So what on earth is "real"?

Now what kind of psychological baseballs are you going to throw, at what psychological spaces, and what are you going to catch the kickbacks with, and what hunches will you have about what kinds of surfaces you missed and what kinds of kickbacks you missed?

Maybe we can see facts as Type A surfaces—standardized baseballs, thrown by standardized throwers, using standardized kickback receivers, in a standardized research context. However, change any component—change the surface, or the baseball, or the throwers, or the detectors, or the reporter, or the context—and you change the picture of multilayered experience. So is it surprising then that as we change our probes (baseballs), our points of view (our hypotheses), our detector system (our dependent variables, logics, statistics), or our research context (our caves) that we report different or changing surfaces? Hardly!

Perhaps then we might consider sciencing as the exploration of multilayered surfaces, with given surfaces occupying the center stage of a given discipline almost as temporary reference points, or base camps, from which reconnaissance parties spread out in concentric circles, with different bags of baseballs, seeking new semistable surfaces, new base camps.

Thus from the point of view of a multilayered reality, the basic unit of analysis becomes a surface—an observational checkpoint surrounded by a region of uncertainty ⦶ and harboring a region of uncertainty ⦿ . Examples include the uncertain boundary of the atom and the uncertain structure of the nucleus it harbors; the uncertain chemical boundary of the neuron and the uncertain electrochemical interactions it harbors; the uncertain cognitive boundaries of a concept and the uncertain structure of the subconcepts it harbors; and the uncertain social boundaries of individuals and the uncertain cognitive-emotional network they harbor.

In everyday language, we acknowledge not only the existence of these outer and inner regions of uncertainty but also acknowledge the necessity of assuming that they are benign, of assuming they harbor no immanent ill will, no surprising tricks—otherwise we can't manage the uncertainty, we become paralyzed or frenetic, like someone fighting off a swarm of wasps.

We recognize the negative consequences of threats to such implicit assumptions when we witness major breakdowns of trust such as: The paranoid individual who "sees" ill will and dirty tricks aimed at him or her from the *outside* (government; neighbors; T.V. sets; satellites); and from the *inside* (ominous messages emanating from tooth tingles; stomach rumbles; "voices"). We see it too in marriage breakdowns and abortive union-management negotiations when we conclude that there is insufficient trust or good will to sustain a viable relationship, or to continue reasonable negotiations. We acknowledge it too when we distinguish between the spirit and the letter of the law—without implicit agreement on the former, the latter gets lost in minutia and hairsplitting.

In other words, in order to go about our daily business of making sense of our world, we need to operate within a set of more or less shared assumptions about our outer and inner regions of uncertainty; otherwise we experience such symptoms as anxiety, depression, indecision, overload, stress, conflict, hairsplitting, even paranoia. To withstand the buffeting and banging of life, such assumptions must be robust and resilient; they must be more or less wired in. To the extent they are open to discussion and revision by those relying on them, the outer and inner floodgates of uncertainty open and inundate the mind, the relationship, the negotiations, the research.

We propose, for example, that most university-based Ph.D.'s don't do research, or if they do, don't publish their observations or speculations because they lack an ingrained set of guiding assumptions; so they become lost in uncertainty, procrastination, endless revisions. They lack an *ingrained* theory or intuition that enables them to focus in on a particular region of the network, to "see" important antecedents and consequences, and so "believe" and argue convincingly for a particular interpretation of their findings.

True, some will be denied publication initially because their ingrained theory or intuition runs counter to those of the journal editors, but if their work is driven by robust assumptions they will probably persevere, perhaps starting a new journal, and even a new "school" of thinking. Notice, we are not proposing that history will judge them to be "right," but only that a minimum condition for getting on with the job, in life or in science, is the possession of robust assumptions about outer and inner regions of uncertainty—excuse me while I take my vitamin C, D, E, B12 . . . boil my drinking water . . . turn on the air ionizer . . . triple-lock the doors . . . go back and check the locks . . . make my yogurt . . . read the labels on all the stuff my wife bought . . . but can you believe the labels? . . . cancel my airline reservation since I read on the back page of the *Times* that the morale of the maintenance workers is low . . . study consumer reports, my horoscope, the Bible, the Koran, Alvin Tofler, critical reviews of Tofler, critical reviews of the critical reviews . . . and take my sleeping pills!

Our emphasis on the need for robust assumptions may be seen as challenging Popper's proposal that the researcher be his or her own strongest critic—indeed, we see it as highly probable that researchers who are strongly critical of their own basic assumptions will lose themselves in speculative space, and so become overwhelmed by alternatives. Thus we view productive researchers as being driven not only by persistent curiosity but also by robust assumptions about powerful antecedents and particular linkages. On the other hand, operating within a set of strong assumptions, good researchers do a thorough job of controlling "local" antecedents and addressing "local" alternatives. In a Kuhnian sense they do excellent research (puzzle solving) within the limits of their paradigm. But critical evaluation of the paradigm—the surrounding and embedded assumptions—is more likely to come from outsiders, from theorists and researchers driven by a different set of assumptions—as provided by Stephen Gould concerning the assumptions underlying sociobiology, given at the end of the last chapter. Of course, others will in turn examine Gould's implicit assumptions more critically than he.

We "see" the need for robust control—blinders—for managing outer and inner regions of uncertainty not only in managing observational and speculative space but also in managing logical and mathematical space; mathematicians get lost as well.[3]

In brief, we are proposing that we use common sense and scientific problem-solving methods to manage the residual uncertainty not managed by our robust personal, social, and scientific biases and paradigms, and furthermore, that such residual uncertainty represents an infinitesimal region of "actual" uncertainty—the latter obviously including infinite uncertainty networks stretching into the past and the future, to say nothing of the potential permutations and combinations of antecedents and consequences involved in any current "natural" event.

In other words, a given observational checkpoint, or logical concept, is nested within an unspecified superstructure of linking surfaces and harbors an unspecified infrastructure of linking surfaces. Furthermore, the surfaces of these surrounding superstructures and harbored infrastructures remain undetected, some by design (by controls to ensure internal validity) but most by ignorance (by unresolved internal and external validity issues). For example, if you perform surprisingly poorly on a math quiz, we as experimenters usually have no idea why. It may be due to a harbored inner surface structure (a full bladder), or it may be due to pressure from an external superstructure surface—for example, an impending interview about a scholarship. However, it may be due to surfaces about which we *and* you are unaware—toxic inhalations in the classroom from asbestos

---

[3]For those interested in set theory, we are proposing that the basic unit of scientific information not be a fact, or a set, but rather a "class-set-class" unit. Class is derived from von Neumann-Bernays-Gödel set theory—as an undefined, primitive category into which we can intuitively put members. Thus a class can contain, not only a set, but also members too vague, or weird, or too numerous to fit the set. A class provides not only a crude surrounding category into which a set can dump its garbage but also serves as a constant reminder that the set is sustained by a surrounding, and embedded, network of presuppositions and "invisibles." A set, category, or operational definition is always nested in a primitively defined class— ⊙ —and harbors a primitively defined class— ☺ . Such class-set-class units are quasi-stable as a function of the interactions between the surface to be detected and the detector system. Such class-set-class units constitute the structure of the puzzle box model of reality—a model we derive from Popper's discussion of a nested hierarchy of plastic controls (Campbell, 1974b).

insulation used in the construction of the building or from influences distant from the research context—the arrival of a full moon, which influences your hormonal balance. These then are crude examples of what we mean by a surface—an observational checkpoint—being surrounded by, and harboring, uncertainty regions and linkages.

As humans with more or less standard light, sound, and touch receptors, we locate many similar, shareable surfaces. We miss others that dogs, or bees, or bats detect and share. As we extend our repertoire of baseballs and detectors (as we extend our technical and conceptual detector systems), we locate more surfaces. We note that other surfaces, which perhaps appeared stable, are linked to still further superstructure and infrastructure surfaces that are less stable than we once believed.

As the surfaces we wish to locate become very large (for example, the future, human nature) and the observational checkpoints sparse, we are hard put to know what to throw at such problem spaces—should we throw a hatful of various-sized baseballs? But we are dealing with such a gigantic target space, such a research context! Some scientists throw large theories at these massive dark spaces and hope the response they hear is not merely the echo of their own beliefs. Some choose a small target area and fire a shotgun and try to locate the resulting splashes. Still others select a highly specific target area and fire a rifle, then wait for the yelp, or the ricochet. All of them will locate a surface. Determining to what degree the surface they locate resides in their own mind (believing is seeing), to what degree it resides "out there" (seeing is believing), and to what degree it is a combination of both becomes the object of the science game.

Some current theorists emphasize the "believing is seeing" side of science, emphasizing the role of the tribal detector system. Others, while acknowledging the biasing influence of the group detector system, emphasize the additional and critical role of stable "out there" surfaces—"reality" surfaces and rhythms, "seeing is believing."

Finally, neither side in this argument can afford high arrogance—the Kuhnians rest their case on the historical method—on the flimsy after-the-fact method. The empiricists rest their case on tiny finite sampling from infinite space-time frames—an open invitation to the tricks of chance. Remember Einstein's observation: "Whoever undertakes to set himself up as a judge in the field of Truth and Knowledge is shipwrecked by the laughter of the gods" (Einstein, 1972, p. 920).

Perhaps Newton provides a fitting phrase on which to close this discussion, and the book:

> I do not know what I may appear to the world, but to myself I seem to have been only a boy playing on the seashore, and diverting myself in now and then finding a smoother pebble or a prettier shell than ordinary, whilst the great ocean of truth lay all undiscovered before me (Newton, 1972, p. 929).

References and Suggested Readings

As well as citing articles referred to in the text, the following list includes a sampling of classic references concerning research design and theory construction.

ADAIR, G., DUSHENKO, T.W., & LINDSAY, R.C.L. (1985). Ethical regulations and their impact on research practice. *American Psychologist, 40,* 59–72.

AGNEW, N.M. (1964). The relative value of self report and objective tests in assessing the effects of amphetamine. *Journal of Psychiatric Research, 2,* 85–100.

AGNEW, N. McK., and BROWN, J. L. (In Press) Bounded rationality: Fallibility decisions in unbounded problem space. *Behavioral Science.*

AGNEW, N. McK., & BROWN, J.L. (1982, Autumn). From skyhooks to walking sticks: On the road to nonrational decision making. *Organizational Dynamics,* 40–58.

AGNEW, N.M., & ERNEST, C.H. (1971). Dose-response and biased set study of an amphetamine and a barbiturate. *Psychopharmacologia, 19,* 282–296.

AGNEW, N.M., & MILLER, G. (1975–76). An epidemiological paradigm for alcohol studies. *Drug Forum, 5,* 5–38.

AGNEW, N. McK., & PYKE, S.W. (1982). *The science game: An introduction to research in the behavioral sciences* (3rd ed.) Englewood Cliffs, NJ: Prentice-Hall.

AGNEW N. McK., PYKE, S., & PYLYSHYN, W.W. (1966). Absolute judgment of distance as a function of induced muscle tension, exposure time and feedback. *Journal of Experimental Psychology, 71,* 649–654.

AJZEN, I., & FISHBEIN, M., (1970). The prediction of behavior from attitudinal and normative variables. *Journal of Experimental Social Psychology, 6,* 466–487.

AJZEN, I., & FISHBEIN, M. (1980). *Understanding attitudes and predicting social behavior.* Englewood Cliffs, N.J.: Prentice-Hall.

ALSIP, J.E., & CHEZIK, D.D. (1974). *Research guide in psychology.* Morristown, NJ: General Learning Press.

ALVAREZ, L.W. (1965). A pseudo experience in parapsychology. *Science, 148,* 1541.

AMERICAN PSYCHOLOGICAL ASSOCIATION. (1981). *Ethical principles of psychologists,* 1981 revision. Washington, DC: Author.

AMERICAN PSYCHOLOGICAL ASSOCIATION. (1982). *Ethical principles in the conduct of research with human participants.* Washington, DC: Author.

AMERICAN PSYCHOLOGICAL ASSOCIATION. (1983). *Publication manual of the American Psychological Association,* (3rd ed.) Washington, DC: Author.

ANDERSON, B.F. (1966). *The psychology experiment* (Chapter 8). Belmont, CA: Brooks/Cole.

ANDERSON, F.G. (Ed.). (1960). *The new organon and related writings by Francis Bacon.* New York: Liberal Arts Press.

ARDREY, R. (1970). *The social contract.* New York: Atheneum.

ASIMOV, I. (1960). *The intelligent man's guide to science.* New York: Basic Books.

AUGUSTINE, SAINT. (1972). On the Gospel of St. John. In G. Seldes (Ed.), *The great quotations* (p. 340). New York: Pocket Books.

BAKAN, D. (1966). The test of significance in psychological research. *Psychological Bulletin, 66,* 423–437.

BAKAN, D. (1975). Speculation in psychology. *Journal of Humanistic Psychology, 15,* 17–25.

BARKER, R.G., & SCHOGGEN, P. (1973). *Qualities of community life.* San Francisco: Jossey-Bass.

BARZUN, J. (1964). *Science: The glorious entertainment.* Toronto: University of Toronto Press.

BAUMRIND, D. (1964). Some thoughts on ethics of research: After reading Milgram's "Behavioral study of obedience." *American Psychologist, 19,* 421–423.

BAUMRIND, D. (1985). Research using intentional deception: Ethical issues revisited. *American Psychologist, 40,* 165–174.

BEACH, F.A. (1955). The descent of instinct. *Psychological Review, 62,* 401–410.

BEM, S.L. (1975). Sex role adaptability: One consequence of psychological androgyny. *Journal of Personality and Social Psychology, 31,* 634–643.

BENEDICT, R. (1938). Continuities and discontinuities in cultural conditioning. *Psychiatry, 1,* 161–167.

BEVERIDGE, W.I.B. (1957). *The art of scientific investigation.* New York: W.W. Norton.

BLALOCK, H.M., Jr., & BLALOCK, A.B. (1968). *Methodology in social research.* New York: McGraw-Hill.

BLEIR, R. (1984). *Science and gender.* New York: Pergamon Press.

BLOCK, J.H. (1976). Debatable conclusions about sex differences. *Contemporary Psychology, 21,* 517–522.

BRACHT, G.H., & GLASS, E.V. (1968). The external validity of experiments. *American Educational Research Journal, 5,* 437–474.

BROWN, C., & SEITZ, J. (1970). "You've come a long way baby": Historical perspectives. In R. Morgan (Ed.), *Sisterhood Is Powerful.* New York: Vintage Books.

BROWN, J.L., & AGNEW, N. McK. (1982, March/April). Corporate agility. *Business Horizons,* 29–33.

BRUNSWIK, E. (1952). The conceptual framework of psychology. In O. Neurath, R. Carnap, & C. Morris (Eds.), *International Encyclopedia of Unified Science* (Vol. 1, No. 10). Chicago: University of Chicago Press.

BUSS, A. (1976). Galton and sex differences. *Journal of the History of the Behavioural Sciences, 12,* 283–285.

BYRNE, D., ERVIN, C., & LAMBERTH, J. (1970). Continuity between the experimental study of attraction and real-life computer dating. *Journal of Personality and Social Psychology, 16,* 157–165.

CAMPBELL, D.T. (1960). Blind variation and selective retention in creative thought as in other knowledge processes. *Psychological Review, 67,* 380–400.

CAMPBELL, D.T. (1969). Reforms as experiments. *American Psychologist, 24,* 409–429.

CAMPBELL, D.T. (1974a). "Downward causation" in hierarchically organized biological systems. In P. Dobzhansky & F.J. Ayala (Eds.), *Studies in the philosophy of biology.* London: Macmillan.

CAMPBELL, D.T. (1974b). Evolutionary epistemology. In P.A. Schlipp (Ed.), *The philosophy of Karl Popper* (Vol. 14, No. 1–2). The library of living philosophers, La Salle, Ill.: Open Court Publishing.

CAMPBELL, D.T. (1975a). On the conflicts between biological and social evolution and between psychology and moral tradition. *American Psychologist, 30,* 1103–1126.

CAMPBELL, D.T. (1975b). Assessing the impact of planned social change. In G.M. Lyons (Ed.),

Social research in public policies. Hanover, NH: Dartmouth College, the Public Affairs Center.

CAMPBELL, D.T. (1975c). Degrees of freedom and the case study. *Comparative Political Studies, 31,* 178–193.

CAMPBELL, D.T., & ROSS, H.L. (1968).. The Connecticut crackdown on speeding: Time-series data in quasi-experimental analysis. *Law and Society Review, 3,* 33–53.

CAMPBELL, D.T., & STANLEY, J.C. (1966). *Experimental and quasi-experimental design for research.* Chicago: Rand McNally.

CAMPBELL, N.R. (1928). *An account of the principles of measurement and calculation.* London: Longmans Green.

CARLSON, E.R., & CARLSON, R. (1960). Male and female subjects in personality research. *Journal of Abnormal and Social Psychology, 61,* 482–483.

CARLSON, R. (1971). Where is the person in personality research? *Psychological Bulletin, 75,* 203–219.

CARROLL, L. (1939). *Alice's adventures in wonderland* and *Through the looking glass.* London: Wm. Collins Sons.

CARROLL, M.A., SCHNEIDER, H.G., & WESLEY, G.R. (1985). *Ethics in the practice of psychology.* Englewood Cliffs, NJ: Prentice-Hall.

CHEIN, I., COOK, S.W., & HARDING, J. (1948). The field of action research. *American Psychologist, 3,* 43–50.

COILE, D.C., & MILLER, N.E. (1984). How radical animal activists try to mislead humane people. *American Psychologist, 39,* 700–701.

CONANT, J.B. (1953). *Modern science and modern man.* Garden City, NY: Doubleday.

COOK, T.D., & CAMPBELL, D.T. (1979). *Quasi-experimentation and analysis issues for field settings.* Boston: Houghton Mifflin.

Council for the Society for the Psychological Study of Social Issues. (1969). Statement by SPSSI on current IQ controversy: Heredity versus environment. *American Psychologist, 24,* 1039–1040.

CRICHTON, M. (1972). *The terminal man.* London: J. Cape.

DAMON, A. (1965). Discrepancies between findings of longitudinal and cross-sectional studies in adult life. *Human Development, 8,* 16–22.

DANZIGER, K. (1985). The origins of the psychological experiment as a social institution. *American Psychologist, 40,* 133–140.

DARWIN, C. (1936). *The origin of species.* New York: Random House.

DAWKINS, R. (1976). *The selfish gene.* New York: Oxford University Press.

DELGADO, J. (1969). *Physical control of the mind.* New York: Harper & Row.

DENZIN, N.K. (Ed.). (1970). *Sociological methods: A source book.* Chicago: Aldine.

DOHERTY, M.A. (1973). Sexual bias in personality theory. *The Counselling Psychologist, 4,* 67–75.

EGGAN, D. (1943). The general problem of Hopi adjustment. *American Anthropologist, 45,* 357–373.

EINSTEIN, A. (1972). Aphorism for Leo. In G. Seldes (Ed.), *The great quotations* (p. 920). New York: Pocket Books.

EINSTEIN, A., & INFELD, L. (1966). *The evolution of physics.* New York: Simon & Schuster.

ELLSBERG, D. (1973). Women and war. In F. Klagsbrun (Ed.), *The first Ms reader.* New York: Warner Paperback Library.

EYSENCK, H.J. (1979). *The structure and measurement of intelligence.* New York: Springer-Verlag.

FAVREAU, O.E. (1977). Sex bias in psychological research. *Canadian Psychological Review, 18*(1), 56–65.

FEE, E. (1976). Science and the woman problem: Historical perspectives. In M.S. Teitlebaum (Ed.), *Sex differences.* Garden City, NY: Anchor Books.

FEE, E. (1981). Is feminism a threat to scientific objectivity? *International Journal of Women's Studies, 4,* 378–392.

FREEDMAN, D., PISANI, R., & PURVES, R. (1978). *Statistics.* New York: W.W. Norton.

FRIEDAN, B. (1963). *The feminine mystique.* New York: Dell.

FROHMAN, M.A., SASHKIN, M., & KANANAGH, M.J. (1976). Action research as applied to organization development. *Organization and Administrative Science, 7,* 129–161.

GAINES, B.R. (1983). Precise past–fuzzy future. *International Journal of Man-Machine Studies, 19,* 117–134.

GAINES, B.R. (1984). Methodology in the large: Modeling all there is. *Systems Research, 1,* 91–103.

GOULD, S.J. (1981). *The mismeasure of man.* New York: W.W. Norton.

GRADY, K.E. (1981). Sex bias in research design. *Psychology of Women Quarterly, 5,* 628–636.

GRAY, V.A. (1977). The image of women in psychology textbooks. *Canadian Psychological Review, 18*(1), 46–55.

GREENGLASS, E., & STEWART, M. (1973). The underrepresentation of women in social psychological research. *Ontario Psychologist, 5,* 21–29.

GREGSON, R.A.M. (1983). *Time series in psychology.* London: Lawrence Erlbaum.

GRONER, R., GRONER, M., & BISCHOF, W.F. *Methods of heuristics.* London: Lawrence Erlbaum.

GUILFORD, J.P. (1965). *Fundamental statistics in psychology and education,* (4th ed.). New York: McGraw-Hill.

HALL, J.E., & HARE-MUSTIN, R.T. (1983). Sanctions and the diversity of ethical complaints against psychologists. *American Psychologist, 38,* 714–729.

HALLOWELL, A.I. (1940). Aggression in Saulteaux society. *Psychiatry, 3,* 395–407.

HALMOS, P.R. (1960). *Naive set theory.* New York: Von Nostrand.

HANEY, C., BANKS, C., & ZIMBARDO, P. (1973). Interpersonal dynamics in a simulated prison. *International Journal of Criminology and Penology, 1,* 69–97.

HANSON, D.J. (1980). Relationship between methods and findings in attitude-behavior research. *Psychology, 17,* 11–13.

HARPER, T. (1985). Abortion bombers like "knights" not terrorists, lawyers tell trial. *Toronto Star,* April 17, A25.

HEBB, D.O. (1970). A return to Jensen and his social science critics. *American Psychologist, 25,* 568.

HEISENBERG, W. (1975, March). The great tradition. *Encounter,* 52–58.

HELLER, J. (1961). *Catch-22.* New York: Simon & Schuster.

HOFSTADTER, D.R., & DENNET, D.C. (1982). *The mind's I: Fantasies and reflections on self and soul.* New York: Bantam Books.

HOWARD, I.P. (1978). Recognition and knowledge of the water-level principle. *Perception, 7,* 151–160.

IVANCEVICH, J.M., & MATTESON, M.T. (1978). Longitudinal organizational research in field settings. *Journal of Business Research, 6,* 181–201.

JANIS, I.L., & MAN, L. (1977). *Decision making.* New York: Free Press.

JENSEN, A.R. (1969a). How much can we boost IQ and scholastic achievement? *Harvard Educational Review, 39,* 1–123.

JENSEN, A.R. (1969b). Criticism or propaganda? *American Psychologist, 24,* 1040–1041.

JICK, T.D. (1979). Mixing qualitative methods: Triangulation in action. *Administrative Science Quarterly, 24,* 602–611.

KAHL, R. (Ed.). (1963). *Studies in explanation.* Englewood Cliffs, NJ: Prentice-Hall.

KAMIN, L.J. (1981). Intelligence. In J.M. Darley, S. Glucksberg, L.J. Kamin, R.A. Kinchla (Eds.), *Psychology,* Englewood Cliffs, NJ: Prentice-Hall.

KELLY, G.A. (1955). *The psychology of personal constructs.* New York: W.W. Norton & Co., Inc.

KEYES, A., BROZEK, J., HENSCHEL, A., MICKELSEN, O., & TAYLOR, H.L. (1950). *The biology of human starvation.* Minneapolis: University of Minnesota Press.

KIMBLE, G.A. (1978). *How to use (and misuse) statistics.* Englewood Cliffs, NJ: Prentice-Hall.

KING, F.A. (1984, September). Animals in research: The case for experimentation. *Psychology Today,* 56–58.

KLUCKHOHN, C., & LEIGHTON, D. (1949). The Navaho view of life. In L. Wilson, & W.L. Kalb (Eds.), *Sociological Analysis.* New York: Harcourt, Brace.

KOEING, K.P., & MASTERS, J. (1965). Experimental treatment of habitual smoking. *Behaviour Research and Therapy, 3,* 235–243.

KOESTLER, A., & SMYTHES, J.R. *Beyond reductionism.* London: Hutchinson.

KUHN, T. (1970). *The structure of scientific revolutions,* (2nd ed.). Chicago: University of Chicago Press.

LANCASTER, J.B. (1976). Sex roles in primate societies. In M.S. Teitlebaum (Ed.), *Sex differences* (pp. 22–61). Garden City, NY: Anchor Books.

LANDSBERGER, H. (1958). *Hawthorne revisited.* Ithaca, NY: Cornell University Press.

LATANÉ, B., & DARLEY, J.M. (1968). Group inhibition of bystander intervention in emergencies. *Journal of Personality and Social Psychology, 10,* 215–221.

LATANÉ, B., & RODIN, J. (1969). A lady in distress: Inhibiting effects of friends and strangers on bystander intervention. *Journal of Experimental Social Psychology, 5,* 189–202.

LEONARD, M.M., & COLLINS, A.M. (1979). Women as footnote. *The Counseling Psychologist, 8*(1), 6–7.

LESTER, J.D. (1976). *Writing research papers: A complete guide,* (2nd ed.). Agincourt, Ontario: Gage.

LEWIN, K. (1946). Action research and minority problems. *Journal of Social Issues, 2,* 34–46.

MACCOBY, E.E., & JACKLIN, C.N. (1974). *The psychology of sex differences.* Stanford, CA: Stanford Press.

MACCORQUODALE, K., & MEEHL, P. (1948). On a distinction between hypothetical constructs and intervening variables. *Psychological Review, 55,* 95–107.

MACKIE, M. (1983). *Exploring gender relations.* Toronto: Butterworths.

MAHONEY, M.J. (1976). *Scientist as subject: The psychological imperative.* Cambridge, MA: Ballinger.

MARCEIL, J.C. (1977). Implicit dimensions of idiography and nomothesis: A reformulation. *American Psychologist, 32,* 1046–1055.

MEHLBERG, H. (1958). *The reach of science.* Toronto: University of Toronto Press.

MERCHANT, C. (1980). *The death of nature.* San Francisco: Harper & Row.

MILGRAM, S. (1963). Behavioral study of obedience. *Journal of Abnormal and Social Psychology, 67,* 371–378.

MILGRAM, S. (1965). Issues in the study of obedience: A reply to Baumrind. *American Psychologist, 19,* 848–852.

MILGRAM, S. (1970). The experience of living in cities. *Science, 167,* 1461–1468.

MILGRAM, S., BICKMAN, L., & BERKOWITZ, L. (1969). Note on the drawing power of crowds of different size. *Journal of Personality and Social Psychology, 13,* 79–82.

MILLER, G.A. (1956). The magical number seven, plus or minus two: Some limits on our capacity for processing information. *Psychological Review, 63,* 81–97.

MILLS, D.H. (1984). Ethics education and adjudication within psychology. *American Psychologist, 39,* 669–675.

MONEY, J., & EHRHARDT, A.A. (1972). *Man and woman, boy and girl: The differentiation and dimorphism of gender identity from conception to maturity.* Baltimore: John Hopkins University Press.

MONTAGU, A. (Ed.). (1980). *Sociobiology examined.* New York: Oxford University Press.

MORRIS, C.W. (1955). Scientific empiricism. In O. Neurath, R. Carnap, C.W. Morris (Eds.), *International Encyclopedia of Unified Science* (Vol. 1, Part 1, p. 63). Chicago: University of Chicago Press.

MORRIS, D. (1967). *The naked ape.* Toronto: Bantam Books.

MOULTON, J., ROBINSON, F.M., & ELIAS, C. (1978). Sex bias in language use. *American Psychologist, 33,* 1032–1036.

NASH, M.M. (1975). "Non-reactive methods and the law." Additional comments on legal liability in behavior research. *American Psychologist, 30,* 777–780.

NEWTON, I. (1972). In G. Seldes (Ed.), *The great quotations* (p. 929). New York: Pocket Books.

OPPENHEIMER, J.R. (1956). Analogy in science. *American Psychologist, 11,* 127–135.

ORNE, M.T. (1962). On the social psychology of the psychological experiment: With particular reference to demand characteristics and their implications. *American Psychologist, 17,* 776–783.

OSKAMP, S. (1977). Methods of studying social behavior. In L.S. Wrightsman (Ed.), *Social Psychology,* (2nd ed.). (Chapter 2). Monterey, CA: Brooks/Cole.

PARLEE, M.B. (1981). Appropriate control groups in feminist research. *Psychology of Women Quarterly, 5,* 637–644.

PERCIVAL, B. (1984). Sex bias in introductory psychology textbooks: Five years later. *Canadian Psychology, 25,* 35–42.

PILIAVIN, J.A. & PILIAVIN, I.M. (1972). Effect of blood on reaction to a victim. *Journal of Personality and Social Psychology, 23,* 353–361.

POPPER, K. (1969). *The logic of scientific discovery.* New York: Basic Books.

POPPER, K. (1972). *Objective knowledge: An evolutionary approach.* Oxford: Clarendon.

POPPER, K. (1973, April). Indeterminism is not enough. *Encounter,* 20–26.

PREMACK, D. (1970). Mechanisms of self-control. In W. Hunt (Ed.), *Learning and mechanisms of control in smoking.* Hawthorne, NY: Aldine.

PYKE, S.W. (1976). Children's literature: Conceptions of sex roles. In W.C. Mann & L. Wheatcraft (Eds.), *Canada: A sociological profile,* (3rd ed.). (pp. 158–171). Toronto: Copp/Clark.

PYKE, S.W. (1979). Cognitive templating: A technique for feminist (and other) counsellors. *Personnel and Guidance Journal, 57,* 315–318.

PYKE, S.W. (1982). Confessions of a reluctant ideologist. *Canadian Psychology, 23,* 125–134.

PYKE, S.W., AGNEW, N. MCK., & KOPPERUD, J. (1966). Modification of an overlearned maladaptive response through a relearning program: A pilot study on smoking. *Behaviour Research and Therapy, 4,* 197–203.

PYKE, S.W., RICKS, F.A., STEWART, J.C., & NEELY, C.A. (1975). The sex variable in Canadian psychological journals. In M. Wright (Chair), *The status of women psychologists.* Symposium presented at the meeting of the Ontario Psychological Association, Toronto.

PYLYSHYN, Z. (1973). What the mind's eye tells the mind's brain: A critique of mental imagery. *Psychological Bulletin, 80,* 1–24.

RHINE, J.G., & PRATT, J.G. (1957). *Para-psychology.* Springfield, IL: Chas. C Thomas.

RIMLAND, B., & MUNSINGER, H. (1977). Burt's IQ data. *Science, 195,* 248.

ROBINSON, P.W., & FOSTER, D.F. (1979). *Experimental psychology: A small-n approach.* New York: Harper & Row.

ROETHLISBERGER, F.J., & DICKSON, W.J. (1948). *Management and the worker.* Cambridge, MA: Harvard University Press.

ROSCOE, J.T. (1975). *Fundamental research statistics for the behavioral sciences,* (2nd ed.). New York: Holt, Rinehart & Winston.

ROSENTHAL, R. (1963). On the social psychology of the psychological experiment: The experimenter's hypothesis as an unintended determinant of experimental results. *American Scientist, 51,* 268–283.

SCHULTZ, D.P. (1969). The human subject in psychological research. *Psychological Bulletin, 72,* 214–228.

SELDES, G. (1972). *The great quotations.* New York: Pocket Books.

SHANTZ, F.C. (1972). Individuality in evaluations of treatment effectiveness. *Journal of Counselling Psychology, 19,* 76–80.

SHAW, M.L.G. (1980). *On becoming a personal scientist.* London: Academic Press.

SHIELDS, S.A. (1975). Functionalism, Darwinism, and the psychology of women: A study in social myth. *American Psychologist, 30,* 739–754.

SILVERMAN, I. (1975). Non-reactive methods and the law. *American Psychologist, 30,* 764–769.

SIMON, H.A. (1970). *The science of the artificial.* Cambridge, MA: M.I.T. Press.

SIMON, H.A. (1979, September). Rational decision making in business organizations. *American Economic Review,* 493–515.

STAPP, H.P. (1977). Theory of reality. *Foundation of Physics, 7,* 313–323.

STARK-ADAMEC, C., & KIMBALL, M. (1984). Science free of sexism: A psychologist's guide to the conduct of nonsexist research. *Canadian Psychology, 25,* 23–34.

STEWART, I., & PALL, D. (1977). *The foundations of mathematics.* Oxford: Oxford University Press.

TAYLOR, J.A. (1953). A personality scale of manifest anxiety. *Journal of Abnormal and Social Psychology, 48,* 285–290.

TESHER, E. (1981, March). Tranquilizers tested for link with cancer. *Toronto Star,* March 16, A2.

THOMAS, L. (1974). *The lives of a cell: Notes of a biology watcher.* New York: Bantam Books.

TIGER, L. (1969). *Men in groups.* Don Mills, Ontario: Nelson's University Paperbacks.

TULVING, E. (1985). How many memory systems are there? *American Psychologist, 40,* 385–398.

TVERSKY, A. (1977). Features of similarity. *Psychological Review, 84,* 327–352.

TVERSKY, A., & KAHNEMAN, D. (1981, January). The framing of decisions and the psychology of choice. *Science, 211,* 453–458.

TYLER, L.E. (1983). *Thinking creatively.* San Francisco: Jossey-Bass.

UNGER, R.K. (1979). Toward a redefinition of sex and gender. *American Psychologist, 34,* 1085–1094.

WALKER, M.J. (1963). An orientation toward modern physical theory. In R. Kahl (Ed.), *Studies in explanation.* Englewood Cliffs, NJ: Prentice-Hall.

WALLSTON, B.S. (1981). What are the questions in psychology of women? A feminist approach to research. *Psychology of Women Quarterly, 5,* 597–617.

WATSON, D.L., & THARP, R.G. (1977). *Self-directed behavior: Self-modification for personal adjustment.* Monterey, CA: Brooks/Cole.

WATSON, J.B. (1913). Psychology as the behaviorist views it. *Psychological Review, 20,* 158–177.

WEBB, F.J., CAMPBELL, D.T., SCHWARTZ, R.D., & SECHREST, L. (1966). *Unobtrusive measures: Non-reactive research in the social sciences.* Chicago: Rand McNally.

WEINER, M. (1956). Perceptual development in a distorted room: A phenomenological study. *Psychological Monographs,* LXX (432).

WEYANT, R.G. (1979). The relationship between psychology and women. *International Journal of Women's Studies, 2,* 358–385.

WHITE, A.D. (1955). *A history of the warfare of science with theology in christendom.* New York: George Braziller.

WHITE, M.S. (1975). Women in the professions: Psychological and social barriers to women in science. In J. Freeman (Ed.), *Women: A feminist perspective* (pp. 227–237). Palo Alto, CA: Mayfield.

WHYTE, W.F., Jr. (1943). *Street corner society.* Chicago: University of Chicago Press.

WIESENTHAL. D.L. (1974). Reweaving deception's tangled web. *Canadian Psychologist, 15,* 326–336.

WILSON, D.W. & DONNERSTEIN, E. (1976). Legal and ethical aspects of nonreactive social psychological research: An excursion in the public mind. *American Psychologist, 31,* 765–773.

WILSON, E.O. (1975). *Sociobiology: The new synthesis.* Cambridge, MA: Harvard University Press.

WILSON, E.O. (1978). *On human nature.* Cambridge, MA: Harvard Unversity Press.

WILSON, H.T. (1983). Anti-method as a counterstructure in social research practice. In M. Morgan (Ed.), *Beyond method: Strategies of social research.* Los Angeles: Sage.

WINER, B.J. (1962). *Statistical principles in experimental design.* New York: McGraw-Hill.

WISPE, L.G., & THOMPSON, J.R., Jr. (1976). The war between the words, biological versus social evolution and some related issues. *American Psychologist, 31,* 341–384.

WOODWARD, B., & ARMSTRONG, S. (1981). *The brethren.* New York: Avon.

WOOLSEY, L. (1977). Psychology and the reconciliation of women's double bind: To be feminine or to be fully human. *Canadian Psychological Review, 18*(1), 66–78.

ZADEH, L.A. (1975). Fuzzy logic and approximate reasoning. *Synthesis, 30,* 407–428.

ZIMBARDO, P.G. (1970, April). *Symposium on social and developmental issues in moral research.* Paper presented at the meeting of the Western Psychological Association. Los Angeles.

Index